GLOBAL MONITORING REPORT 2008

GLOBAL MONITORING REPORT

REPORT 2008

MDGs and the Environment:
Agenda for Inclusive and
Sustainable Development

Cover photo: © Robert Wallis/Panos Pictures.

Cover image: Women in Rajasthan, India, carry sand near the village of Paladi Bhopatan to form rainwater collection channels. Rajasthan has been suffering from a drought for the last eight years.

Cover design by Quantum Think.

Contents

Boxes

Figures

Tables

Foreword

The *Global Monitoring Report 2008* comes at an important time. This year marks the halfway point in the effort to achieve the Millennium Development Goals (MDGs) by 2015. This is also an important year to work toward a consensus on how the world is going to respond to the challenge of climate change, building on the foundation laid at the conference in Bali in December 2007. Successfully meeting this challenge will be essential for durable progress toward the MDGs and related development outcomes. In providing an integrated assessment of the agenda for development and environmental sustainability, this year's report offers timely input on issues that will be at the center of discussions at various international forums in coming months.

The report's assessment of the MDGs at midpoint presents a mixed picture. The first MDG calls for reducing extreme poverty and hunger by half. Although the poverty goal is likely to be met at the global level, thanks to a remarkable surge in global economic growth over the past decade, there are serious shortfalls in fighting hunger and malnutrition—the "forgotten MDG." High food and energy prices have brought increased attention to these issues, but more is needed. Reducing malnutrition is the MDG with a "multiplier" effect, because it is essential to

success on a number of other MDGs which are unlikely to be met, including maternal health, infant mortality, and education. Shortfalls in the human development areas are especially serious in South Asia and Sub-Saharan Africa. Within this overall picture, there is considerable variation across countries. The report finds that, on current trends, most countries are off track to meet most of the MDGs, with those in fragile situations falling behind most seriously.

The implication of this assessment is clear. If the world is to get back on track to meet the MDGs, the international community needs to move quickly to generate stronger and broader momentum toward these goals. In the context of expediting and broadening progress toward the MDGs, and ensuring the sustainability of that progress, the report proposes an agenda for inclusive and sustainable development.

Strong and inclusive growth must be at the center of the strategy to achieve the MDGs, including concerted efforts to spur growth in lagging countries in Africa and elsewhere and in fragile situations. While specific policy priorities for growth vary from country to country, looking across countries, several areas emerge as essential to robust growth: sound macroeconomic policies; a conducive private investment climate, including access to energy and other key infrastructure; and good governance. In many countries in Africa, and in low-income countries more generally, a dynamic agricultural sector is crucial for strong and inclusive growth and will help to mitigate the recent upward pressures on food prices. In countries that are severely affected by the food price increases, well-targeted safety nets may also be needed to cushion the impact on the poor.

The recent financial market turbulence and the resulting global economic slowdown pose difficult challenges for policy makers. We will need decisive monetary and fiscal policy action to head off a deterioration of growth prospects in advanced and developing economies, and stronger prudential supervision to put the financial system on a firmer footing.

We must accelerate progress toward the human development goals. There is a clear need to step up programs in health and education, but it is also clear that increased public spending alone is not the answer. The quality and equity of spending are equally important. And policy interventions must factor in the strong links that exist between health and education outcomes, nutrition, and environmental factors—water and sanitation, pollution, and climate change.

We must integrate environmental sustainability into core development work, maximizing synergies. For natural resource–dependent countries, sound resource management is critical for sustainable growth. Poor countries will suffer the most from climate change and are the least able to adapt. For them, the best way to adapt is to develop—by diversifying their economies, strengthening infrastructure, and developing health systems. Mitigation of carbon emissions will require financing and technology transfer to developing countries. Such sup-

port should not divert resources from other development programs.

Donors must scale up aid in line with their commitments. Sizable shortfalls loom if current trends in aid persist. Thanks to reforms, a number of developing countries are in a position to utilize increased resources productively. The changing aid architecture, including new sources and modalities of aid, promises more resources and innovation but also poses new challenges for aid effectiveness and coherence. We should use the opportunity provided by the Accra High Level Forum in September 2008 to address the new, dynamic dimensions of the aid effectiveness agenda. We also need to catalyze and leverage more private capital in support of development.

We can and should harness trade more effectively to contribute to strong and inclusive growth. The international community must achieve a successful outcome of the Doha trade negotiations in 2008. The current high food prices provide a window of opportunity to break the impasse on agricultural trade liberalization. We should increase aid for trade; together with behind-the-border reforms of key trade-related services, it can help poor countries take advantage of trade opportunities, promoting more inclusive globalization.

The international financial institutions (IFIs) have a crucial role to play in supporting this agenda through their financing, knowledge, and coordination services. At the country level, these institutions need to tailor their products and services to the increasingly differentiated needs of member countries. They also need to respond to the expanding agenda of global and regional public goods, such as combating climate change. In a more complex international financial and development architecture, the coordination and leveraging role that the IFIs play will be increasingly important.

Robert B. Zoellick
President
World Bank

Dominique Strauss-Kahn
Managing Director
International Monetary Fund

Acknowledgments

This report has been prepared jointly by the staffs of the World Bank and the International Monetary Fund. In preparing the report, staff have collaborated closely with partner institutions—the African Development Bank, the Asian Development Bank, the European Bank for Reconstruction and Development, the Inter-American Development Bank, the Organisation for Economic Co-operation and Development, the World Trade Organization, and the United Nations. The cooperation and support of staff of these institutions are gratefully acknowledged.

Zia Qureshi was the lead author and manager of the report. The core team for the report included Punam Chuhan, Maureen Cropper, Stefano Curto, Kirk Hamilton, Bernard Hoekman, Homi Kharas, Maureen Lewis, Jamus Lim, Muthukumara Mani, Alessandro Nicita, and Giovanni Ruta (World Bank) and Richard Harmsen and Alexei Kireyev (IMF). Other significant contributions were made by Sebastien Dessus, Mary Hallward-Driemeier, and Linda Lee (World Bank) and Emmanuel Hife and Ioana Niculcea (IMF). Sachin Shahria assisted with the overall preparation and coordination of the report. The work was carried out under the general guidance of Alan Gelb, Acting Senior Vice President and Chief Economist, World Bank.

A number of other staff made valuable contributions, including the following from the World Bank: Issam Abousleiman, Mehdi Akhlaghi, Juan Alonso, Philippe Ambrosi, Jorge Araujo, Elizabeth Ashbourne, Soma Bhattacharya, Iwona Borowik, Eduard Bos, Paul Brenton, Shaohua Chen, Ajay Chhibber, Michael Child., Kenneth Chomitz, Susmita Dasgupta, William Dick, Ariel Dinar, Yvonne Edwards, Nevin Fahmy, Manuela Ferro, Viven Foster, Homa-Zahra Fotouhi, Dianne Garama, Colum Garrity, Batshur Gootiiz, Vincent Gouarne, Gloria Grandolini, Christopher Hall, Michael Jensen, Ellis Juan, Sima Kanaan, Arthur Karlin, Hiau Looi Kee, Jung-Kwan Kim, Jane Kirby-Zaki, Peter Kolsky, Markus Kostner, Aart Kraay, Arianna Legovini, Soe Lin, Andres Londono, Ana Lopes, Mariem Malouche, Aaditya Mattoo, Susan McAdams, Craig Meisner, Gary Milante, Don Mitchell, Lalita Moorty, Richard Newfarmer, Kyran O'Sullivan, Abha Prasad, Xiaolin Ren, Ashok Sarkar, Banafsheh Siadat, Susan Stout, Jana Stover, Gary Stuggins, Gaiv Tata, Margret Thalwitz, Mark Thomas, Sumter Travers, Katherine Tulenko, Gallina Vincelette, Roberto Zagha, and Albert Zeufack.

Other contributors from the IMF included Sonia Brunschwig, David Hofman, Subir Lall, Dustin Smith, Mark Tareen, and Anna Unikovskaya.

Contributors from other institutions included: Philibert Afrika, John Kofi Baffoe, Ferdinand Bakoup, Shen Gao, Onyango Ouma James, Penthesilea Lartey, Mohamed Manai, and Daniele Ponzi (AfDB); Chris MacCormac, Bruce Purdue, Antonio Ressano-Garcia, Manju Senapaty, and Shahid Zahid (ADB); Alistair Clark, James Earwicker, Elisabetta Falcetti, Jacquelin Ligot, Nicolas Mathieu, Terry McCallion, and Alan Rousso (EBRD); Marcelo Barrón, Tracy Betts Sikander Daryanani, Fernando Fernández, Orlando Ferreira, Carlos Herrera, Mercedes Mateo, Patricia Meduña, Fernando Mendoza, Max Pulgar-Vidal, Susana Rubio, Alejandro Soriano, Raul Tuazon, and Natasha Ward (IDB); and Yasmin Ahmad and Brian Hammond (OECD).

Acknowledgments are also due to Joseph Aldy, Robert Mendelsohn, Nicholas Stern, and David Wheeler for valuable contributions and comments.

Guidance received from the Executive Directors of the World Bank and the IMF and their staff during discussions of the draft report is gratefully acknowledged. The report also benefited from many useful comments and suggestions received from the Bank and Fund management and staff in the course of its preparation and review.

The World Bank's Office of the Publisher managed the editorial services, design, production, and printing of the report. In particular, Susan Graham, Denise Bergeron, Nancy Lammers, Stephen McGroarty, and Santiago Pombo-Bejarano, along with Kirsten Dennison and associates at Precision Graphics, Candace Roberts and associates at Quantum Think, and Martha Gottron, provided excellent help with publishing this report on a very tight schedule.

Abbreviations

ACP	African, Caribbean, and Pacific countries		EIF	Enhanced Integrated Framework
ADB	Asian Development Bank		EITI	Extractive Industries Transparency Initiative
AfDB	African Development Bank			
AIDS	acquired immune deficiency syndrome		EPA	Economic Partnership Agreement
AMC	Advanced Market Commitment		EPI	Environmental Performance Index (of the EU ACP)
ASEAN	Association of Southeast Asian Nations		EU	European Union
			FAO	Food and Agriculture Organization (of the UN)
CCT	conditional cash transfer			
CDM	Clean Development Mechanism		FDI	foreign direct investment
			GAVI	Global Alliance for Vaccines and Immunizations
CEA	Country Environmental Analyses (of the World Bank)			
			GDP	gross domestic product
CERs	Certified Emissions Reductions		GEF	Global Environment Facility
CPIA	Country Policy and Institutional Assessment		GFATM	Global Fund to Fight AIDS, Tuberculosis, and Malaria
CRS	Creditor Reporting System (of the OECD DAC)		GHG	greenhouse gas
			GNI	gross national income
DAC	Development Assistance Committee		HIPC	heavily indebted poor country/countries
DALY	disability-adjusted life year		HIV	human immunodeficiency virus
DRF	Debt Reduction Facility (of the World Bank)			
			IBRD	International Bank for Reconstruction and Development
EBRD	European Bank for Reconstruction and Development			
			IDA	International Development Association (of the World Bank Group)
EC	European Commission			
EDF	European Development Fund			
EFA-FTI	Education for All–Fast-Track Initiative		IDB	Inter-American Development Bank

IEA	International Energy Agency		OTRI	overall trade restrictiveness index
IFC	International Finance Corporation (of the World Bank Group)		PEPFAR	President's Emergency Plan for AIDS Relief
IFI	international financial institutions		PPP	purchasing power parity
IFFIm	International Finance Facility for Immunization		PRS	poverty reduction strategy
			PTA	preferential trade agreement
IHP	International Health Partnership		SADC	Southern Africa Development Community
IMF	International Monetary Fund		SME	small and medium enterprise
IPCC	Intergovernmental Panel on Climate Change		SWAp	sectorwide approach
			TTRI	Tariff Trade Restrictiveness Index
ITC	International Trade Centre		UA	unit of account
LDCs	least-developed countries		UN	United Nations
LICs	low-income countries		UNCTAD	UN Conference on Trade and Development
MDG	Millennium Development Goal			
MDB	multilateral development bank		UNFCCC	UN Framework Convention on Climate Change
MDRI	Multilateral Debt Relief Initiative		UNHCR	UN High Commissioner for Refugees
MICs	middle-income countries		UNDP	UN Development Programme
NAMA	non-agricultural market access			
NGOs	nongovernmental organizations		UNRWA	UN Relief and Works Agency
NTM	nontariff measure			
ODA	official development assistance		WFP	World Food Programme
OECD	Organisation for Economic Co-operation and Development		WHO	World Health Organization
OPEC	Organization of Petroleum Exporting Countries		WTO	World Trade Organization

Executive Summary

The central messages of the *Global Monitoring Report 2008* are clear: urgent action is needed to help the world meet the Millennium Development Goals (MDGs) by 2015; and urgent action is also needed to combat climate change that threatens the well-being of all countries, but particularly of poor countries and poor people. The goals of development and environmental sustainability are closely related, and the paths to those goals have many synergies.

MDGs at Midpoint

Assessment of the MDGs at midpoint presents a mixed picture, one of both significant progress and formidable challenges. The first MDG calls for reducing extreme poverty and hunger by half. Although the poverty goal is likely to be met at the global level, thanks to a remarkable surge in global economic growth over the past decade, there are serious shortfalls in fighting hunger and malnutrition. The recent rise in food prices has brought increased attention to these issues, but more is needed. On current trends, the human development MDGs are unlikely to be met. Prospects are gravest for the goals of reducing child and maternal mortality, but shortfalls are also likely in the primary school completion, empowerment of women, and sanitation MDGs.

Within this overall picture, there is considerable variation across regions and countries. At the regional level, Sub-Saharan Africa lags on all MDGs, including the goal for poverty reduction, though many countries in the region are now experiencing improved growth performance. South Asia lags on most human development MDGs, though it will likely meet the poverty reduction MDG. At the country level, on current trends most countries are off track to meet most of the MDGs, with those in fragile situations falling behind most seriously.

Yet most MDGs remain achievable for most countries if stronger efforts are made both by the countries and their development partners. Progress must be accelerated and made more inclusive. International attention associated with the MDG midpoint makes 2008 a crucial year to generate the necessary momentum. The planned high-level meetings during the year provide an opportunity to agree on priorities for action and milestones for monitoring progress.

Development and Environmental Sustainability

Concurrently, building on the outcome of the December 2007 conference in Bali, 2008 is also an important year to make progress on the climate change agenda. MDG 7 underscores the strong links between development and environmental sustainability, the special theme of this year's *Global Monitoring Report*. Ensuring environmental sustainability is necessary for achieving the other MDGs and maintaining long-term growth and development.

Early action to control greenhouse gas emissions will significantly reduce mitigation and adaptation costs. Even if efforts to stabilize emissions are successful, some degree of warming and related impacts will continue to occur into the next decades. Developing countries will be the most affected. In the 1990s about 200 million people a year, on average, were affected by climate-related disasters in developing countries, compared with 1 million in developed countries. Heavier dependence on natural resources and agriculture in poor countries makes them more vulnerable to the impact of climate change, and their poverty and lack of development make them less able to adapt. Thus development, adaptation, and mitigation are closely connected.

Inclusive and Sustainable Development: A Six-Point Agenda

To expedite and broaden progress toward the MDGs, and to ensure the sustainability of that progress, the report proposes a six-point agenda for inclusive and sustainable development.

1. Sustain and broaden the growth momentum

■ Strong and inclusive economic growth must be at the center of the strategy to achieve the MDGs. Poor countries need to achieve annual GDP growth of 7 percent or more to make serious dents in poverty.

■ Stronger, concerted efforts are needed to spur growth in lagging countries in Africa and elsewhere and in fragile states. While growth in Africa has improved, only about one-third of the region's population lives in countries that have achieved sustained GDP growth of 7 percent or more in the past decade.

■ While specific policy priorities for growth vary from country to country, looking across countries, three areas emerge as essential to robust growth: sound macroeconomic policies; a conducive private investment climate, including access to key infrastructures; and good governance. In fragile states, improvement of the governance environment, together with security enhancement, is crucial.

■ In many countries in Africa, and in low-income countries more generally, a dynamic agricultural sector is key to achieving strong and inclusive growth, and will help to mitigate the upward pressures on food prices. An African Green Revolution would provide a strong foundation for growth and poverty reduction in the region.

■ Risks to developing-country growth arising from the financial market turbulence and the rise in energy and food prices need careful monitoring and appropriate policy responses, including prudent fiscal and monetary policies and, where needed, well-targeted safety nets to cushion the impact of the price increases on the poor.

2. Achieve better results in human development

■ Progress toward the human development goals must be accelerated. That will require commitment of more resources, including increased donor support, to key programs in education and health—for example, the Fast-Track Initiative in education, health systems strengthening, and combating malaria.

■ More spending on education and health programs, however, is not the sole answer. The quality and equity of spending are equally important. Improved governance, stronger accountability mechanisms, and sound expenditure management are essential to raising the quality of education and health services and improving the access of poor, underserved populations.

- A stronger focus is needed on combating malnutrition, especially among children, to underpin better human development outcomes.
- Policies and programs must factor in the strong links that exist between health and education outcomes, nutrition, and environmental factors—water and sanitation, pollution, and climate change.

3. Integrate development and environmental sustainability

- Environmental sustainability must be integrated into core development work, maximizing synergies. Environmental management and integration with the development agenda require institutional strengthening in developing countries, including capacity building for related institutions and improvement of policies such as property rights to natural resources.
- For natural resource–dependent countries, sound resource management is critical for sustainable growth. The quality of macroeconomic management and governance can determine whether the resource wealth is a source of development finance or a contributor to the "resource curse." The Extractive Industries Transparency Initiative has laid a good foundation for enhancing international cooperation in support of efficient and transparent management of natural resources.
- Mitigation of carbon emissions will require financing and technology transfer to support transition to low-carbon growth in developing countries. Such support should not divert resources from other development programs.
- Developing countries will also need support with adaptation to climate change,

which is vitally important for them given their greater vulnerability. For poor countries, the best way to adapt is to develop— by diversifying their economies, strengthening infrastructure, developing health systems, and curbing climate-sensitive diseases such as malaria and diarrhea.

4. Scale up aid and increase its effectiveness

- The time to deliver on aid commitments to support the effort to meet the MDGs is now. Donors must expedite aid delivery to meet their commitments. Sizable shortfalls loom if current trends in official development assistance continue; shortfalls will particularly hurt those poor countries and fragile states that, thanks to their reform efforts, offer promising scale-up opportunities.
- The changing aid architecture, including new sources and modalities of aid, promises much-needed increases in resources and creates opportunities for experimentation and innovation in development finance. It also poses new challenges for aid effectiveness and coherence. The opportunity provided by the Accra High Level Forum in September 2008 should be used to address the new, dynamic dimensions of the aid effectiveness agenda.
- Increased private flows to developing countries create opportunities to catalyze and leverage more private capital in support of development, including through innovative public-private partnerships.
- Both borrowers and creditors need to pay attention to debt sustainability considerations to prevent a reaccumulation of unsustainable debts following debt relief.

5. Harness trade for strong, inclusive, and sustainable growth

- The international community must aim for a successful outcome of the Doha trade negotiations in 2008. The current high food prices provide a window of opportunity to break the impasse on agricultural trade liberalization.

- Aid for trade should be increased; together with behind-the-border reforms of key trade-related services, it can help poor countries take advantage of trade opportunities, promoting more inclusive globalization.

- Trade policy can facilitate transfer of environmentally friendly technologies by removing barriers to trade in environmental products and services.

6. Leverage IFI support for inclusive and sustainable development

- The international financial institutions (IFIs) have a crucial role to play in supporting this interrelated development and environment agenda through their financing, knowledge, and coordination services. In a more complex international financial and development architecture, the coordination and leveraging role that the IFIs play will be increasingly important, even as their relative financing role declines.

- At the country level, the IFIs need to tailor their advice, products, and services to the increasingly differentiated needs of their member countries, including a strong focus on low-income countries, fragile states, and concentrations of poverty within middle-income countries to help the "bottom billion" grow and connect to the global economy.

- The IFIs also need to adapt their strategies to respond to the growing importance of global and regional public goods, such as combating climate change, through advice, direct interventions, and working with other development partners and the private sector.

Overview

Declaring a "development emergency," a host of world leaders meeting in Davos, Switzerland, in January 2008 issued an MDG Call to Action to help the world get back on track to meet the Millennium Development Goals. Halfway to 2015, the international community needs to recommit to the development goals and redouble efforts to achieve them. International attention and a series of planned high-level meetings in connection with the MDG midpoint make 2008 a crucial year to build stronger and broader momentum toward the MDGs—to make the midpoint a turning point for the development goals.

While many developing countries are making impressive progress toward the MDGs, many others are falling behind. On current trends, a majority of countries will fall short of most MDGs. Yet, the MDGs remain achievable for most countries if stronger efforts are made both by the countries themselves and their development partners—in the spirit of mutual accountability for these goals agreed at Monterrey, Mexico, in 2002.[1] Assessment at the MDG halfway point shows a clear, urgent need to accelerate progress and make it more inclusive. The planned high-level international meetings in 2008 provide an opportunity to agree on priorities, including setting possible interim milestones

toward the goals to focus the action and measure progress.

Building on the outcome of the Bali climate change conference, 2008 is also an important year to make progress on the climate change agenda. MDG 7 underscores the strong links between development and environmental sustainability. Ensuring environmental sustainability is important for achieving the other MDGs and sustaining long-term growth and development. Climate change and loss and degradation of natural resources have the potential to severely reverse hard-earned development gains of the past and constrain prospects for the future. Developing countries will suffer the most and are the least able to adapt. As World Bank President Robert B. Zoellick observed at the Bali conference, "Climate change is a development, economic, and investment challenge, not just an environmental issue. . . . Addressing climate change is a critical pillar of the development agenda."[2]

This report addresses the interrelated challenges of development and environmental sustainability. It assesses progress and priorities in the agenda to achieve the MDGs. It assesses the challenge of environmental sustainability and its implications for developing countries, and monitors progress at national and global levels to address the challenge. Based on its assessment, the report sets out an integrated agenda for development that is inclusive and sustainable.

MDGs at Midpoint: Significant Progress, Yet Formidable Challenges

Poverty reduction: strong but uneven progress. First the good news. The world is on course to achieve the first target under MDG 1—halving extreme poverty between 1990 and 2015. This success owes much to a remarkable surge in economic growth. The world economy and the developing countries have rarely grown faster over a sustained period. Growth in developing countries has averaged over 7 percent in the past five years. The number of extreme poor—those living under $1 a day—in the developing world declined by 278 million between 1990 and 2004, and by a stunning 150 million in the last five years of that period. The sizable reduction in the absolute number of poor people is all the more remarkable as it was achieved notwithstanding a rise in the population of the developing world by about 1 billion between 1990 and 2004. The decline in poverty has been the largest in regions with the strongest growth. East Asia, the fastest growing region, has already reached the poverty-reduction MDG. Other regions have also shared in the rise in economic growth and reduction of poverty.

Yet progress has been uneven, with many countries lagging behind, especially in Africa. While the MDG 1 poverty-reduction target will be met at the global level, Sub-Saharan Africa is likely to fall well short. There has been a very encouraging pickup in growth in the region. Some 18 countries with better-managed economies have grown at an average rate of about 5.5 percent over the past 10 years. But roughly as many countries in the region, some 20 in number, many affected by conflict, have remained trapped in low growth, averaging only about 2 percent. Even among the faster growers, only a few, mainly resource-rich countries, have managed to achieve growth in the 7–8 percent range that

is needed to make serious dents in poverty and reach the poverty-reduction target under MDG 1. In Africa as well as in other regions, progress in poverty reduction has been slowest in fragile states. Indeed, in aggregate, the incidence of extreme poverty *rose* in this group of countries. Fragile states, wracked by conflict and hampered by weak governance and capacities, account for about 19 percent of the population of low-income countries but more than one-third of their poor people. Globally, around 1 billion people continue to live in extreme poverty. Excluding China, extreme poverty between 1990 and 2004 declined by a much smaller 32 million.

Human development goals: more serious shortfalls. Notable progress has been made on human development–related MDGs, but the risks of falling short are far greater for these goals than for the income poverty MDG. Again, the good news first. Halfway to 2015, about 40 million more children are in school; gender disparity in primary and secondary schools has declined by 60 percent; 3 million more children survive every year; 2 million lives are saved every year by immunization; and 2 million people now receive AIDS treatment. Yet, about 75 million children of primary school age are still not in school; 10,000 women die every week from treatable complications of pregnancy and birth; more than 190,000 children under five die of disease every week; over 33 million people are infected with HIV, with more than 2 million dying every year from AIDS; more than 1 million people die of malaria, a preventable disease, every year, including 1 child every 30 seconds; and about half of the developing world lacks basic sanitation.

Despite progress, on current trends most human development MDGs are unlikely to be met at the global level. While some regions will meet some of these goals, Sub-Saharan Africa and, in some cases, South Asia are likely to fall seriously short. Prospects are gravest in health, with large shortfalls likely at the global level and in several regions in reducing child and maternal mortality by two-thirds and three-quarters, respectively, and halving the proportion of those without access to basic sanitation (there is greater progress on the related goal of halving the proportion of those without access to safe water). While much progress has been made in reducing child malnutrition, shortfalls are likely in reaching the goal of halving its incidence, especially in Sub-Saharan Africa and South Asia. The HIV prevalence rate has shown some decline in Africa but has risen in some other regions, albeit from much smaller levels than in Africa. Mortality from malaria remains high but lack of data makes it difficult to monitor incidence over time.

Prospects are better in education. The world is likely to miss the goal of universal primary school completion, though it will come close. However, sizable shortfalls are likely in Sub-Saharan Africa and South Asia. The goal of eliminating gender disparity in primary and secondary education seems attainable by 2015, although Sub-Saharan Africa is likely to fall short. Prospects for achieving gender parity in tertiary education and other gender-related targets are less promising. The regional shortfalls in Sub-Saharan Africa and South Asia in part reflect the lower base they started from.

Overall outlook: daunting challenges, but grounds for hope. In sum, while many countries have made impressive progress, most countries are currently off track to meet most of the MDGs, with fragile states falling behind most seriously. At a regional level, Sub-Saharan Africa lags on all MDGs, including MDG 1 for poverty reduction. South Asia lags on most human development goals, although it will likely meet the poverty reduction MDG.

With the world already at the halfway point, recovering lost ground on some of the MDGs seems daunting. Indeed, it is a huge challenge. But rapid progress is possible. The success of better-performing regions and countries inspires and gives reasons for hope. One such example is Vietnam's achievement in reducing poverty from around 58 percent in 1993 to 16 percent in 2006. Even in many

lagging countries, including in Africa, progress is being made. The strengthening of economic growth in a number of African countries is especially significant. Some African countries recently have achieved impressive results: for example, Ghana, Mozambique, Tanzania, and Uganda in accelerating growth and reducing poverty; Malawi in achieving particular success in boosting agricultural productivity; Ghana, Kenya, Tanzania, and Uganda in increasing primary school enrollment; Niger, Togo, and Zambia in combating malaria; Senegal and Uganda in increasing access to water and sanitation; Niger in promoting reforestation; and Rwanda in achieving an impressive recovery from conflict. This progress needs to be quickened and broadened—across MDGs, across countries, and across populations within countries.

Development and Environmental Sustainability: Integrally Linked

Urgency of action to accelerate and broaden progress toward the development goals is paralleled by urgency of action to combat climate change that threatens the well-being of all countries but particularly that of poor countries and poor people. Development and environmental sustainability are fundamentally complementary objectives (although in the short term they may appear as trade-offs). Environmental sustainability is essential for continued economic growth and reduction of poverty. It also exerts positive impacts on human development goals—health, nutrition, and education outcomes. Economic growth and development in poor countries in turn can contribute to environmental sustainability by improving their access to modern energy and cleaner and more efficient technologies and by reducing reliance on activities, such as cutting forests, that are detrimental to the environment. Deforestation contributes about one-fifth of total greenhouse gas (GHG) emissions. At present, 1.6 billion people, about a third of the developing world's population, are without access to modern energy, forced to rely on more carbon-emitting biomass and fossil-fuel energy. Economic development also expands the resources and capacities of poor countries to adapt to environmental impacts.

Sound natural resource management essential. For developing countries, most of whom have a high dependence on natural resources, carefully managing those resources and the environment is especially important for the sustainability of growth and development outcomes. On average, natural capital constitutes more than 40 percent of the national wealth of low-income countries (close to 60 percent if the more advanced emerging market countries are excluded from this group), compared with only 5 percent in high-income countries. Issues of sustainable use of natural resources are typically raised in relation to subsoil assets, notably oil, but extend to other resources such as forests and water. An area of forest equivalent to the size of Panama or Sierra Leone is lost every year to land use changes, with most of the loss concentrated in Latin America and Sub-Saharan Africa. Per capita freshwater availability could fall below critical levels in the near future in many countries in the Middle East and South Asia. Pollution threatens the quality of air and water. The major urban air pollutant affecting human health is particulate matter whose concentrations in low-income countries are on average nearly three times higher than in high-income countries. How these resources are managed will be critical to longer-term sustainability of growth.

Climate change: poor countries most affected. Heavier dependence on natural resources and agriculture and lack of development also render poor countries more vulnerable to the impact of climate change and less able to adapt. These include impacts on agriculture and human health, and the effects of sea level rise and extreme weather events. Estimates of the impact of global warming through 2080 based on nonmitigation

scenarios show developing countries in Sub-Saharan Africa, South Asia, and parts of Latin America, which are home to 1 billion of the world's poorest people, suffering the largest losses in agricultural output, ranging from 15–60 percent. Environmental risk factors play a role in 80 percent of diseases globally, and the economic burden of environmental health hazards has been estimated at 1.5–4 percent of GDP. The cost of climate change in disability-adjusted life years was estimated at 5.5 million annually in 2000, an estimate that will only rise if climate change is not checked. Children of the developing world bear the brunt of the health impact of climate change through increased incidence of diseases such as diarrhea, malaria, and respiratory infections. More than 200 million people in developing countries live in potential impact zones where they would become refugees from coastal flooding at a three-meter sea level rise. Even at a one-meter sea level rise, a number of countries would be significantly affected: for example, without adaptation efforts, more than 10 percent of Vietnam's population would be affected, and the country would lose 10 percent of its GDP and 29 percent of its wetlands. During the 1990s, 200 million people per year, on average, were affected by climate-related disasters in developing countries, compared with about 1 million in developed countries.

Inclusive and Sustainable Development: A Six-Point Agenda

What is the agenda implied by this assessment? Progress toward the MDGs must be quickened and broadened to include the many countries that are lagging behind. To ensure the sustainability of this progress, the environmental challenges must be addressed in a manner that is supportive of developing countries' growth and development. To meet these challenges, the report sets out a six-point agenda for inclusive and sustainable development (box 0.1).

BOX 0.1 MDGs and the environment

A six-point agenda for inclusive and sustainable development

- *Sustain and broaden the growth momentum*
  - Strong and inclusive growth must be at the center of the strategy to achieve the MDGs.
  - Concerted efforts are needed to spur growth in lagging countries in Africa and fragile states; a dynamic agricultural sector is crucial for strong and inclusive growth in many poor countries.
  - Sound macroeconomic policies, a conducive private investment climate (regulatory environment, infrastructure), and good governance are essential for growth.
  - Risks to developing-country growth arising from recent financial market turbulence and rises in oil and food prices need careful monitoring and appropriate responses.

- *Achieve better results in human development*
  - Key programs in health and education must be stepped up—for example, the Fast-Track Initiative in education, eradication of malaria, and health systems strengthening.
  - Increased public spending alone is not the answer; quality and equity of spending are equally important.
  - A stronger focus is needed to combat malnutrition, especially among children, and to underpin better human development outcomes.
  - Policies and interventions must factor in the strong links between health and education outcomes, nutrition, and environmental factors—water and sanitation, pollution, and climate change.

- *Integrate development and environmental sustainability*
  - Environmental sustainability must be integrated into core development work, maximizing synergies.
  - For natural resource–dependent countries, sound resource management is critical for sustainable growth.
  - Developing countries will suffer most from climate change and are least able to adapt; for them the best way to adapt is to develop.
  - Transition to climate-resilient and low-carbon growth will require financing and technology transfer to developing countries. Such support should not divert resources from other development programs.

- *Scale up aid and increase its effectiveness*
  - Donors must expedite aid delivery in line with commitments. Sizable shortfalls loom if current ODA trends persist, which will particularly hurt poor countries and fragile states that offer promising scale-up opportunities.
  - The changing aid architecture promises more resources and innovation but also poses new challenges for aid effectiveness and coherence. The Accra High Level Forum provides a timely opportunity to address the new, dynamic dimensions of the aid agenda.
  - Increased private flows to developing countries create opportunities to catalyze and leverage more private capital in support of development, including through innovative public-private partnerships.
  - Both borrowers and creditors need to pay attention to debt sustainability to prevent a reaccumulation of unsustainable debts following debt relief.

- *Harness trade for strong, inclusive, and sustainable growth*
  - Countries must aim for a successful Doha outcome in 2008. High food prices provide a window of opportunity to move on agricultural trade reform.
  - Aid for trade to strengthen trade logistics, supported by services liberalization, is important for poor countries' competitiveness and ability to benefit from trade opportunities.
  - Trade policy can facilitate transfer of environmentally friendly technologies by removing barriers to trade in environmental products and services.

- *Leverage IFI support for inclusive and sustainable development*
  - The declining relative financing role of the international financial institutions (IFIs) does not imply less relevance. Their impact through leverage remains key in achieving collective action on development (MDGs and related outcomes) and the increasingly important global and regional public goods such as combating climate change.
  - Adaptation of operational strategies initiated by several IFIs in response to increasing client differentiation and global change is important and timely.

1. Sustaining and Broadening the Growth Momentum

Strong and inclusive growth is central to achieving the MDGs and related development outcomes. It reduces poverty directly and expands resources and capacities for achieving the other MDGs related to human development and environmental sustainability.

Implications of Global Economic Developments

Financial turbulence, global slowdown. An immediate priority is to contain the international financial market turbulence and limit its impact on developing country growth. Thus far the effects on developing countries have been relatively contained, thanks to improved macroeconomic policies and stronger fundamentals. Global GDP growth in 2008 is projected to slow to 3.7 percent from 4.9 percent in 2007, with growth in developing countries slowing by about a percentage point but still remaining relatively strong at 6.7 percent.

Nonetheless, the persistence of financial market turbulence and its knock-on effects on growth pose downside risks to this outlook. Also, private capital flows, which have become much more important as a source of external financing in developing countries, could reverse. Countries with large current account deficits and asset bubbles are particularly vulnerable, especially in emerging Europe, and bear close monitoring. Given current uncertainties and country differences, there is no single policy prescription for developing countries in addressing the implications of the financial market turmoil. Vulnerabilities and the appropriate policy responses must be assessed on a country-by-country basis. Prudent policies that allow automatic stabilizers to operate may be preferable to policy activism for many countries. Renewed attention to fundamentals—prudent external debt management, fiscal discipline, and flexible exchange rate policies—can cushion shocks and facilitate adjustment in vulnerable countries.

Rise in oil and food prices. Another, and related, immediate concern is the implications of the sharp rise in the prices of oil and food. Both supply constraints and rapid growth in demand have contributed to the rise in prices—including, in the case of food prices, the increasing use of food crops for biofuels. Thus far the macroeconomic impact on importing countries in general has been relatively limited, offset by rising prices of other commodity exports and higher capital inflows. But the situation of net oil and food importers could worsen if oil and food prices rise further or if the favorable offsetting developments reverse. Poor people in developing countries spend as much as a half of their income on food. The urban poor are the most directly affected. Possible policy responses range from energy demand management and targeted safety nets for affected poor in the short term to longer-term measures to increase energy production and promote agricultural growth. To cushion the impact of price shocks on the poor, reliance should be placed on targeted safety net programs, avoiding recourse to price controls and trade restrictions that are distortive, ineffective, and ultimately unsustainable. If needed, the International Monetary Fund (IMF) and the World Bank could provide financial support through the Exogenous Shocks Facility or IDA (International Development Association) financing.

Policies and Institutions for Strong and Inclusive Growth

Looking to the medium term, a key challenge is to spur stronger growth in lagging countries that have not shared in the surge in growth witnessed in much of the developing world over the past several years. Specific policy priorities and sequencing of actions to promote growth necessarily vary by country. Across developing countries there is considerable diversity in economic circumstances. The specifics of the policy agenda for growth at the country level must be defined as part of individual country development strategies. Looking across countries, three broad areas emerge as being essential to robust growth: sound macroeconomic policies; a conducive private investment climate, including a business-friendly regulatory environment and access to key infrastructure; and good governance. Policies in all three areas have been improving in developing countries but progress has been uneven, which is mirrored in the improving but uneven growth performance across countries in recent years. Deeper and more consistent progress on reforms in these key areas will be needed to achieve sustained and more broadly based growth.

The growth agenda in Africa. Sub-Saharan Africa perhaps illustrates the diversity of countries' growth performance most strikingly. About 20 countries, accounting for a third of the region's population, continue to record very low rates of economic growth that imply stagnant or even declining per capita incomes. Many of these are fragile states affected by conflict. Their policy agenda comprises a mix of security enhancement, political reform and consolidation, capacity building, and actions to build private sector opportunities. They need international aid, but they also need to strengthen basic governmental capacity to ensure its effective use.

Another group of African countries accounting also for roughly a third of the region's population has improved growth performance in recent years to an average of 5–6 percent, with some achieving higher growth. This group includes countries such as Ghana, Mozambique, Rwanda, Tanzania, and Uganda, which a decade ago appeared to have rather grim prospects. Their main challenge is to build on reforms to strengthen the foundations for strong, sustained, and broad-based growth. Solidifying macroeconomic stability, further improving the climate for private investment through regulatory and institutional reform and strengthened physical infrastructure, and deepening regional and global links are key elements of their growth agenda. These countries demonstrate capacity to utilize scaled-up external assistance effectively to further their growth prospects.

In many countries in Africa, and in low-income countries more generally, a dynamic agricultural sector is crucial for strong and inclusive growth and will help to mitigate the upward pressures on food prices that became visible in 2007. An estimated 900 million rural people in the developing world live on less than $1 a day; most of them are engaged in agriculture in some form. A recent World Bank study estimated that GDP growth originating in agriculture is about four times more effective in reducing poverty than GDP growth originating outside the sector.[3] An African Green Revolution would provide a strong foundation for growth and poverty reduction in the region.

Managing natural resource revenues. Some African countries that are rich in natural resources, and that together account for most of the remaining one-third of the region's population, have achieved average growth rates as high as 9 percent, fueled by the boom in resource prices. Their main challenge lies in managing and transforming their natural resource wealth into long-term sustainable growth. This calls for good governance to support extracting and managing the resource wealth efficiently and transparently and transforming resource revenues into productive investments that help diversify the economic base. Explicit resource rent policies are often needed: the chain from rent capture to the management and use of resource rents can determine whether rich resource stocks are a source of development finance or a contributor to the "resource curse." Countries should be encouraged to participate in the Extractive Industries Transparency Initiative (EITI), which is making headway, with 24 implementing countries (of which 17 are in Sub-Saharan Africa) including 7 with national EITI reports out and a system in place for validating performance.

Rise in income inequalities: Is globalization to blame? Besides disparities in growth performance across developing countries, there has been an increase in income inequality within many countries. That increase has been more pronounced in countries with higher growth rates. A recent IMF study analyzing the impact of globalization on inequality found that the major factor contributing to the rise in inequality has not been globalization, but rather technological progress, which has reduced demand for low-skill workers and increased opportunities and rewards for higher-skill workers. Financial globalization has contributed too, but its effect has been more than offset by the equalizing effect of trade liberalization. Broadening access to education and financial services would help counter the disequalizing effects of technological progress and financial globalization.[4] Also important is an investment climate that expands opportunities by providing a level playing field to firms. In poor countries, boosting agriculture is crucial for inclusive growth, as noted above.

2. Achieving Better Results in Human Development

Progress toward the human development MDGs must be expedited if serious shortfalls are to be avoided. A major scaling up of efforts is needed in education and health, and especially in health, where on current trends shortfalls are likely to be the most serious. This will require commitment of more resources, including donor support, to programs in these sectors—for example, the Fast-Track Initiative in education, health systems strengthening, and combating malaria. But more spending alone is not the answer. The quality and equity of spending are equally important. More attention needs to be paid to early childhood interventions, such as improved nutrition, that can establish a stronger foundation for better human development outcomes later in life. Policies and programs must also factor in the strong links that exist between health and education outcomes and environmental risk factors, such as lack of access to clean water and basic sanitation, pollution, and climate change.

Raising quality of health services. Complementing the focus on quality in education in the 2007 *Global Monitoring Report,* this report assesses the quality of programs and services in health and the role of quality in achieving the desired health outcomes. Addressing the issue of quality in public health care can make a significant contribution toward reducing child mortality, improving maternal health, checking the spread of major diseases, and reducing malnutrition. Health care quality is highly uneven, both across and within countries, whether measured by the breadth of medical facility and treatment coverage, health care provider competence and motivation, or medical outcomes. Thanks to expanded health programs, access to health care is improving, but poor outcome measures in many instances suggest low or falling quality as access rises. Research shows that rising per capita income is positively related to health care quality, but rising public health spending alone is not. Effectiveness of spending and service delivery matters. Improved governance is critical for raising quality, including attention to the competency of providers, incentives to improve performance, and accountability mechanisms to ensure better outcomes. Sound expenditure management, better information (real-time data, oversight, including checking the extensive prevalence of absenteeism, and monitoring and auditing), and a focus on results are essential to more effective service delivery. Strategies to make effective use of the private sector and to strengthen the voice of clients at the point of service delivery and within communities also contribute to better quality services.

Achieving more equitable outcomes. In addition to quality issues, progress toward the MDGs is undermined by inequity in health and education spending and outcomes. Health and education spending is often skewed toward higher-income households. Analysis of the incidence of public health and education spending shows the top income quintile benefiting substantially more than the bottom quintile in practically all developing regions—by a factor of more than two in South Asia and Sub-Saharan

Africa. Inequity in outcomes is illustrated by the fact that in Latin America a child born in the poorest quintile is almost three times as likely to die before the age of five as a child born in the richest quintile, almost six times as likely to be malnourished, and only two-thirds as likely to receive medical treatment for a simple complaint such as a fever. Low service quality exacerbates inequity as the poor are much more likely to receive sub-standard services and could be discouraged from using the services altogether—even if these are free. Achieving gender parity in service access and outcomes has been a rela-tive success, but large disparities persist for poorer segments of the population, those in rural areas, and minority groups. Better targeted and tailored programs are needed to reach the underserved and marginalized groups. Where feasible, conditional cash transfer (CCT) programs can help.

Tackling malnutrition. Malnutrition, espe-cially among children, directly affects the incidence of disease and the probability of mortality. Malnutrition is the underlying cause of at least 3.5 million deaths annually and accounts for 35 percent of the disease burden of children under age five. Better nutrition in early years influences children's subsequent educational performance and their prospects for finishing school. Malnu-trition during pregnancy increases the risk of a mother's death at delivery and accounts for more than 20 percent of maternal mortality. Combating malnutrition, part of MDG 1, is thus important also to the achievement of MDGs 2, 4, and 5. While much progress has been made in reducing child malnutrition in the developing world, it remains widespread in many countries, especially in Sub-Saharan Africa and South Asia where severe to mod-erate stunting affects as many as 35 percent of children under five. South Asia has the highest incidence of child malnutrition; the child malnutrition rate in India is double the African average.

Food security is important for combat-ing malnutrition, but factors such as the mother's education and family income are equally, if not more, important. Through reducing the risk of diseases such as diar-rhea, access to clean water and basic sani-tation also matters. Technical interventions to combat malnutrition already exist. They need to be expanded to scale and placed in a wider multisectoral context. Donor pro-grams to combat nutrition typically have been dominated by food aid and supply-led technical assistance. An integrated, multi-sectoral approach is needed that recognizes the multiple factors involved and exploits related synergies, emphasizes education for mothers, explores innovative delivery mech-anisms such as school feeding programs with locally purchased food and CCTs, and engages communities and the private sector. The recent sharp rise in world food prices only increases the urgency of action.

Addressing environmental health risks. Principal environmental risk factors for health include water and sanitation (diar-rhea and malaria), indoor and urban out-door air pollution (respiratory infections), and climate change (tropical vector-borne diseases such as malaria). About a quarter of all deaths in the developing world are princi-pally attributable to environmental risk fac-tors. Unsafe drinking water and poor sani-tation and hygiene account for around 90 percent of diarrhea cases worldwide. More than 40 percent of the global burden of malaria can be prevented through improved environmental management. An estimated 1.5 million deaths annually caused by respi-ratory infections are attributable to environ-mental pollution.

In addressing the environmental risk factors, a key priority is to improve access to clean water and basic sanitation and to promote better hygiene, a vital comple-ment to water and sanitation expansion in poor countries. It is estimated that meeting the water and sanitation MDG will require annual investment on the order of $30 bil-lion, roughly double the current level.[5] But it is not only a matter of public investment in new systems. Better operation and maintenance of existing systems, and use of tariffs to help finance that while protecting the poor, are essential, as is the exploitation of opportunities for private participation. Institutional strengthening of sector agencies will be necessary, as will coordination across sectors given the strong linkages to health. Responses to environmental health risks arising from pollution and climate change are part of the broader agenda of mitigation and adaptation addressed below.

3. Integrating Development and Environmental Sustainability

Environmental sustainability must be integrated into core development work, maximizing synergies. Countries have over the years increasingly incorporated into their growth and development strategies important aspects of environmental management, including energy access and efficiency, control of pollution, improvement of water and sanitation systems, forest resource and land use management, and preservation of fisheries and biodiversity. Building on this progress, the growing threat of global warming now necessitates an increased emphasis on integration of climate change prevention in development strategies—not to curtail development but to sustain it by permitting continued economic growth through reductions in carbon intensity and by strengthening capacity to adapt to climate risks.

Early action to control GHG emissions will significantly reduce mitigation and adaptation costs. Even if efforts to stabilize GHG emission are successful, some degree of warming and related impacts will continue to occur into the next decades. An effective response to climate change must combine both mitigation and adaptation.

Moving forward on mitigation. The international community must work toward a timely agreement on a post-Kyoto framework for mitigation. Stabilization of GHG concentrations within levels that keep the effects of climate change manageable will require a significant reduction of carbon emissions by developed countries along with a curbing of growth in emissions by developing countries with eventual stabilization in the longer term. This accords with the principle of "common but differentiated responsibilities and respective capabilities" that recognizes developing countries' lower historical contribution to GHG concentrations and much lower energy use and carbon emissions per capita. However, even if total carbon emissions of developing countries are allowed to rise for some time, efforts must be made to reduce the carbon intensity of GDP (emissions per unit of GDP). Key elements of a mitigation framework include:

- pricing of carbon to provide market-based incentives to mitigate
- development and diffusion of cleaner and more energy efficient technologies and of renewable energy sources
- financing and technology transfer to support transition to low-carbon growth in developing countries
- reducing deforestation.

Low-cost, high-impact opportunities should be fully exploited, such as investing in "no-regrets" options for improving energy efficiency—investments that are based on existing technologies or approaches and would pay for themselves if subsidies to energy consumption and production were removed.

Strengthening adaptation: vital for developing countries. Adaptation is particularly important for developing countries as they will suffer the most from climate change and are able to adapt the least. For them, the best way to adapt is to develop, which will strengthen adaptation options and capacities by diversifying their economies and expanding the resources they need to adapt—by strengthening infrastructure, developing health systems and curbing climate-sensitive diseases such as malaria and diarrhea. Programs to reduce vulnerability and "climate proofing" of investments can have immediate payoffs, such as implementing early warning systems for heat waves, floods, and droughts; building dams to accommodate increased runoff; and making roads and bridges climate proof. As vulnerability to climate impacts varies widely across developing countries, adaptation programs must be country specific.

Financing mitigation and adaptation. The Secretariat of the UN Framework Convention on Climate Change has estimated that by 2030, annual financial flows to developing countries will need to be on the order of $100 billion to finance mitigation and $28 billion to $67 billion for adaptation. While over 80 percent of these flows are expected to come from the private sector, with carbon markets playing an increasingly important role, public sector financing also will be essential to create the enabling environment for private financing. Assistance for mitigation and adaptation should be additional to current levels of official development assistance so that resources are not diverted from other development programs.

Institutional strengthening. Environmental management and its integration with the development agenda will also require institutional strengthening in developing countries. This includes both capacity building for related institutions and improvement of key policies such as property rights to natural resources. While progress is being made, institutions for environmental management in developing countries are particularly weak. Progress has been strongest in Eastern Europe and Central Asia whereas South Asia and Sub-Saharan Africa have lagged behind. Progress on environmental policies in many cases is undermined by weak institutional capacities for enforcement.

4. Scaling Up Aid and Increasing its Effectiveness

Developing countries must make stronger efforts to mobilize more domestic resources

to accelerate progress toward the MDGs—moving vigorously to spur economic growth, strengthening revenue administration, and improving the efficiency of spending. They must also build on reforms to mobilize private investment—domestic and foreign. Still, for most low-income countries, official development assistance (ODA) remains a major source of development finance. In Sub-Saharan Africa, home to most of these countries, official flows account for about two-thirds of all capital inflows. Even with stronger efforts to mobilize more domestic resources and attract more private capital inflows, these countries will need a substantial increase in ODA to improve their prospects for achieving the MDGs. In middle-income countries aid plays a much smaller but still important role, by catalyzing reforms, supporting efforts to tackle concentrations of poverty, helping to counter negative shocks, and assisting with global or regional public goods such as climate change.

Increasing aid to exploit scale-up opportunities. The time to deliver on aid commitments to support the effort to achieve the MDGs is now. Donors must expedite aid delivery. If current ODA trends persist, sizable shortfalls loom, which would particularly hurt poor countries and fragile states that offer promising opportunities to scale up development results. Many countries have improved their policies and capacities and are able to utilize increased aid productively. But donor response has tended to fall short. Both aid recipients and donors need to deliver on their commitments if the MDGs are to be achieved.

The latest aid numbers give cause for concern. The rise in ODA appears to have stalled. After rising during 2002–05, total net ODA from Development Assistance Committee (DAC) donors fell by 5 percent in real terms in 2006, and preliminary indications are that it declined by a further 8.4 percent in real terms in 2007. At $103.7 billion in 2007, DAC net ODA was about $15 billion higher than its 2004 (pre-Gleneagles) level, but much larger and sustained increases in aid will be needed to reach the target of a $50 billion increase in real terms by 2010 that was set at the 2005 Group of Eight summit in Gleneagles, United Kingdom (which would raise total net ODA to $130 billion in constant 2004 dollars). Aid to Sub-Saharan Africa shows broadly the same pattern: it has risen but at well short of the rate that would achieve the targeted doubling of aid by 2010. Moreover, the bulk (about 70 percent) of the increase in ODA post-Gleneagles has been in the form of debt relief. Core development aid—program and project aid—has shown relatively little increase. Debt relief has significantly reduced the debt burden of beneficiary countries and expanded the fiscal space for development spending. As debt relief operations wind down, core development aid will need to rise quite sharply to reach the Gleneagles target for total ODA. However, preliminary evidence from DAC's 2007 forward survey of donors' aid intentions suggests that, overall, these are not yet sufficiently ambitious to meet the targets set for 2010.

While traditional donors remain the dominant source of development aid, the aid landscape is changing rapidly. New sources of aid have emerged, both from new official bilateral donors, including some developing-country donors such as China and India, and from private donors, who are playing an increasing role in aid. New modalities of aid include global vertical funds focused on specific objectives, such as the Global Fund to Fight AIDS, Tuberculosis, and Malaria and the Global Alliance for Vaccination and Immunization, and innovative financing modalities, such as the International Finance Facility for Immunization, Advance Market Commitments, and the solidarity levy on airline tickets. These new sources and modalities of aid, whose role in the overall aid architecture is likely to increase, are expanding the potential aid envelope and creating new opportunities for experimentation and innovation in development finance. They also pose new challenges for aid effectiveness and coherence, to maximize their development impact.

Ensuring aid effectiveness in a changing aid architecture. Overall, there is some encouraging progress in the implementation of the Paris Declaration on Aid Effectiveness. Progress on aid alignment and harmonization has been notable though uneven. The predictability of aid is improving. However, much of that improved predictability relates to the near term. Medium-term predictability, important for countries' planning and implementation of development strategies and programs, remains low. Longer time horizons for aid commitments and clearer rules for qualification and disbursement are needed. Even as gains are made on the Paris aid alignment and harmonization agenda, new challenges have arisen as the aid architecture has become more complex with more donors, the potential for increased fragmentation of aid, and increased earmarking through vertical approaches.

The increased complexity of the aid architecture enhances the role of strong country-led strategies as a critical element in aid effectiveness. Empowered by clear, coherent national development strategies that are linked to budgetary frameworks and underpinned by stronger country systems and capacities, countries themselves will be best positioned to engage with a plurality of aid sources and ensure coherence of aid with their development priorities. A challenge for the Paris agenda is the integration of the new sources and modalities of aid in the aid alignment and harmonization framework. The Accra High Level Forum in September 2008 provides a timely opportunity to address the new, dynamic dimensions of the aid agenda.

Health sector financing. The health sector epitomizes the challenges to aid effectiveness in the new aid architecture. New donors and aid channels—global vertical funds, earmarked funds from bilateral sources, private donors—have brought much needed attention and financing. Aid to health has increased sharply, more than doubling between 2000 and 2006. But the multiplicity of donors and aid channels and a vertical focus on specific communicable diseases have also made aid effectiveness and coherence more challenging. Issues of alignment with country strategies and priorities are illustrated by the fact that in seven African countries support from vertical funds for fighting HIV/AIDS ranges from one-third to one-half of total spending on health. Donor funding for HIV/AIDS exceeded that for malaria by 40 percent in Ghana and 160 percent in Rwanda, even though in both countries malaria is the leading cause of morbidity and mortality. Issues of efficiency of use are illustrated by the fact that roughly one-half of health aid is off budget and by mismatches between rapid increases in earmarked funds and absorptive capacity. In Ethiopia health systems strengthening has recently received only about 15 percent of donor financing for health, compared with 60 percent for HIV/AIDS.

Such consequences, however, are not inevitable. The key is to better align and integrate vertical and earmarked funds with country strategies and systems and improve donor coordination and complementarity. The strengthening of health systems—human resources, financial management and procurement, information, the governance framework—needs greater attention in donor support. This is important to bolster country capacities to plan and implement effective and integrated health programs—for communicable diseases but also for other programs such as mother and child health that are interrelated. The need for greater coordination and integration is recognized by recent initiatives such as the International Health Partnership that brings together traditional and new donors and the selection of health as a special focus sector in monitoring the application of the Paris principles.

Securing debt sustainability. While debt relief provided under the Heavily Indebted Poor Countries (HIPC) Initiative and the Multilateral Debt Relief Initiative (MDRI) has improved the debt indicators, long-term debt sustainability remains a challenge for several post completion–point countries. Prudent debt management as part of a sound macroeconomic framework and reforms to build resilience to exogenous shocks will help prevent debt burdens from becoming unsustainable again. Creditors need to take debt sustainability considerations into account in their lending decisions. The Bank-Fund Debt Sustainability Framework is a tool that can be used by borrowers and creditors alike to assess and manage risks.

5. Harnessing Trade for Strong, Inclusive, and Sustainable Growth

Strong expansion in world trade has been a powerful force boosting global economic growth. Worldwide merchandise exports grew 14 percent in value in 2007, well above the average 9 percent growth recorded in the previous 10 years, with developing-country exports rising still faster at 17 percent. Research shows that economic growth has been faster in countries that have liberalized their trade more. Trade restrictiveness has been on a declining trend in developing countries in this decade, with middle-income countries seeing the largest declines.

Unleashing trade. A successful Doha Round is crucial for sustaining strong trade growth and making the sharing of its benefits more inclusive—even more so now as protectionist pressures may intensify with the prospective slowing of the global economy. A key bottleneck holding up progress has been the lack of agreement on agricultural trade liberalization. The current high prices for food provide a window of opportunity that World Trade Organization (WTO) members should use to break the impasse on reforming agricultural trade policies in high-income countries. The highly restrictive and distortive agricultural support policies maintained by these countries hurt both their consumers and producers in developing countries, including some of the poorest countries.

The linkage to agricultural growth in poor countries makes reform of these policies especially important for achievement of the MDGs. The Doha outcome must aim for a major reduction of barriers to agricultural trade. The bulk of the potential benefits from Doha are dependent on that.

Significant trade policy commitments by developing countries also are essential for realizing the potential of trade for development, including tapping the considerable scope for expanded trade among them. Developing countries have higher average levels of trade restrictiveness than high-income countries but more neutral trade policy regimes between agriculture and manufacturing. The traditional policy of taxing agriculture in many developing countries has become much less prevalent. Since the mid-1980s, gross subsidy equivalents of support to farmers in high-income countries have remained high, at about $200 billion a year, but have moved in developing countries from a negative amount (implying effective taxation) of about $100 billion a year to positive amounts, signifying small to moderate positive support (except in Africa where the trade policy regime on balance continues to tax farmers). Doha offers an opportunity to developing countries to lock in the current relatively neutral cross-sectoral trade policy stance and to reap the efficiency gains of further lowering applied levels of protection.

Promoting inclusiveness in exploitation of trade opportunities. Enabling firms to exploit opportunities created by trade liberalization and expanded market access requires complementary behind-the-border policies to improve competitiveness and supply response capacities. Of particular importance are services policies. The quality and cost of services such as transportation, telecommunications, and finance are major determinants of competitiveness. Research shows that countries with better trade logistics are more successful in integrating into global markets. Poor countries' competitive-ness typically is hampered by weaker trade logistics. Many developing countries have sought to improve the quality of key logistical services by opening them to foreign competition. However, services trade regimes in most developing countries remain relatively restrictive. Most services liberalization so far has been undertaken unilaterally. The Doha Round provides an opportunity to use the WTO as a mechanism to further services liberalization.

Aid for trade needs to be scaled up substantially to help countries address the behind-the-border constraints on their capacity to exploit trade opportunities. It is particularly important for the least developed countries (LDCs), most of which are in Africa, for whom lack of trade capacity and competitiveness arising from poor logistics such as trade-related infrastructure and customs services, rather than market access, is often the binding constraint. Progress has been made recently on aid for trade, as illustrated by the initiative to enhance the Integrated Framework for trade-related assistance for LDCs and the willingness of donors to make commitments to the associated trust fund to support its operations. Aid for trade rose 10 percent in 2006 to reach an estimated total of about $23 billion, with well over half of it directed to economic infrastructure. Only half of the total flowed to low-income countries, and only about a quarter to LDCs.

Facilitating transfer of environmentally friendly technologies. Trade policy and aid for trade also have a role to play in fighting global warming and supporting sustainable development by promoting the transfer and adoption of environmentally friendly technologies. Trade barriers confronting environmental goods and services, such as products that generate energy in more environmentally friendly ways or use energy more efficiently, tend to be highest in low-income countries, paralleling the overall pattern of trade restrictiveness. From an environmental perspective, the best trade policy is one that encourages the use of the most efficient environmental goods and services. Removing policies that restrain trade in such products, and assisting producers in developing countries to benefit rather than lose from initiatives such as carbon labeling, can help harness the potential of trade to support strong and inclusive growth and improve environmental outcomes. Complementing trade policy, streamlining of intellectual property rights and investment rules can further aid in the transfer and assimilation of environmentally more efficient technologies, which can help with both the mitigation and adaptation aspects of the fight against climate change.

6. Leveraging IFI Support for Inclusive and Sustainable Development

How should international financial institutions (IFIs)—multilateral development banks (MDBs) and the IMF—strengthen and sharpen support for the foregoing agenda for inclusive and sustainable development? Net financial flows to developing countries from IFIs relative to other sources of financing have been declining. In 2007 the IFIs had a share in net ODA of only 8 percent. Net nonconcessional flows turned slightly positive in 2007 after four years of large negative flows. But the IFIs' declining relative financing role does not imply less relevance. The true measure of their impact must consider the development leverage they achieve beyond their narrow financing role. Their impact through leverage remains key in achieving collective action on the MDGs and related development outcomes and on the increasingly important global and regional public goods. Shareholder recognition of this broader impact through leverage is reflected in record pledges made in the past year for IDA15 and AfDF (African Development Fund) XI.

Responding to change: new strategic frameworks. IFIs face a challenging context of rapid change brought about by globaliza-

tion, an evolving international financial architecture, and increasingly differentiated client needs across low-income countries, fragile states, and middle-income countries. They must adapt their strategies to this change. While a process of adaptation has been under way for some time, all IFIs over the course of the past year initiated major strategic reviews and introduced important shifts. These strategic shifts have three common themes:

- First is a shift in client and business focus to promote inclusive and sustainable globalization. One aspect of this shift has been a sharpened focus on low-income countries and fragile states, and also on major concentrations of poverty within middle-income countries, to connect the "bottom billion" to the global economy. Another is a strengthening of private sector operations, as private sector supply response is essential to reap the full benefits of globalization. Common to these shifts is a sharper differentiation of products and services across clients.
- Second is an orientation toward knowledge services as a critical means of achieving development leverage and as the glue that binds development partners—by building country absorptive capacities, strengthening country strategies, underpinning aid effectiveness, disseminating best practice, and developing a shared knowledge base. There is demand for knowledge services from both low- and middle-income countries, but innovation is required to increase flexibility and responsiveness. Middle-income countries also offer practical experiences that the IFIs can increasingly tap for dissemination to low-income countries.
- Third is an increased emphasis on global and regional public goods, through direct interventions and by creating an enabling environment to leverage private sector. These public goods span global macroeconomic and financial stability,

international financial architecture, trade, control of communicable diseases, global environmental commons, regional economic integration, and global and regional knowledge goods. The increased focus on global and regional public goods poses a challenge for IFIs whose business model has in large part been structured around country platforms.

Success in carrying out these strategic shifts will be crucial to the IFIs' ability to increase impact by leveraging their assets and activities. Progress in ongoing efforts to adapt governance structures—members' quotas, voice, participation—also will be important for continued effectiveness.

Ensuring strong operational outcomes in a context of change. Amid this process of strategic change, MDBs posted an overall strong performance in their financial operations during 2007. Their gross disbursements reached a record $49 billion. Concessional flows and nonconcessional flows to nonsovereign entities have been the most dynamic elements. Gross concessional flows rose by 11 percent to over $12 billion, with flows to Africa showing the fastest increase. MDB support to Sub-Saharan Africa has more than doubled since 2000. Implementation capacity (including fiduciary) constitutes the key bottleneck in scaling up concessional finance. MDB nonconcessional flows to nonsovereign entities rose to over $13 billion in 2007, a quadrupling since 2000. Half of these flows are accounted for by the International Finance Corporation (IFC) and the other half by private sector arms of other MDBs. Encouragingly, nonsovereign flows to Africa have also more than doubled since 2000. An important IBRD-IFC innovation in 2007 was the establishment of a Global Emerging Markets Local Currency Bond Fund (GEMLOC). Guarantees, cofinancing, and trust fund operations have also expanded (guarantees from IDA and the International

Bank for Reconstruction and Development have an average leverage ratio of almost 10 to 1). On the other hand, nonconcessional lending to sovereigns, about $23 billion in 2007, has been generally flat, with large fluctuations depending on circumstances in individual countries.

Challenges to effective engagement are especially complex in fragile states. The needs in these countries are huge, as they are farthest away from reaching the MDGs, but they present difficult political and governance contexts for effective delivery of development finance and services. Nonetheless, MDB financial flows to fragile states rose by about 55 percent in the five-year period 2002–07, reaching $2.4 billion. As some of these states move from peace-building to state-building, demand for MDB support will rise further. Developing and implementing effective operational strategies for fragile states is a key element of the IFIs' contribution to the agenda for inclusive and sustainable development.

Strong country-led development strategies (poverty reduction strategies or equivalent strategic frameworks) are central to development effectiveness, even more so in a changing aid architecture characterized by a plurality of aid sources and modalities. Strengthening country strategies is an important focus of IFI knowledge services and capacity building. In 2007, 13 percent of low-income countries were deemed to have well-developed operational frameworks while another 67 percent had taken significant action to develop such frameworks (comparable figures for 2005 were 8 percent and 56 percent, respectively). These figures show progress but also a continuing challenge. Both the IMF and the MDBs are engaged in efforts to strengthen analytic support and policy advice, tailor it better to different client needs, and enhance its impact.

The IFIs are making progress on alignment and harmonization in the framework of the Paris Declaration, but monitoring surveys show room for improvement on several dimensions: use of country systems and implementation frameworks; efficient modalities for joint operations and programmatic and sectorwide approaches; and predictability of support. Harmonization in the context of the changing aid architecture, with the emergence of new players such as vertical funds that committed around $3.5 billion last year, poses new challenges. In 2007 the report of an External Review Committee (Malan report) identified areas for strengthening collaboration between the IMF and the World Bank, including in crisis management, work on fiscal and financial sector issues, and technical assistance.[6] Implementation of the committee's recommendations is proceeding under a Joint Management Action Plan drawn up during the year.

Better tracking results. IFIs are making progress in strengthening the results orientation of their operations and supporting partner countries' capacity to manage for results. A range of internal and external monitoring and evaluation methodologies have been developed to track IFI performance and results. Findings from these exercises over the past year show mixed results. Improvements have been made in implementation of key programs such as the development outcomes targeted in the IDA14 Results Measurement System, and the World Bank's Africa Action Plan and Infrastructure Action Plan. MDBs' Comparative Assessment System (COMPAS) indicators show progress on several dimensions of the results agenda, such as results orientation of country assistance strategies and processes related to projects and program design and implementation. But the indicators also point to the need for stronger efforts to link resource allocation, incentives, and institutional learning to results. Findings from IFI independent evaluations conducted over the past year included the need to further streamline conditionality,

correct underinvestment in regional public goods, achieve further progress in decentralization, and improve the development impact of private sector projects. Overall, results tracking methodologies need to develop a stronger focus on real results on the ground, such as the MDGs, rather than processes. Also, stronger, concerted support is needed to build country development data capacity.

Rising to the environmental challenge. Programs supporting environmental sustainability exemplify the IFIs' increasing engagement in the provision of global public goods. Over the years, the IFIs have considerably expanded their environmental activities—in energy, pollution control, water, land, biodiversity, environmental institutions. These activities have accounted for 12–15 percent of their lending in recent years. Going forward, a major priority will be responding to the increasing challenge of climate change. The IFIs have a crucial role to perform in supporting global collective action to combat climate change. They are actively developing new strategies to scale up work in this area. An example is the Clean Energy Investment Framework. Key elements of their engagement will include:

- Integrating climate action into core development work
- Providing innovative and concessional financing, such as the Global Environment Facility and carbon finance
- Expanding the role of markets, such as the Carbon Partnership Facility and Forest Carbon Partnership Facility
- Facilitating new technology development and diffusion
- Creating an enabling environment to tap the private sector—engaging the IFC and other MDB private sector arms
- Expanding research on mitigation and adaptation, such as low-carbon country growth studies.

Notes

1. The MDGs flowed from the Millennium Declaration adopted by 189 countries at the UN Millennium Summit, held in New York in 2000. The Monterrey mutual accountability compact (also known as the Monterrey Consensus) emerged from the UN Conference on Financing for Development, held in Monterrey, Mexico, in 2002.

2. Robert B. Zoellick, speech at the United Nations Climate Change Conference in Bali, Indonesia, December 12, 2007.

3. World Bank. 2008, *World Development Report 2008: Agriculture for Development*. Washington, DC: World Bank.

4. IMF. 2007. *World Economic Outlook: Globalization and Inequality*. Washington, DC: IMF.

5. This estimate does not include costs of all related water infrastructure, such as wastewater treatment.

6. IMF and World Bank. 2007. *Report of the External Review Committee on Bank-Fund Collaboration*. OM2007-0014, Washington, DC.

I

Monitoring the Development Agenda

Millennium Development Goals at Midpoint: Where Are We?

At midpoint between the adoption of the MDGs in 2000 and their target date in 2015, the review of progress gives a mixed picture of significant improvement and formidable challenges ahead. It is mixed because progress is uneven across MDGs, with goals related to human development (primary school completion, child and maternal mortality) recording slower progress than those more immediately influenced by economic growth or the expansion of infrastructure networks (income poverty, gender parity at school, access to water and sanitation); mixed because progress differs significantly across countries, regions, income groups, or institutional status—with fragile and conflict-affected states lagging behind on all counts.[1]

Progress toward the MDGs: A Mixed Picture

Accelerated economic growth makes the MDG 1 of halving extreme poverty by 2015 likely at the global level (figure 1). Thanks to a more conducive global environment—for trade, finance, technology, and migration—per capita GDP growth accelerated in most low- and middle-income countries in the past decade, paving the way for substantial poverty reduction.[2] Faster growth was in many cases accompanied by rising inequalities. But with better economic management, it was also characterized by a much lower incidence of recessions and crises, events that most often hurt the poor.[3] As a result, current estimates[4] suggest that two-third of the poverty

FIGURE 1   At the global level, progress and prospects vary widely across MDGs

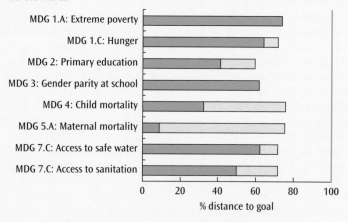

□ Distance to goal achieved   □ Distance to goal to be achieved
  by 2006[a]   by 2006[a] to be on track

Source: Staff calculations based on World Development Indicators.
a. Most recent year for which data are available.
Notes: MDG 1.A: Poverty headcount ratio (PPP93 US$1.08 a day); MDG 1.C: Underweight under-five children (U.S. child growth standards); MDG 2: Primary education completion rate; MDG 3: Gender parity in primary and secondary education; MDG 4: Under-five mortality rate; MDG 5.A: Maternal mortality ratio (modeled estimates); MDG 7.C: Access to improved water source; MDG 7.C: access to improved sanitation facilities.

reduction effort to be accomplished between 1990 and 2015, had been realized by 2005, and that a prolongation of current GDP trends would most probably allow achievement of MDG 1 before 2015.[4] While most of the poverty reduction between 1990 and 2004 took place in East Asia and the Pacific, South Asia would contribute the most to global poverty reduction in the next decade. Nonetheless, significant progress could also be registered in other regions—Sub-Saharan Africa and Latin America and the Caribbean notably, but Sub-Saharan Africa is likely to fall short of the MDG 1 target.

Conversely, slower progress made in terms of child and maternal mortality casts doubts on the prospects of reaching MDGs 4 and 5. Between 1990 and 2006, the probability for a child born in a developing country dying before the age of 5 declined from 10.1 to 7.9 percent, an achievement hardly sufficient to cover half the distance needed to meet MDG 4 of reducing child mortality by two thirds. Countries with higher mortality rates face greater difficulties in reducing them (in rela-

tive terms) than countries starting from more favorable positions. HIV/AIDS and malaria significantly contribute to slowing progress in the former group of countries, mostly located in Sub-Saharan Africa. Similarly, maternal mortality progress between 1990 and 2005—an estimated reduction from 430 to 400 deaths per 100,000 births—represents less than one-tenth of the distance to be covered to meet the MDG 5 of reducing maternal mortality by three quarters between 1990 and 2015. On current trends, these two MDGs will unlikely be met at the global level, in Sub-Saharan Africa and South Asia, and in most countries (see box 1 on country-level assessment).

Rising enrollments are paving the way for reaching universal primary education completion and gender parity at school, though likely not by the target date. In recent years, school enrollments rose sharply, in Sub-Saharan Africa and South Asia in particular—often in response to comprehensive educational reforms such as the abolition of tuition fees.[5] With higher enrollments, gender disparity in primary and secondary education declined by 60 percent between 1990 and 2005. In turn, the MDG 3 of eliminating gender disparity at school is now attainable by 2015 (it had originally been hoped that this target would be met by 2005).Yet, enrollments—even universal enrollments—do not ensure that all children will be able to complete a full course of primary schooling (MDG 2) by 2015. Enrollment measured with administrative data often significantly exceeds attendance measured with surveys, revealing the extent of absenteeism. Furthermore, substantial drop-outs, repetition, and late entry at school (above the official age) make the MDG 3 very ambitious at the global level, if not unrealistic, given the little time left to have all children enrolled in time to complete primary school by 2015. Between 1990 and 2006, only 41 percent of the total distance to the MDG was covered using the primary completion rate[6] as an indicator of progress, and even less ground was covered when using instead the proportion of a cohort persisting to the fifth grade. The challenge is particu-

BOX 1 Assessing whether countries are on or off track

When at least two observations are available after 1990, with a sufficient number of years separating them, the World Bank determines whether a country is on or off track to meet a given MDG by 2015. To do so, it compares the progress recorded so far with that needed to reach the MDG. Technically, this is equivalent to comparing the annual growth rate between 1990 and today with the constant growth rate required to reach the MDG in 2015 from the situation in 1990. The assessment assumes that progress becomes increasingly difficult the closer countries get to the goal. Such a methodology to assess progress toward MDGs is based on two premises. First, historical records suggest that MDG progress is not linear. Countries starting from less favorable positions make more rapid progress on most MDGs.[a] This is consistent with the idea of decreasing returns: as countries get closer to a goal, they face increasing difficulties to make additional progress and need to further increase their levels of policy effort. For instance, public service delivery in remote areas is more costly than in cities, making it difficult to maintain the same pace of progress when cities are already covered.

Second, if understood as a means to focus the attention of donors, governments and citizens on lagging sectors and countries, a geometric approach (in comparison to a linear one) reduces the risk of underestimating the problem, while possibly increasing the risk of overstating it. In the face of possible irreversible damage (to human capital and the environment), which increases the cost of inaction over time, it would seem advisable to minimize the first risk.

Obviously, being off track does not mean that the related MDG will necessarily not be met. Many factors—policies and shocks—can affect the progress rate toward MDGs. It is hoped that the designation of sectors and countries as off track will focus increased attention on them and expedite progress.

a. World Bank. 2007. *World Development Indicators 2007*. Washington, DC: World Bank.

larly acute in Sub-Saharan Africa, which is far off track to meet both MDGs 2 and 3.

The prevalence of HIV/AIDS and tuberculosis started to stabilize at the turn of the decade. It is estimated that 31 million to 36 million people worldwide were living with HIV in 2007; of these, 21 million to 24 million were in Sub-Saharan Africa, and 3 million to 5 million were in South Asia. Most of the recent progress originates in Sub-Saharan Africa, where the proportion of people living with HIV decreased from 6 percent to 5 percent between 2001 and 2007. But progress was not noticeable elsewhere. Europe and Central Asia and Latin America and the Caribbean even recorded significant increases, although the two regions started from much lower levels than Sub-Saharan Africa. Conversely, the prevalence of tuberculosis is on the decline everywhere but in Sub-Saharan Africa (which has the highest prevalence rates), where it has been roughly

stable since 2003. As such, MDG 6 is attainable except that it is still very difficult to monitor the incidence of malaria (mostly located in Sub-Saharan Africa).

Substantial progress has been registered in terms of people's access to water and sanitation, less so in terms of integrating the principles of sustainable development into countries' policies. Data from 2004 suggest that 60 and 50 percent, respectively, of the distance to MDG 7 of halving the proportion of people without access to safe water and sanitation facilities had been covered. A significant part of the remaining distances is likely to be covered before 2015. But broader progress to integrate the principles of sustainable development into country policies is much slower. In fact, the cost of resource depletion and air pollution was estimated to amount to 15 percent of developing countries' GNI in 2005, up from 11 percent in 1990. Some of the environmental costs remain localized, such as those originating from particulate emissions, which rose sharply in East Asia and the Pacific between 1990 and 2005. But others (CO_2 emissions) have global consequences for the environment.

The Challenges Ahead

Looking ahead, the challenge to reach the MDGs will increasingly be concentrated in low-income countries, and especially fragile states, where progress is slower—although many middle-income countries, especially those with large concentrations of poverty, will continue to face substantial challenges. On all MDGs, fragile states lag behind other developing countries (figure 2).[7] This group of countries poses particular development challenges, as many are dealing with conflict or post-conflict environments that make the delivery of development finance and services especially problematic.

At the country level, on current trends most countries are off track to meet most MDGs

(figure 3).This picture is somewhat masked by the influence of large and better-performing developing countries, such as China and India, on aggregates. But observation at the country level provides a more heterogeneous, less positive picture. On all MDGs—except MDG3—the proportion of off-track countries exceeds that of on-track countries. On several MDGs, data gaps remain large.

Notwithstanding the progress made on country statistical capacity, it is still challenging to assess countries' progress toward the MDGs. As noted above, global poverty is likely to be halved by 2015. But it is still the case that 78 out of 149 developing countries lack adequate data to monitor poverty trends—the more so in countries where poverty reduction is believed to be particularly slow. Data are especially weak for some MDGs such as maternal mortality. In the absence of hard numbers, reliance has to be placed on modeling estimates of maternal mortality (or on some indirect measures of policies assumed to influence mortality outcomes). Stronger efforts are needed to build on progress in developing countries' statistical capacity (box 2).

FIGURE 2 Progress toward MDGs is slowest in fragile states

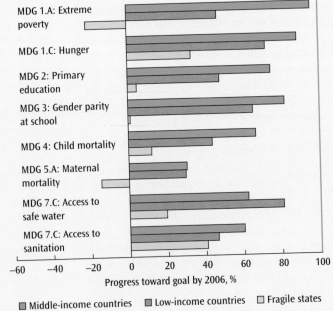

FIGURE 3 Most countries are off track to meet most MDGs

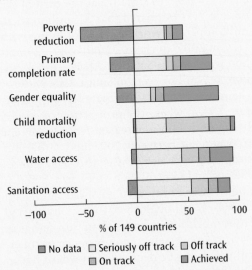

Source: Staff calculations based on World Development Indicators.
Note: Indicators defined as for figure 1.

Source: Staff calculations based on World Development Indicators. Indicators are defined as in figure 1.

BOX 2 Statistical capacity building: furthering progress

Developing countries are making progress in improving statistical capacity, as measured by a World Bank statistical capacity index for 117 low- and middle-income countries between 1999 and 2007. Progress is being recorded on the availability of statistics (MDG indicators in particular), adherence to international statistical standards (statistical practice), and to a lesser extent, frequency with which data are being collected.

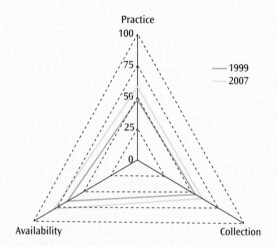

Progress is also being made in terms of designing and implementing National Strategies for the Development of Statistics (NSDS) to strengthen countries' statistical systems: by February 2007, more than 100 developing countries had developed or initiated an NSDS. Such strategic framework of action (the centerpiece of the Marrakech Action Plan for Statistics, MAPS, agreed upon in 2004) was reaffirmed in Hanoi in February 2007 at the third international roundtable on managing for development results. Consultations between donors and partner countries produced an agreement on the need to pool (greater) resources and to better coordinate efforts through NSDS mainstreamed in poverty reduction strategies.

But several issues remain. Without stronger incentives to produce and use statistics, it is difficult to ensure adequate allocation of attention and resources by donors and governments to statistical capacity building against competing claims of other sectors—even if progress in those sectors might not be measurable because of the lack of good statistics. Notwithstanding the fact that it might pay to be ignorant (to protect the continuation of ineffective public programs), the high fixed costs required to overhaul statistical systems might also discourage decision makers.

There are some options that can be considered to strengthen incentives to give high priority to statistical work. Raising user demand for reforming statistical systems may be achieved through greater awareness of the quality of available statistics. For instance, the statistical capacity index (shown above) could be improved by incorporating an assessment of statistical institutional sustainability (political and financial independence), which is ultimately linked to the quality of statistics. From a supply perspective, the use of catalytic vertical funds could protect resources from being used for purposes other than implementing NSDS. A further option is to incorporate measures of statistical capacity into aid allocation and evaluation processes.

The foregoing assessment of progress at the MDG halfway point shows a clear need to generate a stronger and broader momentum toward the MDGs and related development outcomes. Part I of the report addresses key elements of that agenda. It assesses progress on policies and actions for achieving the development goals and identifies priorities going forward. The assessment covers the roles of all parties in that effort—the developing countries themselves, developed countries, and international institutions. Part II of the report provides a more in-depth assessment of progress and priorities relating to environmental sustainability, the special theme of this year's report.

Notes

1. More details on trends in progress toward the MDGs are provided in the annex, Monitoring the MDGs.

2. Related to income poverty, progress in terms of reducing malnutrition (as measured by the proportion of underweight under-5 children) has also been substantial. Data are currently being revised to account for new child growth standards. But trends observed using older U.S. growth standards are not likely to be radically affected. Using such standards, malnutrition declined from 34 to 23 percent between 1990 and 2006 in developing countries.

3. The number of developing countries experiencing prolonged economic recessions (negative per capita GDP growth) went down from 26 to 13 between 1985–95 and 1995–2005. The observation of countries' poverty reduction and growth performances suggests that the relationship is particularly pronounced on the negative side. While worst poverty reduction performances are strongly associated with worst growth performances, best growth performances are less significantly associated with best poverty reduction performances (World Bank. 2007. *World Development Indicators 2007.* Washington DC: World Bank).

4. The recent release (World Bank. 2007. 2005 International Comparison Program Preliminary Report, Washington, DC) of a new set of purchasing power parities (PPP), based on 2005 prices, will lead the World Bank to revise its estimates of global poverty. Compared with the PPPs based on 1993 prices and used until now to compute international poverty lines, PPPs in 2005 show different patterns due to economic transformation over the period 1993–2005 and improved methodologies to compare prices across a larger sample of countries. Inevitably, the use of more recent PPPs will modify poverty estimates estimated and published so far. It is not expected, though, that it could affect fundamentally the projection that global poverty will likely be halved in 2015.

5. Low-income countries' gross enrollment ratios in primary schools went up from 81 percent in 1991 to 102 percent in 2005.

6. This indicator is computed by dividing the number of students in the last grade (excluding repeaters in that grade) by the total number of children of graduation age. It typically includes in the numerator a large number of children above graduation age, who repeated in previous grades or started school late. As such, it tends to overestimate the genuine proportion of graduation age children actually graduating.

7. While individual countries may transition into and out of such status, this status actually tends to be persistent for many countries (World Bank. 2007. Meeting the Challenges of Global Development, Washington DC).

1

Sustaining and Broadening the Growth Momentum

ollowing a long uninterrupted period of strong global expansion, world economic growth has begun to moderate in response to the continuing financial market turbulence that started in August 2007. Although downside risks have increased, global growth prospects remain broadly positive, with world GDP growth in 2008 slowing to a projected 3.7 percent, from 4.9 percent in 2007. What makes this period of economic expansion different from previous periods is the broad-based character of the growth momentum: emerging market economies and other developing countries have rapidly increased their shares in global production and trade.[1] The resulting convergence of income levels between advanced and developing economies helps in the fight against poverty, because poverty reduction will be elusive without strong, private sector-based economic growth. The increasing significance of developing countries as attractive places to invest, the international migration of labor, and the emergence of new donors have also changed the composition of international financial flows: private capital and workers' remittances have grown in importance as main sources of financing in many developing countries. The benefits of the global expansion, however, have not reached all developing countries, especially the many fragile states where per capita growth rates remain negative. Also, income inequality has risen within many countries, mainly as a result of the effects of technological progress on relative wages of unskilled workers, confirming the importance of improving access by low-income workers to high-quality education.

A stable macroeconomic policy framework, strong private sector development, and good governance are key to strong growth and poverty reduction. Many developing countries have made steady progress in improving macroeconomic policies, the investment climate, and governance in recent years. The World Bank's *Doing Business 2008* and Enterprise Surveys show that changes are occurring across many areas, although governments need to step up their reform efforts in areas such as labor laws, property rights, and contract enforcement. Also, the depletion of natural resources and environmental degradation undermines the long-term growth prospects of many developing countries.

The Global Economy: Recent Developments and Prospects

Notwithstanding the tightening of global credit conditions following problems in the

U.S. subprime mortgage markets and the spread to other segments of financial markets, global growth eased only modestly in 2007, to 4.9 percent, supported by robust expansions in emerging market and other developing countries (table 1.1). Rapid growth in most emerging markets counterbalanced the slowing of growth in the United States, which grew at about 2.2 percent in 2007 (compared with 2.9 percent in 2006), as the correction in the housing market continued to act as a drag on the economy. Growth in the Euro area and Japan slowed in the last quarter of the year after two years of strong gains. Global growth is projected to slow in 2008 to 3.7 percent. As a result of revisions to estimated purchasing power parity exchange rates, historical data for world economic growth were revised in early 2008 (see box 1.1).

Core inflation has increased since mid-2007 in both advanced and emerging economies, driven by the spillovers of higher energy and food prices to other sectors of the economy. While prices in Japan have essentially been flat, headline inflation in the United States and the Euro area increased in February 2008, to 4.1 percent and 3.3 percent, respectively. Inflation has also picked up in a number of emerging market and developing countries, reflecting strong domestic demand and rising food prices. The upward pressure on food prices reflects the increasing use of corn and other food items for biofuel production, poor weather conditions, supply disruptions in a number of countries, and global demand growth. Meanwhile, oil prices rebounded to new highs in March 2008.

Global credit market conditions have deteriorated sharply since August 2007 as a repricing of credit risk sparked increased volatility and a broad loss of liquidity (box 1.2). Rising delinquencies on U.S. subprime mortgages have led to higher yields on securities collateralized with such loans and a sharp widening of spreads on structured credits, particularly in the United States and the Euro area. Market strains are amplified by uncertainty about the distribution of asso-

TABLE 1.1 Summary of world output
annual % change

	2002	2003	2004	2005	2006	2007[a]	2008 (projected[b])	2009 (projected[b])
World output	3.1	4.0	5.3	4.4	5.0	4.9	3.7	3.8
Advanced economies	1.6	1.9	3.2	2.5	3.0	2.7	1.3	1.3
of which								
United States	1.6	2.5	3.6	3.1	2.9	2.2	0.5	0.6
Euro Area (15)	0.9	0.8	2.0	1.5	2.8	2.6	1.4	1.2
Japan	0.3	1.4	2.7	1.9	2.4	2.1	1.4	1.5
United Kingdom	2.1	2.8	3.3	1.8	2.9	3.1	1.6	1.6
Canada	2.9	1.9	3.1	3.1	2.8	2.7	1.3	1.9
Other advanced economies	3.9	2.6	4.9	3.9	4.5	4.6	3.3	3.4
Emerging market and developing countries	5.1	6.7	7.7	7.0	7.8	7.9	6.7	6.6
Africa	3.6	4.7	5.8	5.9	5.9	6.3	6.3	6.4
Central & Eastern Europe	4.5	4.8	6.7	5.6	6.6	5.7	4.4	4.3
Commonwealth of Independent States	5.3	7.9	8.4	6.6	8.2	8.5	7.0	6.5
Developing Asia	7.0	8.3	8.8	9.0	9.6	9.7	8.2	8.4
Middle East	4.0	6.6	5.6	5.6	5.8	5.8	6.1	6.1
Western Hemisphere	0.3	2.4	6.0	4.6	5.5	5.6	4.4	3.6

Source: IMF.
Note: Real effective exchange rates are assumed to remain constant at the levels prevailing during January 30–February 27, 2008.
a, b. Country weights used to construct aggregate growth rates for groups of countries were revised from those reported in the October 2007 *World Economic Outlook* to incorporate updated purchasing power parity (PPP) exchange rates released by the World Bank.

BOX 1.1   Recent revisions of purchasing power parities

The International Comparison Program (ICP) has recently revised its estimates of purchasing power parities (PPP) for exchange rates of developing countries. The PPP rate is defined as the amount of currency that would be needed to purchase the same basket of goods and services as one unit of the reference currency, usually the U.S. dollar. The ICP project, coordinated by the World Bank, produces PPP estimates based on statistical surveys of price data for a basket of goods and services for 100 developing countries. The Eurostat-OECD (Organisation for Economic Co-operation and Development) PPP program provides estimates for another 46 countries. In December 2007 the ICP released preliminary PPP estimates for the 2005 benchmark year, replacing previous benchmark PPP estimates, which date back to 1993 or earlier for most emerging market and developing countries.

The PPP rate can deviate by a large amount from the market exchange rate between two currencies. For example, developing countries typically have relatively low prices for nontraded goods and services, and a unit of local currency thus has greater purchasing power within a developing country than it does internationally. Whereas PPP-based GDP takes this into account, conversions based on market exchange rates typically underestimate the value of economic activity and output of a developing country relative to an advanced economy. PPP exchange rates are used in estimating aggregate economic activity across the world, because they tend to lead to a more accurate estimate of global economic activity than is produced by simply using market exchange rates.

The ICP revisions have implications for the share of global GDP accounted for by individual countries and aggregate global growth based on PPP exchange rates: the International Monetary Fund's estimate for global growth in 2007 has been revised down to 4.9 percent from 5.2 percent in the October 2007 *World Economic Outlook*. Downward revisions for PPP-based GDP of two of the world's fastest-growing economies, China and India, are mainly responsible for the overall reduction of global growth estimates. For 2007 China's share of global output is now estimated at 10.9 percent (down from 15.8 percent) while India's share has declined to 4.6 percent (from 6.4 percent). Reflecting the overall reduction in GDP in PPP terms of other countries, the share of the United States in global GDP has been revised up from 19.3 percent to 21.4 percent. Notwithstanding these changes, it remains true that emerging market countries have been the main recent driver of global growth in PPP terms—led by China, which alone contributed nearly 27 percent to global growth in 2007.

Inevitably the new PPPs will also lead to revisions of poverty estimates, such as the number of people living under US$1 a day. The new PPP-based poverty estimates, being prepared by the World Bank, are likely to become available later this year. While poverty levels (number of poor) for some countries may change appreciably, changes in poverty levels over time are likely to be less affected.

ciated losses and the exposures of financial institutions through off-balance-sheet liabilities. These strains have led to a drying up of high-yield corporate bond issuance, a sharp contraction in the asset-backed commercial paper market, a sharp reduction in liquidity in the interbank market, and stress on financial institutions relying on wholesale markets for funding. The resulting flight to quality has served to drive down yields on government debt. Although emerging markets have thus far been less affected by the financial turmoil, sovereign spreads have widened, with some scaling back of capital flows, and stock market volatility has increased considerably. Although the liquidity tensions in the interbank market eased somewhat in early 2008, the problems in the structured credit markets put pressure on some financial institutions' balance sheets and have also started to affect the financial guarantors of over US$3 trillion in securities (monoline insurers), which could undermine the functioning of other financial markets in 2008.

Overall, economic activity in emerging economies remained buoyant in 2007. Direct spillovers from the turmoil on emerging economies have been largely contained to date. In contrast to previous episodes of financial turbulence, the effects on emerging and other developing economies have thus far been relatively limited although trade

BOX 1.2 The recent financial market turbulence

Mature financial markets have been experiencing significant turbulence since July 2007. In the summer of 2007 problems that surfaced in the U.S. subprime mortgage and leveraged loan markets prompted a retrenchment from risky assets and a process of deleveraging, causing severe disruptions in money markets, funding difficulties for several financial institutions, a widening of credit spreads in riskier asset classes, and more volatile bond and equity markets. Major central banks have responded with exceptionally large liquidity injections, and the U.S. Federal Reserve has lowered interest rates six times since August.

Although immediate pressures in mature money markets have eased somewhat, financial sector problems have both widened and deepened in recent months as the size of the credit losses and their impact on banks' balance sheets have become more evident. Spillover effects on other segments of financial markets, in particular credit insurance, have also emerged. Meanwhile, the combination of financial sector weakness and an ongoing deepening of the slump in the U.S. housing sector have increased the risk of a sharp slowdown in U.S. output growth and dampened the outlook for global growth. This worsening outlook has been reflected in substantial corrections in global equity markets.

The problems in credit and asset markets have been principally a mature market phenomenon, and—in contrast to previous episodes of financial turbulence—the effects on emerging markets and other developing countries have thus far been less severe than in previous crises. This is not to say, however, that these countries have not been affected. Emerging markets have seen a marked increase in risk premiums (EMBIG spreads have roughly doubled since June 2007) and orderly but substantial reductions in equity valuations, in line with mature markets.

Generally, however, these developments have not given rise thus far to acute financing difficulties in developing countries, although private external debt market issuance has declined. Some repricing of risk was inevitable, and even desirable, because risk appetite had risen to unprecedented levels and was contributing to demand booms and excessive borrowing, fueling vulnerabilities in some countries.

Several factors help explain why developing countries have been relatively resilient. The recent turbulence has been closely related to innovative financial instruments that so far are less prevalent in less-developed markets. More important, many of these countries exhibit stronger fundamentals and improved policies than in the past. In particular, in many countries current account positions are more favorable this time around, with developing countries as a group showing a significant surplus. And several emerging economies benefit from high levels of foreign exchange reserves and are thus more resilient to short-term funding disruptions.

This improved resilience notwithstanding, the persistence and recent deepening of turbulence in mature markets, and the knock-on effects on world growth that are gradually becoming evident, pose significant risks to economic conditions in developing countries.

There is a risk that a continuation and further deepening of problems in mature financial markets, and a further retreat of risk appetite, may start to affect flows to emerging markets in a more profound way. In particular, this would seem a risk in countries that have large current account deficits, that have experienced sharp increases in asset prices fueled by foreign currency lending, or that have large balance-sheet vulnerabilities, including substantial currency and maturity mismatches (examples include various countries in Central and Eastern Europe, some of which exhibit all of these characteristics).

But more important, emerging economies and other developing countries will be affected through the channel of lower global economic growth. Against the backdrop of lower global demand, trade flows and commodity prices may potentially see substantial corrections. Since the boom in commodities prices has been one of the key factors underpinning the strong performance in many commodity exporters, a sustained decline in commodity prices may have significant adverse effects on economic performance and balance of payments positions.

For low-income commodities exporters, to the extent that they are less diversified, the direct effects of falling commodities prices on economic growth may be particularly acute. For emerging markets, however, a sharp worsening of the external environment could trigger a vicious cycle of lower growth, weaker fundamentals, higher risk premiums, and faltering asset prices. Commodity importers, however, may experience beneficial effects from lower commodity prices.

Given current uncertainties and country differences, there is no single policy prescription for developing countries: vulnerabilities and the appropriate policy responses must be assessed on a country-by-country basis.

BOX 1.2 The recent financial market turbulence *(continued)*

However, countries with prudent external debt management, fiscal discipline, and flexible exchange rate policies will be in a better position to cushion shocks and facilitate adjustment when faced with external shocks such as the current financial market turbulence. Financial sector supervisors—in financial systems that have not yet been tested—also need to learn from the fault lines exposed in the current market turmoil and strengthen their arrangements to facilitate the continued capacity of their financial systems to support growth.

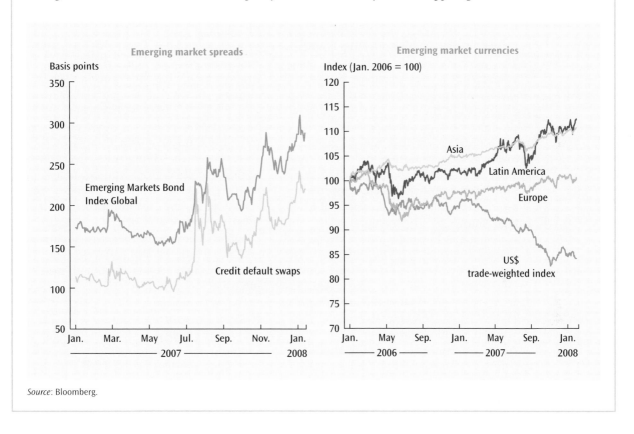

Source: Bloomberg.

and industrial production are beginning to moderate. This is not to say, however, that these countries have not been affected. Not only have emerging markets seen a marked increase in risk premiums and substantial reductions in equity valuations, but aggregate capital flows to these economies have also moderated since August 2007. Overall flows, however, remain well sustained, and international reserves have continued to rise.

For 2008 growth for emerging and developing economies as a group is projected to slow to 6.7 percent, from 7.9 percent in 2007.

Although the underlying driving forces and economic policy settings differ from country to country, the growth trends are broadly based, affecting all major regions. Growth performance in emerging Asia reflects high productivity growth and sound economic policies in general. The regional expansion in Asia continues to be led by China and India, where real GDP growth is projected to reach 9.3 percent and 7.9 percent in 2008, respectively, reflecting strong exports and gains in domestic investment demand. Economic activity remains buoyant in most other emerging economies in the region as well, including Indonesia and the Philippines. Emerging economies in the Middle East continue to benefit from high oil prices and strong domestic demand, with GDP growth projected to reach 6.1 percent on average in 2008. Economic activity in the oil-exporting countries is particularly buoyant in the non-oil sectors, fueled by increasing public investment in infrastructure, social spending, and consumer demand. Oil-importing countries in the region are benefiting from the favorable external environment in the region and beyond: their GDP growth rates outpace growth in the oil-exporting countries. Although economic developments in emerging Europe have benefited from the sustained recovery in Western Europe and further integration in the global economy, the outlook is clouded because of the recent slowdown in Western Europe and the prospect of lower capital inflows on which a number of countries are reliant. Regional growth is expected to reach 4.4 percent in 2008, with the Baltics in the lead. By historical standards, growth in emerging economies in Latin America remains robust, although the growth prospects for 2008 are vulnerable to the slowdown in the United States.

Many emerging economies should be relatively well-prepared to deal with a less favorable external environment, as their underlying vulnerabilities have declined to the lowest level in a decade. Underlying trends, however, vary considerably across regions. While emerging Asia, the Middle East, and Latin America are showing continuous improvements, less progress has been made in reducing vulnerabilities in emerging Europe. External and financial sector vulnerabilities in emerging Europe have edged up in recent years, reflecting weak current account positions, rapid credit growth, and extensive foreign currency lending to unhedged borrowers.

Continuing the trend that started in the beginning of the decade, many low-income countries are benefiting from strong demand for commodities. Growth performance in

Sub-Saharan Africa, projected to reach 6.3 percent in 2008, will be led by the expansion of oil production and the traditional nonfuel commodity exporters, although the slowing of the global economy could threaten the outlook in some countries. Many low-income countries in the region are experiencing positive spillovers in the non-commodity sectors, as evidenced by broad-based domestic demand growth. The positive domestic growth dynamics, against the backdrop of continued progress in macroeconomic stabilization, steady improvements in the business climate, the favorable impact of debt relief, and increased capital inflows, may put Sub-Saharan Africa on a sustained path toward more rapid poverty reduction. Growth performance in the region is uneven, however, with some subregions and countries (e.g., countries in the CFA franc zone, fragile states) remaining on a low growth path, and most countries will need to make further progress in improving the business climate to attract investment and foster growth in the nontraditional sectors. Although resource-intensive low-income countries in Asia and the Commonwealth of Independent States (CIS) are benefiting from high commodity prices and expansion of production capacity in traditional export sectors as well, achieving higher productivity growth and attracting investment in the nontraditional sectors remains a challenge.

The overall balance of risks to the global outlook is tilted to the downside. The main risk to the outlook for global growth is that ongoing turmoil in financial markets will further reduce domestic demand in the advanced economies with more significant spillovers into developing countries, leading to sharper downturns. Emerging market countries that are heavily dependent on capital flows could be particularly exposed. In addition, a number of other risks remain elevated. Oil and nonfuel commodity prices continue to pose risks to both activity and inflation, so that monetary policy could face the difficult challenge of balancing the risks of higher inflation and slow economic activity. Heightened financial sector vulnerabilities also raise risks of a disorderly unwinding of global imbalances should investor preferences shift abruptly.

Growth in Developing Countries: Strong but with Widening Gaps

The favorable global economic environment of the past years has contributed much to the fight against poverty in the world. Overall, developing countries remain on track to meet the first Millennium Development Goal (MDG), with the population share of the extremely poor (living on less than $1 a day) projected to fall from 29 percent in 1990 to 10 percent in 2015. By 2004 this share had already dropped to 18 percent. Preliminary estimates suggest that the number of extremely poor people in developing countries fell by about 278 million between 1990 and 2004. There are, however, significant differences between groups of countries. Most Sub-Saharan African countries remain a long way off the path that would take them to MDG 1, even assuming projected growth rates higher than the historic averages since 1990. Progress among fragile states with relatively low growth rates, most of which are in Sub-Saharan Africa, is particularly disappointing: income poverty rates in these countries have not declined much since the early 1990s (figure 1.1).

Per capita growth performance shows marked differences within regions and groups of countries, with implications for progress in reaching the poverty MDG (figure 1.2). To get a clearer picture of the differences in performance and the potential impact of growth on poverty reduction, figure 1.3 presents developing countries' per capita growth performance in four subcategories: countries with negative average growth; with less than 2 percent average growth; with between 2 percent and 5 percent average growth; and with more than 5 percent average growth during the period 2003–07. In about one-fourth of developing countries, per capita growth during the

FIGURE 1.1 Poverty head count
percent of population living on less than $1 a day and $2 a day

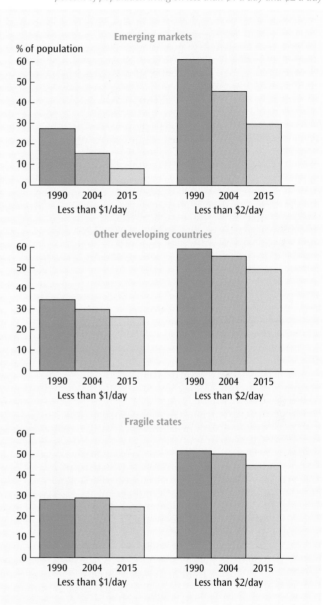

Source: World Bank.
Note: Figures for 2015 reflect poverty headcount projections. Poverty numbers based on new estimates of purchasing power parities are forthcoming.

past five years remained on average below 2 percent a year, which was in most cases insufficient to make a serious dent in income poverty rates. This group of countries includes some emerging market economies

FIGURE 1.2   Per capita GDP growth rates by country group 2003–07

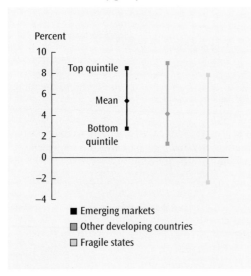

Source: IMF.

FIGURE 1.3   Number of emerging-market and developing countries by annual real GDP per capita growth rates, 2003–07

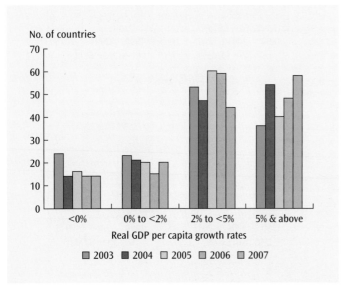

Source: IMF.

and a number of other developing countries (mainly low-income countries in Sub-Saharan Africa and Latin America) and fragile states. The situation of the 17 fragile states in the low-growth category is particularly worrisome: over this period, per capita income contracted annually by about 1 percent on average. Although many fragile states in this group showed some improvement in growth trends in recent years, their overall performance remains disappointing.

The diversity of development in Sub-Saharan Africa is particularly striking (box 1.3). Countries with good growth performance, such as Ghana, Mozambique, Tanzania, and Uganda, which a decade ago appeared to have grim prospects, are making solid progress toward the MDGs. These countries are also stepping up investment in infrastructure and energy, thereby strengthening the foundation for sustained, broad-based growth. At the same time, about a third of Africa's population lives in countries that are facing economic conditions severely constrained by internal conflict and weak governance. These countries are facing a mixture of security, political, legal, economic, and developmental challenges. Poverty in many of them has increased, and problems in some cases have spilled over to their neighbors.

Per capita growth performance in the majority of developing countries, however, improved significantly during the past years, including in some fragile states. Most countries achieved average per capita growth rates above 2 percent during 2003–07, laying the basis for steady progress in reducing poverty rates. Emerging market economies in this category (including countries in emerging Europe, Latin America, and Southeast Asia) led in this respect, with per capita growth rates roughly doubling in comparison with the 1990s. Several fragile states experienced a strong acceleration of growth in recent years, reflecting the transition from a conflict situation (Sierra Leone), or the effects of higher oil and gas exports (Angola, Chad, and Sudan).

Rising Commodity Prices: Impact and Implications

The positive growth trends in developing countries in recent years occurred against

BOX 1.3 Growth in Africa: rising but uneven

Economic growth in Africa has been rising, from a low of 2.3 and 2.1 percent annnually in the 1980s and 1990s, respectively, to an average of 5.6 percent in the past five years. The growth performance, and related policy challenges, however, vary considerably across countries (see map below for growth dispersion during 2004–06). Reviewing trends over the past 10 years, three broad groups of countries can be distinguished. The first group has enjoyed strong growth averaging about 9 percent annually during that period. It comprises 7 resource-rich countries accounting for about one-third of the region's population. The main challenge they face is in managing and transforming their natural resource wealth into long-term sustainable growth. This calls for good governance to support extracting and managing the resource wealth efficiently and transparently and transforming resource revenues into productive investments that help diversify the economic base.

The second group has achieved moderate to strong growth averaging about 5.5 percent in the past 10 years. This group comprises some 18 countries, home to roughly one-third of the region's population. These countries have fairly well-managed economies and potential to improve their growth performance. Their main challenge is to build on reforms to strengthen the foundation for strong, sustained, and broad-based growth. Further improving the climate for private investment, through regulatory and institutional reform and strengthening physical infrastructure, and deepening regional and global links are key elements of the policy agenda. In support of this agenda, they need scaled-up assistance from development partners.

The third group is characterized by low, and in some cases negative, growth. It comprises some 20 countries, accounting for the remaining one-third of the region's population, that achieved average growth of only 2.1 percent in the past 10 years. These countries have much weaker policies and institutions, with many affected by conflict. Their policy agenda consists of a challenging mixture of security enhancement, political reform and consolidation, capacity building, and actions to build private sector growth opportunities. They need international aid but must build basic governmental capacity to ensure its effective use.

GDP per capita growth in Africa

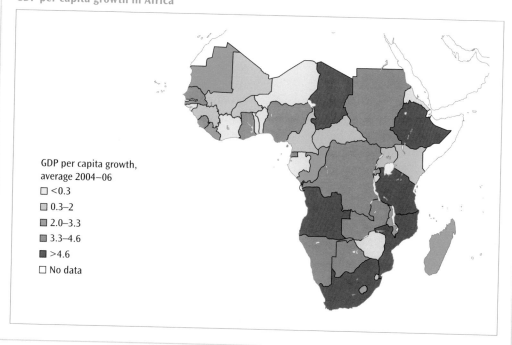

GDP per capita growth, average 2004–06

- ☐ <0.3
- ◻ 0.3–2
- ▨ 2.0–3.3
- ▦ 3.3–4.6
- ■ >4.6
- ☐ No data

the background of strong upward movements in world commodity prices (figure 1.4).[2] World prices for key commodities exported by developing countries increased by 100–300 percent during the past four years. Exporters of copper and uranium experienced the steepest world market price increases, which more than quadrupled, while oil prices tripled and aluminum, coal, and gold prices doubled.

Nonfuel and fuel commodities constitute about one-fifth of world trade. Developing countries are highly dependent on commodity exports: On average commodities represented about 74 percent of developing countries' exports during 2003–06. Oil exporters are among the countries having the least diversified export base, with oil exceeding 70 percent of total exports. At the same time, developing countries are affected, as importers, by the commodity price boom. Rising energy and food prices affect the external payments positions and growth prospects of those developing countries that are less well-endowed with natural resources.

The commodity price boom has led to important shifts in the terms of trade of developing countries. Terms-of-trade changes have been a factor contributing to the differential growth performance of these countries (figure 1.5).[3] Staff calculations of the effects of terms of trade on domestic purchasing power show that the recent commodity price boom has positively affected most oil exporters among emerging countries (Kazakhstan, República Bolivariana de Venezuela), other developing countries (Azerbaijan, the Islamic Republic of Iran), and the fragile states (Angola, Sudan). Other commodity exporters, in particular of metals such as copper, gold, nickel, cobalt, and uranium (Mongolia, Niger, Papua New Guinea, and Zambia) have also benefited from the terms-of-trade gains. For these countries sound management of the rise in natural resource revenues will be important to translate this boom into laying stronger foundations for sustainable growth (box 1.4).

At the same time, many countries experienced a negative terms-of-trade shock, with particularly damaging effects on the urban poor faced with high petroleum and food prices: for example, El Salvador among emerging markets, Jordan, Madagascar, and Mauritius among other developing countries, and Haiti and Togo among the fragile economies. The large group of fragile states with weak growth performance and deteriorating terms of trade is particularly hard hit: during the period 2003–07, their domestic per capita purchasing power declined by an average annual rate of 2 percent, as against an annual per capita GDP decline of almost 1 percent (figure 1.6). For countries negatively affected by oil and food price increases, possible policy responses range from energy demand management and targeted safety nets for the affected poor to longer-term measures to encourage energy production and diversification and to promote agricultural growth (boxes 1.5 and 1.6).

FIGURE 1.4   Commodity price indexes, 1991–2007

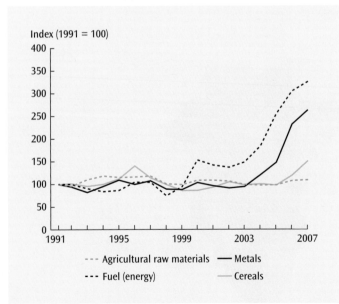

Source: IMF.
Note: Price index in special drawing rights.

Rising Income Inequality within Countries

Although high growth rates have helped reduce global poverty, they have been accompanied by rising income inequality in many developing countries. A recent study by International Monetary Fund (IMF) staff shows that since the beginning of the 1980s, per capita incomes rose in most countries, making most people in developing countries better off.[4] However, income inequality within countries, as measured by the Gini coefficient, also increased in most cases (figure 1.7). The increase in inequality in general was more pronounced in countries with relatively high growth rates. At the same time, income inequality tended to decline or remain relatively stable in countries with lower growth rates, primarily CIS countries and countries in Sub-Saharan Africa. In some of these countries, the poorest quintiles of the population have benefited from rapidly growing private transfers and higher agricultural exports.

Technological progress has had the greatest impact on increasing income inequality within countries (figure 1.8).[5] It has been found to affect adversely the distribution of income in both developed and developing countries by reducing demand for low-skill activities and therefore the incomes of low-skilled workers. Financial globalization has also been a factor contributing to increased inequalities. Although financial deepening promotes higher growth, it can also increase income inequality because richer segments of society have better access to financial services. The strong growth of foreign direct investment in recent years has been directed mainly to technologically intensive sectors, pushing up wages of skilled labor relative to those of unskilled labor. In contrast, trade liberalization has had the effect of reducing income inequality in developing countries. It has helped increase exports and incomes in agriculture, an important source of income for less-skilled workers. The overall effect of

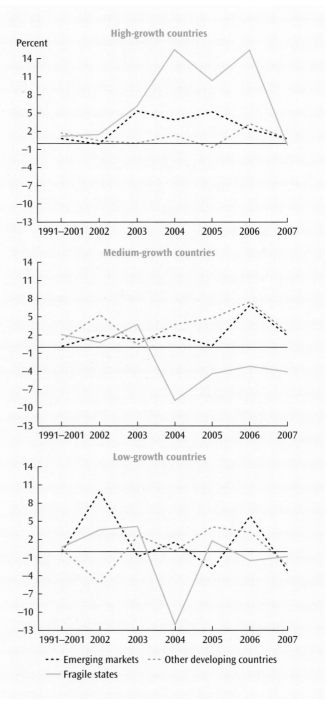

FIGURE 1.5   Terms-of-trade changes by country group, 1991–2007

Source: IMF.
Note: Low-growth countries have per capita growth rates of less than 2 percent.
Medium-growth countries have per capita growth rates between 2 percent and 5 percent.
High-growth countries have per capita growth rates above 5 percent.

BOX 1.4   Management of natural resource revenues

Economies benefiting from additional revenue inflows face a fundamental choice on how to manage the resulting gains. The windfall from high prices on oil and other primary commodities accrues to both public and private sectors in many commodity-exporting developing countries. For the public sector, such a windfall translates into higher fiscal revenues, but its potentially destabilizing effects are a challenge for macroeconomic management.

Experience in macroeconomic management of the recent resource revenue windfall suggests that policy responses can be guided by the following principles:

- *The medium-term fiscal policy should be guided by estimates of the magnitude and permanency of additional fiscal revenue.* If the increase is substantial and is considered permanent, the government can build a gradual increase of spending into its expenditure plans. Such an increase should be made effective with a certain lag from the initial rise of revenue to create a safety margin and ensure that the price increase is indeed permanent. If the gains are expected to be reversed soon—either because of a price reversal or because of the depletion of natural resources—the increase in permanent income will be limited and most of the windfall should be saved. Countries faced with a rapid decline in their natural resources and permanent income should consider allocating the windfall revenue to investments that will generate alternative sources of permanent income in the future. Depending on the circumstances, this could include higher public investment in growth-enhancing projects and the accumulation of foreign financial assets.

- *One-off increases in spending financed by temporary windfalls are possible, as long as they are limited in duration and address a specific problem.* Natural and health disasters and crucial development needs where short-term investment may make an immediate and substantial difference are the obvious target areas for the one-off increases in spending. Such additional spending of part of the temporary windfall should be limited to projects that do not entail sizable recurrent spending in the future and in areas where the implementation capacity is not a binding constraint. The windfall can be also spent on retirement of public—domestic or external—debt, in particular the repurchase of nonconcessional debt held by external commercial creditors. In all cases, the absorptive capacity and the quality of spending should remain the guiding posts.

- *The overall macroeconomic policy mix should be geared to reconciling the effective use of all resources with price stability.* Under a flexible exchange rate regime, to control inflation the authorities have a policy choice between sterilization through higher fiscal surpluses and nominal exchange rate appreciation. As time passes, however, sterilization through higher fiscal surpluses may not be sustainable, as pressing spending needs translate into an adjustment of spending levels to higher permanent fiscal income. Therefore, some appreciation of the nominal exchange rate seems to be the appropriate medium-term policy response. In the case of a fixed exchange rate regime, temporary higher domestic inflation and real appreciation may be unavoidable. Improvements in productivity are the main way to address the resulting loss of competitiveness in these countries.

- *Sound institutions, governance, and public finance management are essential to ensure quality spending of the windfall.* Windfall gains should be considered in a medium-term framework, which would link annual budgets to longer-term policy objectives. The development of special institutions to manage resource windfalls (i.e., oil and stabilization funds, oil accounts, special fiscal rules and legislation, and the like) is in general useful, if such institutions are well-designed, transparent, and accountable. Integration of the special institutions with the budget and the legislated budgetary procedures generally helps strengthen their transparency and quality of spending of the windfall gains. Countries also should be encouraged to participate in the Extractive Industries Transparency Initiative, which is making headway with 15 confirmed candidate countries and 7 countries with reports out and a system in place for validating performance.

globalization in most developing countries has been to lower inequality marginally, with the effect of financial globalization being more than offset by the effect of trade liberalization.

These findings point to the importance of expanding access to education to broaden opportunities for workers to participate in more technologically advanced and remunerative sectors of the economy. They also suggest the need to broaden access to financial services. Finally, they underscore the opportunities for countries to harness trade for stronger and more inclusive growth, a topic discussed in chapter 4. Vietnam provides an example of a successful reform strategy for growth with equality (box 1.7).

Continuing Shifts in Foreign Public and Private Financing Flows

The favorable global economic environment in the past years was associated with a strong increase in net capital flows and current transfers to developing countries, both in U.S. dollar terms and as a share of GDP (table 1.2). Emerging market economies benefited most from the expansion in financial flows, but flows to some other developing countries and fragile states also increased.

In many developing countries, private sources of external financing have grown in importance relative to official sources.[6] During the 1990s about half of external financing available to developing countries (as a percentage of GDP) consisted of private financing in various forms; by 2007 the share of private financing had increased to about two-thirds of total external financing. Much of private financing went to resource-rich economies, such as Guyana and, until recently, Azerbaijan. The increase in private financing has also been particularly clear in some fragile states, where private flows have almost doubled as a share of GDP. However, among the fragile states only a handful of countries can be seen as relatively stable destinations for private financing.

These are either countries with a substantial mining potential (e.g., Chad and Sudan) or small economies, where a significant part of the private flows consist of workers' remittances. In emerging market economies, official financing has not been very significant in relative terms since the beginning of the 1990s and, on average, became negative (on a net basis) in the past few years, as many countries accelerated the repayment of their official debt. With improved fundamentals and high growth rates, demand for private equity and bonds in emerging markets was already high in the 1990s, in particular in emerging European economies (Bulgaria, Hungary, Serbia, Ukraine) and some other emerging economies (China, Kazakhstan).

Debt-generating financing (official and private) has become less important in comparison to nondebt forms of financing. Foreign direct investment and workers' remittances have grown considerably in emerging markets, other developing countries, and some fragile states. Although much of the growth in foreign direct investment is related to investment in extractive sectors in resource-rich countries, macroeconomic stabilization and improvements in the investment climate

FIGURE 1.6 Real per capita GDP growth rate for low-growth fragile states, adjusted for terms-of-trade changes, 1991–2007

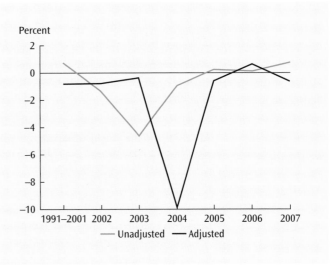

Source: IMF.

BOX 1.5 Impact of oil price increases on low-income countries

Oil prices have tripled in the past five years to record nominal highs of over $100 a barrel. The rise in oil prices has been mainly the result of strong growth in demand in combination with two decades of limited investment in production capacity. New capacity is only slowly coming onstream because of investment lags of several years and because of rising development costs, shortages of services and trained workers, and constraints on access to reserves in some oil-producing countries. Oil prices are also sensitive to geopolitical developments.

In real terms, oil prices are near their historical peak of $96 a barrel (in today's dollars) reached in 1979. Part of the large increase in prices results from to the depreciation of the U.S. dollar. Expressed in euros, oil prices have only doubled over the last five years. Oil prices are expected to stabilize and fall gradually in the coming years. High oil prices have led to slowing demand growth and increasing supply, with rising capacity in OPEC (Organization of Petroleum Exporting Countries) and non-OPEC countries. Nevertheless, on current projections, prices could remain well above $60 a barrel this decade, before declining to $50 a barrel by 2015. Risks to this outlook are mainly to the upside.

The oil price shock has had a mixed impact on oil-importing low-income countries. In a recent working paper on the effects of the 2003–05 oil price increases on 62 of these countries, International Monetary Fund (IMF) staff concluded that:

- For 16 countries there was a decline in the oil import bill relative to GDP owing to a contraction in the volume of oil imports. Many countries passed on world market price increases to domestic prices. The oil price rise did not lead to an adverse impact on the balance of payments for this set of countries, as they saw improvements in both the current and capital accounts during 2003–05.
- Another 12 countries faced higher oil imports but benefited from substantial current account offsets in the form of improved exports or grant receipts, or both.
- A third category of 12 countries faced both higher oil imports and a worsened current account but a substantial improvement in the capital account.
- The remaining 22 importers benefited from neither current account nor capital account improvements sufficient to offset the oil shock and thus saw a deterioration in their international reserves. Within this group, however, a majority of countries maintained relatively comfortable reserve coverage levels and could thus accommodate the drawdown in reserves. Only in a subset of 7 countries did reserves fall to very low levels.[a]

Although more recent detailed cross-country analyses are not yet published, country-by-country information points to similar factors at work in 2006–07, underscoring the variable impact on countries.

The impact, however, of higher oil prices—compounded by rising food prices—on the most vulnerable segments of the population may be severe. Even in countries that benefited from offsetting price increases in commodity exports or capital inflows, the oil shock may have disproportionate effects on the poorest. Going forward, it cannot be excluded that the current mitigating factors reverse if oil and commodity prices decouple, a scenario in which oil prices soar (as a result of political developments) while commodity prices deflate in a context of lower global demand.

The IMF and the World Bank stand ready to assist their members in dealing with exogenous shocks of this nature. Under the IMF's Exogenous Shocks Facility, balance of payments support can be provided to countries faced with a significant increase in world market prices for major import products, such as oil or food. International Development Association financing could help prevent costly disruptions to priority spending and mitigate the impact on the poorest. At the same time, countries need to pursue policies to reduce their vulnerability to oil shocks through energy diversification and improved energy efficiency. The World Bank can assist countries in this endeavor with development policy and sector support operations.

a. Dudine and others 2006.

BOX 1.6 Rising food prices and their policy implications

Over the past 12 months, the world has experienced an average food price increase of 15 percent. Although this price shock does not necessarily translate into higher sustained inflation, it is bound to have adverse effects on poor urban residents in low-income countries. On the positive side, farmers in low-income countries may benefit from higher prices for their crops. A major driver of the food price increases has been high rates of global economic growth in recent years. Demand growth in emerging markets has been particularly strong. Price developments have also been affected by serious droughts and animal diseases in some parts of the world.

More recently food prices have jumped sharply, at least in part because of an attempt to encourage the use of biofuels in industrial countries. Although the use of biofuels has the advantage of diversifying energy sources, the production of ethanol from corn does not generate much net energy, and it has led to a doubling of corn prices during the past two years. This has had knock-on effects on other crops, as land is switched from wheat on the margin, for example, into corn or, as has been most marked in Europe, out of dairy production and into crops used for biodiesel.

The industrial-country policy on biofuels is partly driven by agricultural protectionism. A number of countries, including Brazil, can produce ethanol much cheaper, with a greater saving of nonrenewable energy and lower emissions, for example, by using sugar. But this sugar-based ethanol is subject to prohibitive trade barriers in the United States and Europe. In addition, production subsidies in industrial countries, which are intended to encourage innovation in this sector, seem to have led to excessive entry into the U.S. ethanol distillery business.

Farm subsidies of various kinds in industrial countries have long affected the international trading system and currently make it difficult to move forward with further trade liberalization in the context of the Doha Round. With high food prices, subsidies are less compelling and—depending on how they are structured—may not even pay out when prices are above a certain level. Industrial countries need to seize this moment and eliminate subsidies. Industrial-country tariffs on ethanol should also come down. Allowing free trade in biofuels should generally help agricultural sectors everywhere and bring benefits to poor, rural societies. Opportunities to expand land use will be greater if all countries have a fair chance to produce biofuels.

At the same time, developing countries should pursue policies aimed at increasing growth in agricultural production through small-holder productivity gains. In the short term, there will likely also be the need to cushion the impact of food price increases on the affected poor. In particular, actions in the following areas will be needed:

- Trade reforms to facilitate flows within and among developing countries. Reducing barriers to regional trade can help improve the efficiency of regional markets. Also, improved infrastructure would reduce transportation cost.
- More investment in the generation of improved technologies and improved extension services to promote the adoption of better crop varieties.
- Well-designed, targeted safety nets to provide transitory support to the affected poor in response to price shocks, avoiding recourse to distortive price controls and trade restrictions.
- Access to weather-based index insurance, which can reduce weather risks and cover loans necessary to finance new technologies.

The World Bank is actively engaged in supporting countries in these efforts and could respond with additional financing if necessary.

have facilitated the expansion of investment in other sectors as well. As a result of the shifts in the composition of external financing and debt reduction operations, net liabilities to official creditors have dropped noticeably. Also, in many countries the accumulation of foreign reserves during the past five years exceeded the growth in capital inflows and current transfers, reflecting the improvements in their trade accounts. As a result, the external asset/liability profiles of many developing countries have changed considerably over

FIGURE 1.7 Annual change in Gini coefficient in 59 developing countries

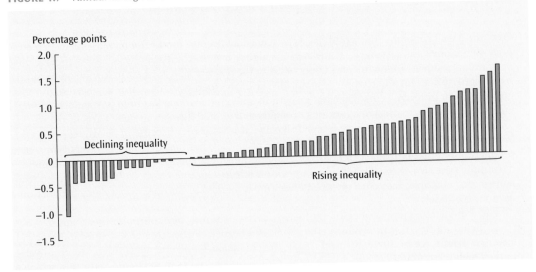

Source: World Bank staff calculations based on latest available country surveys.

time: short-term debt instruments held by the monetary authorities have increased as a percentage of GDP.

Private capital flows have a broadly positive impact on growth. Recent studies generally find bidirectional causality between foreign direct investment and growth, although the impact of foreign direct investment on growth is almost always stronger than that of growth on investment.[7] Most country studies confirm that foreign direct investment and private loans are usually associated with higher growth as they help increase production capacity, technology transfer, and improvements in quality standards. Research on the impact of foreign direct investment on growth at the industry level underlines the importance of the quality of investment. Some studies of specific countries actually find an opposite direction of causality, from GDP to foreign direct investment (e.g., in the case of Chile). There have been no conclusive studies on the impact of portfolio investments on growth, although they may contribute to a deepening of financial markets and enhanced financial intermediation, which promote growth in recipient economies.

The Growing Importance of Workers' Remittances

The growth of workers' remittances as a source of foreign financing for the economy has been particularly strong in recent years (table 1.3). Remittance flows represent the single largest source of foreign exchange for many countries, exceeding total development assistance.[8] Cross-border movements of people and labor are increasingly important factors affecting growth and poverty, with very sizable positive realized or potential welfare effects. Nearly 200 million people now live outside their country of birth. Recorded remittance flows to developing countries grew fourfold between 1991 and 2006 and exceeded US$200 billion in 2006—twice the amount of official assistance to developing countries. If unrecorded flows through formal and informal channels are included, the actual flows would be significantly larger.

The economic gains for both receiving and sending countries may be significant (box 1.8). According to one estimate, an increase in migrants that would raise the workforce in high-income countries by 3

FIGURE 1.8   Decompositions of change in the Gini coefficient

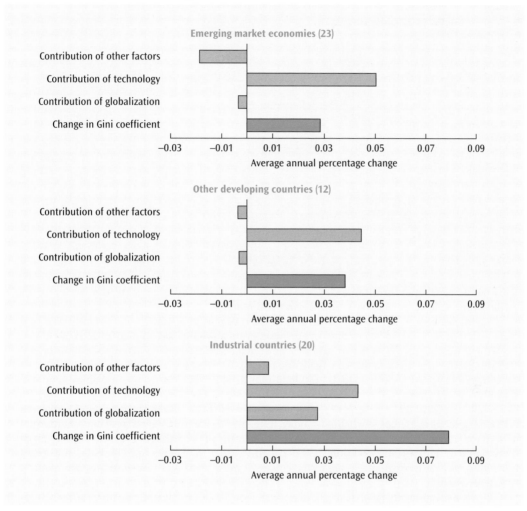

Source: IMF 2007.
Note: 1991–2006, or shorter periods dependent on data availability. "Globalization" includes both trade and financial globalization.

percent by 2025 could increase global real income by 0.6 percent, or US$356 billion.[9] On average, the gains are higher for developing-country households than for rich-country households. Improved flows of migrants and remittances by reducing international impediments, transaction costs, and red tape would help realize these gains.

Remittances have had a positive impact on poverty alleviation. Remittances mainly finance primary consumption, critical for the poorest segments of the population. For example, a survey of remittances in Tajikistan showed that most remittances are under US$1,000 a year and tend to be spent mainly on consumption, primarily food, clothing, and medical care.[10] In the period of booming remittances in 2000–06 the poverty rate in Tajikistan declined by 20 percent. Poverty-reducing effects are particularly large in the countries where migrants are associated with the lower part of income distribution. For example, extreme poverty fell by 35 percent in El Salvador and Mexico, and moderate poverty fell by 21 percent in El Salvador and 15 percent in Mexico.[11]

BOX 1.7 Vietnam: Growth with equality leads to dramatic success in reducing poverty

Over the last 15 years, Vietnam has achieved one of the world's fastest declines in poverty. Vietnam's income poverty rate declined from about 58 percent in 1993 to about 16 percent in 2006 and some 34 million people have come out of poverty. Steady and rapid growth in income, of 7–8 percent, has been a key factor in reducing poverty.

The high growth rates have been accompanied by only limited increases in inequality. The Gini coefficient increased from 0.34 in 1993 to 0.36 in 2006, a much lower increase than in many other emerging economies. Growth and poverty reduction have come in both rural and urban areas. While urban poverty is much smaller—about 4 percent in 2006—rural poverty has declined from two-thirds of the population in 1993 to about one-fifth today. The reduction in poverty has occurred in all parts of the country. Poverty is much lower in the Mekong and Red River delta than in other parts of the country, but the decline in poverty has also been felt in the Northern Mountains and Central Highlands where poverty is relatively higher. Three factors have led to Vietnam's inclusive growth—literacy, trade, and infrastructure.

Vietnam's drive towards literacy began as early as 1945 and was reinforced throughout the 1970s and 1980s. A final major push for universal literacy was made between 1990 and 2000, when provincial and commune level literacy campaigns were launched. Today Vietnam has achieved over 95 percent literacy. Access to schools has improved dramatically, with average travel time to lower secondary school down to 15 minutes.

Vietnam's openness to trade—the ratio of exports plus imports to GDP is about 150 percent—has been a second key to inclusive growth. From a food-deficit country in the early 1990s Vietnam has emerged as a major exporter of agricultural products. Bilateral and multilateral trade agreements have also helped to generate foreign direct investment and have made it a major exporter of apparel, wood products, and light industrial products, with major employment benefits to the economy.

Finally, infrastructure, especially rural electrification and rural roads programs, has ensured that remote areas are not left behind. Today, almost 95 percent of Vietnamese households have electricity connections, compared with only 50 percent in the early 1990s, and 90 percent of the population is within two kilometers of an all-weather road. This has allowed connectivity between rural and urban areas and to the country's main ports and transport and communication networks.

Can Vietnam sustain its inclusive development model as it rapidly approaches middle-income-country status? Vietnam will need to help its citizens access higher education, just as it did with basic education, to ensure that rural productivity is lifted as it industrializes further and to see that its ethnic minorities are provided opportunities to develop. It will also need to build modern social safety nets to assist those affected by future transitions and to ensure that its growth does not come at the cost of its environment.

A study of 76 countries (of which 24 are in Sub-Saharan Africa) that utilized poverty surveys beginning in 1980 found that every 10-percent increase in remittances led to a 1-percent decline in poverty.[12]

The evidence on the impact of remittances on social outcomes is ambiguous. Remittances have contributed to better access to health care and education by providing additional means to recipient households for financing their educational and health needs. For example, a study of three country cases (Guatemala, Mexico, and the Philippines) showed that remittances had reduced poverty and increased private spending on education and health.[13] At the same time, in most developing countries international migration involves relatively better-educated people,

TABLE 1.2 Net financial flows to developing countries
in % of GDP

	Average 1991–2001	2002	2003	2004	2005	2006	2007
Emerging market economics	**6.7**	**6.4**	**7.5**	**7.3**	**8.3**	**8.2**	**9.9**
Private capital flows (net)	3.4	2.3	3.6	3.7	5.0	5.0	6.3
Private current transfers (net)	2.3	3.2	3.5	3.6	3.6	3.6	3.5
Official capital flows and transfers (net)	1.0	0.9	0.4	0.0	−0.3	−0.4	0.1
Memorandum item:							
Reserve assets[a]	*−1.2*	*−1.0*	*−3.4*	*−2.7*	*−3.0*	*−4.0*	*−4.4*
Other developing countries	**12.9**	**13.5**	**14.0**	**14.8**	**16.5**	**16.2**	**15.9**
Private capital flows (net)	2.4	4.8	5.0	5.3	6.4	5.7	5.8
Private current transfers (net)	3.0	3.7	4.0	4.7	5.3	5.5	5.7
Official capital flows and transfers (net)	7.4	5.0	5.0	4.8	4.8	5.0	4.4
Memorandum item:							
Reserve assets[a]	*−1.5*	*−1.6*	*−2.3*	*−2.3*	*−2.9*	*−4.7*	*−3.9*
Fragile states[b]	**14.0**	**19.3**	**17.8**	**17.9**	**21.7**	**20.5**	**18.9**
Private capital flows (net)	2.8	4.9	2.4	1.1	4.7	5.7	3.5
Private current transfers (net)	3.2	4.7	6.1	7.0	6.8	6.4	6.3
Official capital flows and transfers (net)	8.0	9.7	9.3	9.8	10.2	8.5	9.1
Memorandum item:							
Reserve assets[a]	*−0.5*	*−1.7*	*0.5*	*−1.2*	*−2.3*	*−2.1*	*−1.4*
Memorandum item:							
Total net private financial flows including							
current transfers (US$ billions)	*166.0*	*206.4*	*297.7*	*411.0*	*502.5*	*496.9*	*872.3*
Of which:							
China	*19.0*	*44.5*	*70.6*	*128.3*	*87.7*	*34.8*	*119.9*
India	*15.7*	*27.2*	*42.1*	*42.0*	*42.3*	*64.3*	*119.6*

Source: IMF staff estimates.
Note: Percentage numbers represent unweighted averages.
a. A minus sign denotes an increase.
b. Calculations exclude Sierra Leone, Timor-Leste, and Zimbabwe.

TABLE 1.3 International remittances
US$ billions

	Average 1991–2001	2002	2003	2004	2005	2006
Emerging market economies	43.5	76.9	95.3	100.2	118.9	128.0
Inflows	50.9	90.9	112.3	123.5	146.2	161.2
Outflows	7.4	14.0	17.0	23.3	27.3	33.2
Other developing countries	11.9	17.0	22.2	27.4	32.1	35.5
Inflows	15.8	22.4	27.9	33.7	39.4	43.2
Outflows	3.9	5.4	5.7	6.3	7.3	7.7
Fragile states	0.1	1.1	1.6	1.8	1.5	1.5
Inflows	1.0	2.2	2.8	3.1	2.7	2.7
Outflows	0.9	1.0	1.2	1.3	1.2	1.2

Sources: World Bank; IMF.
Note: Remittances include workers' remittances, compensation of employees, and migrant transfers.

BOX 1.8   Private remittances: positive effects and risks

Remittances may have significant positive effects on the receiving countries:

- *Poverty reduction.* In countries without a developed social insurance system and efficient domestic labor market, labor migration and remittances often play an important role in addressing poverty. By financing primary consumption, remittances help alleviate extreme poverty, in particular in the countries where migrants represent the lower part of income distribution.
- *Public finances.* Imports boosted by remittances are a source of additional revenue collection in the form of value added taxes and import duties. Emigration helps ease the unemployment problem and contain the associated fiscal expenditures.
- *Financial intermediation.* As more recipients gain the confidence needed to deposit remittances, the scope for financial intermediation will grow. Remittances have also helped strengthen microfinance institutions, which in turn will be important in channeling remittances to productive use. Several banks in Brazil, the Arab Republic of Egypt, El Salvador, and Kazakhstan have raised cheaper international long-term financing by the securitization of future remittance flows. The inflow of remittances to a bank helps mitigate its currency convertibility risks and makes its securities more attractive for international investors.
- *Investment, and entrepreneurship.* There are strong indications that remittances in excess of a certain amount tend to be used for investment, rather than on subsistence consumption. Although a substantial part of large-scale remittances is directed to residential construction and imports, these remittances represent a financial source for establishing small business and equity participation.

At the same time, reliance on remittances presents certain risks:

- *Monetary management.* In a small economy with a shallow foreign exchange market and insufficient monetary policy instruments, the magnitude of remittances may create challenges for monetary management. Like other large inflows, they may entail currency appreciation and inflationary pressures and may call for greater exchange rate flexibility.
- *The risk of a brain drain.* The current flood of emigration from many developing countries is a mixture of unskilled and skilled labor (teachers, doctors, engineers), which is already depriving the country of its future manpower. Although the returning workers provide additional qualified labor for low-income countries, on a net basis the flow of remittances continues to reflect the dominance of emigration.
- *Diminishing pressure for reforms.* Remittances may create an illusion of growing and sustainable affluence. The ability of the private sector to address its immediate needs independently from the government can create a disincentive for the authorities to deal with the underlying problems that forced the people to leave the country initially.

reducing the number of doctors, teachers and engineers in those countries. The brain drain exhibits significant regional differences and dynamics, with more serious implications for isolated smaller economies. Smaller low-income countries, such as Haiti and Jamaica, tend to suffer a greater brain drain with a large negative social impact than do larger countries like India and China. While skilled emigration may raise the incentive to acquire skills for those who stay, the departure of skilled labor can adversely affect the livelihood of the majority left behind.[14]

Remittances-receiving countries need to develop a strategy to maximize the benefits of remittances while minimizing their negative repercussions. As a first step, it is important to determine whether or not remittances are likely to be a permanent phenomenon. Most developing countries already grant tax exemptions for remittances, and some match investments by migrant organizations in development projects with public funds. Also, many countries have simplified banking procedures for deposits and withdrawals of remittances and increasingly involve microfinance institutions in the remittance market. Reducing the costs of sending remittances would increase the disposable income of migrants' families and would encourage them to use the official banking channels. However, banking regulations in some sending countries, in particular those related to anti-money-laundering, while necessary for security purposes, remain unfavorable for remittances and are demanding on the migrants, for whom sending money home may be the only contact with the banking system. Encouraging partnership between the international banking and postal services and money transfer operators would help reduce remittance costs while preserving high security standards.

Policies for Strong and Inclusive Growth

Strong and inclusive growth is central to achieving the MDGs and related development outcomes. A key challenge is to spur growth in lagging countries that have not shared in the surge in growth witnessed in much of the developing world over the past several years. Factors underlying the different growth experiences in developing countries are only partly known and continue to be the subject of much research (box 1.9). Specific policy priorities and sequencing of actions to promote growth necessarily vary by country. Across developing countries there is considerable diversity in economic circumstances. The specifics of the policy agenda for growth at the country level must be defined as part of individual country development strategies. Looking across countries, three broad areas emerge as being essential to robust growth: sound macroeconomic policies, a conducive private investment climate, and good governance. This section reviews progress in these areas.

Quality of Macroeconomic Policies

Since 2003 IMF staff have used annual surveys to monitor the quality of macroeconomic policies mainly in low-income countries (table 1.4). The assessment of fiscal policies remains mixed, although there have been marked improvements. Almost half of the monitored countries consistently have scored good ratings on fiscal policy during the past five years, and the number of countries with unsatisfactory policies has declined substantially. Although the composition of public spending has also improved, the quality of policies in this area remains weak, as policies in almost half of the countries continue to be rated unsatisfactory.

Monetary policy, access to foreign exchange, and governance of financial institutions remain relatively strong areas of macroeconomic policies. In particular, there have been improvements in access to foreign exchange and governance in monetary and financial institutions in a number of countries. Consistency of macroeconomic policies remains mixed, as a number of relatively strong-performing countries scored lower in 2007 compared with 2006 and policies in some new countries were rated as unsatisfactory.

The overall quality of policies in countries with low growth rates and in fragile states remains clearly inferior to that of other countries. The composition of public spending, fiscal transparency, and governance of the public sector remain weak in these countries. Monetary policies and access to foreign exchange represent the few relatively strong areas of their macroeconomic policies, but still remain weak relative to many other low-income countries. However, some fragile states (Afghanistan, Haiti, and Liberia) have undertaken efforts in the past few years to improve their macroeconomic policies.

Improvement of Private Investment Climate

Many developing countries have made further progress in improving the investment climate (table 1.5). The World Bank's

BOX 1.9   The Commission on Growth and Development

The Commission on Growth and Development was established in April 2006 to learn from the growth experience of the past couple of decades and to assess the opportunities and challenges arising from globalization. Its objective is "to take stock of the state of theoretical and empirical knowledge on economic growth with a view to drawing implications for policy for the current and next generation of policymakers." The commission does not seek to design a blueprint, but instead aims to provide policy makers and others with the most current assessment of the forces that drive economic growth and with a framework to help design and implement strategies and policies to achieve and sustain rapid growth. The independent commission comprises 21 members (15 are political and policy leaders from developing countries), most with policy-making and business experience. There are two academics on the commission: the chair, Michael Spence; and Robert Solow, both Nobel Laureates. It is funded by the William and Flora Hewlett Foundation; the governments of Australia, the Netherlands, Sweden, and the United Kingdom; and the World Bank (www.growthcommission.org).

The commission invited world-renowned academics, practitioners, and experts to write papers exploring the state of knowledge on growth-related issues, which were reviewed and discussed at several workshops. The commission's final conclusions and report are scheduled to be published in May 2008. They are expected to cover a range of issues that were discussed at the workshops.

One set of issues relates to the changing growth strategies and role of government in the course of development. Successfully making the strategic and policy transitions as the economy evolves is key to achieving sustained growth. Since World War II, 12 countries, most of them in East Asia, have managed to grow at rates in excess of 7 percent for 25 years or more—rates that allow "catch-up" with advanced economies in a generation or two. However, many more countries—mostly in Africa, Latin America, and the Middle East—have been able to achieve high growth but have been unable to sustain it over time.

Another set of issues discussed by the commission concerns the implications of the new global environment for developing countries' growth strategies: globalization; global imbalances and financial risks; the demographics of aging in many countries and high youth unemployment in others; and global warming. Also on the commission's agenda have been the equity dimensions of growth and key sectoral issues in growth including infrastructure, education, health, and labor markets where public sector investment is an important enabler of sustained growth dynamics.

Doing Business 2008 report shows that reforms have been most frequent in the area of starting a business. Within the last five years, 92 of the 175 countries covered have reduced the number of days needed to register a business, with 57 reducing the number of procedures needed to do this. The time and number of procedures needed to trade goods across borders have been other areas where improvements have been made in a large number of countries. Notable progress is also indicated in information and legal processes for getting credit. The Bank's Enterprise Surveys confirm that changes are occurring across many areas—although not always uniformly within a country.

Results show that governments are relatively reluctant to pursue reforms in more sensitive areas, such as labor regulations or bankruptcy law, where social considerations or the existence of significant interest group pressures may be important. Overall, there has been slower progress made in areas where reform requires larger institutional changes, such as labor laws, property rights, and contract enforcement.

Rankings on the "ease of doing business" index generally improve with the income level, but there is considerable varia-

TABLE 1.4 The quality of macroeconomic policies in low-income countries, 2003–07
share of countries falling in each category, %

	Fiscal policy	Composition of public spending	Fiscal transparency	Monetary policy	Cosistency of macro policies	Governance in monetary and financial institutions	Access to foreign exchange
2007 survey							
Unsatisfactory	18.5	45.7	22.5	9.9	17.3	8.6	4.9
Adequate	34.6	45.7	45.0	18.5	37.0	28.4	12.4
Good	46.9	8.6	32.5	71.6	45.7	63.0	82.7
2006 survey							
Unsatisfactory	20.5	48.7	21.8	10.3	15.4	15.4	3.9
Adequate	33.3	38.5	43.6	19.2	32.1	28.2	12.8
Good	46.2	12.8	34.6	70.5	52.6	56.4	83.3
2003 survey							
Unsatisfactory	33.8	49.4	..	11.7	22.4	17.1	9.2
Adequate	19.5	32.5	..	11.7	29.0	22.4	13.2
Good	46.8	18.2	..	76.6	48.7	60.5	77.6
Fragile states (2007 survey)							
Unsatisfactory	31.3	71.9	45.2	12.5	28.1	18.8	12.5
Adequate	37.5	25.0	35.5	6.3	37.5	28.1	18.8
Good	31.3	3.1	19.4	81.3	34.4	53.1	68.8
Fragile states (2006 survey)							
Unsatisfactory	46.7	70.0	40.0	20.0	30.0	30.0	10.0
Adequate	26.7	20.0	43.3	10.0	30.0	33.3	20.0
Good	26.7	10.00	16.7	70.0	40.0	36.7	70.0

Source: IMF Staff.
Note: The 2007 survey includes countries absent in the 2006 survey: Cape Verde, Central African Republic, and São Tomé and Principe. It also includes Montenegro and Serbia, two new and separate countries.

tion within each income group. A number of lower-middle-income counties—and even some low-income countries—rank in the top half of countries (figure 1.9), illustrating that fostering a stronger business environment does not require a lot of resources.

In 2006 Sub-Saharan Africa had the third-highest share of reforming countries. In 2007 the region slipped to fifth place on that score. However, some countries made impressive gains: Ghana rose in the Doing Business rankings from 109 to 87, Madagascar from 160 to 149, and Kenya from 82 to 72.

Research confirms impact of reforms. The top constraints to growth of firms vary by country and firm characteristics. Recent

analysis of the investment climate in 34 Sub-Saharan countries, using data from Enterprise Surveys, shows that unreliable or costly infrastructure is particularly constraining in landlocked countries, where it hampers access to markets, and in countries with greater concentration of manufacturing exports, where timely delivery is increasingly important (table 1.6). A more developed financial system and supportive but prudent regulatory frameworks are associated with better outcomes, particularly in lower-income countries. Addressing skill shortages and improving access to finance are most helpful to expanding firms, while labor regulations and corruption are most constraining to declining firms.[15] Another recent study

TABLE 1.5 Status of investment climate reform, 2003–07

Regulatory action	2005–07			2003–07		
	Reform	Reversal	No change	Reform	Reversal	No change
Starting a business						
Number of procedures	43	7	125	57	8	110
Time (days)	66	6	103	92	5	78
Dealing with licenses						
Number of procedures	11	6	158	—	—	—
Time (days)	34	12	128	—	—	—
Employing workers						
Hiring index	23	20	132	23	28	124
Firing index	4	5	166	6	7	162
Restrictions on hours worked	6	3	166	7	3	165
Labor firing costs	3	7	164	6	12	156
Getting credit						
Legal rights index	20	2	153	—	—	—
Credit information index	50	7	118	—	—	—
Protecting investors						
Disclosure index	10	0	165	—	—	—
Extent of director liability index	4	1	170	—	—	—
Ease of shareholder suits index	5	0	170	—	—	—
Registering property						
Number of procedures	8	3	160	11	4	156
Time (days)	32	5	134	36	7	128
Paying taxes						
Number of procedures	19	8	148	—	—	—
Time (days)	10	5	150	—	—	—
Trading across borders						
Number of procedures (exporting)	31	14	130	—	—	—
Time (days) (exporting)	50	11	114	—	—	—
Number of procedures (importing)	47	6	122	—	—	—
Time (days) (importing)	50	8	117	—	—	—
Enforcing contracts						
Number of procedures	23	6	146	32	6	137
Time (days)	10	0	165	31	0	144
Closing a business						
Time (years)	11	1	137	14	3	132

Source: Doing Business database.
Note: The table shows the number of countries that have reformed, reversed, or made no change in regulations regarding various investment climate indicators. The number of countries has increased over time from 133 in 2003 to 175 in 2007. Because some indicators are available for five years and others for three years, both time frames are shown. Only countries with at least two years of data are included in the chart.
—Not available.

based on Enterprise Surveys in Latin America highlights the importance of the governance agenda (figure 1.10).[16] The study calls for strengthening of the rule of law and of institutional frameworks to enforce compliance as key priorities for improving firm performance in the region. Additional areas highlighted include expanding access to credit, followed by policies to encourage innovation and investments in human capital.

FIGURE 1.9 Average ranking of "ease of doing business," by region and income group

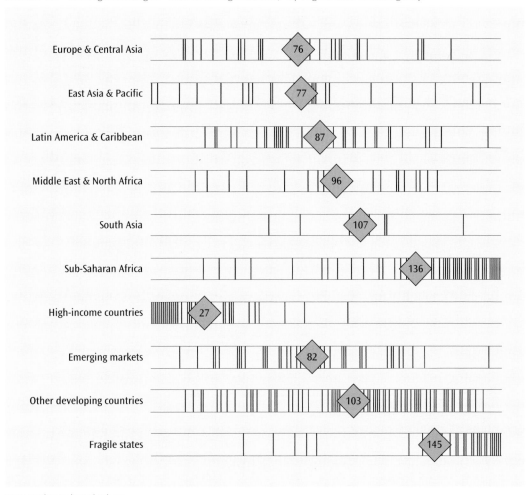

Source: Doing Business database.
Note: Each line shows the rank of one country in the group.

Investment climate reform promotes a level playing field and broad-based growth. Weak investment climates affect the prospects of small, medium, and large enterprises in different ways. One dimension by which the impact of the investment climate varies across firms is by size. The impact has something of a u shape—with a weak investment climate generally hurting small and medium enterprises (SMEs), while often encouraging the growth of micro- and informal firms and having less of a detrimental impact on the large firms. Weak infrastructure and corruption are most strongly associated with

encouraging the growth of microfirms. In the case of the former, the effect comes through the choice of technology and greater reliance on labor-intensive processes. In locations where the incidence of bribes is higher, firms have the incentive to remain small and "fly below the radar screen" of officials.

Among formal firms, a weak investment climate generally lowers productivity and growth prospects. It is often SMEs that are hurt most as they have fewer alternative ways of compensating for limited access to finance, inefficient government services, and poor infrastructure. SMEs not only have

TABLE 1.6   Low coverage and high cost of Africa's infrastructure

	Coverage deficit			High costs	
Item	Sub-Saharan Africa	Other developing countries	Item	Sub-Saharan Africa	Other developing countries
Paved road density (per 1,000 sq. km)	31	134	Power tariffs (US$c/kWh)	0.05–0.30	0.05–0.10
Total road density (per 1,000 sq. km)	137	211			
Mainline density (lines per 1,000 people)	10	78	Road freight tariffs (US$c/ton-km)	0.05–0.25	0.01–0.04
Mobile density (lines per 1,000 people)	55	86			
Generation capacity (MW per million people)	37	326	International phone call (US$/3-min. call to the United States)	0.80	0.20
Electricity coverage (% of population)	16	41			
Improved water (% of population)	60	72	Internet dial-up service (US$/month)	50	15–25
Improved sanitation (% of population)	34	51			

Source: World Bank Africa Region Infrastructure Country Diagnostic project.

less access to formal finance and pay more in bribes than larger firms, their growth opportunities are more sensitive to financing constraints. In contrast, larger firms can be disproportionately hurt by a weak judicial or property rights system. Weak property rights lower the ability of firms to undertake arms-length transactions, activities most associated with larger firms.[17] Strengthening the investment climate is thus an important way of leveling the playing field and ensuring a dynamic SME sector with incentives—and opportunities—to grow and prosper.

Interactions across policy areas are important. The effectiveness of reforms can depend importantly on the broader quality of institutions. For example, using data from 27 countries in Eastern Europe and Central Asia, a recent study shows that changing the formal rights of creditors has little effect on the share of bank financing available to firms.[18] However, the effect is larger when complemented by an efficient court system,

which affects enforcement. An evaluation of the impact of Mexico's reform of the time and costs associated with registering a business on new business entry also confirms the importance of regulatory complementarities.[18] The impact was greater in states that had lower regulatory burdens overall.

Need for greater emphasis on implementation and enforcement. Reforming what is on the books is an important step but only part of the story. What matters is how measures are actually implemented or enforced. The gap between what is on the books and what happens on the ground can be large. In many cases the gap can be explained by corruption. Greater numbers of procedures and longer delays open opportunities for demands for extra payments or offers of speed money, particularly if democratic institutions are weak.[20] The effectiveness of investment climate reforms is enhanced by broader improvement in the quality of a country's institutions and governance.

FIGURE 1.10   Aggregate labor productivity gains in Latin America, by firm size

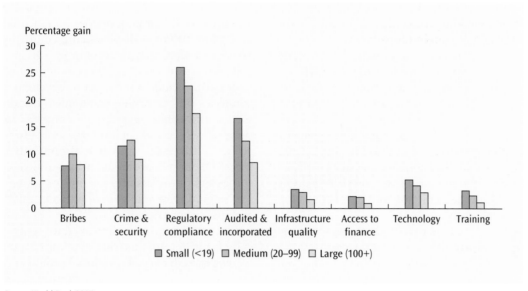

Source: World Bank 2007.
Note: The figure depicts the potential percentage gains that could be achieved if firms were to move to the 75th percentile of the same industry and firm size.

Governance Reform

Good governance has a positive impact on growth. Research shows that it can also support growth that is more inclusive (box 1.10). An increased focus on governance reform is yielding progress, but institutional weaknesses remain a key obstacle to better growth and development outcomes in many countries.

The World Bank's Country Policy and Institutional Assessment (CPIA) ratings suggest that governance in developing countries improved between 2000 and 2006 (figure 1.11). Governance in low- and middle-income countries has incrementally improved in almost all categories. All groups of countries experienced the most progress on revenue mobilization and budget management and the least progress on property rights and quality of public administration. As a group, fragile states showed only limited progress in most areas and did not advance on the quality of public administration and transparency, accountability, and corruption.

Important progress has been made in implementing the Public Expenditure and Financial Management (PEFA) indicator system.[21] At end-February 2008, 74 countries had completed or substantially completed a PEFA assessment, with 4 countries having had repeat assessments. Since the PEFA framework was launched only in 2005, it is too early to have a broad assessment of progress over time. A recent analysis of data on poverty-reducing public spending in heavily indebted poor countries (HIPCs), however, shows some improvements in public financial management between 2001 and 2006.[22] As of end-February 2008, only 28 PEFA reports had been made public and posted on the PEFA Web site. Efforts toward increased disclosure of these reports must be continued.

Environmental Sustainability and Growth

In the previous sections, progress toward the income poverty MDG is analyzed on the basis of traditional economic variables: per capita GDP, corrected for variations in the external terms of trade. The discussion shows that developing countries' strong growth performance in recent years has made a crucial contribution to the poverty reduction effort; without strong growth, achieving the MDGs will remain illusory. The traditional measures of economic growth, however, do not take into account the long-term effects of natural resource depletion and environmental degradation on growth and poverty. One of the defining characteristics of developing countries is their high dependence on natural resources. This resource dependence can have implications for the sustainability of poverty reduction if growth is heavily based on the depletion and depreciation of natural assets.

Development policy challenges depend importantly upon whether a country has abundant produced or human capital, crop-land or pastureland, forests or fish, minerals or energy. Tables 1.7 and 1.8 present asset accounts for developing regions and income groups in 2005.[23] Oil-producing countries are shown separately to account for the special characteristics of their economies. The tables also include a breakout of developing countries into emerging economies, fragile states, and other developing countries. In these tables natural capital consists of crop-land, pastureland, timber and nontimber forest resources, protected areas, and subsoil assets (minerals and energy). "Intangible" capital is an amalgam of human capital and institutional quality.

Natural capital as a share of total wealth is high for developing countries but falls as income rises. It exceeds produced capital as a

---

BOX 1.10   Institutions, inequality, and growth

Research shows a negative relation across countries between income inequality and institutional quality (see box figure). This modern-day association between inequality and institutions is the result of long and complex historical processes in which both inequality and institutions have influenced each other: a process the 2006 *World Development Report* (WDR) referred to as virtuous and vicious circles between the two. In countries where wealth and income were concentrated in the hands of the few, exclusive institutions developed to concentrate power in the hands of the few and perpetuate the privileges. In other countries where the distribution of wealth was more equal, more open and inclusive institutions developed that protected the property rights of the many rather than the few. The 2006 WDR calls on a variety of historical examples, including the contrast between the developments of North and South America to illustrate this point. The interaction between inequality and institutions has in many countries undermined growth in the long term, with more-unequal societies with weaker governance ending up poorer than their more-equal and better-governed counterparts.

A vivid illustration of how weak institutions that protect only the property rights of the few can undermine economic growth comes from recent work by Klapper and others.[a] They construct data on entrepreneurial activity, as measured by rates of new business formation, across a large set of developed and developing countries. They find a strong association between institutional quality and business entry rates that persists after controlling for per capita income and de jure regulatory barriers to firm entry. In particular, weak institutions that protect the property rights of the few shield incumbents from competitive pressure by stifling entrepreneurial activity. This can contribute to the perpetuation of both high inequality and weak institutions. And it can also undermine growth: in a related paper, Klapper, Laeven, and Rajan[b] find that when weak institutions stifle entrepreneurial activity, growth of incumbent firms thus sheltered from competition is also significantly lower.

a. Klapper and others 2007.
b. Klapper, Laeven, and Rajan 2006.

BOX 1.10   Institutions, inequality, and growth *(continued)*

High inequality and weak institutions go together across countries

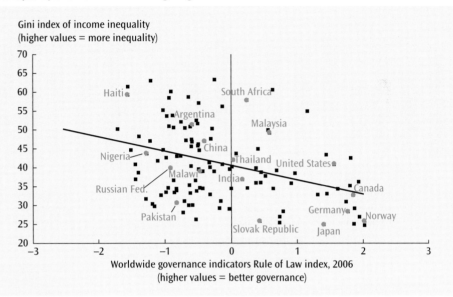

Note: Data on the Gini Index are taken from 2007 World Development Indicators, table 2.7, and refer to the most recent year for which data are available. Data on Rule of Law come from the Worldwide Governance Indicators project, www.govindicators.org, and refer to 2006, the most recent year available.

Entrepreneurial activity is stronger in countries where property rights are protected

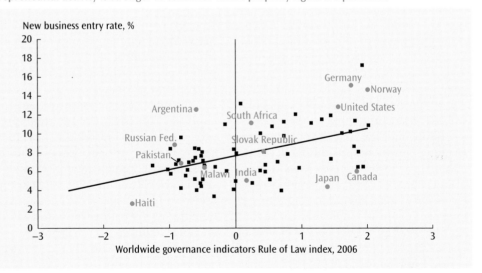

Note: Data on new business entry rates are taken from Klapper and others (2007) and refer to the number of newly registered businesses in a year as a fraction of the total number of registered businesses in the previous year. Data are averaged for 2003–05. Data on Rule of Law come from the Worldwide Governance Indicators project, www.govindicators.org, and refer to 2006, the most recent year available.

FIGURE 1.11   CPIA governance indicators, 2000–06

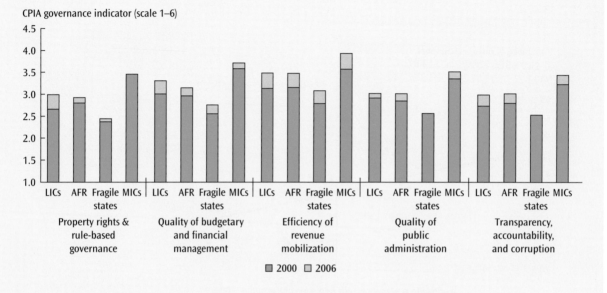

Source: World Bank CPIA database.
Note: CPIA is on a scale from 1 to 6, with a higher score denoting better performance. LICs = Low-income countries; MICs = middle-income countries;
AFR = Sub-Saharan African countries.

share of wealth in these countries, but not in high-income countries. The share of intangible capital tends to rise with income and is particularly important in Europe and Central Asia (72 percent of total wealth). Fragile states are notable for having extremely low levels of produced assets per person.

Agricultural land is an important share of total natural wealth in developing countries. Preserving soil quality in these countries will be particularly important for maintaining wealth and sustaining development. Similarly, fragile states show a relatively large share of forest resources in total natural wealth, suggesting that sound forest management could be important for maintaining the wealth of these countries. Total natural wealth per capita rises with income, reflecting high population-to-land ratios in lower-income countries, and the much greater productivity of agricultural land in higher-income countries.

Net Savings, Environmental Resources, and Sustainable Growth

Recent growth theory suggests a link between current net savings and changes in future consumption.[24] Measures of saving should account for the depletion of natural resources and damage to the environment in addition to the depreciation of produced capital. "Adjusted net savings" provides such a measure, altering the measure of net saving in the National Accounts to include investment in human capital (an addition to saving); depletion of minerals, energy, and forests; and damages from emissions of particulate matter and carbon dioxide (CO_2). Negative adjusted net savings indicates that an economy is potentially on an unsustainable long-term path.

The positive relation between adjusted savings and economic growth is illustrated in figure 1.12. Because there is a lag

TABLE 1.7 Total per capita wealth and its components, by developing region and economy type, 2005
2000 US$ thousands

	2000 US$ per capita				Percent		
	Total wealth	Produced capital	Natural capital	Intangible capital	Produced capital	Natural capital	Intangible capital
East Asia & Pacific	16.4	4.7	5.6	6.1	28	34	37
Europe & Central Asia	36.2	9.2	11.5	15.5	25	32	43
Latin America & the Caribbean	66.3	10.2	16.6	39.5	15	25	60
Middle East & North Africa	22.3	5.5	12.2	4.5	25	55	20
South Asia	8.3	1.6	2.7	4.1	19	32	49
Sub-Saharan Africa	10.5	1.4	3.9	5.2	13	37	49
Emerging market economies	22.7	4.8	6.6	11.2	21	29	50
Other developing countries	12.6	3.0	7.2	2.4	24	57	19
Fragile states	4.9	0.7	5.4	−1.3	15	111	−26
High-income countries	453.4	78.6	21.0	353.9	17	5	78
World	93.1	16.9	9.0	67.3	18	10	72
Major oil producers	30.9	10.4	31.6	−11.1	34	102	−36

Source: World Bank estimates. All dollar figures are at nominal exchange rates.

TABLE 1.8 Per capita natural wealth and its components, by developing region and economy type, 2005
2000 US$ thousands

	2000 US$ per capita					Percent			
	Natural capital	Agricultural land	Forest resources	Protected areas	Subsoil assets	Agricultural land	Forest resources	Protected areas	Subsoil assets
East Asia & Pacific	5.6	2.6	0.4	0.2	2.4	47	7	4	42
Europe & Central Asia	11.5	2.2	0.7	0.6	7.9	20	6	6	69
Latin America & the Caribbean	16.6	4.8	2.6	0.9	8.4	29	16	5	50
Middle East & North Africa	12.2	2.1	0.1	0.1	10.0	17	1	1	81
South Asia	2.7	1.7	0.2	0.1	0.7	62	8	5	25
Sub-Saharan Africa	3.9	2.0	0.8	0.2	1.0	51	19	4	26
Emerging market economies	6.6	2.5	0.6	0.3	3.2	38	9	5	48
Other developing countries	7.2	2.1	0.9	0.2	3.9	29	13	3	55
Fragile states	5.4	1.9	1.0	0.1	2.4	36	18	1	45
High-income countries	21.0	5.6	1.1	2.1	12.2	27	5	10	58
World	9.0	3.0	0.7	0.6	4.7	33	8	7	52
Major oil producers	31.6	1.7	0.8	1.2	27.8	5	3	4	88

Source: World Bank estimates. All dollar figures are at nominal exchange rates.

between investment and growth in output, these figures scatter adjusted net saving rates averaged over 2000–02 against per capita growth rates averaged over 2002–06. As figure 1.12 shows, there is some tendency for higher net saving rates to be associated with higher growth in output per capita over the short run. Robust evidence on the linkage between net savings and growth over the longer term is reported in a forthcoming

FIGURE 1.12   GDP growth vs. adjusted net savings

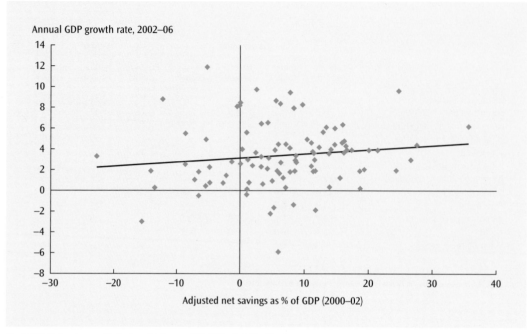

Source: World Development Indicators database and World Bank staff estimates.
Note: Includes all countries except major oil producers.

FIGURE 1.13   Adjusted net saving trends, 1990–2005

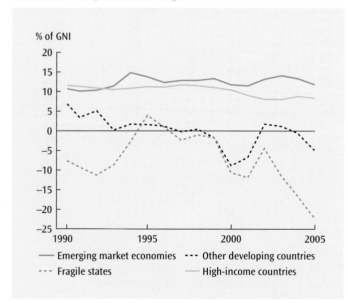

Source: World Development Indicators 2007.

study, which shows, using historical series in per capita terms from 1970 to 2000, that adjusted net savings is correlated with future changes in consumption in developing countries.[25]

Reflecting high rates of natural resource depletion, adjusted net savings are negative in many developing countries, putting these countries on an unsustainable long-term path (table 1.9 and figure 1.13). In fragile states, adjusted net savings in 2005 were estimated at minus 22 percent of GNI. On average, other developing countries (excluding emerging markets and fragile states) also had negative adjusted saving rates (minus 5 percent of GNI) as a result of high natural resource depletion. Environmental health damages—which measure deductions to the stock of human capital caused by particulate matter pollution—are particularly important in East Asia and the Pacific and in South Asia, as are the damages caused by

TABLE 1.9 Adjustments to savings, 2005
% of GNI

	Gross national savings	Education expenditure	Consumption of fixed capital	Natural resource depletion	Environmental health degradation	CO_2 damages	Adjusted net savings
East Asia & Pacific	44.4	2.2	10.3	7.8	1.2	1.2	26.1
Europe & Central Asia	23.9	4.1	10.4	17.5	0.6	1.2	−1.7
Latin America & the Caribbean	21.0	4.3	12.0	8.6	0.4	0.4	3.9
Middle East & North Africa	33.7	4.5	10.9	32.2	0.6	1.2	−6.7
South Asia	29.4	3.5	9.1	5.5	0.8	1.2	16.5
Sub-Saharan Africa	17.3	3.8	10.7	16.1	0.4	0.7	−6.8
Emerging market economies	30.6	3.5	10.7	9.9	0.8	1.0	11.7
Other developing countries	30.0	3.7	10.2	27.0	0.6	0.9	−5.0
Fragile states	19.9	3.4	10.0	33.4	0.9	1.1	−22.2
High-income countries	18.6	4.6	13.1	1.4	0.3	0.3	8.2
World	22.1	4.3	12.3	4.9	0.4	0.5	8.1
Major oil producers	34.6	3.6	9.1	41.7	0.5	1.5	−14.4

Source: World Development Indicators 2007.

carbon dioxide pollution. In contrast, emerging markets showed positive rates, reflecting the robust saving efforts in countries such as China and India, but also the much smaller impact of natural resource depletion.

Notes

1. This chapter discusses growth and poverty reduction in emerging market economies, other developing countries, and fragile states. Emerging economies include those developing countries with substantial access to international capital markets. They include mainly middle-income countries, although some low-income countries (such as India) are also included in this group. The "other developing countries" category includes mainly low-income countries.

2. See also IMF 2008.

3. The terms-of-trade changes had a sizable impact on domestic incomes and purchasing power in many developing countries. In countries with large terms-of-trade fluctuations, gross domestic income (GDI) offers a more reliable measurement of changes in purchasing power than GDP. Real GDP measures the value added of physical output in the economy but says nothing about its purchasing power. Changes in output at constant prices may differ from the income generated by this output as a result of shifts in the terms of trade. If the terms of trade improve compared with the base year, income generated by a given level of real GDP increases, and vice versa.

4. IMF 2007.

5. IMF 2007.

6. See also Dorsey and others, forthcoming.

7. Hansen and Rand 2006; Alfaro and Charlton 2007; Chowdhury and Mavrotas 2006.

8. The data on remittances remains patchy, although significant improvements have been achieved recently. The World Bank has developed the most comprehensive database on skilled migration to date.

9. World Bank 2006.

10. Kireyev 2008.

11. Ozden and Schiff 2007, p. 5.

12. Gupta, Pattillo, and Wagh 2007. See also Adams and Page 2003.

13. Ozden and Schiff 2005.

14. Ozden and Schiff 2005.

15. Aterido, Hallward-Driemeier, and Iarossi 2007.

16. World Bank 2007.

17. Aterido, Hallward-Driemeier, and Pages 2007.

18. Safavian and Sharma 2007.

19. Kaplan, Piedra, and Seira 2007.

20. Gonzalez, Lopez-Cordova, and Valladares 2007.

21. PEFA is a partnership of the World Bank, the IMF, the European Commission, the United

Kingdom's Department for International Development, the Swiss State Secretariat for Economic Affairs, the French Ministry of Foreign Affairs, the Norwegian Ministry of Foreign Affairs, and the Strategic Partnership with Africa. See http://www.pefa.org. It includes 28 indicators covering aspects of budget formulation, execution, and reporting as part of an overall diagnostic Performance Measurement Framework report on the quality of a country's public financial management (PFM) systems.

22. de Renzio and Dorotinsky 2007.

23. The estimates are based on the methodology presented in World Bank 2006. Note that China dominates the East Asia figures in table 1.7.

The relatively low total wealth and high produced capital share in this region reflect difficulties with the methodology of estimation for China. The negative values for intangible capital reported for fragile states and major oil producers reflect very low returns on total assets in these countries.

24. Dasgupta 2001; Hamilton and Hartwick 2005.

25. Ferreira and others, forthcoming. Ferreira and Vincent (2005) show that adjusted net saving is not significantly correlated with future consumption in developed countries, where technological change and knowledge generation are likely to be more important as sources of growth than physical asset accumulation.

2

Achieving Better Results in Human Development

The world has made steady progress toward meeting the numerical targets for the human development Millennium Development Goals (MDGs). Achievements have been impressive in some cases, and even in countries that are lagging, progress is measurable. The glass is, at the very least, half full. Nonetheless, significant challenges still exist as the global community approaches the halfway point of the MDG goals, and some countries and regions are seriously off track for successfully meeting the goals. This chapter provides an overview of the key issues and trends that underpin the human development indicators of the MDGs, with an explicit focus on inequity in spending and access, health care quality, and child malnutrition. The chapter also documents environmental problems that pose barriers to the achievement of the human development MDGs.

One challenge for reaching the health and education MDGs relates to equity: uneven access to resources and the exclusion of marginalized groups mean that the benefits associated with progression toward the MDGs are not widely shared by all. These inequalities are closely related to quality concerns, because the costs of low-quality education and health care are likely to be disproportionately borne by the poor. Moreover, poor quality discourages the use of services even if they are free. The quantitative nature of the MDGs masks important variations in quality, which in turn holds up the attainment of the MDGs in education and in health.

For education, while several regions are on track to meet the targets of universal primary completion and gender parity (MDGs 2 and 3), neither of these goals necessarily translates into learning or human capital development. The quality of education is as important, if not more so, as its quantity, as the *Global Monitoring Report 2007* emphasized. In addition, addressing the issue of quality in public health care provision can make a significant contribution toward combating malnutrition, reducing child mortality, improving maternal health, and limiting the spread of HIV/AIDS, malaria, and tuberculosis (MDGs 1, 4, 5, and 6).

Malnutrition—"the forgotten MDG"—has received limited attention and investment, and it continues to be a major concern in many countries, especially in South Asia and Sub-Saharan Africa.[1] Malnutrition lowers the immune system and undermines the individual's ability to deal with adverse environmental hazards, in particular those associated with unsafe drinking water and lack of sanitation. Water, sanitation, and good hygiene are increasingly recognized as important for improving health and nutrition status.

Exposure to environmental health risks in early infancy can lead to stunting, wasting, lowered immunity, and increased mortality. Indoor air pollution stemming from reliance on biomass for energy raises morbidity, especially among children, and it is a major contributor to mortality. Outdoor air pollution increasingly places both children and adults at risk, a problem particularly acute in urban areas of fast-growing economies. Climate change is expanding the exposure to tropical vector-borne diseases, such as malaria, as average temperatures rise and as new areas become infested. All of these environmental hazards have a negative influence on health, and bringing these hazards under control will help not only to achieve environmental goals but also to improve the health status of children and infants.

Equity Considerations in Meeting the MDGs

Inequalities in access to health and educational services exist almost everywhere in the world: the poor tend to be less healthy and less educated than the rich. But income is not the only factor leading to unequal access. So too are differences in ethnicity, gender, and social status. In addition, the quality of education and health services is often unequally distributed. Nonetheless, poverty remains the largest roadblock to good health and education and can lead to a vicious cycle of deteriorating health, low demand for education, and increased poverty.

How equitable are countries' education and health systems?

Analyzing health inequality requires some measures of living standards along with objective measures of the quality of health services provision, which can be disaggregated and also collected for different groups of the population. Three commonly employed outcome measures are child survival rates, anthropo-

metric indexes, and an aggregated measure of adult health.[2] Education inequality is analyzed by examining outcome measures such as school completion rates and student achievement on standardized tests. There are also input-based measures, such as public expenditure in health and education. These measures can be used to understand the current state of inequities in health and education, as well as their evolution over time.

There are a few places in the developing world, such as Sri Lanka or Kerala, India, where disparities in income and educational attainment are small, where health access is equal, and where outcomes are similar across the population. Virtually everywhere else, however, and by almost any available measure, the richest quintile is healthier than the poorest on an aggregate regional basis, and the disparities can be sobering (table 2.1). For example, in Latin America and the Caribbean, a child born in the poorest quintile is almost three times as likely to die before his or her fifth birthday, almost six times as likely to be malnourished, and about two-thirds as likely to receive medical attention for a fever as is a child born in the richest quintile. In all regions, the concentration indexes—which are a measure of the extent of socioeconomic-related inequality in health outcomes—suggest the existence of inequalities that are detrimental to the poor (box 2.1). Health inequalities tend to be the most acute in upper-middle-income countries, consistent with patterns of income inequality worldwide.

Educational outcomes also appear to reflect this same inequality. With the exception of Europe and Central Asia, school participation and completion rates are significantly higher for the richest quintile of the population (figure 2.1). In regions such as the Middle East and South Asia, where intraquintile female completion rates are already significantly lower than male completion rates, the difference in the likelihood of completion for a boy in the richest quintile compared with a girl in the poorest is particularly acute. While inequalities in par-

TABLE 2.1   Selected measures of health inequality, by region and income group, 2000–present

	Poorest quintile	Richest quintile	Ratio of poorest to richest quintile	Concentration Index
Under-five mortality rate (per 1,000 live births)				
Latin America & the Caribbean	86.5	34.8	2.95	−0.17
Middle East & North Africa	101.0	44.0	2.27	−0.13
South Asia	131.7	65.8	2.10	−0.12
East Asia & Pacific	96.1	37.9	2.89	−0.18
Europe & Central Asia	78.9	41.3	1.97	−0.11
Sub-Saharan Africa	171.1	100.5	1.86	−0.09
Low-income countries	166.4	96.7	1.84	−0.09
Lower-middle-income countries	78.9	30.8	2.76	−0.16
Upper-middle-income countries	91.1	35.8	2.81	−0.18
World	**136.0**	**73.6**	**2.17**	**−0.12**
Medical treatment of fever (% of under-five child population)				
Latin America & the Caribbean	37.2	58.7	0.66	0.10
Middle East & North Africa	26.6	36.2	0.72	0.09
South Asia	31.6	59.8	0.49	0.17
East Asia & Pacific	35.3	54.2	0.65	0.07
Europe & Central Asia	15.2	36.4	0.42	0.09
Sub-Saharan Africa	27.8	49.3	0.54	0.14
Low-income countries	27.2	48.8	0.54	0.14
Lower-middle-income countries	36.4	55.4	0.68	0.08
Upper-middle-income countries	30.3	56.1	0.53	0.12
World	**30.2**	**51.1**	**0.58**	**0.12**
Medical treatment of adult illnesses (% of female population)				
Latin America & the Caribbean	23.5	37.0	0.87	0.07
South Asia	17.2	49.6	0.35	0.20
Europe & Central Asia	32.6	51.8	0.63	0.06
Sub-Saharan Africa	39.4	63.7	0.61	0.12
Low-income countries	35.8	61.6	0.57	0.13
Lower-middle-income countries	23.9	35.2	0.89	0.06
Upper-middle-income countries	52.3	73.3	0.72	0.07
World	**34.2**	**56.0**	**0.66**	**0.11**

Source: Adapted from Gwatkin and others 2007 based on DHS data.
Note: Averages are unweighted means for latest available years.

ticipation rates apply across regions, they are especially dramatic in South Asia and Sub-Saharan Africa.

Much of the concern about the role of equity in reaching the MDG goals for health and education revolves around the skewed allocation of public resources for programs in these areas. Although there are variations across countries, public spending on health care and education tend to be skewed toward high-income segments of the population.[3] With the exception of Latin America and the Caribbean, public spending on health services consistently favors the rich

(figure 2.2), while spending on public education favors the rich across all regions (figure 2.3). In Sub-Saharan Africa, for example, the highest quintile receives more than twice as much public funding for health care and education as the lowest quintile. This is typically also the case when countries are grouped by income.

Out-of-pocket payments by patients and parents for publicly provided services are also an equity concern. Fees for education and health, both formal and informal, can represent a significant portion of household income. In health, the proportion of out-of-pocket

An examination of outcomes by income quintiles provides a crude summary measure of inequalities. A smoother measure can be obtained from "concentration curves" for health, which capture the distribution of a given health measure against living standards. The concentration index derived from this curve quantifies the magnitude of socioeconomic-related inequality in health (and education).[a] For example, using data for India and Mali, it is possible to cumulate the relative percentages of births for each quintile, order them by increasing wealth, and plot this against the cumulative percentage of under-five deaths. The resulting concentration curves show that child deaths are concentrated among the poor (since both curves exceed the line of equality), although there is relatively less inequality in Mali than in India (since the curve is less bowed outward).

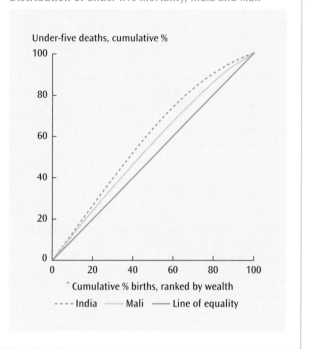

Distribution of under-five mortality, India and Mali

Source: O'Donnell and others 2008.
Note: Curves based on DHS 1982–92 (for India) and 1985–1995 (for Mali).
a. The concentration index is analogous to the Gini index. An index of zero suggests no inequality, and since health outcomes can be measured as "bads," such as ill health, negative values mean that ill health is higher among the poor. Inequality is greater the larger the absolute (positive or negative) value of the index.

FIGURE 2.1   Regional disparities in primary school completion and participation, 1990–2005

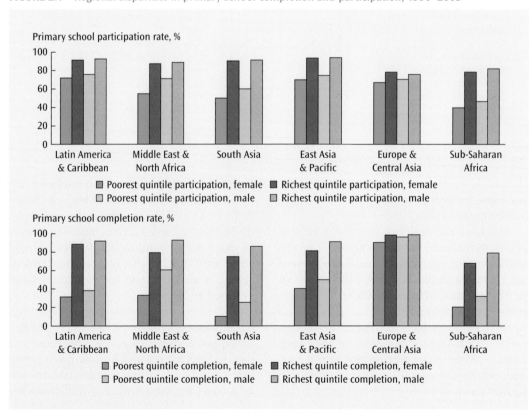

Source: World Bank calculations, based on DHS data.
Note: Regional values are unweighted averages.

FIGURE 2.2 Incidence of public health spending on poorest and richest quintiles, 1989–2001

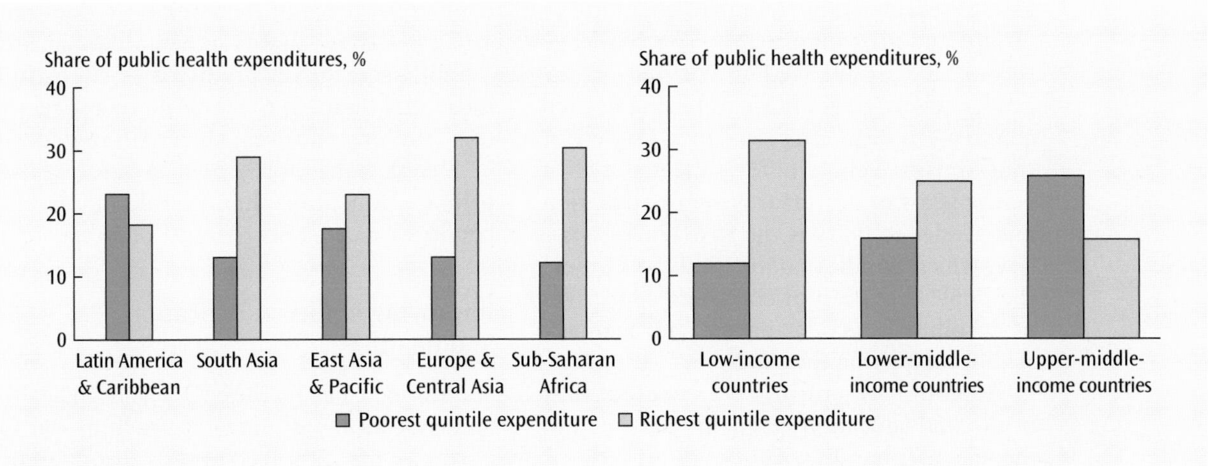

FIGURE 2.3 Incidence of public education spending on poorest and richest quintiles, 1985–2001

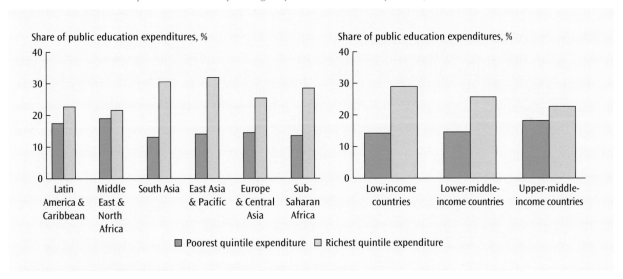

Source: Filmer 2003 and World Bank calculations.
Note: Regional and income averages are unweighted averages.

Source: Filmer 2003 and World Bank calculations.
Note: Regional and income averages are unweighted averages.

payments tends to be higher for countries with lower levels of national income. At the household level that leads to inadequate health care utilization and households being driven into poverty.[4]

Progress on gender equity in primary education has been dramatic over the past four decades, and in some regions, such as Europe and Central Asia and Latin American and the Caribbean, girls are surpassing boys.

But some inequities persist, even in successful countries, particularly among excluded groups and among rural populations. Girls in both of these communities tend to lag significantly behind boys.[5] In Lao People's Democratic Republic, for example, disparities continue to exist in the average years of school completion for boys and girls between urban and rural areas, and between the majority Lao-Tai population and minority groups, highlighting the importance of targeting rural areas and, within them, minority groups and girls (figure 2.4). The challenge is to reach marginalized groups and—if the gender education goals are to be met in each country—to focus efforts on girls. One effort that aims to help countries meet the twin equity goals of universal primary education and gender equality is the Fast-Track Initiative, which bundles donor funds to support the implementation of countries' objectives of enrollment, gender parity, and primary school completion (box 2.2).

Although it could be expected that health and education inequality is related to income distribution within a country, this is not the case. Concentration ratios for health and education, reflecting the distribution of health and education outcomes, generally display a weak and statistically insignificant negative relationship with the income Gini coefficient (figure 2.5). In other words, countries that are more unequal in terms of income distribution do not necessarily have

a more unequal distribution of health outcomes. The level of income per se does not affect health inequality either, although it is a highly significant predictor of education inequality (figure 2.6).[6] This finding suggests that poorer countries, such as Bangladesh or Nepal, have more unequal outcomes in primary education than do middle-income countries such as Brazil and Colombia.

Improving equity in education and health

Success in achieving the MDG goals in health and education will hinge on reaching out to poor and marginalized groups through targeted interventions. Tailored programs are often necessary to bridge language differences between marginal groups and the majority population, and cultural barriers often need to be accommodated to ensure participation in education and health programs.

In Argentina, for example, public health and nutrition programs are targeted to the

FIGURE 2.4 Differences in Laotian education achievement across age, gender, and ethnic group, 2002–03

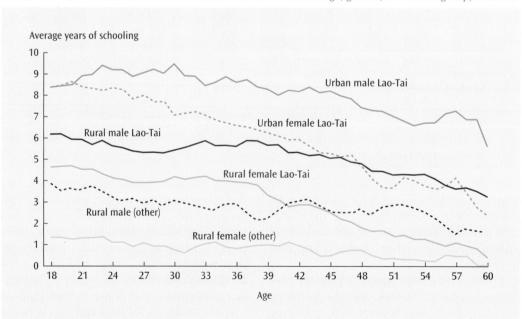

Source: King and van de Walle (2007).
Note: Figures are drawn after taking three-year moving averages. Data for the urban non-Lao-Tai are not included because of lack of observations.

BOX 2.2   The Education for All Fast-Track Initiative

The Education for All Fast-Track Initiative (EFA–FTI) is a global partnership launched in 2002 to help low-income countries meet the education MDGs and the EFA goal that all children complete a full cycle of primary education by 2015. It is among the largest global partnerships (in which the Bank is a participant) and is a platform for collaboration at the global and country levels.

FTI Achievements. FTI is widely regarded as a partnership with promise for achieving development impact; its achievements include:

- strengthening harmonization at both the global and country level around country plans
- raising the political profile of education and deepened country commitment to reform
- increasing domestic resource allocation for basic education (albeit unevenly across countries)
- generating momentum for accelerating progress on primary education in terms of primary school enrollment (an increase of 4.4 percentage points in all countries and 8.2 percentage points in Sub-Saharan countries), gender parity (from .87 to .92 between 2000 and 2006 and from .82 to .89 in Sub-Saharan countries), and primary completion rates (an average increase of 12 percentage points, from 57 to 69 percent in all countries, and a 17 point increase, from 37 to 54 percent, in Sub-Saharan countries)
- mobilizing external funding for education, through bilateral and multilateral channels as well as through the FTI Catalytic Fund, which grew rapidly in 2006-07 to over $1 billion in donor pledges.

FTI Catalytic Fund. The Catalytic Fund was established in 2003 to provide transitional financial assistance to FTI-endorsed countries. The fund was designed both to complement other bilateral and multilateral funding and to ensure that countries' FTI-endorsed education sector plans could be adequately funded. As a joint agreement across 17 donor countries, the initiative puts into practice the harmonization and alignment goals of the Paris Declaration by:

- fostering collaboration among donors, and
- relying on local decision making to drive activity and ensure that countries' needs are met flexibly and in a timely manner.

To date, fifteen donors have pledged $1.2 billion through 2009, and $301 million in grant agreements have been signed with 18 countries. Current requests for funding are estimated at $878 million and further pledges of funding are pending.

FTI's Challenge. FTI's challenge is to stimulate strengthened dialogue, decision making, and commitment in four critical areas:

- enhancing local capacity to implement education sector plans more effectively to obtain results faster, more deeply, and more efficiently
- introducing strategies, policies, and interventions in partner countries to provide education to children living in marginalized communities, children with disabilities, and children living in situations of fragility or conflict
- aligning education reforms on the key objective of ensuring learning outcomes, and not just on school enrollment and completion
- strengthening the international aid architecture to facilitate more reliable, robust, and harmonized financial and technical support.

---

poor even though their health coverage is universal. Argentina's child-feeding programs deliver between 40 and 75 percent of their benefits to the poorest 20 percent of the population; similarly, between 20 and 50 percent of all government-administered immunizations were given to children from lower-income groups.[7] In contrast, such clear progressive outcomes were not found in two reproductive health programs— mobile reproductive health camps and education sessions—conducted in the rural part of Gujarat state in India. In this case, program beneficiaries were clustered among

FIGURE 2.5   Relationship between health and education inequality and income inequality

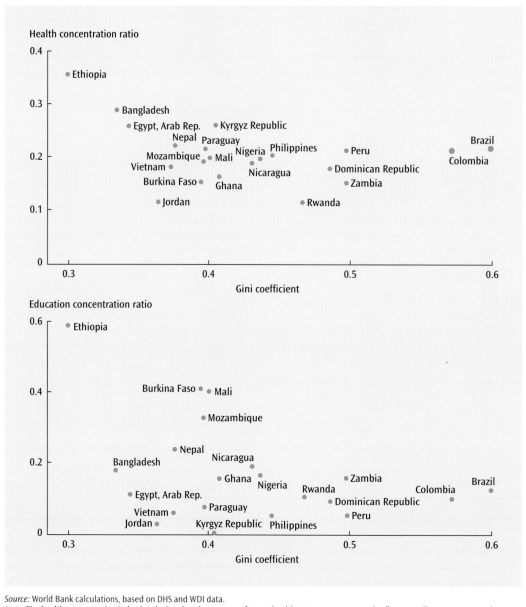

Source: World Bank calculations, based on DHS and WDI data.
Note: The health concentration index is calculated as the average of seven health status measures: under-five mortality rate, percent of children with moderate and severe stunting, percent of children without all essential vaccinations, percent of children receiving medical treatment for fever, percent of women with births receiving antenatal care, percent of women with births with delivery attended by trained medical personnel, and percent of women receiving medical treatment for adult diseases. The education concentration index is the average of school participation and completion rates.

middle-income groups, with smaller numbers among both the rich and the poor.[8]

In some cases, the results of health interventions are potentially regressive even where absolute improvements are achieved. A program to expand the use of maternal

health services in the Matlab subdistrict of Bangladesh increased the number of facility-based births among the population as a whole but did not improve service usage by the very poor.[9] As a result, the distribution of health benefits across income groups

FIGURE 2.6 Relationship between health and education inequality and per capita income

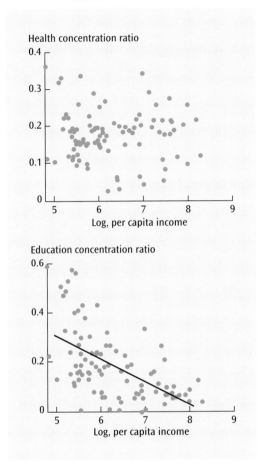

Source: World Bank calculations, based on DHS and WDI data.
Note: For definitions of health and education concentration indexes, see figure 2.5.

remained essentially unchanged between 1997 and 2001, and in the most unequal years service usage by the poor was so low that a woman in the richest quintile of the population could be up to 3.5 times as likely to be a beneficiary of the program as a woman in the poorest quintile.

The success of health equity interventions varies according to country, strategy, disease, or service. The large-scale delivery of primary health care services by nongovernmental organizations (NGOs) generated improved services for the poor in Cambodia and Nicaragua, but the same medium of

delivery led to more mixed results in Gujarat state in India.[10] Similarly, while a campaign to distribute insecticide-treated bednets in conjunction with measles immunization in Ghana and Zambia was successful in raising bednet ownership rates among the poor, the long-term sustainability of bednet programs in reducing malaria incidence and transmission is not so clear.[11] In some cases, these contextual factors may even be region specific. In rural Guatemala, different models of delivery of government health services provided mixed results, depending on the service area and population served.[12] Overall, trends in health equity vary across countries and time periods.

Educational interventions to promote equity can improve enrollment, completion, and test scores for the poor. However, targeted interventions do not always achieve the intended outcome of increasing access for disadvantaged groups for a number of reasons.

For example, recent evidence suggests that when preschool and compulsory education is more extensive—in terms of enrollment and duration—equality of opportunity in education is increased.[13] Achieving such an outcome is not simply a result of increasing educational spending and resources for students from targeted groups, whether at the class or school level.[14] One recent finding of relevance to countries striving to meet the MDGs is that neglect of nutrition and cognitive stimulation in the first six years of life permanently affects an individual for life. Longitudinal studies show the serious behavioral, health, and income effects of neglect in early life.[15] Access to early childhood interventions is highly specific to the income and education of parents, partly because infants and small children are kept at home.

Where financially feasible, targeted conditional cash transfers (CCTs), whereby parents are paid to ensure that their children receive education and health services, have been shown to be highly effective in encouraging school enrollment and completion and in ensuring child health checkups.[16] Among the most challenging aspects of CCTs are the administrative difficulties, especially in remote areas, and the supply of services that are often insufficient to meet the demand triggered by CCT programs.

Health Care Quality Critical to Reaching the MDGs

The quality of health care services matters because it reflects the extent to which investments in national health care systems are able to raise both human capital and individual welfare. Efficient and accountable health care systems provide good returns on such investments, and in the long run the quality of health care matters more to improving health outcomes than increases in health care spending per se.

Health care quality can be defined as the "proper performance (according to standards) of interventions that are known to be safe, that are affordable to the society in question, and that have the ability to produce an impact on mortality, morbidity, disability, and nutrition."[17] This definition is broad, and the specific dimensions or criteria chosen can influence assessments of the quality of health care.

Health Care Quality Measurement: Complex. The measurement of the quality of health care provision is complicated and not standardized across countries and diseases. Unlike the case of education quality, there is an absence of a small number of universally agreed-upon indicators for the quality of health care delivery, and existing measures are often not systematically available for all countries.

Inherent in the definition of health care quality is the notion that quality can be evaluated from the perspective of inputs, processes, or outcomes.[18] Input measures are often aspects of structure; for example, whether medical facilities possess and maintain medical equipment, or the extent to which they are stocked with essential drugs. Indicators of process attempt to gauge service delivery from the supply-side—such as

whether doctors correctly diagnose medical conditions and prescribe the appropriate treatment—or the demand side, such as patients' subjective evaluations of the quality of care received. Measures of outcomes, such as mortality rates, are indirect; moreover, they often capture quantity as well as quality aspects of health care. Nonetheless, outcome indicators are typically correlated with health care quality in other dimensions and can serve as important complements to these measures of health care quality.

Why Improve Quality?

By almost any measure, improvements in health care quality benefit not only the individual but households and society more broadly. Better-quality health care may positively affect nutritional and mortality outcomes, infant health, and usage rates among the underserved.[19] Moreover, health quality improvements need not be entirely precluded by cost considerations: there is ample evidence that even low-income households are willing to pay higher user fees, if they obtain improved access to, and enhanced reliability of, health care services in return. Most important, higher one-time costs incurred as a result of receiving higher quality care may mean lower costs in the long run, since post-consultation complications are less likely to arise when the initial quality of care is high.[20] The fact that formal and informal out-of-pocket payments are so widespread in low-income countries suggests a willingness to pay for perceived failures in public services, either in terms of limited access or poor quality.[21]

In Ghana, improvements in public health care services and infrastructure led to improvements in child nutritional status, as captured by anthropometric measures.[22] Children were taller in communities where there were more doctors, lower consultation fees, and basic drug availability. In addition, these health services had a positive impact on the probability of child survival. These results were particularly strong for children living in rural areas, although there was no distinguishable effect between the quality of health services received by the poor versus nonpoor. This last result stands in contrast to a similar study of the Côte d'Ivoire, which—while echoing the findings that doctor and drug availability positively influences child health—also notes that the quality of health services received were systematically different between children in poor and nonpoor households.[23]

Within countries, health care quality tends to depend on socioeconomic status, ethnicity, and whether the medical provider is public or private. Doctors treating the poor tend to be of lower quality than those treating the better off, even after taking into account differential abilities to pay. In India, the generally lower-quality medical training of physicians in the private sector—relative to the public sector—was more than offset by higher effort in performance. As a result, the private sector in India delivers an overall higher quality of care.[24] Racial inequalities may also be operative, as in the case of Mexico, where a large and significant difference was found in the quality of health care provided to indigenous versus nonindigenous patients.[25]

Well-trained doctors can make a dramatic difference in improving health care quality. In a study of doctors in India, Indonesia, and Tanzania, more competent doctors—as measured by an index of competency—were more likely to ask the right questions during treatment.[26] For example, doctors in the top quintile of competence more frequently performed common diagnostic procedures for diarrhea—such as checking for blood or mucous in stools, or for fever—as compared to doctors in lower quintiles.

One measure of effort (or lack of it) is absenteeism, which is both chronic and pervasive in primary health care facilities in many developing countries.[27] In Bangladesh, absenteeism by physicians in larger clinics was 40 percent, while the rate was much higher, 74 percent, in smaller subcenters with a single doctor. Meanwhile, absenteeism rates were lower for other health care professionals, such as nurses and paramedics. The absence rates across five developing countries

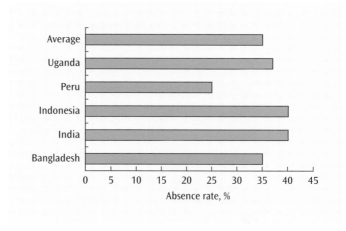

FIGURE 2.7   Absenteeism among primary health care workers, 2002–03

Source: Adapted from Chaudhury and others 2006.
Note: Absenteeism was defined as not being found in the facility for any reason at the time of the unannounced random visit.

averaged 35 percent between 2002 and 2003 (figure 2.7), and it is possible that this figure underestimates the severity of the problem, because health care personnel can be present without actually providing medical care.

Low absenteeism is correlated with well-functioning facilities—as measured by objective criteria such as whether the facility has potable water—and greater utilization. Chronic absenteeism leads to low usage, because health care personnel are not available, and dissuades future use because of unreliable service. Evidence for low-income, rural communities in Cameroon, Tanzania, and Uganda suggest that NGOs charging modest fees provide higher quality of care than free government clinics, as well as higher rates of utilization. This is true even for NGOs that pay their health care personnel less than the government rate. Greater accountability and more consistent and reliable health services result in higher quality care from NGOs.[28]

High Variability of Health Care Quality

Although health care quality is notoriously difficult to measure, there is little doubt that quality of care varies from country to country and within countries, raising equity concerns as well as health care concerns. The role that public spending plays in this variation is a matter of some controversy. Most studies have been unable to find strong links between health outcomes and government health spending, although some recent work has questioned this result.[29] For example, the relationship between infant and under-five mortality rates and public health spending is weak overall, and may depend on the specific set of countries or variables being considered.[30]

This weak link between spending and health outcomes is consistent with strong evidence in education of an insignificant relationship between spending and learning. Even taking into account the one-time nature of mortality, the statistical insignificance of health care spending for mortality rates suggests that the quality of service delivery is likely to be low. However, variations in the quality of service delivery across countries are relatively large (table 2.2).

Measures of performance illustrate this point. The provision of assistance during delivery by a doctor or health care professional, for example, ranges from 78 percent of all live births in the Middle East and North Africa, to 18 percent in South Asia. In contrast, the use of oral rehydration treatment for children suffering from diarrhea in South Asia is almost double that in the Middle East and North Africa. Even within Sub-Saharan Africa, the vaccination coverage of children ages 1–2 years ranges from a low of 8.1 percent in Uganda to a high of 75.9 percent in Eritrea.

Despite this seemingly large cross-country variation, evidence suggests that cross-country differences may be smaller than intra-country variations. Studies have also found large intracountry variations by type of facility, medical condition, and domain of care.[31]

Relation of Quality to Income and Economic Growth

Ultimately, the goal of a quality health care system is improved health status. Healthy populations are more likely to invest in human capital via education, and this improves productivity, spurs greater overall economic growth, and raises incomes. Higher-quality health care is especially important for children, as healthy children are more likely to go to school, finish school, and learn more, which in turn has a positive effect on future productivity and household income.[32] Cross-country evidence for education shows the insignificance of education spending in spurring economic growth, but the central importance of education quality (box 2.3).

While the quality of health is often multifaceted and can involve strong value judgments, aggregate measures of health quality, as captured by selected outcome indicators, provide some broad generalizations. Health quality is positively related to national income, but there is little relationship between public health spending levels and quality measures (figure 2.8). This apparent paradox—that income matters for health quality but health spending does not—suggests that other drivers of health quality are important.

There are several possible factors accounting for this finding. As noted above, public health care expenditures are skewed toward expensive secondary and higher-level care that benefits higher-income quintiles. Second, health care expenditures are a proxy for structural measures such as whether a clinic has certain medical equipment or essential drugs, and these measures may be a relatively poor determinant of health care quality. For example, a study to assess the quality of clinics providing prenatal care in Jamaica found that clinic processes—such as examination and counseling procedures—exerted a positive, significant impact on birth weights, while structural factors alone did not.[33] Failure to monitor health care delivery services adequately can also lead to poor outcomes.[34] This combination of inequality of spending, poor governance, and difficulties in capturing meaningful measures of quality health care services may result in weak associations. More balanced spending and raising service performance therefore offer important tools for reaching the human development MDGs.

TABLE 2.2 Selected proximate measures of health care quality for selected countries
by region, 2002–06

Country	Year of data	Assistance during delivery by doctor or health care professional (% of all live births)	Receipt of full set of vaccinations in first year of life	Children with acute respiratory infection treated at health care facility (% of all under-five children)	Treatment of diarrheic children with oral rehydration therapy
Sub-Saharan Africa					
Burkina Faso	2003	37.9	27.8	35.9	26.5
Cameroon	2004	61.7	38.1	40.6	24.2
Chad	2004	16.1	5.4	6.5	17.7
Ghana	2003	47.1	49.8	44.0	46.4
Guinea	2005	38.1	29.1	42.0	36.6
Kenya	2003	41.6	43.7	49.1	29.2
Malawi	2004	57	47.1	36.5	61.1
Mozambique	2003	47.7	42.8	55.4	54.1
Niger	2006	17.7	16.8	47.2	26.2
Rwanda	2005	28.4	66.3	27.9	18.6
Senegal	2005	51.9	40.9	47.2	26.7
Uganda	2006	42.6	9.7	73.5	43.4
Zimbabwe	2005/06	68.5	34.1	26.3	61.6
Regional average		*45.9*	*34.7*	*40.9*	*36.3*
Middle East & North Africa					
Egypt, Arab Rep. of	2005	74.2	81.4	63.4	35.7
Jordan	2002	98.3	23.0	76.4	22
Morocco	2003/04	62.6	82.4	37.8	28
Regional average		*78.4*	*62.3*	*59.2*	*28.6*
Europe & Central Asia					
Moldova	2005	99.5	2.1	59.7	34.9
Regional average		*99.0*	*2.1*	*59.7*	*34.9*
South Asia					
Bangladesh	2004	13.2	67.0	19.9	74.6
Nepal	2006	22.8	77.8	34.3	29.3
Regional average		*18.0*	*78.0*	*27.1*	*52.0*
East Asia & Pacific					
Cambodia	2005	43.8	52.3	45.4	35.8
Indonesia	2002/03	66.3	42.1	61.3	48.4
Philippines	2003	59.8	58.9	54.8	57.6
Regional average		*56.6*	*51.1*	*53.8*	*47.3*
Latin America & the Caribbean					
Bolivia	2003	60.8	12.1	51.5	38.2
Colombia	2005	90.7	25.2	0	55.4
Dominican Republic	2002	97.8	22.3	63.5	32.3
Haiti	2005	26.1	27.0	31.5	43.8
Honduras	2005	66.9	2.2	53.9	55.7
Regional average		*72.0*	*17.8*	*40.1*	*45.1*

Source: Demographic and Health Surveys, various years.
Note: Full range of vaccinations include BCG, diphtheria, polio, and measles.

BOX 2.3   Improving educational quality and stimulating growth

An emerging body of evidence shows the major role that the quality of learning and the skills acquired through the educational system plays in spurring growth. Recent work commissioned by the World Bank draws on the traditional human capital model to show the sizable effect that improvements in quality may have on long-term income growth. Using a set of international standardized test score for the last 40 years for a group of 50 countries, Hanushek and Wößmann reach two key conclusions. First, educational quality has a strong causal impact on individual earnings and economic growth. The authors find that one standard-deviation increase in international standardized test scores contributes to higher growth in long-term GDP per capita of 2 percent. Second, the role of educational quality in economic development differs between developing and developed countries. The payoff to increasing quality, per year of schooling of the population, is 80 percent higher for developing countries.

Hanushek and Wößmann also make a strong case that improving educational quality requires a focus on efficient education spending, bolstered by sound institutions that encourage competition, autonomy, and accountability. Simply increasing educational spending does not guarantee improved educational quality.

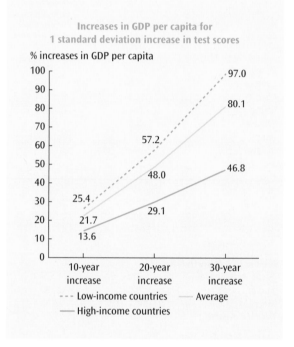

The long-term quality-of-education payoff

Source: Adapted from Hanushek and Wößmann 2007.

Quality of health care deserves greater attention and measurement if reaching the health MDGs is to be realized. As in education, quality matters to outcomes, but the tools in health are more complex and less comparable across countries, making meaningful comparisons difficult. This is clearly an area for additional effort and financing.

Child Malnutrition: Tackling Hunger and Mortality

Reducing child malnutrition is one area that holds great potential not only for improving child health but also for improving education outcomes and ultimately the welfare of individuals and families. A close epidemiological link exists between childhood malnutrition and mortality across a range of diseases, such as diarrhea, measles, and pneumonia; malnourishment not only increases the risk of contracting these diseases, it also influences the severity and likelihood that the outcomes resulting from them are fatal. Malnutrition is also closely related to performance in education; undernourished children display reduced school achievement and inferior cognitive abilities that diminish their lifetime accumulation of human capital. Child malnutrition also has consequences for adult health, because malnourishment in childhood can result in a higher disease risk in adulthood.[35]

Understanding the impact of malnutrition on early childhood and subsequent adult development is complicated by the presence of other factors in households with malnourished children, notably poverty, limited demand for education, and an adverse physical environment—all of which contribute

FIGURE 2.8 Relationship of health quality to income and public health care expenditures

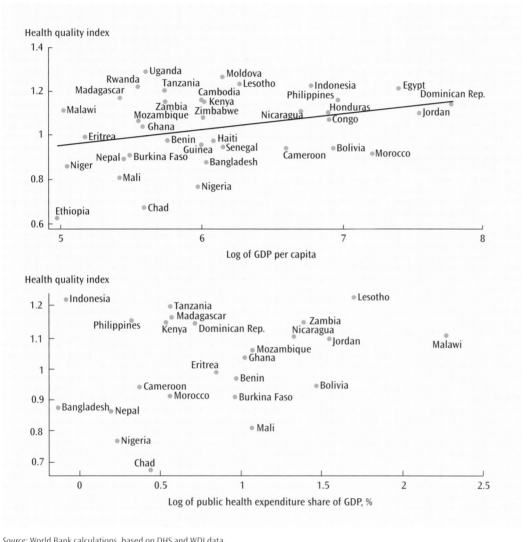

Source: World Bank calculations, based on DHS and WDI data.

Notes: Health quality includes 8 measures of health quality outcomes: percent live births with no antenatal care, percent live births with no tetanus injections, percent live births with no trained medics during delivery, percent children with no cocktail of essential vaccinations, percent women with births receiving key components of antenatal care, percent women with births receiving no postnatal care, percent children with acute respiratory infection not treated in a medical facility, and percent children with diarrhea with no treatment.

to malnutrition. Because risks accumulate and are compounded over time, total accumulated risks are important,[36] although there are certain sensitive periods of physiological development where the appropriate intervention can make a major difference. Of particular significance is the increasing evidence pointing to the narrow "window of opportunity" for preventing malnutrition, which starts at conception and ends at two years of age. Nutritional deficits during this period can lead to irreversible physical and cognitive impacts.[37]

The most readily available and observable indicators for malnutrition outcomes are based on the anthropometric criteria of height and weight. Two accepted measures are stunting (low height for age, a measure of chronic malnutrition) and wasting (low weight for height, which captures more transient episodes of malnutrition). In addition, intake of micronutrients—principally iron, iodine, and vitamin A—are increasingly being monitored as important metrics for gauging malnutrition. And the implications of inaction are serious. For example, sustained iron and iodine deficiencies in pregnant women can lead to reduced cognition in babies.[38]

Long-term Consequences of Malnutrition

Nutritional deficits in childhood interfere with human capital accumulation. Starting with primary education, malnutrition can result in lower enrollment levels, grade repetition, failure to complete grades, and inferior performance on cognitive tests. Evidence from country studies is instructive.

In rural Pakistan between 1986 and 1990, school enrollment rates rose as a result of improvements in nutrition. By one estimate, an increase of 0.25 of a standard deviation in average nutrition translated into an increase of 5.5 percent in the probability of school enrollment for the entire cohort. This would mean an increase in average productivity equal to a 0.65 percent increase in lifetime earnings. Moreover, this nutrition effect was seven times greater for girls than for boys.[39] A similar study that tracked Filipino children born between 1983–84 and 1994–95 found that an increase of one standard devi-

ation in nutrition would lead to enrollment improvements equivalent to between 11 and 21 months of school attendance.[40]

In rural Zimbabwe, nutritional deficits sustained by children—as a result of civil war in the late 1970s and two episodes of drought between 1982 and 1984—led to delayed school entry by five months and an estimated reduction in lifetime earnings of 14 percent.[41] A study of a randomized, community-level nutritional intervention in rural Guatemala that ran from 1969–77 found persistent effects from the intervention. Twenty-five years after the program, women who received nutritional supplements as children had up to 1.2 years of additional schooling compared with those who had not received the supplement, as well as higher levels of economic productivity.[42]

Nutritional deficits also exert a direct effect on lifelong cognitive abilities and well-being. In Jamaica a study that followed a cohort of children from ages 9–24 months into adolescence found that the beneficiaries of childhood nutritional interventions significantly outperformed those without the interventions in 11 of 12 cognitive and educational tests.[43]

Steady Progress in Reducing Malnutrition

Nutrition outcomes have been steadily improving over time, as reflected in the downward trend in the incidence of stunting in most developing regions (table 2.3).[44] Today just 36 countries account for 90 percent of all stunted children worldwide.[45] Since the mid-1990s, the prevalence of stunting has fallen throughout Asia, with notable reductions in East and Southeast Asia. The notable exception to the trend is Sub-Saharan Africa, where declines have been modest, at best.

This steady progress can potentially be derailed by increases over the past four years in the worldwide prices of commodities (see chapter 1). Rising food and fuel prices lower the real income of households that do not produce these products, which may lead to substitution toward less food or cheaper, but

TABLE 2.3 Downward trends in under-five malnutrition, 1990–2005

	Moderate and severe stunting (as a % of under-five children)			
	1990	1995	2000	2005
Latin America & the Caribbean	18.0	15.3	13.0	11.1
Middle East & North Africa	26.2	23.1	20.2	17.6
South Asia	50.8	45.2	39.7	34.5
East Asia & Pacific	35.9	29.2	23.5	18.9
Sub-Saharan Africa	36.7	35.8	34.9	34.1
Developing countries	37.9	33.5	29.6	26.5
Developed countries	2.8	2.8	2.7	2.6
World	33.5	29.9	26.7	24.1

Source: Adapted from de Onis and others 2004, based on WHO data.

less nutritious, substitutes for current diets. That could raise malnutrition levels, especially among the poorest households.

Post-2000 data on stunting from the World Health Organization (WHO) suggest that reductions in child malnutrition vary significantly from country to country (figure 2.9). Income is clearly correlated with the prevalence of malnutrition, as measured by stunting outcomes. The incidence of moderate and severe stunting in low-income countries exceeds that in high-income countries by a factor of 16. Much of this difference stems from the high incidence of severe

FIGURE 2.9 Stunting and wasting for under-five children, 2000–present

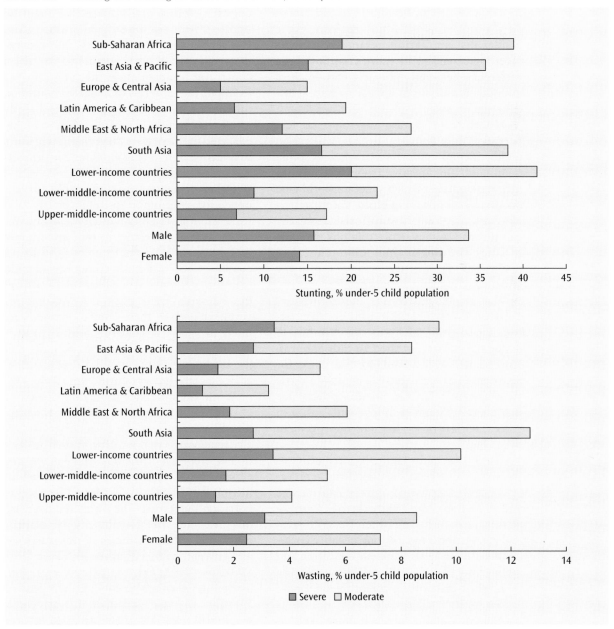

Source: WHO Global Database on Child Growth and Malnutrition, various years.

stunting among children under age five in Sub-Saharan Africa. South Asia actually has a slightly higher incidence than Sub-Saharan Africa of moderate stunting, but a lower incidence of severe stunting.

Stunting prevalence differs between males and females. Using severe stunting as the measure of malnourishment, under-five females are *less* malnourished than males. In countries in the Middle East and North Africa and in South Asia—regions where gender discrimination against females is often perceived to be more common—the difference between male and female child malnutrition does not appear to be statistically significant.

Moderate and severe wasting is far less pervasive than stunting. In fact, wasting in middle-income countries as a whole is statistically indistinguishable from that of high-income countries, which suggests worldwide progress in improving child malnutrition among those countries. Unfortunately, the gap in wasting prevalence remains between middle- and low-income countries, and pockets of malnutrition persist even in the upper-middle-income countries.[46]

Worldwide, patterns of micronutrient deficiencies are very similar to the pattern for stunting and wasting. Vitamin A deficiency is concentrated in Sub-Saharan Africa and South Asia. High-risk areas for zinc deficiency are, likewise, mainly in those two regions.[47] Finally, anemia prevalence is highest in South Asia and Sub-Saharan Africa, with little evidence of improvement over time.[48]

Two of the main factors contributing to the notable differences in malnutrition prevalence across regions and countries are income and education. Empirically there is a strong positive association between poverty rates and malnutrition and a strong negative correlation between levels of female education and malnutrition (figure 2.10), and this is the case even when controlling for other factors.[49] A country with a high poverty rate, such as Rwanda or Zambia, is much more likely to have a high child malnutrition rate compared with those with lower rates of poverty, such as Colombia and the Islamic Republic of Iran. Similarly, countries such as Niger and Rwanda that have low primary education completion among females tend to demonstrate higher rates of child malnutrition.

The importance of education and income as determinants of child malnutrition has been confirmed by household and cross-country empirical evidence.[50] Education improvements seem particularly important. Household analyses suggest that insufficient maternal schooling is frequently the main constraint to adequate child nutrition. For example, higher levels of maternal education influence feeding practices, which directly affect child health. In Ghana, the most highly educated mothers were more than three times as effective in reducing child malnutrition as the least educated mothers.[51]

Other evidence from household surveys underscores the importance of income growth for reductions in child malnutrition. Assuming an annual per capita income growth rate of 2.5 percent from the 1990s to 2015 for 12 countries, projections of reductions in child malnutrition range from a low of 13 percent (for Romania) to as much as 63 percent (for Peru).[52] However, these simulation results are likely to be overoptimistic because, in reality, only 3 of the 12 countries actually met the study's assumption of a 2.5 percent per capita income growth during the 1990s.

While the influence of income growth is positive and statistically significant, the magnitude of the effect can be relatively small. The impact of economic growth on malnutrition is tempered by the relatively low income elasticity of nutrition, so that changes in income have a relatively limited impact on nutrition outcomes. The estimated decrease in a given measure of malnutrition is dramatically affected by estimates of this elasticity, and current evidence suggests a range from −0.01 to −0.82 (figure 2.11). For example, assuming an annual income growth rate of 5 percent and an elasticity of −0.5 percent, it would still take Tanzania until 2026 to meet the MDG malnutrition goal.[53]

FIGURE 2.10 The relationship between malnutrition, poverty, and education

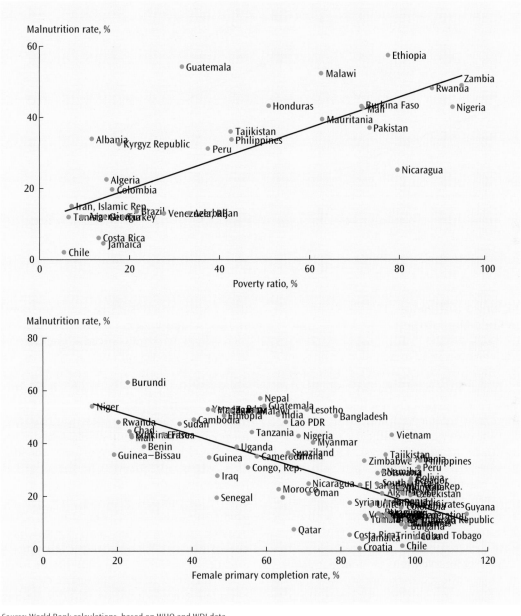

Source: World Bank calculations, based on WHO and WDI data.
Note: Partial regression plots of bivariate regression of height two standard deviations below median on: (a) poverty headcount ratio ($2 day PPP adjusted basis) as percentage of population; and (b) female primary education completion rate, as percentage of relevant age group.

Rising nutrition levels can lead to a virtuous cycle of improvements in health and increases in income. Evidence from northwestern Tanzania between 1991 and 1994 on the role of supplementary child feeding programs found that such nutritional interventions would allow the income poverty MDG to be attained at an annual income growth rate of 1.5 percent, lower than the 2.2 percent rate required in the absence of such a policy.[54]

FIGURE 2.11 Relation of reductions in under-five malnutrition to increases in income

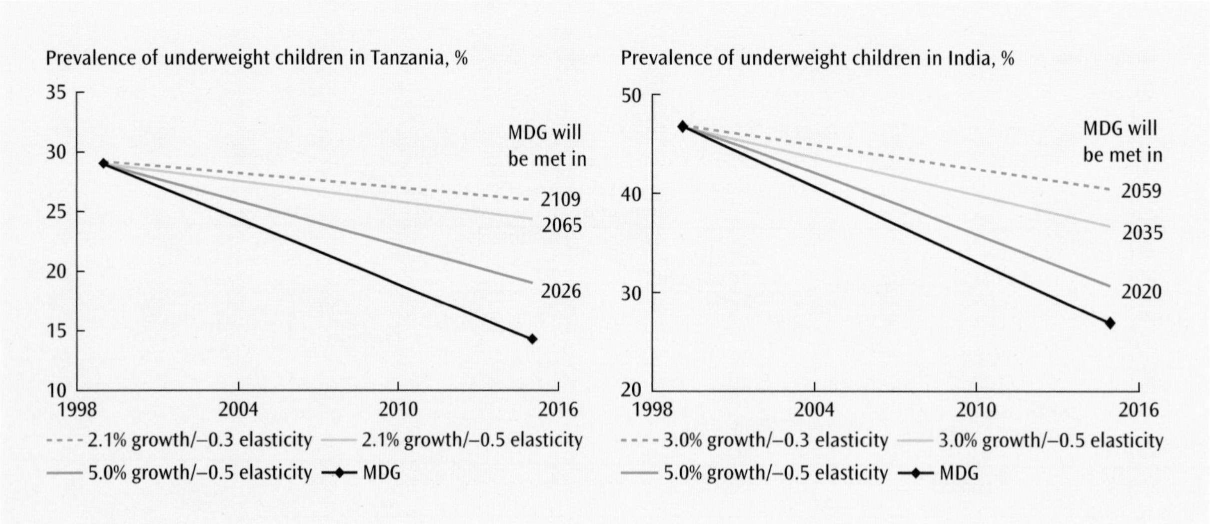

Prevalence of underweight children in Tanzania, %

MDG will
be met in

2109
2065

2026

---- 2.1% growth/−0.3 elasticity ——— 2.1% growth/−0.5 elasticity
——— 5.0% growth/−0.5 elasticity ◆ MDG

Prevalence of underweight children in India, %

MDG will
be met in

2059

2035

2020

---- 3.0% growth/−0.3 elasticity ——— 3.0% growth/−0.5 elasticity
——— 5.0% growth/−0.5 elasticity ◆ MDG

Source: World Bank 2006c.

Making a Difference in Child Malnutrition

Malnutrition is often assumed to be caused by food insecurity. Recent evidence suggests that household behavior and assets are equally important (or perhaps even more important) determinants. Food security, while necessary, is not sufficient to guarantee positive nutrition outcomes. The potential for interaction and feedback effects between child nutrition, education, and income suggest a role for policy interventions in child health that work concomitantly with other investments.[55] Addressing nutrition reinforces other efforts to improve child health.

Several interventions to stem both short- and long-term malnutrition are well known and simple to achieve—examples are oral rehydration therapy and the promotion of exclusive breastfeeding. Ensuring adequate levels of iron, iodine, vitamin A, and zinc for pregnant women, infants, and children can often be effectively achieved through fortifying common foods such as flour and salt with micronutrients, and promoting the use of iron cookware.[56] These offer inexpensive but effective means of implementation as they harness the private sector in distribu-

tion. Except where subsistence is the norm and consumption of commercial foods rare, such efforts are highly effective and deserve to be priority interventions.

Recent evidence on the importance of nutrition during pregnancy and during the first two years of life suggests that focusing investments on nutrition supplements for pregnant women and children under age two would have a high payoff over the long term. Maternal education makes a big difference in ensuring adequate nutrition, as does rising household income, but shorter-term efforts such as teaching mothers about hygiene and sound feeding practices have been shown to be effective even among uneducated women.[57] Availability of fortified snack foods at home or school can compensate for poor nutrition without leading to substitutions for meals, which is a common practice in some countries. Community nutrition interventions can also have an impact on how communities compensate for inadequate food for children and mothers.

As with health care quality, these interventions will be effective only to the extent that they are targeted to the populations in need. The quality of the delivery of these services will also affect their success.

The Environment and Health Goals

The interrelationships among environmental factors, child health, nutrition status, and education are strong and multifaceted, and together significantly influence progress toward the MDGs. Environmental risk factors such as access to water and sanitation play a role in many diseases. It has been estimated that 23 percent of all deaths are principally attributable to environmental factors. Children are among those most vulnerable and adversely affected. Diarrhea, malaria, and lower respiratory infections are most closely linked to environmental factors.

Malnutrition is among the most important determinants of child mortality, together with respiratory infection (largely caused by indoor air pollution), diarrheal diseases (mostly from inadequate water, sanitation, and hygiene), and malaria (from inadequate environmental management and vector control).[58] Lack of food and nutrients, along with the consequences of lack of access to clean water, poor hygiene and sanitation, and repeated infections, lowers resistance to disease, which in turn, leads to a cycle of illness and chronic malnutrition.[59] The WHO estimates that the environment—in particular poor water, sanitation, and hygiene—accounts for about half of the health burden of malnutrition.[60] Recent evidence also points to the negative effects on child growth of infections and of exposure to environmental health risks in early infancy that lead to permanent growth faltering, lowered immunity, and increased mortality.[61]

Impacts of Environment on Health

Environmental health refers to all the physical, chemical, and biological factors external to a person, as well as to all the related factors affecting individuals' behaviors, and encompasses the assessment and control of those environmental factors that can potentially affect health status.[62] Modifiable environmental risks are deemed to be those that are "reasonably amenable to management or change" and that can be classified into either traditional or modern forms.[63] Traditional hazards are those environmental health risks closely linked with poverty and development: lack of access to clean water, poor sanitation, poor waste disposal, indoor air pollution, and vector-borne diseases such as malaria. Modern hazards include environmental health risks such as urban air pollution, agro-industrial waste, and toxic chemicals. The sources of these environmental challenges vary widely, their implications are broad, and interventions range from highly private goods and services (such as cleaning up indoor air pollution) to public goods (such as provision of sanitation).

Environmental risk factors play a role in more than 80 percent of diseases globally. An estimated 24 percent of the global disease burden from all causes is attributable principally to environmental factors (box 2.4). In developing countries, 25 percent of all deaths were found to be attributable to environmental risk factors, compared to 17 percent in developed countries (figure 2.12).[64]

BOX 2.4   Indicators of environmental risk factors—DALYs

The disability-adjusted life year (DALY) is a measure used to quantify the burden of disease by combining years of life lost due to premature death and years of healthy life lost due to morbidity, with one DALY representing the loss of one year of equivalent full health. The use of the DALY measure allows quantification and comparison of the impact of different environmental risk factors on health. In calculating the burden of disease attributable to an environmental risk factor, it is often not practical to assume that exposure to the risk factor can be reduced to zero. Instead, the contribution of environmental risk factors is estimated by how much the disease burden would decline if exposure to a given factor were reduced to a certain achievable baseline level.

FIGURE 2.12 Environmental disease burden in DALYs per 1,000 of population, 2002

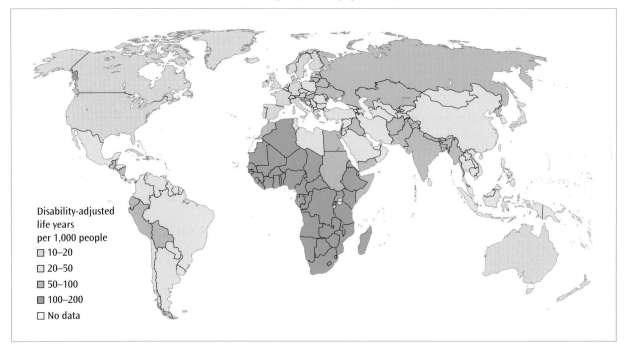

Disability-adjusted
life years
per 1,000 people
☐ 10–20
☐ 20–50
☐ 50–100
☐ 100–200
☐ No data

Source: Prüss-Üstün and Corvalán 2006.

In addition, the poorest and most vulnerable populations—women, children, migrants, people living with HIV/AIDS—are generally the most adversely affected by environmental risk factors as they tend to reside in areas with the worst environmental conditions or have greater exposure to risk factors. Moreover, these populations typically have lower resistance to infection. Among children under five, over 40 percent of the global disease burden is linked to environmental risk factors: an estimated 4.7 million children under five died in 2000 from illness related to unsafe environments.[65]

For the lowest-income countries striving to reach the MDGs, the diseases estimated to have the largest epidemiological burden attributable to environmental factors include diarrhea, lower respiratory infections, and malaria. These diseases also constitute the greatest burden on children ages 0–14 years. Together, the three conditions account for 24 percent of all deaths in children under age 15 (figure 2.13).[66]

Roughly 94 percent of diarrheal cases worldwide can be attributed to the environment, primarily to unsafe drinking water, poor sanitation, and hygiene, resulting in 1.5 million deaths annually, many of them children. Another estimated 1.5 million deaths annually result from respiratory infections caused by environmental factors. In developing countries alone, approximately 24 percent of upper respiratory infections and 42 percent of lower respiratory infections were attributable to environmental risk factors, such as outdoor and indoor air pollution, and contributing risk factors, such as tobacco smoke, solid fuel use, and housing conditions.[67]

Roughly two-fifths of global malaria cases could be prevented through improved environmental management, such as modifications to the natural environment or to human habitation. Behaviors, such as the consistent use of bed nets, can also enhance prevention.[68] Climate change, which raises malaria incidence through meteorological effects on pathogens and vectors, is expected to expand

FIGURE 2.13   Environmental contribution to disease burden

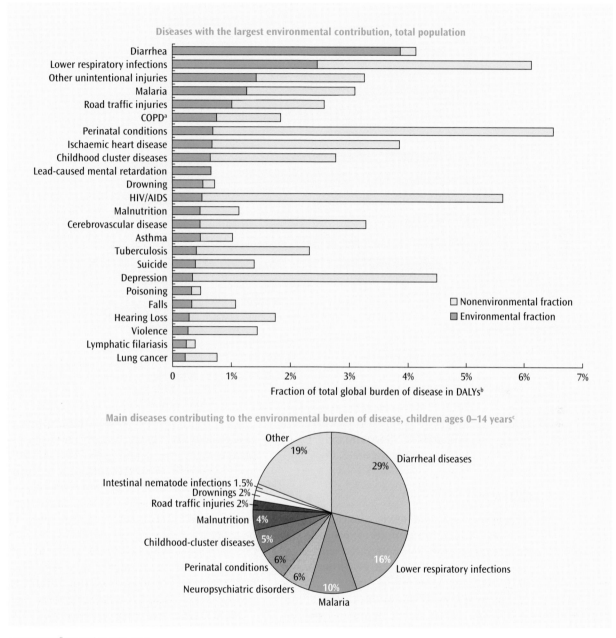

Source: Prüss-Üstün and Corvalán 2006.

a. COPD = Chronic obstructive pulmonary disease.

b. DALYs represents a weighted measure of death, illness, and disabilities.

c. The environmental disease burden is measured in DALYs.

the geographical distribution of several vector-borne diseases, including malaria, and may even come to extend transmission seasons in some regions. Even small temperature

increases could potentially cause large relative increases in the risk of malaria.[69]

Environmental effects on health status also affect incomes. The economic burden on

FIGURE 2.14 Economic burden associated with poor environmental health
percentage of GDP

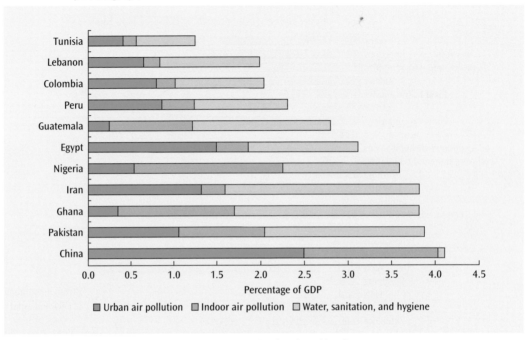

Source: World Bank Country Environmental Analyses, various years, and Baris and Ezzati (2007).
Note: The economic burden of health costs are typically measured as costs of poor health in terms of DALYs and adjusted by either human capital or value of statistical life methods. Since different methodologies and parameters may have been used for estimating costs across countries, these cross-country comparisons are only indicative.

society caused by poor environmental health has been estimated at approximately 1.5–4 percent of GDP annually (figure 2.14).[70]

Water and Sanitation

While wide agreement exists on the need for adequate water and sanitation, progress has been slow, particularly compared with progress on other MDGs.[71] According to the WHO's Joint Monitoring Programme for Water Supply and Sanitation, over a billion people do not enjoy reasonable access to a safe drinking water supply, and a staggering 2.6 billion people (40 percent of the world's population) do not have access to basic sanitation. While these needs may appear basic, the challenges involved in meeting them are complex. Political, economic, and institutional demands have complicated efforts to close the gap. Facilities typically require large initial fixed costs. The economic and institutional costs of operating and managing them are relatively high and are best financed by users, and government has a necessary role in overseeing and regulating their operation. Clean water is vital and demand for it is high. But sanitation generates large externalities and low demand because the beneficiaries of sanitation are not only those who create the problem, but particularly those residing "downstream." Hygiene entails behavior changes that are notoriously difficult to achieve rapidly.

Almost all diseases associated with the lack of drinking water supply and sanitation are transmitted by fecal material that has not been disposed of properly. Contamination from fecal material can occur through many transmission routes. Adequate water and sanitation can interrupt some of these routes but not all of them, and recent evidence suggests that behavioral changes are also needed. Changes in hygiene behavior

FIGURE 2.15 Trends and projections of access to water and sanitation in developing countries, 1990–2015

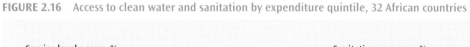

Source: WHO and UNICEF 2006.

must accompany infrastructure investments in water and sanitation systems if the full set of health benefits is to be realized.

The most recent assessment suggests that the world is roughly on target for reaching the MDG goal of halving the proportion of people without sustainable access to safe drinking water, but it is expected to miss the goal for access to basic sanitation by half a billion people (figure 2.15).[72] The data also show that levels of access to improved water and sanitation in urban areas have been static, whereas access to water supply and sanitation in rural areas has been improving. Nonetheless, significant disparities continue to exist in urban and rural levels of access.

In addition, the summary global statistics are averages and conceal major disparities by income group. When disaggregated, it is clear that access to different levels of service varies with income quintile.[73] As figure 2.16 shows for 32 countries in Africa, the distribution of access to clean water and proper sanitation is highly unequal: while less than 10 percent of the bottom expenditure quintile has access to improved water

FIGURE 2.16 Access to clean water and sanitation by expenditure quintile, 32 African countries

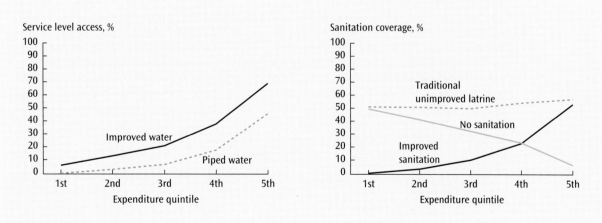

Source: Banerjee and others 2008.

supply, nearly 70 percent of the top quintile has such access. Similarly, over half of the bottom quintile has no access to sanitation of any kind, while only 6 percent of the top quintile has no access to sanitation. Given the fundamental nature and cost of water and sanitation services, it is not surprising that service levels are linked to expenditure levels; that is, as incomes increase, many families will invest in these basic services, and they are willing and able to pay at least for water.

Air Pollution

A major source of indoor air pollution in developing countries is the burning of solid fuels such as biomass (animal dung, wood, crop residues, and wastes) and coal for heating and cooking. Currently half of the world's population relies on inefficient, highly polluting solid fuels for their daily energy needs.[74] Many use solid fuels that are burned in open fires or simple stoves that release smoke into the home. These practices increase indoor air pollution, posing a serious health threat particularly for women and young children who spend more time indoors close to fires (box 2.5).

Approximately 32 percent of the global burden of disease caused by indoor air pollution occurs in Sub-Saharan Africa, 37 percent in South Asia, and 18 percent in East Asia and the Pacific. In developing countries, solid fuel use is the fourth most important environmental risk factor, and it accounts for approximately 3.7 percent of DALYs lost. Because of their reliance on solid fuels, the poorest regions of the world suffer the most, both in terms of deaths and DALYs (table 2.4). The specific health outcomes associated with indoor air pollution include acute lower respiratory infection, chronic obstructive pulmonary disease, and lung cancer.

Outdoor air pollution is caused mainly by the combustion of petroleum products or coal by automobiles, industry, and power stations. In some countries, major sources include wood or agricultural waste. Outdoor air pollution also stems from industrial processes that involve dust formation (such as that from cement factories and metal smelters) and the release of gases (such as that from chemical production). Outdoor air pollution is believed to contribute 0.6–1.4 percent of the total burden of disease in developing countries, and other forms of pollutants (such as lead in water, air, and soil) may contribute up to 0.9 percent.[75]

BOX 2.5   Exposure to indoor air pollution: Evidence from Bangladesh

A recent study on Bangladesh analyzes individuals' exposure to indoor air pollution at two levels: differences within households attributable to family roles; and differences across households attributable to income and education. The findings revealed high levels of exposure for children and adolescents of both sexes, with particularly high exposure for children under five, as would be expected. Among adults, men had half the exposure of women (women's exposure was similar to that of children and adolescents). Elderly men also had significantly lower exposure than elderly women. Household choices of cooking fuel, cooking locations, construction materials, and ventilation practices were found to be significantly affected by family income and adult education levels (particularly for women).

Overall, the poorest, least-educated households had twice the pollution levels of relatively high-income households with highly educated adults. The study found that the typical household could cut their children's pollution in half by adopting two simple measures: increasing children's outdoor time from three hours a day to five or six hours; and concentrating that outdoor time during peak cooking periods.

Source: Dasgupta and others 2004.

Urban air pollution has become a growing concern for most large cities in developing countries. An estimated 800,000 people die prematurely every year from lung cancer and cardiovascular and respiratory diseases caused by outdoor air pollution.[76] Other health effects from urban air pollution include chronic bronchitis, acute respiratory illness, asthma, and coronary diseases. Quantifying the adverse health effects caused by urban air pollution is difficult because of limited data availability, although this is beginning to change with the World Bank's Country Environmental Analyses (CEAs), which highlight the need for ambient air quality monitoring stations, and for strengthened legal and policy frameworks for urban air quality management.[77]

The health effects of air pollution depend on the nature and level of exposure, as well as individuals' activity patterns. Children are particularly susceptible to environmental risks given that greater exposure to air pollution can severely retard their growth and development. Overall, an estimated 5 percent of global lung cancer cases, 2 percent of deaths from cardiovascular and respiratory conditions, and 1 percent of respiratory infections are attributable to pollution caused by urban particulate matter, resulting in 7.9 million premature deaths.[78] The potential savings from curbing health-related problems caused by urban air pollution can thus be substantial.

Climate Change

Climate change refers to human-induced (anthropogenic) change to the global climate system. Climate change constitutes an environmental risk that has global implications for health, but that requires local interventions to address the sources of the problem.[79] However, a causal relationship between climate change and health is difficult to show, given the numerous factors driving both health outcomes and environmental conditions.

Methods for describing and measuring the health effects of climate change remain in the

TABLE 2.4 Deaths and DALYs lost due to solid fuel use

Region	Deaths (thousands)	DALYs (thousands)	Total burden (%)
East Asia & Pacific	540	7,087	18.4
Europe & Central Asia	21	544	1.4
Latin America & the Caribbean	26	774	2.0
Middle East & North Africa	118	3,572	9.3
South Asia	522	14,237	36.9
Sub-Saharan Africa	392	12,318	32.0
World	**1,619**	**38,532**	**100.0**

Source: Bruce and others 2006.

early stages of development. Estimates of the health effects of climate change are therefore based on measures of current and past effects of climate variation (and other influences) on health, and these derived relationships are then applied to projections of likely changes in future climatic conditions.[80]

Climate change has the potential to affect a variety of health outcomes (table 2.5). It directly effects heat waves, floods, and storms and indirectly affects the distribution and transmission intensity of infectious diseases and the availability of fresh water and food. In addition, climate change affects exposure to various communicable and noncommunicable diseases. A global estimate measured the burden of disease in 2000 attributable to climate change at 925 DALYs per million, with strong regional variations exhibited. The largest burdens were found in Sub-Saharan Africa, Asia, and the Eastern Mediterranean.[81] These regions are generally located at lower latitudes, where the most important climate-sensitive health outcomes—such as malnutrition, diarrhea, and malaria—are already pervasive, and where vulnerability to climate change is greatest. Changes in climate are believed to have caused over 150,000 deaths, or the loss of over 5.5 million DALYs annually, since the year 2000.

Addressing Environmental Health Risks

Addressing environmental health risks is challenging because of the political, financial,

TABLE 2.5   Projected health effects of climate change

Health effect	Confidence
Increased malnutrition and consequent disorders, including those related to child growth and development	High
Increased number of people dying and suffering from disease and injury due to heat waves, floods, storms, fires, and droughts	High
Continued change in the range of some infectious disease vectors	High
Mixed effects on malaria; in some places the geographical range will contract, elsewhere it will expand, and the transmission season may change	Very high
Increased burden of diarrheal diseases	Medium
Increased cardiorespiratory morbidity and mortality associated with ground-level ozone	High
Some increased benefits to health, including fewer deaths from cold. These benefits are expected to be outweighed by the negative effects of rising temperatures worldwide, especially in developing countries	High

Source: Confalonieri and others 2007.
Note: The Intergovernmental Panel on Climate Change assigns confidence levels according to the scientific evidence available.

TABLE 2.6   Cost per DALY of alternative interventions for addressing environmental hazards
US$ per healthy year gained

Intervention	Cost per DALY	Assumptions/Comments
Insect-treated bed nets	9–31	Two net treatments with insecticide per year
Insecticide residual spraying	11–34	Two rounds of spraying per hear
Breastfeeding promotion and diarrhea treatment	930	Two interventions during first year of life
Measles immunization	981	
Cholera immunization	2,945	
Water and sanitation upgrading		
Hand pump or standpost	94	
House connection	224	
Sanitation construction and hygiene promotion	< 270	
Acute respiratory disease in children (pneumonia)	398	Four case management interventions

Source: Jamison and others 2006.

and implementation difficulties. Simple investments, such as bed nets, can produce large benefits at modest cost relative to more complex interventions (table 2.6). However, the manner in which bed nets are obtained, treated, and used varies widely across countries, which accounts for some of the observed ineffectiveness of this simple and cheap technology. Poor governance, for example, can raise the costs significantly. Breastfeeding promotion is relatively inexpensive, but this is an awkward intervention because demand is uncertain and reaching the right mother is not always straightforward, particularly in rural areas. Residual spraying, if done consistently, is inexpensive and can protect households without any behavioral shift.

Measles immunization is also relatively inexpensive; moreover it has a positive effect on reducing morbidity and mortality from diarrhea, so its effects are quite powerful beyond simply preventing measles. Thus, there are options for preventing and treating the major environmentally driven diseases that plague the lowest-income countries. The challenge is devising effective programs that actually reach families and investing in the education that helps households prevent illness and use treatment options.

Water supply and sanitation. Water and sanitation infrastructure investments are not cheap, and although health benefits are likely to be significant, they are only part of the considerable economic and environmental benefits that accrue to households and society from these investments. An estimated US$30 billion in annual investments is needed to reach the MDG targets of halving the fraction of the population without basic access to water and sanitation, and these costs do not include wastewater treatment, which is particularly expensive. Currently only US$15 billion is spent globally per year.

The high costs and other problems associated with building and maintaining water and sanitation infrastructure suggest that future investments should be subjected to the following considerations. First, institution building should accompany infrastructure construction, something that has been achieved even in small rural areas through local professional operators (a local entity willing to handle the operations and maintenance for a fee). The World Bank has found such programs to be effective in Rwanda, and programs are currently being tested in Haiti, Mali, and Madagascar.[82] Second, urban water and sanitation networks need to be extended to peri-urban areas and smaller towns. Third, technical standards could be adjusted so that the standards of the developed world are not imposed on low-income countries that cannot afford the gold standard. Fourth, hygiene promotion should be included as part of the investment, as has been the case in recent World Bank water projects in China, Egypt, and Vietnam.

Of greatest concern, however, is the need to build the institutions that can ensure long-term operation and maintenance of water supply and sanitation systems. Not doing so during the "Drinking Water Supply and Sanitation Decade" of the 1980s led to the failure of the costly initiative. Part of the challenge is ensuring an adequate financial base through charges on users, something that often succumbs to political pressures and leads to deterioration of the physical infrastructure and water and sanitation services. Thus a strengthening of the institutional and policy framework must accompany water supply and sanitation investments if they are to have a sustainable impact.

Indoor air pollution. A study that compared the differences in healthy years gained for four alternative solid fuels found that cleaner fuels yielded the greatest gains across all regions, but that improved stoves also had a significant impact.[83] In Sub-Saharan Africa and South Asia, regions with the largest burden of disease attributable to solid fuel use, an improved biomass stove was the most cost-effective intervention. Cleaner fuels, such as kerosene, were the most cost-effective in East Asia and the Pacific.

Conclusion

Halfway to 2015 the world has made serious, if uneven, progress in numerical outcomes toward achieving the MDGs for health and education. Stronger and more targeted efforts are needed to improve the access of the poor and underserved populations to these services. Greater attention also needs to be focused on the quality of education and health investments—and to the governance and accountability of public programs—if they are to meet MDG objectives. Many countries are falling short on the malnutrition goal, and new evidence is pointing to the need to reach pregnant women as well as young children if nutritional status is to improve and education goals are to be realized. Finally, it is clear that environmental hazards pose a major risk to health status. Efforts to mitigate the effects of climate change, reduce indoor and outdoor air pollution, and expand water and sanitation coverage have positive impacts on health that must be considered in weighing the value of such investments. Ultimately, there are positive synergies across the goals, and these synergies need to be exploited.[84]

Notes

1. For more details on progress on the various MDG targets, see Annex: Monitoring the MDGs.
2. O'Donnell and others 2008.
3. O'Donnell and others 2007.
4. Lewis 2006.
5. Lewis and Lockheed 2007b.
6. Indeed, even in OECD countries, the inequality of health outcomes tends to exceed income disparities.
7. Victora and others 2003.
8. Ranson and others 2005.
9. Anwar and others 2005.
10. Schwartz and Bhushan 2005; Ranson and others 2005.
11. Grabowsky and others 2005; Lengeler 2004.
12. Danel and La Forgia 2005.
13. Ranson and others 2005.
14. Wößmann and Peterson 2007.
15. Grantham-McGregor and others 2007; Young and Richardson 2007.
16. Coady, Filmer, and Gwatkin 2005.
17. Roemer and Montoya-Aguilar 1988.
18. Donabedian 2005.
19. Thomas, Lavy, and Strauss 1996; Collier, Dercon, and Mackinnon 2002.
20. Alderman and Lavy 1996; Leonard, Mliga, and Mariam 2002; Fronco and others 2002.
21. Narayan and others 2000; Lewis 2006.
22. Lavy and others 1996.
23. Thomas, Lavy, and Strauss 1996.
24. Das and Hammer 2007.
25. Barber, Bertozzi, and Gertler 2007.
26. Das, Hammer, and Leonard 2008.
27. Chaudhury and others 2006; Banerjee, Deaton, and Duflo 2004.
28. Leonard and Leonard 2004; Leonard and Masatu 2007; Reinikka and Svensson 2007.
29. Bokhari, Gai, and Gottret 2007.
30. Filmer and Pritchett 1999; Lewis 2006; Wagstaff and Claeson 2004.
31. Peabody and Liu 2007.
32. Jack and Lewis 2007.

33. Peabody, Gertler, and Leibowitz 1998. The estimated magnitude of the impact of clinical process quality was large. Increasing the frequency of one element of a given clinical exam (such as checking blood pressure) from once in the prenatal period to checks at every visit would increase average birth weights by approximately 128 grams.
34. Lewis 2006.
35. Grantham-McGregor and others 2007; Victora and others 2008.
36. Sameroff and others 1993.
37. Victora and others 2008.
38. Verhoef and others 2003.
39. Alderman and others 2001.
40. Glewwe and King 2001.
41. Alderman, Hoddinott, and Kinsey 2006.
42. Maluccio and others 2006; Hoddinott and others 2008.
43. Walker and others 2005.
44. de Onis and others 2004.
45. Black and others 2008.
46. World Bank 2006c.
47. Black and others 2008.
48. Mason, Rivers, and Helwig 2005.
49. Multivariate analyses produce similar results: Even after the inclusion of various controls that affect malnutrition outcomes-such as the size of the rural population and the regulatory quality of the country-education and income per capita are both negative and significant predictors of child malnutrition outcomes.
50. Smith and Haddad 2000; Alderman, Behrman, and Hoddinott 2007.
51. Armar-Klemesu and others 2000.
52. Haddad and others 2003.
53. World Bank 2006c.
54. Alderman, Hoogeveen, and Rossi 2006.
55. Wagstaff and Claeson 2004.
56. Bhutta and others 2008.
57. Behrman, Alderman, and Hoddinott 2004.
58. Prüss-Üstün and Corvalán 2006.
59. de Garbino 2004; Wagstaff and Claeson 2004.
60. Prüss-Üstün and Corvalán 2006.
61. World Bank 2008.
62. This definition follows that of WHO (2007). Others have defined environmental health more broadly to include all those aspects of human health determined by social and psychosocial factors within the environment.
63. Lvovsky 2001.
64. Prüss-Üstün and Corvalán 2006.
65. WHO 2005.

66. Prüss-Üstün and Corvalán 2006.
67. Prüss-Üstün and Corvalán 2006.
68. Prüss-Üstün and others 2004.
69. McMichael and others 2004.
70. Johnson and Lvovsky 2001.
71. The terms *sanitation* and *hygiene* can unfortunately mean many different things. Within this chapter, *sanitation* refers to infrastructure and service provision required for the safe management of human excreta, as exemplified by latrines, sewers, and wastewater treatment. As such, important environmental health services, such as solid waste management, vector control, and surface water drainage, are not included, nor are they tracked by the UN system for measuring progress toward MDG Target 10. *Hygiene* refers to the set of human behaviors related to the safe management of human excreta, such as the wash-ing of hands with soap at appropriate times and the safe disposal of child feces.

72. WHO and UNICEF 2006.
73. Banerjee and others 2008.
74. Bruce and others 2006.
75. Kjellström and others 2006.
76. WHO 2002.
77. The CEA report for Pakistan is an example (World Bank 2006b).
78. Kjellström and others 2006.
79. Campbell-Lendrum and Woodruff 2007; chapter 7 of this volume.
80. Campbell-Lendrum and Woodruff 2007.
81. Campbell-Lendrum and Woodruff 2007.
82. Prevost 2008.
83. Bruce and others 2008.
84. Wagstaff and Claeson 2004.

3

Scaling Up Aid: Opportunities and Challenges in a Changing Aid Architecture

The global aid landscape is undergoing profound changes in the way aid is financed and delivered. The new aid architecture is marked by the emergence of global funds and nontraditional bilateral donors; a growing role in aid of private foundations, nongovernmental organizations (NGOs), and corporations; and more public-private partnerships. Changes to the aid architecture are expanding the availability of resources for poor countries and spurring new and innovative ways of addressing pressing development needs. But they also pose new challenges for aid effectiveness.

The latest aid numbers point to mixed progress on aid volumes from traditional Development Assistance Committee (DAC) donors. Aid declined in 2006 and 2007 as major debt relief operations tapered off. To meet the commitment of the Group of Eight and other donors to increase aid by $50 billion (from 2004 levels) by 2010, donors will need to sharply accelerate the expansion of core development aid to an estimated 12 percent annual growth rate. However, preliminary evidence from the forward survey of donors' aid allocations suggests that these rates are not yet sufficiently ambitious to meet the targets set for 2010. Yet, a substantial number of African countries and fragile states remain dependent on external assistance. Scaling up of aid is

a priority if these countries are to attain the Millennium Development Goals (MDGs).

Assistance from non-DAC donors, both official and private, has grown in size and importance. The most dynamic parts of the aid system are the new players who are bringing fresh funding, enthusiasm, and business models into the system. Although traditional official donors remain major players in the development business, new public and private actors are committing growing volumes of financial assistance to the developing world.

The increasing complexity of the aid architecture also presents challenges. In particular, a proliferation of aid channels, fragmentation of aid, and a trend toward vertical programs and earmarking of funds pose new challenges for coherence and predictability in the delivery of aid. These developments call for better donor coordination, division of labor, harmonization of the new sources of aid with the principles of the Paris Declaration, and alignment of global public needs with national development interests. The upcoming Accra High Level Forum provides a timely opportunity to address these new, dynamic dimensions of the aid agenda.

The health sector epitomizes many of the challenges to aid effectiveness in the new aid architecture. A wide range of new donors and aid channels has contributed to a sharp increase in aid to health. At the same time, the multiplicity of donors and channels and a vertical focus on specific communicable diseases have made aid effectiveness and coherence more challenging. The need to address these issues is recognized by initiatives such as the International Health Partnership launched in September 2007. Health has been selected as a special focus sector in deepening and widening the Paris principles and monitoring their application.

Climate change is becoming an urgent concern, and addressing climate change activities in mitigation and adaptation will require significant increases in development finance. It is important that support to developing countries for mitigation and adaptation be additional and not divert resources from other development programs. New and innovative sources of funding will be required to support climate change activities.

The Heavily Indebted Poor Countries (HIPC) Initiative and Multilateral Debt Relief Initiative (MDRI) have substantially lowered debt burdens. Yet, vulnerability of economic activity to terms-of-trade and climate-related shocks presents a challenge to long-term debt sustainability of several post-completion-point HIPCs. Strong debt management as part of a sound macro framework and reforms to build resilience to exogenous shocks will help prevent debt burdens from becoming unsustainable again. On their part, creditors need to take debt sustainability considerations into account in their lending decisions.

Aid Trends and Prospects

Mixed Progress on Aid Volumes

A growing number of public and private actors are boosting global aid volumes. But the overall picture is mixed. Aggregate trends in volumes mask important differences across donor groups.

DAC Donors

Stalling aid volumes. The commitment of the Group of Eight and other donors to increase aid

by $50 billion (from 2004 levels) by 2010, with half of the increase going to Africa, is becoming harder to achieve. Between 2002 and 2005, DAC donors managed a creditable increase in aid by relying on major debt relief operations, which have been instrumental in significantly reducing poor countries' debt burdens and increasing fiscal space for priority spending. The latest DAC numbers show that the upward trend in official development assistance (ODA) stalled in 2006–07; after contracting by 4.5 percent in real terms in 2006, net ODA fell an additional 8.4 percent in real terms to $103.7 billion in 2007 (figure 3.1).[1] Aid levels were pulled down as the exceptionally large debt-relief operations for Iraq and Nigeria tapered off.[2] Most eligible countries will already have had their debts written off by 2010, so to meet the 2005 Gleneagles commitments, which were reaffirmed at Heiligendamm in 2007, donors need to find other channels through which incremental aid can flow.

Of the $104.4 billion aid envelope from DAC in 2006, $73 billion was for core development assistance, which excludes bilateral debt relief, bilateral emergency assistance, and administration costs.[3] The growth of this component of aid slowed to about 4 percent in real terms in 2006, below the 10.3 percent expansion reached in 2005 and also below the average annual growth of 5 percent during 2002–06. Prospects for meeting 2010 targets will depend on accelerating the growth of core development aid. To put this in perspective, assuming that debt relief falls back to levels of the early 2000s and the share of humanitarian assistance continues at current levels, core development aid would need to grow by about $40 billion or at an average annual growth rate of around 12 percent.[4] Without such expansion, 2010 targets will not be met.

The decline in aid volumes pulled down the size of donors' net ODA relative to gross national income (GNI). At 0.31 percent, combined net ODA/GNI in 2006 was below the level of the early 1990s and also below the 2010 projected target of 0.35 percent (based on announced commitments). The ODA/

FIGURE 3.1 DAC members' net ODA flows and 2010 target

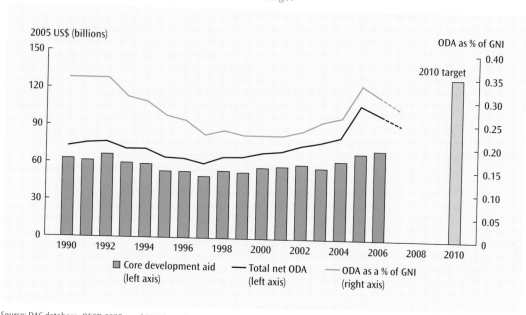

Source: DAC database, OECD 2008a and 2008b, and staff estimates. Data for 2007 are preliminary.
Note: Targets are based on DAC members' announced commitments.

GNI ratio for DAC members of the European Union (EU) was 0.43 percent. There is considerable variation across donors, with five donors reaching or exceeding the United Nations ODA target of 0.7 percent of GNI, and two donors with net ODA less than 0.2 percent of GNI (figure 3.2).

DAC members' ODA shows a substantial shift in composition during 2004–06 (figure 3.3). The share of debt relief doubled, to almost one-fifth of the total. DAC donors' contributions to multilateral institutions fell from nearly a third to a quarter, as a larger share of aid was provided bilaterally through exceptional debt relief. The share of technical cooperation also trended down—from 24 percent in 2004 to 21 percent in 2006.

Mixed response to scale-up opportunities.
Thanks to the progress countries are making in strengthening their development strategies and institutional frameworks for implementation, a broad range of countries can productively absorb increased aid flows. A recent World Bank report found that there are several strong performers, typically

second-generation poverty reduction strategy (PRS-II) countries, where the strengthening of the strategic and institutional framework is sufficiently advanced to merit early delivery on the Gleneagles commitments.[5] Also, a larger proportion of aid can be provided to these countries in the form of budget support. Some examples include Burkina Faso, Ghana, Madagascar, Mozambique, Rwanda, Tanzania, and Vietnam. There is scope as well for scaling up of aid in many first-generation PRS countries, starting with moderate increases but building to larger amounts as absorptive capacities expand. In these countries aid programs could comprise a mix of modalities such as budget support, investment projects, including sectorwide approaches, and technical assistance, depending on specific country circumstances. Examples include Armenia, Bangladesh, Honduras, the Kyrgyz Republic, and Mali. Fragile states, particularly postconflict and reengagement countries, also present opportunities for selective, focused, and carefully sequenced increases in aid for projects and programs tailored to their weaker governance contexts.

FIGURE 3.2   DAC members' ODA

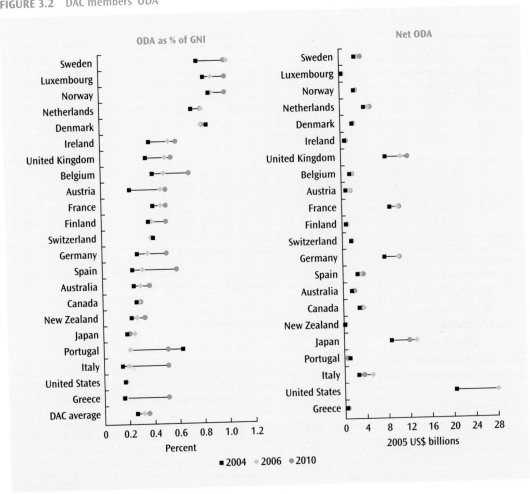

Source: OECD 2008a.
Note: 2010 ODA/GNI are based on announced commitments and are not forecasts. Not all donors have announced forward commitments.

Despite the opportunities for scaling up, much of the expansion in ODA over 2002–06 has been concentrated in a few countries (figure 3.4). The pattern of concentration reflects, in part, global and security concerns—for example, Afghanistan and Iraq account for nearly half of the increase in ODA.[6] Additional aid in the case of Nigeria and the Democratic Republic of Congo mostly reflects debt relief. Scaling up of donor support to countries that are well positioned to absorb more aid has been relatively limited, and there is also wide variation across countries. For example, the expansion in aid flows to PRS-II countries such as Burkina Faso, Ghana, Madagascar, Mozambique, Rwanda, and Tanzania, which had initially been singled out for scale-up efforts by the Organisation for Economic Co-operation and Development (OECD) DAC and the World Bank, is mixed: during 2002–06 aid flows expanded by around 50 percent to Burkina Faso and Madagascar and by about 40 percent to Ghana, while other countries saw modest increases or even a decline.

The challenge of meeting targets. It is not easy to set up new channels to disburse aid effectively. One of the fastest-growing programs, the Global Fund to Fight AIDS, Tuberculosis

FIGURE 3.3 Distribution of DAC members' ODA by type

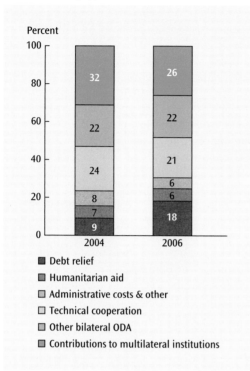

Source: DAC database and staff estimates.
Note: Administrative costs include in-donor country refugee costs.

FIGURE 3.4 Top 10 recipients of the increase in net ODA, 2002–06

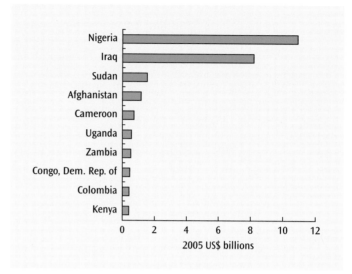

Source: DAC database and staff estimates.

and Malaria (GFATM), was able to reach $1 billion in disbursements in its fourth year of operation. Another new agency, the United States' Millennium Challenge Corporation, had committed $5.5 billion in multiyear aid compacts to 16 countries as of February 2008 but had disbursed only about $180 million.[7] Though the new channels are making a contribution, the bulk of the increase in aid flows in the short to medium term will have to pass through traditional channels. However, the planning in most agencies to scale up to the required degree is not yet under way.

Preliminary evidence from the forward survey of donors' aid allocations suggests that these are not yet sufficiently ambitious to meet the targets set for 2010. The 2007 survey adopted a new methodology—one where information on forward spending plans was collected for a subset of total ODA, defined as country programmable aid. The idea was to measure aid that is planned at the coun-

try level and for which forward spending plans are more likely to be available.[8] Compared with the 2006 survey, donor response to the 2007 survey was higher, at 47 percent of coverage of estimated total country programmable aid for DAC members and 69 percent for multilateral donors.[9] Nevertheless, signs of scaling up in donors' plans are modest. And though Sub-Saharan Africa receives the largest increase, the survey indicates a planned increase in volume of country programmable aid of $100 million or more between 2005 and 2010 for only a handful of poor countries (IDA-eligible). The results also indicate that several fragile states are among those seeing increases in planned country programmable aid.

More encouraging are donors' funding commitments to the replenishment cycles of the International Development Association (IDA) and the concessional windows of other regional development banks and GFATM. New donor pledges for IDA15 (covering the period mid-2008 to mid-2011) amount to $25.1 billion, representing the largest expansion in donor funding in IDA's history and indicating strong support for IDA (see chapter 5 for details). The latest replenishment of GFATM also points to larger contributions by donors.[10]

Innovative financing approaches can help raise funds for short-term needs or provide long-term, sustainable funding for development. The solidarity tax on airline tickets was introduced in France in mid-2006, and has been implemented since then in Chile, Côte d'Ivoire, the Democratic Republic of Congo, the Republic of Korea, Madagascar, Mauritius, Niger, and Norway. Another 15 countries are in the process of implementing the tax. The funds are used to finance UNITAID, an international purchase facility for drugs and treatments for HIV/AIDS, malaria, and tuberculosis. The contributions to UNITAID's budget for 2008, financed primarily through air ticket taxes, are expected to be $364 million. The International Finance Facility for Immunisation (IFFIm) provides frontloading to support development investments that are needed in the short term, even though donor funding is available only over the long term. IFFIm was established as a new supranational in 2006, with some $4 billion in assets in the form of irrevocable donor grants paid over 20 years. IFFIm's first triple-A rated $1 billion bond issuance funded immunization programs of the Global Alliance for Vaccines and Immunizations (GAVI).

Overall, however, DAC donor intentions of scaling up assistance are falling short of promised increases. A stronger and more expeditious donor response is needed to support opportunities that exist in a number of countries for scaling up development results and accelerating progress toward the MDGs.

Expanding Role of Non-DAC Donors

New players such as non-DAC bilaterals, private entities, and vertical funds are the fastest-growing sources of funds. Their increasing role is changing the aid landscape. New donors and modalities promise more resources and innovation for development.

Non-DAC bilateral donors. The number of non-DAC countries that now provide aid has risen steeply to nearly 30. That number includes emerging market countries such as Brazil, China, India, Malaysia, the Russian Federation, Thailand, República Bolivariana de Venezuela, and a number of oil-rich countries. These donors now provide significant resources, totaling perhaps $8 billion annually (figure 3.5a). Non-DAC OECD countries are providing sizable amounts of aid and have plans to substantially scale up flows; for example, Korea, which provided $455 million in 2006, has plans to provide $1 billion of ODA by 2010.[11] Non-DAC OECD countries are expected to double ODA by 2015. New EU member countries (not members of the OECD) could well reach ODA effort of 0.17 percent of GNI by 2010 and 0.33 percent by 2015. Middle Eastern countries provided $2.5 billion in assistance in 2006, with Saudi Arabia contributing $2.1 billion (as reported to the DAC). Firm data on assistance from other bilaterals are not available. Estimates place aid from China and India at about $3 billion annually, and both countries are developing larger aid programs.[12]

Private donors. Private donors now contribute substantial amounts of aid. Net grants from NGOs in DAC countries are estimated by the OECD at $14.6 billion in nominal terms in 2006. Although these grants leveled off in 2006 in real terms, they have grown by nearly 40 percent during 2004–06 (figure 3.5b). Other estimates suggest that the total amount of private international giving, from NGOs as well as other entities such as corporations, educational institutions, and religious organizations, may be substantially larger. One estimate places private international giving from all sources in the United States alone at $33.5 billion.[13] A survey estimates that a little over a third of this amount is related to emergency assistance.[14]

Globally, there are thousands of international NGOs, foundations, and corporations now engaged in transnational development activities.[15] There are also tens of thousands of developing-country NGOs that are increasingly active in raising local funds for development, and possibly millions of community-based organizations that implement development projects. Private players are

FIGURE 3.5   Rising trend in aid from non-DAC bilaterals and NGOs

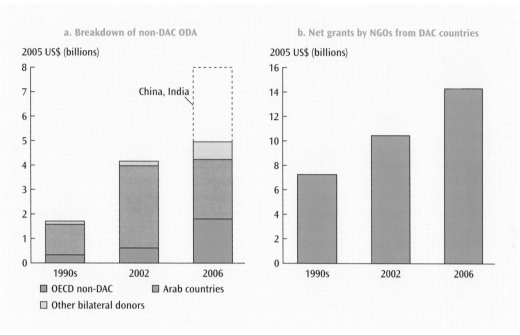

Source: DAC database; Kharas 2007a.
Note: Data for non-DAC bilaterals are for countries that report to the DAC; OECD non-DAC countries include the Czech Republic, Hungary, Iceland, Korea (Rep. of), Poland, the Slovak Republic, and Turkey; Arab countries are Kuwait, Saudi Arabia, and the United Arab Emirates; and other bilateral donors are Israel, Taiwan (China), and Thailand. Data for China and India are estimates.

changing the aid landscape in two ways. They are providing significant sums of money to complement official aid, and prospects for continued strong expansion are good—for example, the Gates Foundation alone disbursed over $1 billion in 2006, and the outlook is for a ramping up of disbursements to about $3 billion annually in a few years.[16] And they operate largely outside official structures, dealing directly with local beneficiaries.

Innovative approaches to financing development have also spurred increased voluntary contributions from individuals. Individuals holding "affinity" credit cards, for example, agree to make small contributions proportionate to their purchases. Investment funds can also generate contributions; IDA receives a part of the manager fee income of the World Bank Bond Fund established by Japanese financial institutions. (PRODUCT) RED, launched in 2006, raises funds for GFATM HIV/AIDS programs in Africa, as partner corporations design and

sell (RED) products and make corresponding contributions. By the end of 2007, contributions of the corporate partners totaled more than $50 million.

Vertical funds. Vertical funds—or funds that are focused on specific objectives, such as fighting particular communicable diseases, for example, GFATM and GAVI—are one of the most rapidly increasing sources of official aid and have also become platforms where the private and official sectors can cooperate with funding and expertise. New vertical funds have disbursed about $7 billion over the last five years.

Aid to Sub-Saharan Africa Growing, at a Modest Pace

Financial globalization is contributing to a widening range of financing options for developing countries. Yet, for a substantial number of poor countries in Sub-Saharan Africa and for fragile and conflict-affected states, official development assistance remains important. Scaling up of aid is a priority if these countries are to attain the MDGs. For low-income countries in the region, ODA accounts for almost two-thirds of all external financing on average.

Although aid to Africa has risen, new aid has been largely debt relief. DAC donors are providing larger amounts of bilateral aid to the region and are allocating a larger share of ODA to Sub-Saharan Africa—over a third in 2006 compared to about a quarter in 2000. Overall, aid flows from DAC and multilateral donors to the region climbed to $40 billion in 2006, representing an increase of $6.9 billion in real terms over 2005 levels and $12.4 billion over 2004 amounts. The expansion in net ODA, excluding debt relief and humanitarian assistance, has been limited, however, accounting for less than a third of the expansion in ODA to the region in 2006 and a fifth of the increase in aid during 2004–06 (figure 3.6). Debt relief has benefited recipient countries through reduced debt burdens and expanded fiscal space for development spending. As debt

relief operations taper off, other types of aid to the region will need to rise sharply if the Gleneagles commitment to increase ODA to Sub-Saharan Africa to $50 billion (a doubling from the 2004 level) is to be achieved.

Assistance to Fragile States: Issues of Timing and Duration

Fragile states face the toughest challenges in achieving progress toward the MDGs.[17] More than four-fifths of fragile IDA countries have been subject to conflict. Conflict is one of the main reasons why countries slide into fragility. While the number of conflicts in low-income countries has been declining, the risk of reversal in postconflict countries is high: around 40 percent of countries relapse into conflict in the first decade of postconflict recovery.[18] Recent research suggests that conflict risk is particularly high in the first four years of a peacekeeping operation, decreasing thereafter but still remaining significantly above the level of risk in other (non-postconflict) low-income countries. It also appears to be correlated with the timing of elections, with the risk of relapse increasing in the year following an election.[19]

Size and pattern of assistance. Development assistance to fragile states rose from $9.7 billion to $26.2 billion between 2002-06, a doubling in real terms.[20] Bilateral donors, the source of about 90 percent of ODA flows to fragile states, accounted for most of this increase, much of it associated with debt relief. Support to individual countries varied widely; countries affected by conflict and post-conflict countries typically received much more aid than other fragile states.[21] For example, between 60–70 percent of the aid to fragile states in 2005 and 2006 was concentrated in four countries—Afghanistan, Democratic Republic of Congo, Nigeria, and Sudan.

One perspective on the effectiveness of assistance in fragile situations is to evaluate the timing and duration of assistance— namely, whether it was provided during periods of highest conflict risk.[22] Figure 3.7

FIGURE 3.6   Net ODA to Sub-Saharan Africa

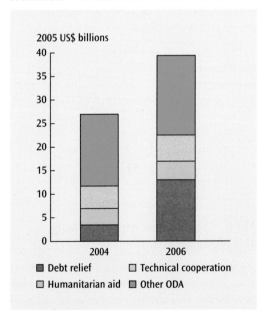

Source: DAC database and staff estimates.
Note: Net ODA received from DAC donors and multilateral donors.

FIGURE 3.7   Conflict risk, aid, and peacekeeping

Pattern of peacekeeping and aid expenditures against conflict risk in the years following the deployment of a new peacekeeping operation

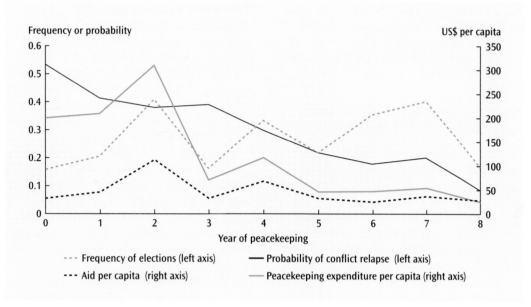

- - - Frequency of elections (left axis)   —— Probability of conflict relapse (left axis)
- - - Aid per capita (right axis)   —— Peacekeeping expenditure per capita (right axis)

Source: Cliffe and Milante 2008.
Note: The first year of peacekeeping is denoted as zero.

shows that in a sample of 54 cases both peacekeeping expenditures and development aid dropped sharply in the fourth year following the deployment of a new peacekeeping operation.[23] This drop coincides with the period directly following the first post-crisis elections and may reflect certain donor considerations: commitments to deploy peacekeepers up to the elections and then draw them down immediately following the election itself, or donor concern over the potential to manipulate aid for political advantage. Evidence on the high risks accompanying post-election periods suggests the need to maintain both peacekeeping and development aid at a consistent level until the risk of conflict relapse has diminished. The data also show that aid tends to taper off mid-decade, even though conflict risks remain significant and just when countries have rebuilt or strengthened capacity to better absorb aid. This pattern of assistance to post-crisis countries may be driven by popular media coverage of crises, or the so-called CNN effect—large-scale

commitments are provided when crises are visible in the mass media, but this support drops off as media coverage declines.[24] But a sharp decline in aid mid-decade may well miss an opportunity to consolidate the early gains of peace.

Strengthening coordination in fragile situations. The international community is taking steps to strengthen coordination of activities across as well as within peacekeeping, humanitarian, and development areas—examples are the OECD's formulation of Principles of Good International Engagement in Fragile States and the establishment of the UN Peace-Building Commission. Recently, the multilateral development banks (MDBs) have agreed to a common goal for MDB engagement in fragile states, a set of guiding principles for MDB engagement, and a set of operational and implementation arrangements that will contribute to improved coordination among the MDBs.[25] As part of this, the MDBs also agreed on a shared approach to identifying fragility and on the need to continue to have regular consultations on priority country situations. OECD DAC is developing practical guidance on state-building in fragile situations. It is also evaluating development effectiveness in situations of fragility and conflict and the applicability of the Paris Declaration in these situations.

Donor Response to Climate Change: Scale-Up of Resources Needed

Climate change has the potential to seriously undermine development progress. The impacts of climate change include, among others, increased frequency and severity of droughts, floods, and storms; decline in agricultural productivity and food security; further spread of water-related diseases (particularly in tropical areas); population displacement; and conflicts over scarce resources. With increasing climate variability and risks, the poorest countries and communities, particularly in Sub-Saharan Africa and Southeast Asia, are likely to suffer the earliest and most because of their geographical location, low incomes, and low institutional capacity, as well as their greater reliance on climate-sensitive sectors like agriculture. Addressing these challenges requires urgent action on several fronts: mitigation, adaptation, and the global humanitarian system. Chapters 6 and 7 address the challenge of combating climate change and promoting environmental sustainability. The focus here is on the donor community's mobilization of resources to assist developing countries in meeting this challenge and dealing with its impacts.

Humanitarian aid. The rising frequency and severity of natural disasters has focused increased attention on humanitarian aid. Humanitarian aid has risen, and new donors and new ways of delivering humanitarian assistance are changing the response to disasters. There is a wider application of good humanitarian donorship principles that call for more adequate and equitable assistance, provided in a timely manner, and

with a larger share being channeled through consolidated appeals processes.[26] Despite the global concern with humanitarian issues, there is still a gap between needs and funds: 72 percent of estimated funding requirements were met in 2006 compared with 59 percent in 2000.[27] High-profile disasters receive more resources and attention than less visible ones: a drought in Niger might see $20 per capita in assistance, while a visible crisis such as the South Asia earthquake might receive $300 per capita.[28]

The total size of global humanitarian assistance is not readily available. The *Global Humanitarian Assistance Report 2006* estimates the amount to be $18 billion in 2005, compared with $10 billion in 2001.[29] Humanitarian assistance from DAC donors shows an upward trend—the size of bilateral emergency and disaster relief was $7.1 billion in 2005 (boosted by the Indian Ocean tsunami and the South Asia earthquake) and $6.6 billion in 2006 (figure 3.8). DAC bilateral humanitarian assistance is highly concentrated, with the top five recipients receiving nearly 50 percent of the resources. The Financial Tracking Service (FTS) of the Global Humanitarian Aid Database shows that private sources of funding rose sharply in 2005 to nearly $4.5 billion, but have since fallen back to much lower pre-2005 levels.

The European Union collectively is the leading provider of humanitarian assistance, providing $3.7 billion of humanitarian aid in 2006. The EU has adopted a common vision, policy objectives, and shared principles to enhance the coherence and effectiveness of EU humanitarian aid.[30] These principles emphasize adequacy and equity in provision of humanitarian aid, partnership, effectiveness and accountability, and capacity to respond rapidly.

Along with seeking to provide more timely and adequate aid, new approaches to humanitarian assistance emphasize prevention and longer-term risk reduction. Poor countries need to develop the capacity to monitor and respond to risks if they are to reduce their vulnerability. An essential component of

FIGURE 3.8 Humanitarian aid, 1970–2006

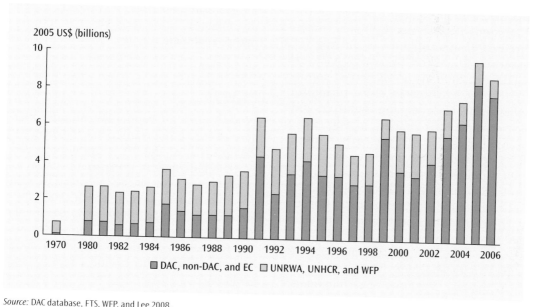

Source: DAC database, FTS, WFP, and Lee 2008.

the EU's approach is promotion of disaster risk reduction strategies and preparedness activities. The World Bank's Global Facility for Disaster Reduction and Recovery (established in 2006) helps developing countries fund projects and programs that enhance local capacities for disaster prevention and emergency preparedness. New approaches to humanitarian response also recognize that a smooth transition from relief to rehabilitation and recovery is critical to aid effectiveness. This calls for strengthened cooperation between humanitarian and development agencies and other actors.

Funding mitigation and adaptation. Addressing climate change in developing countries requires financial flows and technological support much beyond current public funding levels. The UN Framework Convention on Climate Change (UNFCCC) estimates that by 2030 financial flows to developing countries should be on the order of $100 billion annually to finance mitigation and somewhere between $28 billion and $67 billion for adaptation. Focusing on adaptation only, the *Human Development Report* concludes that

the additional cost will be $86 billion a year by 2015—$44 billion for climate-proofing development investments, $40 billion for adapting poverty reduction programs to climate change, and $2 billion for strengthening the disaster response system.[31]

The UNFCCC process has created a number of avenues for increasing financing for mitigation (essentially through the creation of a carbon market, under the Kyoto Protocol) and adaptation (with the Global Environment Facility, or GEF, a key instrument to develop a knowledge base for adaptation). To comply with their obligations under the Kyoto Protocol, industrial countries can, above and beyond domestic emissions reductions, trade emission permits or purchase emission reduction credits from projects in developing countries using the Clean Development Mechanism (CDM), or in economies in transition using Joint Implementation. This has led to a vibrant global carbon market reaching an estimated $30 billion in value in 2006, three times greater than in 2005. According to preliminary estimates, this growth continued in 2007 (roughly doubling over 2006). The CDM unambiguously dominates the project-based market, with more than 1 billion Certified Emissions Reductions (CERs) transacted (from 2002 onward), for a cumulative value exceeding $17 billion. By some estimates, the CDM—in 2006 alone—leveraged approximately $9.2 billion in clean technology investments in developing countries, about 48 percent of their total investments in clean technologies. Finally, the carbon market provides additional resources for adaptation, through a 2 percent share of proceeds on CERs issued for a CDM project activity, collected in the Adaptation Fund (together with other sources of funding). The size of the Adaptation Fund could reach $100 million per year, or more, depending on the activity of the carbon market.

In contrast to the rise of carbon finance, resource mobilization under the GEF has been modest. But the GEF has been a key instrument for addressing climate change (particularly adaptation), through its significant leverage power: during 1991–2007, the GEF allocated $2.3 billion for climate change projects.[32] The GEF continues to rely principally on voluntary contributions—an arrangement that reduces the predictability of finance.

Clearly, new and innovative sources of funding will be required to support climate change activities as highlighted in the Bali Action Plan. The action plan embraces mitigation of climate change (including, for the first time, consideration of reducing emissions from deforestation and land degradation), adaptation, technology development and transfer, and provision of financial resources in support of developing countries' actions. The latter include, in particular, better access to predictable, adequate, and sustainable financial support and provision of additional resources; mobilization of public and private sector funding and investment, including facilitation of climate-friendly choices; and positive incentives for developing countries to enhance mitigation and adaptation actions. There are some encouraging developments in this direction, including joint efforts by the World Bank and other MDBs with interested parties to establish a portfolio of strategic climate investment funds to facilitate early transformational climate actions.[33]

The Challenge of Aid Effectiveness

New donors and modalities promise more resources and innovation, but the increased complexity of the aid architecture adds to the challenge of ensuring effectiveness and coherence of aid. As aid increases and involves more players, three challenges present themselves: how to integrate the new players harmoniously into the overall aid framework; how to develop modalities that would permit new aid commitments to be met in an effective way; and how to improve the efficiency and effectiveness of aid through better aid delivery.

The Paris Declaration addresses some of these issues. The Paris framework represents the international community's consensus and resolve to improve the effectiveness of aid. Implementation of the Paris Declaration is spurring important reforms of the aid system. But many of the new donors bypass traditional channels and institutional arrangements. The Accra High Level Forum scheduled for September 2008 provides an opportunity to address the new, dynamic dimensions of aid harmonization. The forum will review progress on implementing the Paris Declaration, address new challenges, and help shape the evolution of the aid effectiveness agenda moving forward.

Integrating New Players into the Aid Architecture: Competitive Pluralism

The current aid system is organized around a dialogue between a recipient country government and its major aid donors. These country-level platforms coordinate development resources with country priorities and translate broad strategies into specific projects and programs. Donors are asked to be responsive to country development priorities; recipients are asked to be focused on implementation of projects and programs. The challenge of integrating new players into this framework arises on many fronts. The new players may not have the flexibility to respond fully to recipient priorities—they tend to be organized to deliver on a narrower set of areas. Vertical funds have specific mandates, the non-DAC bilaterals may have selected expertise to share, and private donors must specialize to attract funds. At the same time, the new players tend to have limited country presence and participation in the development dialogue. And the sheer number of players implies that the process of face-to-face dialogue between governments and donors is harder to manage.

Other challenges also present themselves. Some new players eschew government agencies for implementation of their projects, either choosing private nonprofits or else undertaking implementation themselves. That raises issues of whether local capacity and institutions are being strengthened or weakened.

The aid architecture must recognize the opportunities and challenges that come with the new players. It will be difficult to bring all sources of aid under the same umbrella of a country-level platform. The most urgent needs are for better information sharing, learning, and evaluation of innovations and scaling up. There is currently not enough information on the operations of the new players. When donors have different approaches to a problem, it is important to do comparative analysis to establish which ones are more cost-effective. A harmonized, coordinated system must be complemented by an openness toward alternative approaches and the innovation they may bring. Competitive pluralism needs to be built into the aid architecture.

Innovative Financing for Development

Recent innovative approaches include creating new competitive markets for undersupplied goods and services, shifting risk to resolve market failures, and using results-based financing. Expanded partnerships involving both donor and developing country governments, multilateral institutions, the private sector, and civil society are also exploring innovative approaches to development financing. The Bill and Melinda Gates Foundation, for instance, has been a substantial supporter of innovative initiatives, funding exploration and design work for many new initiatives, in particular in the health sector. In cooperation with the International Finance Corporation (IFC), it seeks to encourage the private sector to invest in health care in Africa. The IFC plans to set up a $300 million–$350 million equity fund to invest in health care businesses and a $400 million–$500 million debt vehicle to provide long-term finance to health care organizations.

Several initiatives link funding with performance or results-based outcomes. The U.S. Millennium Challenge Corporation provides assistance to countries showing good performance according to key indicators. Debt buy-downs link debt relief with successful project implementation. The $1.5 billion Advanced Market Commitment (AMC) pilot is results based, subsidizing vaccines against pneumococcal diseases, which kill 1.6 million people every year (including 1 million children), overwhelmingly in poor countries. Donors commit to fund an AMC of a specified market size and price for vaccines that meet set specifications to ensure public health impact in developing countries. AMCs encourage the development of target products, but only subsidize actual product sales to interested governments.

Other new mechanisms linked to results include output-based aid. This aid provides direct subsidies to service providers for the delivery of specified basic services or outputs.[34] For example, a recent output-based scheme in Uganda aims to give a subsidy (of $2.5 million) for connecting poor households in slum and peri-urban areas of Kampala to water services.[35] The output-based approach to aid delivery uses explicit performance-based subsidies to help the poor afford access to basic services.[36] The subsidies target poorer consumers and are paid to the service provider only after the delivery or provision of the agreed-to service. This approach harnesses the private sector to deliver results.

Improving the Impact of Aid through Better Aid Delivery

DAC peer reviews of aid programs point to 12 lessons for effective aid management.[37] Among these are the need for DAC donors to focus their assistance on fewer countries, fewer sectors, and fewer activities, and to develop a stronger culture for managing for results and aligning incentives accordingly, but in ways that strengthen local structures of accountability. These issues have been taken up through the Paris Declaration. Partner countries, donors, and the international financial institutions are taking substantial actions toward meeting the Paris commitments on aid alignment and harmonization.

Alignment and harmonization. The findings of the 2006 Survey on Monitoring the Paris Declaration indicate mixed progress on

alignment and harmonization.[38] For example, the survey results show that donors provide 43 percent of their aid to governments through program-based approaches such as budget support and sectorwide approaches, relative to the Paris target of 66 percent.[39] In addition, the extent to which donors conduct joint missions is low—the survey found that 18 percent of missions were undertaken jointly, while 42 percent of country analytic work was prepared jointly with another donor, relative to the 2010 Paris targets of 40 percent joint missions and 66 percent joint analytical work. Greater donor efforts are going to be needed if the 2010 targets in these areas are to be met. The 2008 survey, which is under way and which will cover nearly twice as many countries as the 2006 survey, will provide stronger and more up-to-date information on the progress and prospects for reaching the 2010 Paris targets.

Fragmentation. Aid fragmentation has emerged as a serious issue, with multiple aid agencies from each country joining the new players. *Fragmentation* refers to a large number of donors each with a small share of total aid. Projects have become smaller. Each agency makes requests for studies and for individual meetings with country officials;[40] they often also establish separate project management units and procurement practices for their own projects. High fragmentation can have negative implications for aid quality. DAC data for 61 PRS countries and fragile states show that over 60 percent of countries had 20 or more donors and over 75 percent of countries had 10 or more donors together accounting for 10 percent or less of aid (figure 3.9).

Division of labor. The EU has recently adopted a voluntary Code of Conduct on Complementarity and Division of Labor in Development Policy to facilitate division of labor as a way to improve aid effectiveness. Among the 10 operational principles of the code of conduct for donors' actions are concentration in a limited number of sectors in a country based on a donor's comparative

FIGURE 3.9   Concentration of DAC donors and multilaterals in selected countries, measured by programmable aid

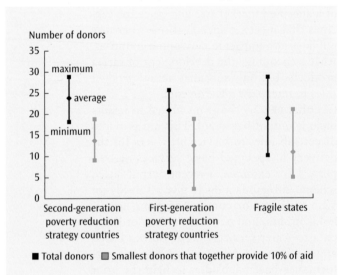

Source: OECD DCD 2007c.
Note: Data are for country progammable aid (gross).

advantage; enhancement of donor coordination by supporting a lead donor arrangement in each priority sector; assurance of adequate donor support in sectors that are relevant for poverty reduction; and establishment of priority countries for EU donor engagement.

Predictability. Aid predictability is an important dimension of aid quality. In aid-dependent countries, the variability and unpredictability of donor funding undermine aid effectiveness by affecting short- and medium-term budget planning and programming, disrupting implementation of expenditure allocations, complicating macroeconomic management, and deepening the challenge of building absorptive capacity. Donors and recipients have focused on both short- and medium-term predictability. While short-term aid predictability is improving, less progress has been made in improving medium-term predictability. The 2007 budget support survey by the Strategic Partnership with Africa finds

that of the $2.7 billion in general budget support committed by donors for 2006, 92 percent was disbursed within the year, compared with 85 percent in the 2006 survey and below 70 percent in the 2003 survey (figure 3.10). Within-year delays are less pronounced as well. The pattern of shortfall in disbursements in the first quarter and a surge in funds in the fourth quarter is less evident.

In contrast, with respect to medium-term predictability, the Strategic Partnership with Africa survey finds that the proportion of current (2006) donor programs committing general budget support for future years falls off dramatically in outer years, to 69 percent for 2008 and 35 percent for 2009. Medium-term predictability has remained relatively low in most cases, despite mechanisms such as multidonor budget support, joint country assistance strategies, and pooled financing through sectorwide approaches, and despite recipient countries taking steps to strengthen public financial management (box 3.1).[41]

FIGURE 3.10 In-year predictability is improving

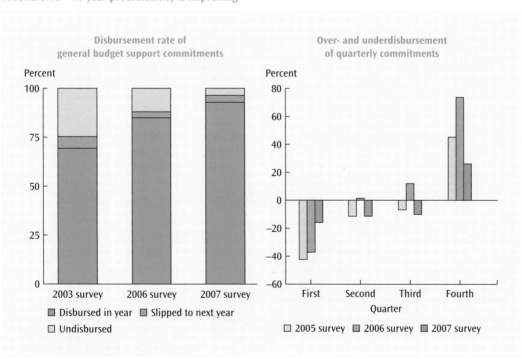

Source: Strategic Partnership with Africa 2008.

BOX 3.1   Improving the predictability of aid: Ghana and Tanzania

The experience of Ghana and Tanzania provides evidence of both continuing challenges and some progress in improving multiyear aid predictability.

Ghana. Ghana has had some success in improving aid predictability, thanks to improved coordination through a multidonor budget support framework. Multidonor budget support (MDBS) partners disburse their budget support based on triggers defined two years in advance and assessed in the year prior to disbursement. This new schedule allows the MDBS partners to inform the government about their budget support before the government's budget proposal is submitted to Parliament. Better predictability was achieved even as donors were scaling up: MDBS disbursements rose throughout 2003–07.[a] The Ghana experience suggests that increasing predictability requires progress across three fronts: mechanisms to improve coordination, ownership within government and among development agencies, and clearly defined measurement yardsticks. In an effort to enhance predictability, the government has involved all active budget support donors in the Ghana Joint Assistance Strategy process.[b]

Tanzania. Total aid to Tanzania climbed from 6 percent of GDP in 2000 to over 12 percent in 2005/06, and accounts for 40 percent of public expenditure. Aid projections have been embedded in the annual budget process in recent years—the authorities ask each donor to provide three-year projections of disbursements as input to the annual budget guidelines and Medium-Term Expenditure Framework (MTEF) preparation. A review of these projections shows a sharp divergence between actual financing and projections; indeed, projections systematically under-predict actual flows (figure and table). The forecasting error is large as a percentage of GDP and larger than that of other components of revenue. In every year donors collectively increased total external financing but forecast significant reductions over the following three years. The substantial size of external financing means that the predictability of medium-term external financing is particularly important to strengthening the country's MTEF.

Tanzania: Aid is not very predictable in the medium term

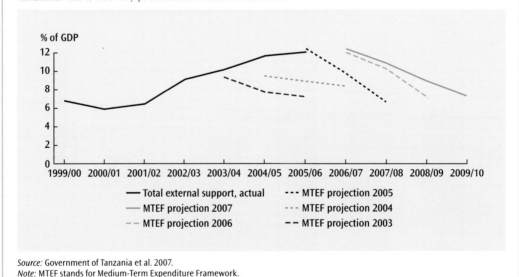

Source: Government of Tanzania et al. 2007.
Note: MTEF stands for Medium-Term Expenditure Framework.

BOX 3.1   Improving the predictability of aid: Ghana and Tanzania (*continued*)

Tanzania: Aid is less predictable than domestic revenue

	Average forecast error in % (2003/04–2005/06)			Average forecast error in % of GDP (2003/04–2005/06)		
	1 year ahead	2 years ahead	3 years ahead	1 year ahead	2 years ahead	3 years ahead
Domestic revenue	0.0	2.3	4.5	0.0	0.3	0.6
Budget support (+HIPC)	28.5	54.0	51.0	1.2	2.6	2.2
Project + basket support	−4.8	35.7	61.3	−0.3	0.9	2.5
Total external support	10.0	43.2	61.9	0.9	3.6	4.6

Source: Moon 2007.

a. Cavalcanti 2007. The one contribution that declined reflected disagreements about measurement of progress.
b. IDA 2007.

The potential costs of variability of aid can be large. One study finds that unforeseen variations in aid primarily impact domestic investment expenditure.[42] It also finds that periods of excess aid are seldom used to accelerate spending on this category so as to catch up with previous shortfalls. Thus, aid volatility may have permanent costs in terms of reduced investment and growth. A recent study attempts to measure the cost of volatile flows by applying the concept of "certainty equivalence" to the flows received by recipient countries.[43] On this basis, the study estimates the cost of volatility to be quite large at 22 percent—that is, the value of aid flows may be discounted by as much as 22 percent on average to take into account the effect of volatility. The cost varies considerably across countries; it is particularly large for countries such as Cambodia, the Democratic Republic of Congo, and Nigeria, which have seen extreme movements in their aid flows.

An encouraging development is the European Commission's MDG contract, which provides a more predictable way of delivering aid.[44] It is not a new EC financial mechanism, but rather an enhanced form of budget support for implementation under the 10th European Development Fund (EDF 10), which will provide €22.7 billion over the period 2008–13. More than half of all EDF general budget support commitments would be disbursed through MDG contracts. About half of the African countries that are to receive general budget support would receive it in the form of MDG contracts. The funds would be committed for the six years of EDF 10. A proportion of funds committed to a country—80 percent—would be virtually guaranteed except when there is a clear failure to meet key criteria. Under the MDG contract, monitoring will be on an annual basis with a focus on results, especially in health and education, and performance assessment will be within a medium-term framework so as to foster more comprehensive analysis and dialogue. The initial focus will be on countries with a strong performance track record and multiyear monitoring framework. Among other mechanisms that have the potential to enhance predictability of aid are the U.S. Millennium Challenge Account and the International Health Partnership.

On their part, aid recipients can take measures to mitigate the adverse effects of aid variability.[45] They can build up reserve buffers that can be drawn down in the event of temporary aid shortfalls. Countries can identify priority spending programs and safeguard these from unexpected cuts in aid. They can also build flexibility into spending programs by designing programs that can respond quickly to aid volatility. By regular stress testing of baseline projections, countries can assess the short-term financing risks to the budget.

Selectivity. Donors' aid allocations indicate that aid is becoming more selective. Empirical estimates of the responsiveness of aid to policy performance and the quality of institutions (as measured by the World Bank's CPIA ratings) show an improving trend. Overall, bilateral donors are found to be less selective than multilateral donors, a trend that has persisted. There is also considerable variation among donors, which suggests that several criteria influence the allocation of aid. A recent study assesses how changes in the international aid architecture have affected the allocation of bilateral aid over 1970–2004.[46] The study finds an improving trend in donor selectivity, reinforcing the above results. Specifically, the study finds that countries that formulate poverty reduction strategies see higher amounts of aid and that debt reduction has reduced defensive lending by donors.

Aligning Global Funds with Country Programs

Global programs have become an important part of the aid landscape. A desire to address specific priorities—global challenges or development goals—and advantages of greater attributability provide strong incentives for the donor community to create new global programs and vertical funds and to earmark funds as part of their effort to scale up aid. Despite broad agreement on the importance of global programs, concerns abound on how to strengthen the broader development effectiveness of these programs and improve the sustainability of the desired outcomes. Global programs illustrate the challenges of applying the Paris principles. An important issue that arises is that of alignment of these programs with country strategies and complementarity with traditional, country-based aid.

Several recent discussions, supported by analysis of country experiences, have focused attention on improving the alignment of global programs at the country level. A workshop for developing coutry policy makers organized by the World Bank and the OECD DAC in Mauritius in June 2007 highlighted several challenges on this front. For example, in cases of weak country capacity and leadership, country strategies and expenditure patterns can be highly influenced by external partners.[47] Often there are differences in priorities of donors and development partners, and this can create imbalances and development gaps. There is also a tendency to neglect implications for accountability. The problem can be especially acute when global programs are the main contributors to a sector and particularly when earmarking is at the level of a subsector (such as HIV/AIDS). Country experiences—as in Benin, Madagascar, Malawi, and Sierra Leone—indicate that global program support was often not integrated into the national development or sector strategies. For example, the President's Emergency Plan for AIDS Relief (PEPFAR) and GFATM support operated in parallel to government health sector policies and systems in Malawi and Benin.

There are signs of progress, however, as several countries have begun to better integrate global programs along with other donor support into sectorwide approaches (SWAps), as is now occuring in the health sector in Malawi. In the case of Mozambique, GFATM support was integrated into a SWAp and in 2006 into a common fund for health (Presaude). This approach allowed "virtual earmarking" of GFATM resources and the use of national systems rather than separate financial management and audit. It also reduced the proportion of aid funds that are off budget.[48] The key lesson that emerges is that global programs should be integrated and mainstreamed into national development strategies and programs and linked to related sector priorities and systems. They should also be brought on budget, to reduce transaction costs and fragmentation of development approaches and to enhance transparency and accountability. Country experiences also suggest the importance of a strong monitoring and evaluation framework. The framework should be focused on results-based indicators relevant to the national development plan, and not simply on global program indicators. There is also a need to adapt donor procedures to local systems and place less reliance on setting up parallel systems, which should help strengthen country processes.

Addressing the Challenge of Aid Effectiveness in Health

Aid for health is changing rapidly. New actors such as private philanthropies have rapidly expanded the funds available for investment in global health. In tandem with rising private philanthropy, the channels through which bilateral, multilateral, and other donors are providing resources for health have grown. The current health aid system encourages innovation, flexibility, and speed.[49] Yet, as indicated in the preceding section, its complexity poses the challenge of ensuring coherence and coordination and aligning global programs with national priorities.

Scaling up of resources. The health sector has seen a rapid scaling up of both traditional and innovative aid flows. There are well over 100 international entities involved in supporting health. Concessional financing for

health more than doubled, from $6.8 billion in 2000 to nearly $17 billion in 2006 (figure 3.11). The spurt in funding is the result of new (bilateral) programs such as the U.S. PEPFAR and increases in funding for health by bilateral donors, private foundations such as the Gates Foundation, and global health funds such as GFATM and GAVI.[50]

External assistance from both traditional and new sources accounts for 7 percent of health sector spending in developing countries. This figure masks large differences across countries and regions: In Africa this share is much larger at 15 percent. Fifteen of the 23 countries where external assistance

FIGURE 3.11 Strong growth in assistance for health, 2000 and 2006

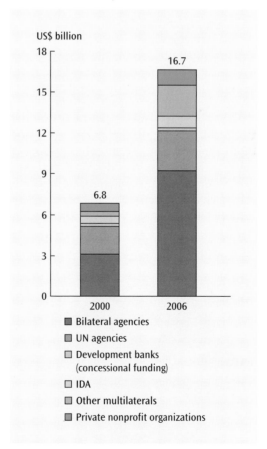

Source: Michaud 2008.
Note: Concessional financing only. Other multilaterals include the European Commission, GAVI, and GFATM. Data for 2006 are provisional.

supports over 20 percent of all health spending are in Africa.[51] Seven African countries receive HIV/AIDS funding that is larger than 30 percent of their total public health budget; in some countries this funding exceeds other public sector health spending.[52]

Effectiveness issues. While the focus on health is bringing much-needed financing to this sector, the narrow focus on a single issue or subsector can have unintended effects, particularly in the short run. For one thing, the pattern of external funding can create imbalances in the health sector and undermine attention to other local health priorities. For example, in Rwanda donor funding in health was unevenly allocated, with $47 million for HIV/AIDS, $18 million for malaria (which is the leading cause of morbidity and mortality in the country), and only $1 million for management of childhood diseases.[53] Likewise, in Ghana malaria is the main cause of sickness and mortality, but donor funding to fight malaria has recently been 60 percent of the amount allocated for HIV/AIDS.

Sharp increases in vertical funds can also strain absorptive capacity. Since earmarked funds typically pay less attention to investment in health service delivery systems, inadequate capacity can translate into low efficiency and effectiveness of spending. An example of absorptive capacity constraints at the sector level is in Ethiopia, where the capital budget execution rate for external assistance has been found to be low at between 15 and 20 percent, compared with 80 percent for domestic resources.[54] But strengthening the absorptive capacity of the health systems usually receives less attention than direct funding for HIV/AIDS in donor commitments (figure 3.12).

A heavy reliance on aid to finance public expenditures, especially in health with a high proportion of recurrent costs, raises issues of sustainability of financing, and in turn of service delivery gains, and has implications for the ability of countries to budget and plan for the medium and long term. Most funding is short term—for example, in Ethiopia and Rwanda 55 percent of foreign-financed projects are negotiated on an annual basis. This short-term pattern of financing introduces uncertainty about aid amounts. Large year-to-year variations in aid levels constrain long-term plans of building capacity in the health sector—that is, hiring nurses and doctors and scaling up health services—especially in the poorest and most aid-dependent countries. The challenges are even more acute in fragile and conflict-affected situations, where aid is even more variable and is usually channeled through parallel systems because of weak public financial systems.

Amid the changing aid architecture and scaling up of financing for health, there is much scope to improve the efficiency and effectiveness of aid delivery and utilization in the sector. Health has been selected as a special focus sector (tracer sector) in applying the Paris principles at the sectoral level.[55] There is growing awareness that health targets cannot be efficiently attained and sustained without appropriate health delivery systems. Adequate investment in health systems is therefore needed. To support effective scale-up of service delivery, donors will need to strengthen coordination and harmonization of aid, increase flexibility in funding, provide more predictable and sustainable assistance, and enhance alignment with country-owned and country-led health plans.

FIGURE 3.12 Ethiopia: Distribution of aid within the health sector

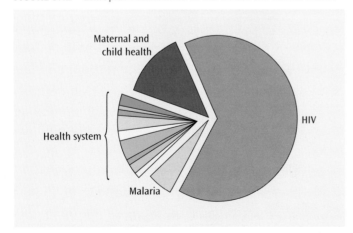

Source: Government of Ethiopia, et al. 2007.

The need for more coherence in aid for health is recognized by several new initiatives. Among these are the creation of the group of eight heads of health agencies and the International Health Partnership. The group of eight heads of health agencies—World Bank, World Health Organization, Joint United Nations Programme on HIV/AIDS, United Nations Children's Fund, United Nations Population Fund, GFATM, GAVI Alliance, and Gates Foundation—was formed by leaders of these institutions to strengthen collaboration to achieve better health outcomes. The International Health Partnership includes a number of bilateral donors, the group of eight agencies, as well as several partner countries. The main goals of the partnership are to improve health systems, provide better coordination among donors, and support countries in developing their own health plans.[56]

Debt Relief

Implementation of the HIPC Initiative and the MDRI

International debt relief efforts have continued within the framework of the HIPC Initiative and the MDRI. The HIPC Initiative has remained the main framework for international coordination of debt relief to the poorest countries since its launch in 1996 by the International Monetary Fund (IMF) and the World Bank. Its primary goals are twofold: to bring the debt of the poorest countries to levels deemed sustainable so that these countries can pursue their developmental and poverty-reducing objectives; and to help HIPCs implement a set of institutional and policy reforms designed to prevent the reemergence of debt problems in the future. In 2005, the HIPC Initiative was supplemented with the MDRI, whereby IDA, the IMF, and the African Development Bank (AfDB) provide additional debt relief with the view to further freeing resources for poverty reduction and achievement of the MDGs. In 2007 the Inter-American Development Bank also decided to provide

debt relief to the five HIPCs in the Latin America and the Caribbean region.

To date, 41 countries have been identified as eligible for, or have already received, assistance under the HIPC Initiative. By the end of March 2008, 33 HIPCs had reached the HIPC Initiative decision point and were receiving debt relief; of these, 23 had also reached the completion point—when creditors provide the full amount of debt relief committed at the decision point. The 23 post-completion-point HIPCs have also benefited from debt relief under the MDRI.

The overall amount of debt relief to be delivered to the 33 post-decision-point HIPCs under the HIPC Initiative and MDRI is currently estimated at $72 billion in end-2006 net present value terms. As a result, the debt stock of the 33 post-decision-point HIPCs is projected to decline by nearly 90 percent in present value terms (figure 3.13).

Debt relief under the HIPC Initiative and MDRI has helped to expand the fiscal space for the 33 post-decision-point HIPCs for their poverty-reducing and other development expenditures. The debt service paid by these countries has declined by about 2 percentage points of GDP between 1999 and 2006, while their poverty-reducing expenditures have increased by about the same

FIGURE 3.13 Reduction of debt stock for the 33 post-decision-point HIPCs

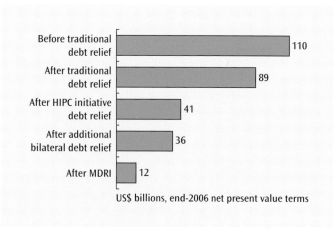

US$ billions, end-2006 net present value terms

Source: IMF–World Bank 2007; staff estimates.
Note: Based on decision-point debt stocks.

magnitude. The HIPC Initiative and MDRI relief is expected to reduce the debt service payments of post-decision-point HIPCs by another 1 percentage point of GDP by 2009.

Despite the significant progress achieved to date in the implementation of the HIPC Initiative and MDRI, important challenges remain. Some eligible HIPCs face difficulties in qualifying for the HIPC Initiative debt relief. Before reaching the decision point, they must exhibit a solid macroeconomic policy track record under an IMF-supported program and develop a poverty reduction strategy. For the eight pre-decision-point HIPCs, progress in building a policy track record has often been hampered by internal conflicts, governance issues, substantial arrears to multilateral institutions (which preclude these countries from engaging in an IMF-supported program), and more generally, difficulties in formulating viable macroeconomic and poverty reduction programs. Several of the ten interim HIPCs also face similar challenges on their way to the completion point. These difficulties are reflected in the long interim periods (between decision point and completion point) experienced by a number of recent and prospective completion-point countries.

Additional donor resources are needed to cover the projected costs of debt relief to countries with protracted arrears to multilateral financial institutions. The IMF, in particular, will require substantial additional resources to provide debt relief to the remaining two protracted arrears cases (Somalia and Sudan). As of end-February 2008, the total arrears of these countries to the IMF amounted to SDR 1.3 billion. As the costs for providing debt relief to these countries were not included in the original financing framework of the HIPC Initiative and the MDRI, additional financing will need to be mobilized.

The participation of non–Paris Club official bilateral creditors and commercial creditors in the HIPC Initiative remains low. Non–Paris Club official bilateral creditors have on average delivered only about one-third of their expected share of debt relief to post-completion-point HIPCs.[57] The participation of commercial creditors has been even lower, with a few exceptions. Moreover, some of these creditors have resorted to litigation against the HIPCs. The low participation of non–Paris Club and commercial creditors undermines the principle of "equal burden sharing" that is at the heart of the Initiative and presents a growing challenge in light of the higher share of these creditors in the debt of the pre-completion-point HIPCs.[58]

Concerted action by the international community is required to encourage fuller participation by all creditors and discourage aggressive litigation against the HIPCs. To that end, IMF and World Bank staffs have stepped up moral suasion, public dissemination of information on the HIPC Initiative, and provision of technical support. The World Bank's Debt Reduction Facility for IDA-only countries can also help extinguish commercial debt of the HIPCs via debt buyback operations at a deep discount.[59] Debt buybacks under two recent operations supported by the facility—for Mozambique and Nicaragua—extinguished nearly US$1.5 billion of commercial external debt on terms fully comparable with those provided by other creditors under the HIPC Initiative.

Maintaining Long-Term Debt Sustainability

Despite substantial debt relief, long-term sustainability remains a challenge for several post-completion-point HIPCs. For example, only nine of 23 post-completion-point HIPCs are now found at a low risk of debt distress, with the remainder being at either moderate or high risk according to their latest debt sustainability analyses (figure 3.14). The issue of sustainability often stems from underlying vulnerabilities in these countries: vulnerability to volatile terms-of-trade shocks and susceptibility to climate-related shocks. Sustainability will require reforms (strengthening of institutions and climate adaptation) to

FIGURE 3.14   Risk of debt distress in post-completion-point HIPCs

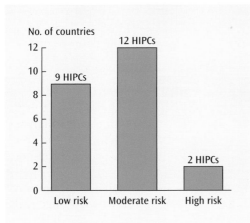

Source: IMF–World Bank 2007; staff estimates.
Note: Debt distress classification of post-completion-point HIPCs refers to the assessment made under the latest available joint IMF-WB debt sustainability analyses as of March 2008 and includes the effects of MDRI.

build resilience to exogenous shocks, a sound macro framework, and strong debt management. Thus, post-debt-relief HIPCs should continue to borrow prudently, in line with their debt repayment capacity. The IMF and World Bank are providing technical assistance to help HIPCs strengthen their debt management capacity and design sustainable financing strategies (box 3.2).

Other creditors are also encouraged to take debt sustainability considerations into account in their lending decisions to help HIPCs avoid reaccumulating unsustainable debt burdens. The joint Bank-Fund Debt Sustainability Framework (DSF) provides a potential coordination point for creditors. Debt sustainability analyses are, with the permission of governments, made public on Bank and Fund Web sites[60] and Bank and Fund staff have conducted vigorous outreach efforts to all creditor classes. This has culminated in several agreements with creditors. Agreements have been signed with the main regional development banks, defining modalities for their staff to contribute to debt sustainability analyses; these institutions have in turn adopted similar financing approaches to that of IDA, adjusting their financial terms to mitigate debt distress risks. In addition, the export credit agencies of the OECD have adopted a set of sustainable lending principles that are harmonized with the Bank-Fund DSF. Activities with other creditor groups have raised awareness of debt sustainability issues and the approach followed by the World Bank and the IMF. Finally, the framework provides useful signals to the market, helping commercial creditors identify default risks and thus reducing the likelihood of another debt crisis.

BOX 3.2   Debt Management Performance Assessment Tool

The World Bank, in collaboration with other stakeholders, has developed the government Debt Management Performance Assessment (DeMPA) Tool. Based on the public expenditure and financial accountability methodology for public financial management, and sound practices in government debt management, the DeMPA uses a set of 15 indicators that represent an internationally recognized and comprehensive methodology for assessing debt management performance. The DeMPA highlights strengths and weaknesses in government debt management practices in the respective country. The indicators are useful in guiding the design of reform programs, monitoring performance over time, and enhancing donor harmonization and capacity building.

The indicators have been field-tested in five low-income countries—Albania, The Gambia, Guyana, Malawi, and Nicaragua. The table summarizes the results of the five field-test assessments. The shaded areas represent indicators where the minimum requirement for effective operation of the debt management system was not met. This signals a priority area for reform. The comprehensiveness of the assessment allows important linkages between indicators to be emphasized. Recently, this assessment framework has been used to guide the design of debt management reforms in Albania and Bangladesh.

(continued on next page)

BOX 3.2 Debt Management Performance Assessment Tool (*continued*)

Synthesis of field tests

2007	Legal framework DPI-1	Managerial structure DPI-2	Debt management strategy DPI-3	Evaluation of debt management operations DPI-4	Audit DPI-5	Coordination with fiscal policy DPI-6	Coordination with monetary policy DPI-7	Domestic borrowing DPI-8
Country 1	A	A	B+	B	C+	B	B	B
Country 2	C	D	D	D	D	D+	C	B
Country 3	C+	C	D	D	D	C+	C+	C+
Country 4	C	C	D	D	D+	C	D+	C+
Country 5	A	D+	D	D	D	B	C	C+

2007	External borrowing DPI-9	Loan guarantees, onlending derivatives DPI-10	Cash flow forecasting and cash balance management DPI-11	Debt administration and data security DPI-12	Segregation of duties, staff capacity and business continuity plans DPI-13	Debt records DPI-14	Debt reporting DPI-15
Country 1	D	C	C+	B	D+	D+	D+
Country 2	D	D	D+	B	D+	C+	C+
Country 3	C	D	D+	B	D+	C+	C+
Country 4	D	C	C+	D+	D+	B	B
Country 5	B+	C	D	B+	C+	A	A

Note: Indicator scores range from A to D where A indicates sound practice in the particular area, B is an in-between score, C indicates the minimum requirement for effective debt management, and D indicates below the minimum required for effective debt management. DPI = Debt management performance indicator.

Notes

1. Preliminary estimate; see OECD 2008b.

2. Debt relief grants from DAC members peaked at $25 billion in 2005 and were $18.9 billion in 2006.

3. Core development assistance also excludes in-donor country refugee costs. Core development aid is similar to the concept of programmable ODA used by DAC, which also excludes imputed student costs.

4. Also see OECD (2008a and 2008b) and Kharas (2007a).

5. World Bank (2007a) assessed in detail the scale-up opportunities for a wide range of countries.

6. Only net ODA (by DAC donors and multilaterals) that is provided at the country level is included in the calculations.

7. Millennium Challenge Corporation, http://www.mcc.gov.

8. OECD DCD (2007a). As part of the DAC 2007 Survey of Aid Allocation Policies and Indicative Spending Plans, a desk study was done on donors' country allocation and budgetary processes. The study found that all DAC donors have annual budgets, although budgetary planning is often multiyear. For example, in at least half of DAC member countries, the budget proposal includes indicative spending plans three to four years forward. An annual budget process means that funds can be disbursed only from approved annual budgets. Budget proposals outline the government's policy priorities in terms of recipients, sectors, and themes. Multilateral donors work with multiyear budget frameworks with regard to core funding and policy and allocation priorities. For example, funding for IDA and the African Development Fund is set during the replenishment negotiations and covers three years. DAC bilateral donors' forward planning is generally limited to their priority partner countries.

Thus, the results of the survey are incomplete in that sense. Multilateral donors' forward planning covers all recipients of their aid.

9. See OECD DCD 2007b.

10. Global Fund 2007. In September 2007 donors provided an initial $9.7 billion in pledges for the second replenishment cycle covering the period 2008–10. Many donors cannot make commitments beyond a year, so there is an expectation that commitments will increase over the cycle.

11. Manning 2006.

12. Kharas 2007a.

13. Hudson Institute 2007; Kharas 2007b.

14. Kerlin and Thanasombat 2006.

15. By one count, at least 18,000 NGOs are active, of which 4,100 are in the United States alone; see Center for the Study of Global Governance 2004, p. 302.

16. Gates Foundation 2007.

17. They also present a risk of adverse global and regional spillovers.

18. Collier, Hoeffler, and Soderbom 2006.

19. There is substantial evidence that UN peacekeeping operations can reduce the likelihood of renewed conflict by up to 50 percent in the immediate two to five years after the end of civil wars. See Sambanis 2007.

20. Fragile states comprise IDA-eligible countries with a country policy and institutional assessment (CPIA) score of 3.2 or below (or no CPIA score). Thirty-five countries were identified as fragile in 2006.

21. *Global Monitoring Report 2007* covered aid to fragile states in more detail.

22. This is certainly a reasonable test for peacekeeping assistance, where the effect on reducing conflict risk is direct and significant in most studies. More work is needed to evaluate the direct effects of aid on reducing conflict risk.

23. Cliffe and Milante 2008.

24. Gaps in funding may also arise because postcrisis financing tends to be fragmented, with different funding sources, implementing agencies, and mandates. For example, early humanitarian and peacekeeping activities require international mandates, whereas recovery, reconstruction, and development require strong national ownership.

25. Statement issued at a meeting of MDB heads held on October 20, 2007.

26. Development Initiatives 2006.

27. United Nations Financial Tracking Service (FTS) database. http://ocha.unog.ch/fts/reporting/reporting.asp.

28. Development Initiatives 2006; also see Stromberg 2007 for an analysis of the determinants of donors' humanitarian assistance.

29. Based on DAC members' humanitarian aid, EC humanitarian aid, multilateral contributions to the UN High Commissioner for Refugees, and the United Nations Relief and Works Agency, and a share of multilateral contributions to the UN World Food Programme.

30. http://ec.europa.eu/echo/whatsnew/consensus_en.htm.

31. UNDP 2007.

32. Until recently, the main multilateral mechanism for adaptation funding is the GEF. In 2001 the GEF received a mandate to finance adaptation projects through three vehicles: the Least Developed Country Fund, which has received pledges of $170 million; the Special Climate Change Fund, with about $75 million in pledges; and the Strategic Priority on Adaptation, which has been allocated $50 million for pilot projects. Additional resources for adaptation will also accrue to the GEF via the Adaptation Fund. The GEF is currently undergoing a change that shifts away from projects toward a more programmatic approach.

33. The proposed portfolio of three funds would provide concessional finance at significant scale in selected countries to encourage early action by both private and public sectors and market-based solutions to the climate change challenge. The funds would build upon and enhance the activities of other existing instruments, such as the GEF and financing products of the International Bank for Reconstruction and Development, and International Finance Corporation. The suite of funds includes the Clean Technology Fund (target size around $5 billion–$10 billion), which is at the most advanced stage of design, to accelerate the deployment of advanced technologies in developing countries; the Forest Investment Fund (target size $300 million–$500 million), which will focus on reducing deforestation and land degradation; and the Climate Resilience Pilot Program (target size around $200 million–$300 million), focusing on the most vulnerable countries to mainstream climate resilience in development planning and programs and demonstrate lessons for scaling up through IDA and the Adaptation Fund.

34. See IDA 2006 and Brook and Petrie 2007. Also see Birdsall and others (2007) for a proposal on progress-based aid, which focuses on results.

35. http://www.gpoba.org/activities/index.asp. The World Bank administers the Global Partnership on Output-Based Aid.

36. These could be one-off subsidies typically involving capital subsidies for access to water, electricity, and the like.; transitional subsidies, which are used temporarily to meet the gap between cost-recovery amount and what the consumer can afford; and ongoing subsidies where this gap persists. See GPOBA 2005.

37. OECD 2008a.

38. *2006 Survey on Monitoring the Paris Declaration: Overview of the Results.* OECD 2007a.

39. The results need to be interpreted carefully because some donors' definitions of program-based approaches may vary.

40. Ashraf Ghani, former minister of finance in Afghanistan, estimated that 60 percent of his time was spent dealing with official aid donors.

41. These mechanisms are designed to address coordination, harmonization, and alignment with country priorities.

42. Celasun and Walliser 2008.

43. Kharas 2008.

44. European Commission 2007.

45. IMF 2007.

46. Claessens, Cassimon, and van Campenhout 2007.

47. By contrast, when country leadership and capacity is strong, the authorities can take the lead in defining priorities and in channeling donor support—whether general budget support, project aid, or earmarked aid—to these priorities. See World Bank 2007b.

48. See World Bank 2007c.

49. Cerrell 2007.

50. For a group of 81 developing countries, Lane and Glassman (2007) find that health aid per capita is positively associated with aggregate disease burden as measured by DALYs (disability-adjusted life years). However, they also find that health aid is more closely associated with certain types of diseases—namely, HIV/AIDS and TB.

51. See GPOBA 2005.

52. Lewis 2005.

53. Republic of Rwanda 2006.

54. Government of Ethiopia Irish Aid, UNICEF, USAID, and World Bank 2007.

55. Education and infrastructure are also beginning to receive special attention for the sectoral application of the Paris framework.

56. See International Health Partnership 2007, 2008.

57. IMF–World Bank 2007.

58. Equal burden sharing, which implies that all creditors provide the same share of debt relief on their claims against the HIPCs, is one of the key principles of the HIPC Initiative. The completion point cannot be reached unless creditors holding at least 80 percent of HIPC-eligible debt agree to participate in debt relief.

59. Since its inception in 1989, the Debt Reduction Facility has implemented 24 operations in 21 IDA-only countries, extinguishing about US$9 billion of external commercial debt.

60. http://www.worldbank.org/debt; www.imf.org/dsa.

4

Harnessing Trade for Inclusive and Sustainable Growth

World trade has been expanding rapidly, and trends in trade policy have continued to be in the direction of fewer barriers to trade.[1] Progress in the multilateral trade negotiations has proved to be elusive, however, reflecting in large part the inability of World Trade Organization (WTO) members to agree on agricultural trade liberalization. Organisation for Economic Co-operation and Development (OECD) countries continue to impose highly distorting agricultural support policies to the detriment of their consumers and producers in developing countries. Developing countries have higher average levels of trade restrictiveness, but the policy of taxing agriculture in many developing countries has become much less prevalent.

A successful Doha Round is important for inclusive and sustainable growth. The current high prices for food provide a window of opportunity that WTO members should use to break the impasse on reforming agricultural trade policies in high-income countries. Doha also offers an opportunity to developing countries to lock in the prevailing, relatively neutral cross-sectoral policy stance for trade in merchandise, and to reap the efficiency gains of lowering further the applied levels of protection.

Access to export markets is important for developing countries, but what matter most are the trade policies and complementary measures that countries themselves adopt. A neutral and liberal trade regime, accompanied by policies and public investments that help communities and firms capture trade opportunities, will largely determine the role that trade will play in achieving the Millennium Development Goal (MDG) poverty targets. "Behind the border" policies are of particular importance in enhancing competitiveness of firms, including policies that affect the quality and costs of services inputs. Many countries are relatively open to trade and investment in services, but restrictions continue to affect the performance of many services sectors in numerous countries. Countries that have undertaken unilateral policy reforms have an opportunity to lock these in via the WTO in the context of the Doha Round. But there is also great scope to do more to use the WTO as a mechanism to commit to future liberalization of trade in services. Not only will this generate gains for the countries that do so, it may help move the overall Doha negotiations forward.

Progress is being made on aid for trade, as illustrated by the initiative to enhance the

Integrated Framework for Trade-Related Technical Assistance for Least Developed Countries and the willingness of donors to make commitments to the associated trust fund to support its operations. The regional and global WTO-facilitated meetings on aid for trade in 2007 have helped raise awareness of the importance of complementing trade policy reform with assistance to help firms and farmers benefit more from trade opportunities. What matters now is delivery. This should target competitiveness-related areas—such as trade logistics—as well as help improve the ability of poor households and disadvantaged communities in rural areas to harness trade opportunities to raise their incomes.

Trade policy and aid for trade have a role to play in fighting and adjusting to global warming by increasing incentives to use the most energy efficient environmental goods and services. Trade barriers confronting more climate-friendly technologies tend to be highest in low-income countries, paralleling the overall pattern of trade restrictiveness. Removing policies that restrain trade in energy-efficient environmental goods and services—ensuring that production of inefficient technologies is not supported and assisting producers in developing countries to benefit rather than lose from initiatives such as carbon labeling—can help both in harnessing the potential of trade to enhance inclusive and sustainable growth and in improving environmental outcomes.

Recent Developments in International Trade

World trade in 2007 continued its strong growth trend of recent years. Worldwide exports of merchandise reached $13.7 trillion in 2007, growing 14 percent in value, well above the average growth of 9 percent recorded in 1997–2006. At 17 percent, developing-country export growth was down slightly from the 2006 rate of 22 percent but continued to outpace industrial countries, which grew 13 percent.

Turning to individual regions, higher energy prices contributed to export growth of 10 percent in Middle Eastern and North African countries. Asian exports expanded by 21 percent, with China and India accounting for the bulk of the increase, with a 27 percent and 18 percent increase in 2007, respectively. Buoyed by higher commodity prices and demand, exports from Sub-Saharan Africa and Latin American and Caribbean countries continued to benefit from the healthy global economy, both recording a 12 percent increase. Least-developed countries, as a group, experienced a remarkable 17 percent growth.[2]

The Doha Round Negotiations

Central to the task of promoting inclusive globalization is bringing down barriers to the products that poor people produce. A successful Doha Round is one of the most important steps nations, acting collectively, could take to enhance inclusive and sustainable growth.

Considerable progress in the complex WTO negotiations, especially in agriculture, has been made. While efforts continue across the broad range of areas covered by the negotiations—including but not limited to agriculture, non-agricultural market access (NAMA), services, rules, regional trade arrangements, special and differential treatment for developing countries, trade and environment, trade-related intellectual property rights, and trade facilitation—the gateway to completing the negotiations is agreement on negotiating modalities in agriculture and NAMA. Draft texts issued on February 8, 2008, by the chairpersons of the agriculture and NAMA negotiating groups as a basis for further discussion lay out the most specific and comprehensive blueprint for global liberalization since the negotiations began in 2001, albeit with bracketed ranges for key numeric parameters.

Agricultural modalities relate to the three core elements of the negotiation—market access, domestic support, and export competition. Progress has been made in recent consultations on export competition, and efforts are ongoing to obtain agreement on market access and domestic support, including the specific targets and approaches for tariff cuts, permitted tariff rate quotas, overall domestic support levels, flexibilities for "special" and "sensitive" products, and a special safeguard mechanism. In the discussions on NAMA modalities, progress has been made on tabling ranges for the coefficients to be applied in a nonlinear tariff-cutting formula, the extent of the application of the formula by different members, and the nature of exceptions and flexibilities that will be permitted for certain members. As with agriculture, agreement is still elusive and many details remain to be worked out.

In services, a plurilateral request-and-offer process has been under way for some time, whereby subsets of members are working toward a set of scheduled market access and national treatment commitments. More recently, attention has also focused on the mandate of the chairman of the negotiating group to consult on a possible services text. On the rule-making front—notably domestic regulation—discussions are proceeding on the basis of a chairman's text issued in April 2007. As with other areas, negotiations are influenced to a degree by what is happening in agriculture and NAMA.

With respect to WTO rules, in early December the chairman of the negotiating group issued a consolidated draft text on antidumping, subsidies (including fisheries subsidies), and countervailing measures. Implicit in this text is a range of trade-offs that members are invited to consider. No member has rejected the text as a basis for further discussion. A revised text will depend on how the negotiations proceed and also on progress in other areas. The work on regional trade arrangements has already produced a concrete result in the form of the decision on a transparency mechanism for the multilateral examination of agreements.

In the area of special and differential treatment for developing countries, discus-sions are continuing in relation to a number of agreement-specific proposals for improved special and differential treatment provisions. At the same time, work is proceeding on the establishment of a mechanism to monitor the implementation of special and differential treatment provisions in WTO agreements. On trade and environment, constructive engagement has been continuing on all aspects of the mandate, although further discussion is required on the approach to environmental services and goods in terms of the mandate. An aspect of this issue is the degree of willingness among some members to identify products qualifying as environmental goods prior to the establishment of modalities in agriculture and NAMA. As regards trade facilitation, consensus is being pursued through a text-drafting exercise and is far along. Progress has been made in addressing special and differential treatment, technical assistance, and capacity-building issues.

For the first time in the history of the trading system, a comprehensive set of binding disciplines on international trade in agricultural products is within reach. Only a WTO agreement can address the global trade-distorting impacts of agricultural subsidies, reduce peak tariffs on labor-intensive goods that discriminate against the poor, reduce barriers in key emerging markets to help stimulate South-South trade, and secure the rules-based trading system. A failure to produce concrete results in the near future will undermine certainty and predictability in trade relations, thus diminishing the scope for trade to play its part in fostering economic progress and reducing poverty. The cost of a deal not done would be paid by those who can least afford it. Negotiators do seem to agree on one issue: the window in time for agreeing on modalities will not stay open indefinitely.

Preferential Trade Agreements

Preferential trade agreements (PTAs) continued to proliferate in 2007, both among developing countries and between developed and developing countries. Approximately 194 still-active PTAs have been notified to the WTO. However, given that many agreements have not been notified, the actual number of agreements in effect is estimated at over 300. Despite the high number of agreements, the amount of trade that actually takes place under PTAs is often limited by the exclusion of sensitive products, complicated and costly rules-of-origin requirements (the cost of which can be as high as the equivalent of a 4 percent tariff),[3] and low preference margins.

Notable PTAs that came into effect in 2007 include the expansion of the European Union to include Bulgaria and Romania; the addition of Albania, Bosnia and Herzegovina, Croatia, Kosovo, the former Yugoslav Republic of Macedonia, Moldova, Montenegro, and Serbia to the Central European Free Trade Agreement (CEFTA); a free trade agreement between the Republic of Korea and the Association of Southeast Asian Nations (ASEAN); and bilateral agreements between the Syrian Arab Republic and Turkey, Chile and China, and the United States and Peru.

EU ACP Economic Partnership Agreements

Since 2000 the European Union (EU) has extended favorable preferential access to the exports of 78 African, Caribbean, and Pacific (ACP) developing countries under a system known as the Cotonou Agreement. Because the trade preferences were unilateral (the EU received no reciprocal preferential access), the Cotonou Agreement was not compatible with WTO requirements for trade agreements and operated under a temporary waiver with an expiration date of December 31, 2007. Anticipating this deadline, the EU began in 2002 to negotiate Economic Partnership Agreements (EPAs) with six regional clusters of countries with the goal of producing WTO-compatible agreements.

Negotiations were difficult and progressed slowly. Only one full EPA—covering goods, services, rules of origin, and development support—was agreed upon before the end-of-year deadline, with the cluster of Caribbean countries. Partial interim agreements were initialed with the East African Community and Southern Africa clusters, and individually with an additional 10 countries—Botswana, Cameroon, Côte d'Ivoire, Fiji, Ghana, Lesotho, Mozambique, Namibia, Papua New Guinea, and Swaziland. Umbrella (framework) agreements on trade and development cooperation were signed with the East African Community (EAC), the Common Market for Eastern and Southern Africa (COMESA), and the Southern Africa Development Community (SADC). As of January 1, 2008, countries with EPAs will have tariff- and quota-free access to EU markets, with a short transition for sugar and rice. Liberalization in the ACP countries to EU exports varies by region and country but will be implemented gradually, with provisions to protect sensitive sectors. Those countries that did not reach agreement on an EPA include 32 least-developed countries (LDCs), which will continue to have duty- and quota-free market access under the EU's "Everything But Arms" initiative for LDCs, and an additional 10 non-LDCs, which will revert to preferences under the EU's Generalized System of Preferences.[4]

Developments in National Trade Policies: Merchandise Trade

Governments use numerous instruments to regulate trade, including import tariffs, specific duties, quotas, technical product regulations, antidumping duties, and discretionary licensing. The commonly used indicators of trade policy, such as average tariffs and frequency measures, only capture partially the impact of trade policies on trade flows. It is preferable to use summary measures that take into account the effect of all policies affecting trade.

Measures of Trade Restrictiveness

What follows uses two measures of the restrictiveness of trade policies affecting merchandise trade: the Overall Trade Restrictiveness Index (OTRI) and the Tariff Trade Restrictiveness Index (TTRI).[5] Both provide a measure of the uniform tariff equivalent of observed policies on a country's imports: they represent the "tariff" that would be needed to generate the observed level of trade for a country. The level of restrictiveness confronting exporters is captured by two similarly constructed indicators: the Market Access OTRI (MA-OTRI) and the Market Access TTRI (MA-TTRI).

The OTRI captures all policies on which information is reported to and by Geneva-based organizations (the International Trade Centre, the United Nations Conference on Trade and Development [UNCTAD], and WTO). These comprise ad valorem tariffs, specific duties, and nontariff measures (NTMs) such as price control measures, quantitative restrictions, monopolistic measures, and technical regulations (box 4.1). The TTRI is narrower in scope; it takes into account only tariffs (both ad valorem and specific).[7]

As many NTMs are not necessarily protectionist in intent (or effect), the OTRI reflects net (overall) restrictiveness; it is not a

---

BOX 4.1 Trade data and trade restrictiveness indicators

The accuracy of the summary measures of trade restrictiveness is largely a function of the underlying data. While the indicators used in this report are based on sound theoretical foundations and are an advance over standard summary indicators such as (weighted) average tariffs, their accuracy inevitably depends on the quality of information on prevailing policies.

Prior to the calculation of these indicators, tariff and nontariff data are collected, validated, and standardized. Tariff data collection is undertaken by UNCTAD and the International Trade Centre (Geneva), working with the WTO. These trade and tariff data are published in a global database and software system (the World Integrated Trade Solution—WITS). In recent years the underlying data have been improved by incorporating more extensive information on tariff preferences and specific duties. Although ad valorem tariff data are generally comprehensive and up-to-date, the database may not have comprehensive coverage of so-called para-tariffs and surcharges, which are usually applied on a temporary basis, leading to underestimation of trade restrictiveness in a given year. Conversely, some measures may continue to be registered in the database even though they have subsequently been removed.

Excise taxes may also affect estimates of the indexes. As long as excise taxes are imposed on both imports and domestic production, they should not be classified as a trade tax. However, some countries report excises in their tariff schedule (as they are collected on imports at the border), and these may therefore be included in the estimate of trade restrictiveness. Several instances where this was the case have been identified, and the underlying data corrected.[6] Specific duties—taxes imposed on the basis of quantities imported rather than values—raise additional issues, as these taxes need to be converted into ad valorem tariff equivalents. Different methodologies can be used to do this. For the indexes of this report, the methodology used by UNCTAD has been used.

The major factor affecting the accuracy of the indexes is the coverage of nontariff measures (NTMs). Comprehensive data on such measures are unfortunately lacking. Resource constraints have impeded the collection of data on NTMs by the organization that historically has taken the lead in this area—UNCTAD. Existing data are therefore not necessarily up-to-date and may not be fully comparable across countries. Given the increasing importance of NTMs in global trade—in part as a result of the steady decline in tariffs in many countries—it is important that a concerted effort be made to mobilize the political attention and resources needed to improve information on NTMs, including to better distinguish between regulatory policies such as product standards and other policies that have as a primary motive the restriction of trade.

The limitations of the data on NTMs are one reason for reporting both the OTRI and the TTRI in this report. Although a downward-biased measure of trade restrictiveness, the advantage of the TTRI is that it is more comparable across countries, and more countries can be included in the calculation of the index.

measure of the level of protection that a government seeks to provide domestic industry. Some NTMs comprise border restrictions, such as quotas or bans, and are motivated by protectionist objectives. Others, such as standards for mercury content or fecal matter, are aimed at safeguarding human, animal, or plant health. Unfortunately the measures do not permit us to distinguish between objectives. Thus, protection is better measured by the TTRI, although, because of its limited coverage of trade policy instruments, it is best seen as providing a lower-bound estimate of the extent of protection prevailing in a market.

Levels of Trade Restrictiveness

Although trade flows are now subject to lower barriers than was the case a decade ago, trade barriers still exert a large impact on world trade. Trade policies are generally more restrictive in developing countries than in the high-income economies (table 4.1). This is due in part to lower tariffs in the latter but also to the higher percentage of trade in manufactured products in the trade of these countries (manufactures generally face much lower trade restrictions than agricultural products, which are relatively more

important in the export basket of developing countries). Trade restrictions on agriculture are on average highest in high-income countries. In general, the higher the level of development of countries, the lower the overall trade restrictiveness, and the higher the level of trade restrictiveness in agriculture.

The impact of NTMs on overall restrictiveness can be assessed by the difference between the OTRI and the TTRI. Nontariff measures are an important component of overall trade restrictiveness, especially for agricultural products. Nontariff measures tend to be more prevalent in high-income and upper-middle-income countries. For higher-income countries, NTMs account for about two-thirds of total restrictiveness. NTMs appear to play a less important role in lower-middle-income and low-income countries. Although NTMs in agriculture tend to be significant, agricultural products also confront much higher tariffs than manufactures do. The TTRI of high-income countries is approximately 12.4 percent for agriculture compared to only 1.4 percent for manufactured products.

Trade restrictiveness levels differ across geographic regions. The level of trade restrictiveness on average is higher for countries in South Asia, the Middle East, and North Africa and lower for countries in East Asia, Eastern Europe, and Central Asia. Sub-Saharan Africa and Latin America have overall restrictiveness levels in between these two extremes (table 4.2). The EU, United States, Japan, and China account for about 60 percent of world trade. All have policies that are more restrictive of trade in agricultural products than manufactures (table 4.3), with Japan and the EU imposing significantly higher restrictions. Manufacturing trade is relatively less restricted: the TTRI is less than 5 percent in China and around 1 percent in the EU, Japan, and United States.

Changes in Trade Restrictiveness

Trade barriers have fallen in many countries, resulting in lower trade restrictiveness.

TABLE 4.1 OTRI and TTRI by income group, 2006
percent

	Total trade	Agriculture	Manufacturing
High-income countries	**7.0**	**43.1**	**4.3**
	2.1	*12.4*	*1.4*
QUAD	**7.1**	**44.5**	**4.0**
	1.9	*11.1*	*1.3*
Upper-middle-income countries	**13.0**	**29.3**	**11.8**
	4.6	*6.6*	*4.5*
Lower-middle-income countries	**11.8**	**26.5**	**10.6**
	6.5	*11.5*	*6.0*
Low-income countries	**17.7**	**26.6**	**16.7**
	10.8	*15.3*	*10.4*

Source: World Bank staff estimates.
Note: TTRI in italics; OTRI in boldface. QUAD comprises Canada, the EU, Japan, and the United States.

Reductions have mostly been the result of unilateral reforms but are also the result of trade negotiations and agreements. Between 2000 and 2006 the OTRI declined in all country and income groups (figure 4.1). Developing economies, especially middle-income countries, saw the largest declines, including in agriculture. By region, countries in East Asia and Latin America reduced overall trade restrictiveness the most during this period, while Sub-Saharan African countries experienced the least reduction. However, it should be noted that Sub-Saharan Africa's OTRI is below that of South Asia and the Middle East and North Africa. With the exception of South Asia and Sub-Saharan Africa, where policy reforms have mainly targeted trade in manufactures and the overall level of agricultural trade restrictiveness increased slightly, trade restrictiveness has fallen for both agriculture and manufacturing.

New Estimates of Distortions to Agricultural Incentives

Trade restrictiveness across products and countries tends to show a clear pattern: richer countries tend to have higher barriers to trade in agricultural products. This is a phenomenon that initially emerged in the late 19th century[8] and has been a persistent feature of global trade policy ever since. For 20 years the OECD Secretariat has been publishing annual estimates of producer support to farmers in OECD member countries.[9] These Producer Support Estimates (PSEs) provide a transparent set of numbers that allow monitoring over time of the extent to which farmers are being assisted by governments through myriad direct payments and agricultural market price support policies. Although PSEs have fallen in some OECD countries since 1999–2001—for example, in Japan and the United States—they have increased in the EU, the Republic of Korea, and a number of other countries (figure 4.2).

The policies included in the PSE are captured in the OTRIs and TTRIs reported

TABLE 4.2 OTRI and TTRI, by developing country region, 2006
percent

	Total trade	Agriculture	Manufacturing
East Asia & Pacific	**11.3**	**26.6**	**10.4**
	5.0	*8.7*	*4.8*
Europe & Central Asia	**10.1**	**25.9**	**9.0**
	4.5	*10.3*	*4.0*
Latin America & the Caribbean	**15.0**	**28.1**	**13.8**
	5.4	*6.6*	*5.3*
Middle East & North Africa	**21.6**	**32.3**	**19.4**
	11.9	*12.1*	*11.8*
South Asia	**19.5**	**46.4**	**18.2**
	14.0	*31.4*	*13.2*
Sub-Saharan Africa	**14.4**	**24.9**	**12.9**
	8.4	*13.8*	*7.6*

Source: World Bank staff estimates.
Note: TTRI in italics; OTRI in boldface font.

TABLE 4.3 OTRI and TTRI for the four largest traders, 2006
percent

	All trade	Agriculture	Manufacturing
United States	**6.4**	**18.4**	**5.7**
	1.6	*3.8*	*1.5*
European Union	**6.6**	**48.7**	**2.9**
	1.4	*5.9*	*1.1*
Japan	**11.4**	**55.8**	**5.7**
	4.5	*31.1*	*1.1*
China	**9.9**	**17.1**	**9.5**
	5.1	*8.8*	*4.9*

Source: World Bank staff estimates.
Note: TTRI in italics; OTRI in boldface font.

above for agriculture. As the membership of the OECD is composed mostly of high-income countries, the type of detailed data used to calculate PSEs is not available for developing countries. As a result agriculture OTRIs are less comparable across developed and developing countries. A recent World Bank research project has sought to fill this gap by compiling annual time series estimates of rates and values of assistance/taxation over the past half century for around 75 countries that together account

FIGURE 4.1 Change in OTRI, 2000–06

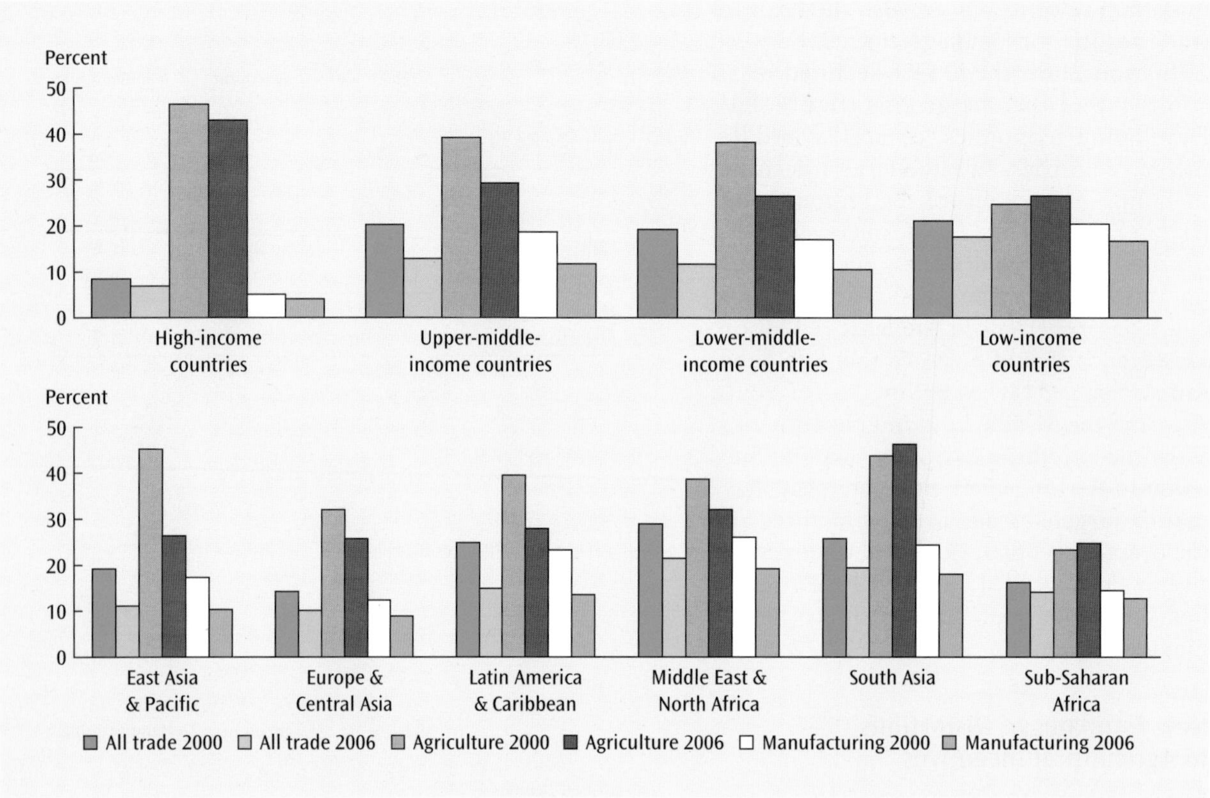

Source: World Bank staff estimates.

for 90 percent of global population, GDP, and agricultural production. For each country, nominal rates of assistance (NRAs)[10] are calculated for key products, which make up an average of 70 percent of the value of total farm production, and are estimated for the residual set of commodities.[11]

An aggregated summary of the NRAs is provided in figure 4.3. This reveals that the growth of agricultural support in high-income countries began to reverse only in the 1990s. If farm income support that is said to be decoupled from production incentives is considered, there is very little decline in the rate of support. Figure 4.3 also supports the widely held view that developing-country governments put in place agricultural policies that effectively taxed their farmers. The extent of taxation was of the order of 20 percent from the mid-1950s to the mid-1980s.

Since then not only has it diminished but, on average, developing countries have moved from taxing to subsidizing their agricultural sector.

Figure 4.4 shows the trends in NRAs by developing-country region. African countries have shown the least tendency to reduce the taxing of farmers—the average NRA has been negative in all five-year periods except in the mid-1980s, when international prices of farm products reached an all-time low in real terms. By contrast, for both Asia and Latin America, NRAs crossed over from negative to positive after the 1980s. In European transition economies, in the initial years of reform, nominal assistance to farmers was slightly negative, but thereafter it has trended upward. As of 2004, however, it still averaged only about half the average rate of Western Europe.

The U.S. dollar values of the gross subsidy equivalents of the NRAs (or taxation) are shown in table 4.4. These estimates suggest that, from the mid-1950s through the mid-1970s, assistance to farmers in high-income countries almost exactly offset taxation of farmers in developing countries. Until the late 1980s, farmers in developing countries were at a double disadvantage in terms of competitiveness: farmers in OECD countries benefited from significant levels of support, whereas agricultural production in developing countries tended to be taxed. Since the early 1980s, the gradual decline in taxation of farmers in developing countries and the growth in assistance to high-income country farmers have combined to see the net global transfer to farmers increase to more than $250 billion per year (figure 4.5). Regionally, outside the high-income group, it is Asia where the payments are largest in aggregate. On a per farmer basis, however, payments are now largest in Europe's transition economies. In Africa, meanwhile, farmers still confront discrimination relative to other forms of economic activity.

The data on gross subsidy equivalents of support to farmers show that the overall level of assistance in high-income countries has

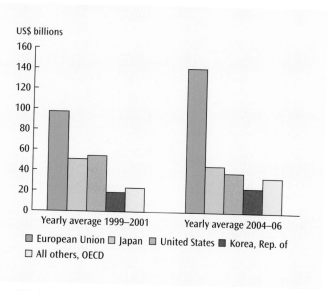

FIGURE 4.2 Producer support estimates for OECD members, 1999–2006

Source: OECD (2007).

been virtually constant for the last 15 years and has been rising in developing countries, perhaps in part as a response to the example set by high-income nations. The high level of production support in high-income countries distorts domestic and world market prices

FIGURE 4.3 Nominal rate of assistance to farmers in high-income and developing countries, 1960 to 2004

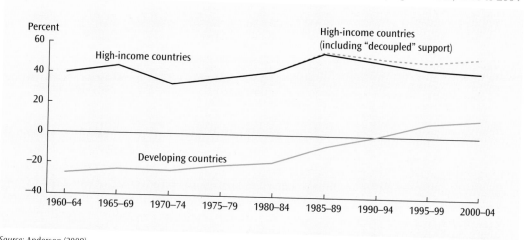

Source: Anderson (2008).
Note: Averaged using weights based on the gross value of agricultural production at undistorted prices. High-income countries include the Republic of Korea and Taiwan, China.

FIGURE 4.4   Nominal rate of assistance to farmers in developing countries, 1960 to 2004

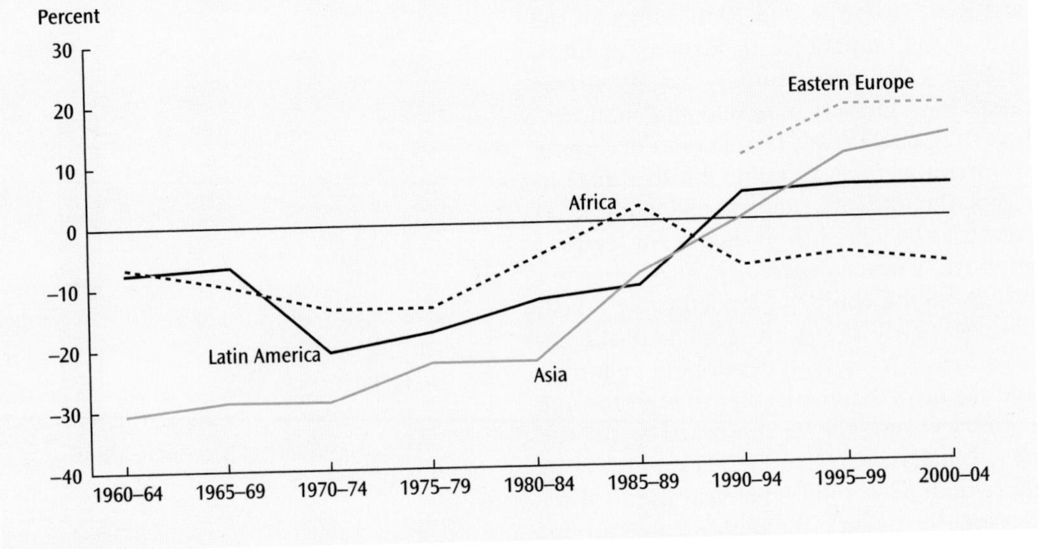

Source: Anderson (2008).

TABLE 4.4   Gross subsidy equivalents of assistance to farmers, by region, 1960 to 2004
current US$ billions per year

	1960–64	1965–69	1970–74	1975–79	1980–84	1985–89	1990–94	1995–99	2000–04
High-income countries[a]	30.3	43.1	49.0	96.4	133.0	174.1	216.3	200.2	190.9
Developing countries	–18.7	–21.9	–46.7	–69.0	–92.0	–35.8	0.8	47.9	65.2
Africa	–0.6	–1.3	–3.3	–5.9	–4.0	1.5	–6.3	–6.0	–7.9
Asia	–17.5	–19.0	–37.8	–55.1	–70.8	–28.9	–1.8	27.1	48.0
Latin America	–0.3	–0.7	–4.9	–6.7	–10.4	–9.3	4.7	6.5	5.3
European transition economies	–0.2	–0.9	–0.6	–1.3	–6.8	0.8	4.2	20.3	19.7

Source: Anderson (2008).
Note: These values have been scaled up to account for the fact that each region is less than fully covered, the assumption being that NRA in the nonstudied group of countries in each region was the same as the regional average for the studied countries.
a. High-income countries are a subset of OECD countries (Western Europe, Japan, United States, Canada, Australia, New Zealand, the Republic of Korea, and Taiwan, China for the periods after 1995), which is why the numbers in this row for the last four columns are below the PSE estimates for the OECD as a whole (the latter includes the Czech Republic, Hungary, the Republic of Korea, Mexico, Poland, the Slovak Republic, and Turkey).

and is detrimental to producers in developing countries and consumers in the high-income countries themselves. Historical policies in many developing countries of taxing agriculture have also been detrimental to farmers, and the more recent trend toward a more neutral policy stance for agriculture relative to other sectors of activity is to be welcomed. However, going beyond this and emulating

OECD members by starting to subsidize agriculture is not desirable.

The trends in agricultural trade policies illustrate the importance of using the opportunity offered by the Doha Round to agree to far-reaching reductions in overall production support to farmers in high-income countries, and of complementing this by agreeing to cap the extent of such support provided

FIGURE 4.5   Gross subsidy equivalents of assistance to farmers in developing and high-income countries, 1960–2004

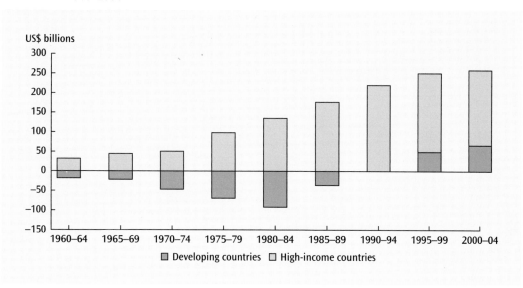

Source: Anderson (2008).

in developing countries and to lock in the relatively neutral sectoral trade policy stance that now prevails in many developing economies. Current high global price levels for food provide a window that may facilitate agreement—lower tariffs will benefit poor households by reducing domestic prices, while farmers will be less affected given robust global demand for food and biofuel feedstocks. An important challenge in this connection has been the recent recourse by some major exporters to export taxes and other controls. These increase the instability of world market prices, have adverse effects on the poor (including net sellers in poor countries), and do systemic damage by eroding the confidence of importing countries in the reliability of world markets as a source of food supply.

The trend toward higher protection of agriculture is driven in part by equity objectives as well as by a desire to shelter farmers from competition from subsidized farmers in OECD countries. Trade policy is not the appropriate instrument to pursue equity objectives or to attain goals such as food security and rural development. This is not just because trade policy distorts consumption and production decisions; it is also because the distributional consequences of protecting agriculture may be harmful to many poor households, especially those that are net consumers and do not derive income from agriculture. Other policy instruments that are aimed at increasing productivity or linking rural communities to markets are much superior to trade policy in helping the poor benefit from trade opportunities. Liberalization therefore needs to be complemented by assistance to developing governments to help put in place such productivity and income-enhancing policies—aid for trade.

Market Access

The effect of trade policies on exporters' access to markets is different across trading partners and geographic regions. This is due both to the discriminatory use of trade policies (i.e., trade preferences) and to the composition of trade. Table 4.5 reports the MA-OTRI and MA-TTRI faced by exporters in each geographic region and country income group. The MA-OTRI measures the

TABLE 4.5   MA-OTRI and MA-TTRI by income group, 2006

Importing Countries	High-income countries	Upper-middle income countries	Lower-middle income countries	Low-income countries	East Asia & Pacific	Europe & Central Asia	Latin America & Caribbean	Middle East & N. Africa	South Asia	Sub-Saharan Africa
High-income countries	**6.3**	**5.7**	**7.9**	**9.1**	**8.3**	**5.1**	**7.0**	**4.3**	**10.4**	**4.4**
	2.4	*1.2*	*2.5*	*2.4*	*2.6*	*1.1*	*1.5*	*0.8*	*3.1*	*0.7*
QUAD	**6.3**	**5.2**	**8.6**	**10.6**	**8.9**	**5.2**	**6.9**	**4.4**	**13.6**	**4.5**
	2.1	*0.9*	*2.5*	*2.5*	*2.7*	*0.8*	*1.2*	*0.5*	*3.3*	*0.5*
Upper-middle-income countries	**15.6**	**11.8**	**15.8**	**14.7**	**19.2**	**10.2**	**13.6**	**6.0**	**14.3**	**5.9**
	5.6	*3.8*	*5.6*	*5.7*	*7.2*	*4.4*	*2.6*	*2.5*	*6.6*	*3.5*
Lower-middle-income countries	**12.4**	**11.1**	**12.9**	**9.4**	**13.6**	**11.2**	**12.6**	**6.7**	**9.9**	**4.0**
	7.1	*4.8*	*6.7*	*5.1*	*6.6*	*6.2*	*5.1*	*2.8*	*6.2*	*2.7*
Low-income countries	**18.2**	**14.3**	**19.5**	**25.4**	**22.2**	**17.7**	**15.9**	**16.3**	**16.2**	**16.3**
	10.9	*8.1*	*12.2*	*12.9*	*13.8*	*6.2*	*9.0*	*10.0*	*10.4*	*12.2*

Source: World Bank staff estimates.
Note: MA-TTRI in italics; MA-OTRI in boldface font.

overall restrictiveness (including nontariff measures) faced by exports; the MA-TTRI measures restrictiveness faced by exports due to tariffs alone.

Sub-Saharan Africa countries benefit from relatively liberal market access as a result of preferential access to the major economies and because of the relatively larger share of exports of commodities for which tariffs are low. Conversely, Sub-Saharan Africa's market access to other low-income countries is restricted by relatively high tariffs. Among other regions, East European and Central Asian market access to high-income countries is facilitated by preferences in the EU, while the low TTRI confronting the Middle East and North Africa is largely due to the composition of exports—oil products are generally subject to low import tariffs.

Changes in Market Access

Market access has improved in recent years, with high- and upper-middle-income countries benefiting relatively more (figure 4.6). This is largely due to export composition, as high-income countries' exports consist mainly of manufactures, for which restrictiveness has declined relatively more. Exports of lower-income countries are more oriented toward agriculture, which faces more restrictive barriers and for which liberalization has been more muted.

Trade Policy, Growth, and Poverty: The Behind-the-Border Agenda

The relationship between trade expansion and economic growth is well documented. Growth in turn is a primary driver for poverty reduction. Developing countries that have registered the largest declines in poverty are generally those that have also expanded their trade faster. Even in instances where economic growth may directly affect the poor only modestly, growth that increases the national wealth as a whole permits government to allocate more resources to measures aimed at alleviating poverty and other social programs.

The level of trade restrictiveness across countries is generally negatively correlated with the level of development. High-income countries tend to have less-restrictive trade regimes than developing countries, and among developing countries, low-income countries are generally more restrictive than middle-income countries. Figure 4.7 plots the correlation between changes in per

FIGURE 4.6   Change in the average MA-OTRI for all exports, 2000–06

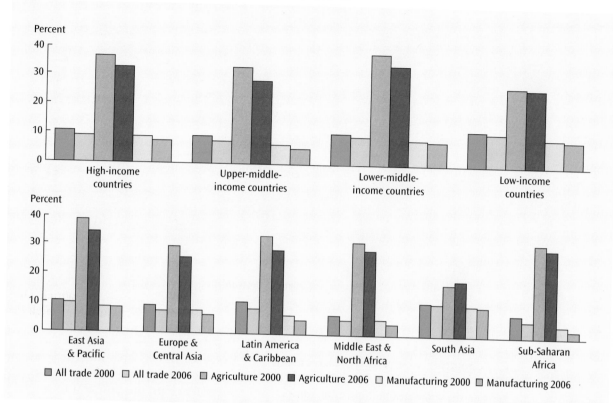

■ All trade 2000   ☐ All trade 2006   ■ Agriculture 2000   ■ Agriculture 2006   ☐ Manufacturing 2000   ☐ Manufacturing 2006

Source: World Bank staff estimates.

capita GDP with changes in the OTRI for developing countries in the period 2000 to 2006. Countries for which per capita GDP has grown more have tended to have liberalized their trade more.

In principle, trade liberalization should enhance national welfare, although there will always be some groups that lose, as the removal of trade policies generates redistributive effects. Trade policies have diverse effects across economic sectors and geographic areas, and gains and losses depend on how individuals are positioned relative to the pre-existing structure of protection. If the transitional costs of trade liberalization fall disproportionately on the poor, complementary reforms are needed to mitigate such costs.

The existing literature is virtually unanimous in finding that trade reforms increase the incomes of the poor as a group. More-

over, the transitional adjustment costs are found to be generally small relative to the overall benefits. Hertel and Winters[12] for example, collect a series of studies that estimate that the effect of complete tariff liberalization on poverty (as measured by the threshold of US$1 per day) in developing countries would be to reduce the poverty headcount index by 5.0 to 6.5 percentage points over a 10-year period. These studies also indicate that effects can be diverse across countries, with poverty potentially increasing in some countries as a result of preference erosion and trade diversion. Another set of recent studies that focuses on a sample of small, low-income countries points to small but generally positive effects of multilateral trade liberalization on poverty.[13] The studies collected in Harrison[14] also find positive effects of trade liberalization on poverty.

FIGURE 4.7 Higher growth is associated with lower trade restrictiveness

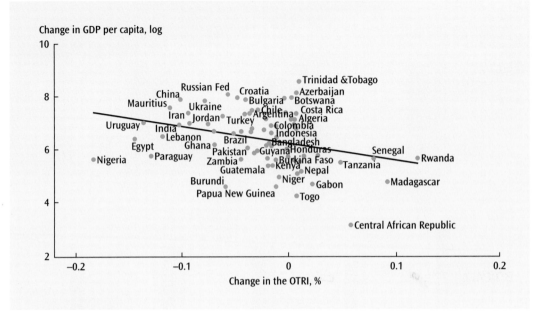

Source: World Bank staff estimates.

Besides pointing to a positive correlation between trade liberalization and poverty reduction, these studies highlight the importance of complementary policies in realizing the full benefits of trade reforms for growth and poverty reduction.

Behind-the-Border Policies Matter

The magnitude of the gains to poor countries from global trade reforms depends on actions to create new and more remunerative jobs and move producers out of subsistence agriculture. Trade reform by itself will not ensure these outcomes. Domestic supply constraints are a major reason for the lack of trade growth and diversification in many of the poorest developing countries. Without action to improve supply capacity, reduce transport costs for remote areas, increase farm productivity, and improve the investment climate, trade opportunities cannot be fully exploited and the potential gains from trade will not be maximized. The reforms that may be called for span several areas, mostly "behind the border."

Research in this area identifies in particular actions to move households out of subsistence production and to improve productivity. Given that poverty is concentrated in rural areas that depend heavily on agriculture, trade opportunities can raise incomes, but only if products are produced for the market. This may require active intervention to help households make the switch—through extension services, access to credit, and investments in infrastructure. Poor roads and ports, poorly performing customs, weaknesses in regulatory capacity, and limited access to finance and business services are all factors determining trade performance.

A major dimension of facilitating trade is action to reduce the burden of administrative hurdles—such as customs and tax procedures, clearance requirements, and cargo inspections. Djankov, Freund, and Cong[15] conclude that each day of delay caused by such hurdles reduces export volumes by 1 percent on average. A recent World Bank initiative provides comparable cross-country data measuring the quality of logistics performance implied by such regulatory policies and related infrastructure in a country (box 4.2). A database compiled as a result of this initiative documents that good trade logistics are critical for developing countries to improve their competitiveness, reap the benefits of globalization, and fight poverty more effectively in an increasingly integrated world.[16] Success in integrating into global supply chains starts with the ability of firms to connect to international markets and to move goods across borders rapidly, reliably, and cheaply. Countries with better performance on logistics experience higher growth in their openness (trade-to-GDP ratio; figure 4.8).

Services Policies

Many of the behind-the-border policies affecting the competitiveness of firms and farmers in a country are services-related. To be able to compete, firms in open economies need access to low-cost and high-quality producer services—telecommunications, transport and distribution services, financial intermediation, and so forth. Global outsourcing, production sharing, and offshoring depend on access to, and the cost and quality of, services.

Low-cost and high-quality telecommunications will generate economy-wide benefits, as the communications network is a

---

BOX 4.2   The World Bank Logistics Performance Index

Launched in November 2007, the Logistics Performance Index (LPI) is an interactive benchmarking tool created to help countries identify the challenges and opportunities they face in improving trade logistics. The LPI and its indicators provide the first in-depth assessment of the logistics gap among countries across several areas of performance.

Based on a worldwide survey of global freight forwarders and express carriers, the LPI develops measures of the logistics friendliness of the countries surveyed. Feedback from the survey is supplemented with objective data on the performance of key components of the logistics chain. The LPI provides a comprehensive picture of countries' supply chain performance. It is built on the following seven areas of performance:

- Efficiency of the clearance process by customs and other border agencies
- Quality of transport and information technology infrastructure for logistics
- Ease and affordability of arranging international shipments
- Competence of the local logistics industry
- Ability to track and trace international shipments
- Domestic logistics costs
- Timeliness of shipments in reaching destination

The LPI and its indicators point to significant differences in logistics performance across countries and regions. Among developing countries, the best logistics performers are also those experiencing economic growth led by manufactured exports. A key insight from the survey of logistics professionals is that, while costs and timeliness are of paramount importance, traders are primarily concerned with the overall reliability of the supply chain. Costs related to hedging against uncertainty have become a significant part of logistics costs in many developing countries. Country performance can be greatly influenced by the weakest link in the supply chain: poor performance in just one or two areas can have serious repercussions on overall competitiveness.

The LPI also suggests that policy makers should look beyond the traditional "trade facilitation" agenda that focuses on road infrastructure and information technology in customs to also focus on improving the operation of logistics services markets and the public agencies active in border control. This demands a more integrated, comprehensive approach to reforms all along the supply chain. International companies can bring global knowledge, but the support of local exporters, operators, and public agencies is crucial.

Source: World Bank (2007a) and http://www.worldbank.org/lpi.

FIGURE 4.8   Countries with better trade logistics have higher trade-to-GDP growth

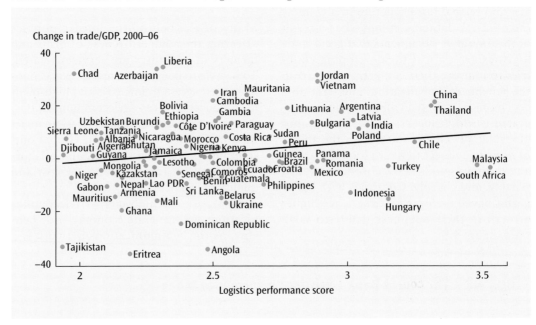

Source: World Bank staff estimates.

transport mechanism for information services and other products that can be digitized. Telecommunications are crucial to the dissemination and diffusion of knowledge—the spread of the Internet and the dynamism it has lent to economies around the world are telling testimony to the importance of telecommunications services. Similarly, transport services affect the cost of shipping goods and movement of workers within and between countries. Business services such as accounting, engineering, consulting, and legal services reduce transaction costs associated with the operation of financial markets and the enforcement of contracts, and are a channel through which business process innovations are transmitted across firms in an industry or across industries. Retail and wholesale distribution services are a vital link between producers and consumers. Health and education services are key inputs into—and determinants of—the stock and growth of human capital.

Permitting foreign firms to compete in services markets is a powerful potential

channel for technology diffusion as well as a mechanism to reduce costs and/or raise the quality of services. A research project by the World Bank is seeking to compile data on the extent to which policies discriminate against foreign services providers, thereby providing a complement to the OTRI and related measures of trade restrictiveness pertaining to trade in goods. To date, surveys have been conducted in 32 developing countries and comparable information obtained for 24 OECD countries, covering five key sectors: financial services (banking and insurance), telecommunications, retail distribution, transportation, and professional services.[17] In each sector, the survey covered the most relevant modes of supplying that service: cross-border trade in services (mode 1 in WTO parlance) in financial, transportation, and professional services; commercial presence or foreign direct investment (FDI; mode 3) in each services sector; and the presence of service-supplying individuals (mode 4) in professional services. Survey results to date are summarized in figure 4.9.[18]

The survey reveals that developing countries have significantly liberalized a range of service sectors over the last couple of decades, but in some areas protection persists. In fact, the overall pattern of policies across sectors is increasingly similar in developing and industrial countries. In telecommunications, public monopolies seem in most countries a relic of history, with at least some measure of competition introduced in both mobile and fixed services. In banking too, domination by state-owned banks has given way to increased openness to the presence of foreign and private banks. Very few countries restrict foreign investment in retail. However, even though the markets for these services are now more competitive, they are in most countries some distance from being truly contestable. In telecommunications, governments continue to limit the number of providers and, particularly in Asia, the extent of foreign ownership. In both banking and insurance, the allocation of new licenses often remains opaque and highly discretionary. In retail, a range of domestic regulations, such as zoning laws, frequently impedes entry in both developing and industrial countries.

Transport and professional services remain a bastion of protectionism in high-income countries and are also subject to high barriers in developing countries (figure 4.10). In maritime transport, even though international shipping is today quite open, entry into cabotage and auxiliary services such as cargo handling is in many countries restricted. In air transport, restrictions on foreign investment coexist with limitations on cabotage and cross-border trade—though conditions for freight transport are much more liberal than those for passenger transport. In professional services, even though there is increased scope for international trade through electronic means, in which many developing countries are also beginning to participate, there remain restrictions on foreign presence. In general, accounting and the practice of international law tend to be more open than auditing and the practice

FIGURE 4.9 Restrictiveness of services trade policies, 2007

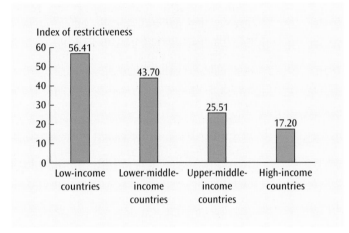

Source: World Bank staff estimates.

FIGURE 4.10 Services trade restrictiveness indices, by sector

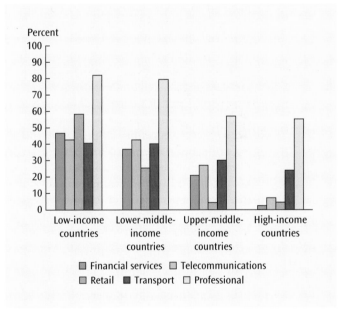

Source: World Bank staff estimates.

of domestic law. The restrictions on foreign investment are far less stringent than the restrictions on the presence of foreign professionals.

The available evidence suggests that increased openness in telecommunications, in combination with dramatic technological progress, has led to striking improvements in access, variety, and quality of services.[19] In retail distribution and transport too, liberalization has generally produced significant benefits for both upstream producers and downstream consumers. Outsourcing of professional and other business services is producing significant cost savings for importing countries and generating new employment opportunities in exporting countries, though the former must also contend with the costs of adjustment. In financial services, while greater openness has eventually improved the efficiency of services, in some cases premature liberalization has had adverse economic effects both on financial stability and on access to services for the poor and small enterprises.[20] This points to the need for liberalization to be accompanied by complementary reforms, ranging from improved prudential and pro-competitive regulation to the implementation of policies to widen access to services along the lines of universal access mechanisms in telecommunications.

While most services liberalization has so far been undertaken unilaterally, services are also the subject of multilateral and regional trade negotiations. These negotiations have led to greater certainty of policy by inducing countries to begin to lock in unilateral liberalization, but the negotiations have so far produced little additional market opening. Bringing services on to center stage in the WTO's Doha negotiations could contribute to deeper reform. These negotiations offer WTO members a key opportunity to secure access to foreign markets and to spur domestic reforms. A negotiated outcome that is balanced, is commercially relevant, and supports development would have four elements: a promise not to impose new restrictions on trade in services, thereby dispelling the specter of protectionism that hangs over outsourcing of business services; a commitment to eliminate barriers to FDI, either immediately or gradually where regulatory inadequacies need to be remedied; a credible promise of international assistance where needed for complementary reforms; and an agreement to allow greater freedom

of international movement for individual service providers in order to fulfill specific services contracts.

Aid for Trade

In the 2005 WTO Hong Kong ministerial declaration, trade ministers called on bilateral and multilateral donors to increase the resources for aid for trade, endorsed the enhancement of the Integrated Framework for LDCs, and established a Task Force on Aid for Trade. The task force highlighted the centrality of recipient-country ownership and political leadership, with governments incorporating trade more centrally into their development and poverty reduction strategies. It provided a definition of aid for trade and recommended, among other things, monitoring and evaluation to ensure that pledges on aid for trade were fulfilled through a body in the WTO, which was to undertake a periodic global review of aid-for-trade delivery.[21]

Several regional meetings were held in the fall of 2007 to encourage information exchange about best practices and to facilitate collective action to maximize the benefits of aid for trade. The regional meetings were followed by the first WTO global aid-for-trade review in November 2007. This global review highlighted the need for improvements in aid for trade and the importance of improving data on aid flows and performance indicators (outcomes) for both donors and recipients, as well as increasing country, regional, and sector focus. Follow-up events planned for 2008/09 will shift from awareness raising and mobilization to monitoring of aid for trade and assessments of progress in implementation.

Progress has been made in trade-related technical assistance for the LDCs with the establishment of the Enhanced Integrated Framework (EIF) in May 2007, with a new executive secretariat to support its operations.[22] Operational decisions are to be made by a new EIF board, comprising voting representatives of three bilateral donors and three LDCs, with a view to making the mechanism more country-driven. To date, over US$100 million has been pledged by bilateral donors to the EIF trust fund. Several challenges remain, including providing adequate in-country support to the IF process, linking the WTO-based EIF secretariat to in-country processes, selecting a manager for the EIF trust fund, and establishing clear lines of responsibility for financial management, monitoring, and evaluation.

Global monitoring of donor pledges for aid for trade in a consistent fashion has proved a challenging exercise. First, donors each use their own definitions of aid for trade. For example, while EU pledges are limited to trade policy and regulations and trade development, U.S. and Japanese pledges contain activities relating to infrastructure. Second, reporting total amounts for economic infrastructure projects that serve both traded and nontraded sectors presents a significant overestimation of the actual volume of aid for trade.

For consistency purposes, this section follows the WTO-OECD first Global Review of Aid for Trade and reports aid-for-trade commitments as defined in the existing centralized OECD Development Assistance Committee (DAC) Creditor Reporting System (CRS). The CRS categories capture only three of the six categories identified by the Task Force on Aid for Trade: trade policy and regulation, economic infrastructure (as a proxy for the category "trade-related infrastructure"), and productive capacity building (which includes the category "trade development"). The reported amounts are, therefore, an imperfect proxy and tend to overestimate total aid for trade-related infrastructure; at the same time budget support associated with support for trade reforms has been excluded. The CRS is being fine-tuned to better reflect the trade component of aid and to include suitable proxies for the categories "trade-related adjustment" and "other trade-related needs."

Leaving aside the methodological limitations, aid-for-trade flows increased by some $2 billion in real terms during 2006, or 10 percent relative to the baseline for 2002–05 established by the task force (table 4.6). Total aid for trade during the 2002–06 period, on the basis of the OECD CRS definition, was roughly 33 percent of total sector-allocable ODA, below the 35 percent registered in 2002.

Japan and the United States dominated global aid-for-trade delivery in terms of volume with $4.9 billion and $4.4 billion in 2006, respectively. In the case of the U.S. aid for trade, this represents a 25 percent increase over the 2002–05 average, much of it devoted to the reconstruction efforts in Iraq and Afghanistan. Other important bilateral donors included France, Germany, the Netherlands, Spain, and the United Kingdom. The European Communities was the largest multilateral donor in 2006, having increased its aid for trade to $3.1 billion (15 percent of total aid for trade), up from $2.5 billion on average during 2002–05. The World Bank, through the International Development Association (IDA), was the fourth largest provider of concessional aid for trade in 2006, and the largest multilateral provider of such assistance during the 2002–06 period—plus it was the largest overall donor to low-income countries, accounting for 24 percent of all aid for trade received by these countries. The Asian Development Bank and the African Development Bank were also important providers of aid for trade in their respective regions and were among the top 10 donors globally. The 10 largest bilateral donors and multilateral agencies funded 90 percent of global aid for trade activities in 2006. In general, a greater portion of multilateral aid for trade goes to low-income countries than bilateral aid for trade.

In terms of composition, aid to support the development of economic infrastructure and productive capacity building dominated overall volumes of aid for trade, at 55 percent and 42 percent, respectively, during the 2002–06 period. At 3.4 percent, aid for trade policy and regulations, usually delivered through

TABLE 4.6 Aid for trade, 2006, and annual average, 2002–06
Official Development Assistance commitments of DAC donors and multilateral agencies
US$ millions, 2005 constant prices

					Annual average, 2002–06		
	Economic infrastructure	Trade policy and regulations	Productive capacity building	Total aid for trade, 2006	As a share of total aid for trade (%)	As a share of total aid for trade received by LICs (%)	As a share of donor sector allocable ODA (%)
Top 10 bilateral donors in 2006							
Denmark	160	0	182	229	1.6	2.7	36
France	424	3	341	909	3.3	3.2	22
Germany	608	14	694	1,845	6.0	4.1	29
Japan	3,738	64	1,007	4,883	22.4	21.3	61
Netherlands	85	26	422	842	2.7	1.1	22
Norway	90	10	150	300	1.2	1.2	19
Spain	295	1	142	660	2.0	0.5	36
Sweden	100	17	122	317	1.1	1.0	17
United Kingdom	281	37	410	612	3.3	3.3	21
United States	2,087	237	1,690	4,391	17.2	7.9	26
Main multilateral donors in 2006							
European Communities	1,365	217	1,003	3,133	11.9	12.0	36
World Bank (IDA)	1,759	32	1,274	2,775	14.2	24.0	46
African Development Bank	280	43	280	513	2.6	4.4	44
Asian Development Bank	274	31	332	373	3.0	5.4	45
Total aid for trade, all donors	*12,035*	*717*	*9,106*	*23,005*	*100*	*100*	*33*

Source: OECD Creditor Reporting System.

technical assistance, accounted for the smallest share.

Iraq, India, Vietnam, Afghanistan, and Indonesia were the top five recipients of aid for trade in 2006, accounting for almost 30 percent of the total. Asian countries received almost half of all aid for trade ($10.6 billion on average during 2002–06) (figure 4.11).[23] Africa followed with 30 percent ($6.5 billion). Ethiopia, with 2.4 percent of total aid for trade, was the only country from Sub-Saharan Africa in the top 10 recipients of aid for trade. The predominance of Asia largely reflects the volume of aid received for economic infrastructure—over two-thirds of total aid for trade in the region. Even when excluding large recipi-

ent countries in Asia, Africa lags behind: the average Asian country receives more than double the aid for trade of the average African country. Low-income countries, including LDCs, received only about half of the total aid-for-trade commitments in 2002–06, of which the LDCs received slightly more than half.

Trade Policies, Climate Change, and Sustainable Development

International technology transfer can be a significant and cost-effective component of climate change mitigation and adaptation efforts. There already exist a number of low-carbon technologies to combat climate change. International trade can play a role in the reduction of greenhouse gases and the use of more energy-efficient production technologies by allowing firms to import environmentally friendly technology embodied in equipment, thus allowing more efficient production and consumption. Trade can also help with adaptation, by enhancing access to relevant technologies—such as genetically modified seeds and efficient irrigation methods—and by encouraging technology transfer and dissemination of knowledge and know-how on available techniques.

An important first step toward the adoption of more environmentally friendly technologies would be to reduce trade restrictions on imports of environmental goods and services. Many such products face relatively high levels of trade restrictiveness, especially in developing countries (figure 4.12).[24]

In general, rates of trade restrictiveness confronting such products are similar to those affecting other manufactured products. However, the negative spillovers associated with policies that restrict trade in such technologies increase their welfare cost. Reducing barriers that have protection of domestic industry as their main objective will help to encourage the adoption of more efficient technologies and more environmentally friendly forms of energy.

A recent study that analyzes global trade in four technology groups—high-efficiency and clean coal technologies, efficient lighting, solar photovoltaics, and wind power—finds that tariffs and NTMs are significant impediments to the diffusion of clean energy technologies in developing countries.[25] It concludes that liberalizing trade in these clean energy technologies could result in large increases in trade volumes, as illustrated in table 4.7. Liberalization of key climate-friendly technologies could be taken up as part of the ongoing WTO Doha Round negotiations on environmental goods and services (box 4.3).

Trade liberalization is just one aspect of enhancing access to cleaner technology by rapidly growing developing economies.

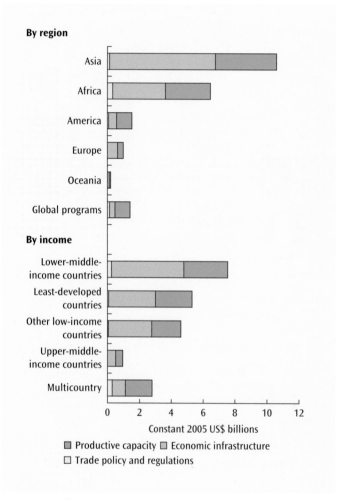

FIGURE 4.11 Distribution of aid for trade by income group and region, and by category, average 2002–06

Source: OECD Creditor Report System and OECD/WTO Trade Capacity Building Database
Note: Asia includes East and South.

Streamlining of intellectual property rights, investment rules, and other domestic policies will further aid in widespread assimilation of existing clean technologies and facilitate long-term investments in emerging technology areas. Trade serves as a major channel for international technology transfer to developing countries, but in many cases FDI may be more important. Weak intellectual property rights in developing countries may inhibit diffusion of specific technologies beyond the project level, and FDI in general may be subject to various restrictive regulations. Many

FIGURE 4.12   Environmental goods confront significant trade restrictiveness

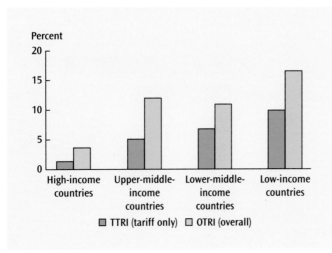

Source: World Bank staff estimates.

TABLE 4.7   Increase in trade volumes from liberalizing clean energy technologies
percent

Technology option	Eliminating tariffs only	Eliminating tarrifs and nontariff measures
Clean coal technology	3.6	4.6
Wind power generation	12.6	22.6
Solar power generation	6.4	13.5
Efficient lighting technology	15.4	63.6
All four technologies	**7.2**	**13.5**

Source: World Bank (2007b).

developing countries also have weak environmental standards, low pollution charges, and weak enforcement capacity. This reduces the incentives to acquire and apply more sophisticated clean energy technologies.

Determining the set of goods or technologies that can help mitigate or adapt to climate change is complex. For example, in principle, the removal of trade taxes on imports of biofuels can help improve sustainability by reducing greenhouse gas emissions and pollutants from tailpipe emissions, but this depends very much on the feedstock used, the alternative use of the land used to produce the feedstock, and the biofuel production process.

Current first-generation biofuel technologies produce two types of fuel in significant quantities: ethanol (either from starch crops such as maize, wheat, or cassava or from sugar crops) and biodiesel (from vegetable oils or animal fats). There is a general consensus that producing ethanol from maize results at best in only a small reduction in greenhouse gas emissions and may not reduce such emissions at all, while production of ethanol from sugarcane juice or molasses will have a more beneficial impact on emissions. Production of certain biodiesels may increase emissions, with impacts a function of the feedstock used (e.g., palm oil produced on land that was previously in tropical forests).

From the perspective of greenhouse gas emissions, trade policy should be targeting the use of the most efficient biofuels. However, determining this is not that simple. In addition to the greenhouse gas emission impacts—on which research comes to different conclusions—there are other costs to be considered. These include the loss of biodiversity when cropland is expanded, the increased use of irrigation water, and the increased fertilizer runoff from crop production. The overall environmental benefit of biofuels needs to consider the full range of benefits and costs, and this has not yet been done. Such costs also include the negative impacts on the welfare of net food-importing countries, which can be important. New technologies that are currently being developed are expected to be able to convert cellulose into biofuels, resulting in net reductions in greenhouse gas emissions that approach those from the reduction in fossil fuel use. While these technologies are not expected to be commercially available for at least a decade, if they become available there is likely to be a major shift in the production of biofuels toward crops that produce large volumes of biomass, such as sugarcane, and away from grain, fats, and oils.

Suggestions have been made in some quarters that tariff policy should be used to raise the cost of imported products that are

---

BOX 4.3 WTO negotiations and climate change

The 2001 Doha Ministerial Declaration (Paragraph 31 (iii)) called for negotiations on "the reduction or, as appropriate, elimination of tariff and non-tariff barriers to environmental goods and services," with a view to enhancing the mutual supportiveness of trade, environment, and development. All WTO members agree that environmental goods liberalization should be geared toward improving the environment. However, not much progress has been made on this front because of differing views on how to define *environmental goods*, a precondition for determining what goods to include for liberalization. Views also differ on how to approach liberalization in a manner that addresses the interests of both developed and developing countries.

High-income countries interested in liberalizing environmental goods support a list approach: identifying and submitting specific lists of goods and then negotiating the elimination or reduction of bound tariffs (and nontariff measures) permanently and on a most-favored-nation (MFN) basis. Some developing countries prefer a "project" approach, under which liberalization would be bound temporally and only for the duration of environmental projects that would benefit from liberalized imports of goods and services on an MFN basis. Although a number of countries have submitted lists with products of interest, not much progress has been made to date.

Building on the list approach, a recent U.S.-European Union proposal suggests that WTO members could first agree to eliminate tariffs and identified nontariff barriers to trade in specific climate-friendly products. The proposal provides for special and differential treatment for developing-country members, including longer phase-in periods. The objective is to have a zero-tariff world for climate-friendly goods in the near future and no later than 2013. But there are disagreements on what should be on the list. For example, the proposal was criticized by countries that believe that ethanol should be included in any list of climate-friendly technologies. A number of developing countries are also concerned about the impact of liberalization on existing domestic industries and in some cases on tariff revenue.

---

deemed to have been produced with environmentally inefficient technologies and encourage countries to participate in international agreements that they may otherwise abstain from.[26] Trade policy has a role to play in instances where governments (or a group of signatories to an environmental agreement) impose carbon taxes or equivalent instruments on domestic production to reduce greenhouse gas emissions. An equivalent tax on imports of the products that are subject to the carbon tax regime will ensure that local output is treated the same as foreign products. Such border tax adjustments can, in principle, help mitigation efforts without affecting international competitiveness while encouraging participation by others. However, border tax adjustments by themselves are second-best instruments—the first-best policy is to levy an environmental tax at the origin. Determining the appropriate (equivalent) tax for a given product is not straightforward. Taxes should accurately reflect the production process used by the exporting firm,

and information on this may not be available. Border tax adjustments also give rise to risks of hiding tariffs or export subsidies and may be inconsistent with WTO regulations.

Trade policy may sometimes have adverse consequences on the environment. For example, agricultural support programs have led to the use of production methods that are excessively polluting; fish subsidies have helped lead to depletion of ocean fish stocks, and by restricting imports of the most environmentally efficient biofuels and subsidizing consumption of less efficient local output, consumers are prevented from switching to less polluting types of energy that originate in parts of the world where the environmental costs of extraction are lower.

Similar considerations apply to proposals to penalize or avoid consumption of lower-cost imported food products that can be produced locally. Often this will not make any sense from an environmental perspective—in that even with the transport-related emissions and other costs, the net impact of imports on the environment will likely be less than if similar products are raised locally. As important, there is a significant danger that use of trade policy for environmental reasons will be captured by protectionist interests, result in retaliation, and further weaken the rules-based multilateral trading system. Proposals to adopt labeling systems that provide consumers with information on the carbon footprint of a product may be better solutions than the use of explicit trade sanctions, but they run the risk of arbitrariness, discrimination, and unintended consequences if not designed carefully (box 4.4).

Mitigation versus Adaptation

To date, the policy response to global warming has focused mostly on the steps that industrial and developing nations should take to mitigate greenhouse gas emissions. Far less attention has been paid to what developing countries should do to adapt to the consequences of foreseeable climate change in the coming decades. Developing countries, particularly the poorest ones, will be most vulnerable to climate change and increasing climate variability because they have the least capacity to adapt. Excessive floods, droughts, heat waves, and rising sea levels will amplify the already existing challenges posed by tropical or arid geography, a heavy dependence on rain-fed agriculture, rapid population growth, poverty, and a limited capacity to cope with an uncertain climate.

According to the recent Stern Review, "adaptation is the only response available for the impacts that will occur over the next several decades before mitigation measures can have an effect."[27] Unlike mitigation, adaptation will in most cases provide local benefits, realized without long lead times. Therefore, some adaptation will occur autonomously, as individuals respond to market signals and environmental changes. Some aspects of adaptation, such as major infrastructure decisions, will require greater foresight and planning. There are also some aspects of adaptation that require the provi-sion of public goods delivering global benefits, including improved information about the climate system and access to more climate-resilient crops and technologies.

International trade in adaptation technologies has received far less attention than the mitigation technologies discussed previously. A United Nations Framework Convention on Climate Change subsidiary body for scientific and technological advice recently invited submissions of adaptation technologies from national governments and other relevant organizations. The objective was to compile a list of technologies for adaptation at the regional, national, and local levels in different sectors and to identify common needs, concerns, and barriers related to their dissemination and transfer. Over 170 technologies were identified as a part of this exercise, with the majority of the technologies being relevant to the agricultural sector, followed closely by those pertaining to the water resources sector.[28] Other identifiable sectors were coastal zones, health, biodiversity, and infrastructure.

The technologies were classified as either hard, such as drought-resistant crop varieties, seawalls, and irrigation technologies, or soft, such as crop rotation patterns. These broad categories of hard and soft technologies were further subdivided into traditional, modern, and high technology. Traditional (indigenous) technologies that have been applied to adapt to weather hazards include methods to build floating vegetable gardens and dikes. Examples of modern technologies include techniques to produce new chemical products such as fertilizers, pesticides, and solvents; improved designs (e.g., of sanitation systems, housing, and commercial buildings); and technologies to produce new crop varieties (e.g., hybrid corn) and reduce water use (e.g., drip irrigation). High technology includes some of the more recently developed technologies resulting from scientific advances, including in information and communications technology, earth observation systems, and geographic information systems.

Many adaptation technologies are in the realm of services rather than goods.

BOX 4.4 Will carbon labeling help or hinder developing-country trade?

Carbon labeling is increasingly attracting popular attention. It offers consumers and companies the opportunity to participate in the fight against global warming by providing information on the total greenhouse gas emissions that a given product generates. While carbon labeling is mainly discussed in developed countries, it can have major impacts on developing countries. The choice of measurement methodologies and of control systems—needed to convince consumers and companies that the measurements are unbiased—can have a major bearing on the competitiveness of developing-country producers.

Some companies in high-income countries are already moving forward with carbon labeling. For example, the U.K. supermarket Tesco has announced that it will use carbon labeling on all its products. The idea is quickly spreading to continental Europe. In the United States, Wal-Mart, the world's biggest retailer, has announced that it is measuring the emissions of selected products. Eventually, its suppliers will be rated by the use of a carbon scorecard.

Designing the appropriate scheme is no small challenge, as carbon labeling is highly technical and data-demanding. To be development-friendly, carbon labeling needs to accurately reflect developing countries' advantages in low carbon emissions wherever they exist. For example, developing-country workers may walk to work or use communal transport, while in developed countries people often drive in their cars. Such differences have potentially large implications on both global warming and developing countries' prospects, depending on whether or not these differences are accurately reflected in carbon labeling. Decisions about which activities in the production chain to include in the analysis are, therefore, crucial from both a scientific and a development perspective. Schemes that concentrate on only specific parts of the production chain will generally be very misleading. Carbon labeling schemes may also have differential impacts, depending on the size of firms. The more complex the schemes, the greater the difficulty small and poor producers in developing countries are likely to encounter in selling their products and benefiting from market access opportunities.

Emission efficiency will likely become a key parameter of competitiveness in a climate-constrained world. This will have differential impacts on countries, depending on their specific circumstances. In agriculture, for example, many developing countries use traditional technology and enjoy a warm climate and, therefore, use few modern inputs like nitrogen-based fertilizer (which cause emissions of one of the most harmful greenhouse gases) and little fuel (with associated emissions of carbon dioxide). However, these countries are often located far from major export markets and thus require more fuel-consuming transportation. Emission-efficient supply chains demand that the advantages of labor-intensive techniques and sunshine (as opposed to developed-country mechanization and heated greenhouses) outweigh the disadvantage of transport-related emissions. Analyses of greenhouse gas emission throughout the supply chain suggest that in many cases products coming from far away may cause lower emissions than products sourced locally.

Source: Brenton, Edwards, and Jensen (2008).

Whether they concern services or goods, liberalization of trade may be complicated by non-environmental considerations and objectives. Examples are dual-use technologies, political sensitivities regarding agricultural liberalization, as well as differences in views regarding the risks associated with the use of—and trade in—genetically modified organisms. However, many of these technologies are not affected by such considerations and can be prioritized along with the mitigation-related products and technologies for liberalization.

Notes

1. WTO 2007.

2. LDC exports of oil grew by 20 percent; exports of other merchandise grew by 14 percent.

3. For example, Francois, Hoekman, and Manchin 2006.

4. Nigeria, Republic of Congo, Gabon, Cook Islands, Federated States of Micronesia, Nauru, Niue, Palau, Marshall Islands, and Tonga.

5. Policies affecting trade and investment in services are discussed in a subsequent section of this chapter.

6. In practice, identification of such problems must be done by national administrations. World

Bank staff have interacted with several governments that classified excise taxes as import duties in national tariff schedules. As a result of such interactions, the data have been corrected.

7. The OTRI and TTRI are calculated as a weighted sum of ad valorem tariffs and ad valorem equivalents of specific duties, and nontariff measures (for the OTRI), where weights are import volumes and import demand elasticities (Kee, Nicita, and Olarreaga 2008a, 2008b). The OTRIs by country and the data used to calculate the OTRI are posted on the DECRG Trade Research Web site under "data and statistics"; see http://go.worldbank.org/C5VQJIV3H0.

8. See, for example, Findlay and O'Rourke 2007, 396ff.

9. See http://www.oecd.org/document/0/0,3343, en_2649_33773_39508672_1_1_1_1,00.html.

10. The NRA is similar to the PSE in that it includes the effects of both farm output and farm input price distortions, but it also includes exchange rate distortions, and it is expressed as a percentage of total farm production valued at undistorted rather than distorted prices.

11. The full set of results from this project will be published in the second half of 2008. A global overview volume (Anderson 2008) will be complemented by four regional volumes, one each for Africa (Anderson and Masters 2008), Asia (Anderson and Martin 2008), Latin America and the Caribbean (Anderson and Valdés 2008) and Europe's transition economies plus Turkey (Anderson and Swinnen 2008). Details of the research project methodology and its working papers are available at http://www.worldbank.org/agdistortions.

12. Hertel and Winters 2006.

13. Hoekman and Olarreaga 2007.

14. Harrison 2006.

15. Djankov, Freund, and Cong 2006.

16. World Bank 2007a.

17. The sectors are further disaggregated into banking (retail and merchant), insurance (life, nonlife, and reinsurance), road transport, railway shipping, maritime shipping and auxiliary services, air transport (freight and passengers), accounting, auditing, and legal services. See Gootiz and Mattoo 2008.

18. Results of the survey are summarized in an index of restrictiveness. For each sector and mode of supply the openness of policy toward foreign suppliers is mapped on a 5-point scale ranging from 0 (for no restrictions) to 1 (highly restricted), with three intermediate levels of restrictiveness (0.25. 0.50 and

0.75). Sectoral results are aggregated across modes of supply using weights that reflect judgments of the relative importance of the different modes for a sector. For example, mode 4 (temporary movement of suppliers) is important for professional services but not for telecommunications, whereas mode 3 is the dominant mode of contesting a market. Sectoral restrictiveness indexes are aggregated using sectoral GDP shares as weights. The country income group indexes are derived using GDP weights for the countries in the sample.

19. Hoekman (2006) and Hoekman and Mattoo (2008) survey the recent literature and empirical evidence; the contributions to Mattoo, Stern, and Zanini (2008) analyze the economics of trade in the various services sectors from a development perspective.

20. World Bank 2008; Mattoo and Payton 2007.

21. The task force identified six categories for aid for trade: (i) trade policy and regulations, (ii) trade development, (iii) trade-related infrastructure, (iv) building of productive capacity, (v) trade-related adjustment, and (vi) other trade-related needs. The task force also proposed a 2002–05 baseline on the basis of which to assess additionality and monitor the adequacy of provided funding.

22. The Integrated Framework is a multiagency, multidonor program to assist the LDCs in addressing national competitiveness priorities. The enhancement of the IF was recommended by a 2005 task force.

23. In the OECD CRS database, Asia includes Middle East Asia, South and Central Asia, and Far East Asia.

24. Environmental goods are products that result in less use of energy or generate energy in more environmentally efficient ways. For the list of environmental products and technologies considered in this chapter, see http://econ.worldbank.org/programs/trade.

25. World Bank 2007b.

26. Draft climate change legislation in the EU includes proposals to impose restrictions on imports unless an international agreement subjecting all industrialized countries to similar climate change mitigation measures is reached. According to the proposal, such a "carbon equalization system" could take the form of a requirement that foreign companies doing business in Europe obtain emissions permits alongside European competitors. Similar proposals have also been tabled in the U.S. Congress (Brewer 2008).

5

Leveraging through the International Financial Institutions

The past year has seen a continuation of a trend of diminishing importance of the international financial institutions (IFIs) in terms of their net financial flows. The multilateral development banks (MDBs) now account for only 8 percent of net official development assistance (ODA). But this does not necessarily imply declining relevance. The true measure of the impact of IFIs in a rapidly changing global environment must consider the leverage—beyond financing—in achieving collective action on development and implementing an ever-more-important global and regional public goods agenda. The IFIs should be assessed on results, on policy change at the country level, on institutional learning, and on harmonization and improved effectiveness of the aid architecture. Through their country operations, as well as their regional and global-level work, the IFIs are supporting the MDGs, linking these with poverty reduction strategies, medium-term expenditure frameworks, annual budgets, specific investments, policies, and programs in each country.

The IFIs are operating in a world of rapid change. Developing countries generated 70 percent of global growth in 2007.[1] Three-fifths of the developing world's population is living in countries that are growing strongly and where poverty is being reduced rapidly.

Some large developing countries are now global exporters of capital, technology, and entrepreneurial know-how. Yet, there are some 40 countries, with one-fifth of the developing world's population, with low incomes, slow growth, and poor progress on poverty reduction. Some countries are seeing a boom based on natural resources or manufactured exports. Others are suffering from deteriorating terms of trade or are losing market share in traditional exports. In this multipolar world, the IFIs face an array of clients with vastly different needs and aspirations.

Nowhere is this change seen more clearly than in financial markets. Eighty-six developing countries have ratings on their international bonds and have access to global capital pools in rich and developing countries. Flows of capital, goods, and technology to most developing countries are now dominated by market forces rather than intermediated through official aid agencies. Many multinational firms are displaying greater social activism through their direct activities and through corporate philanthropy. With thousands of international nongovernmental organizations (NGOs), tens of thousands of developing-country NGOs, and hundreds of thousands of community-based organizations in developing countries, the number of actors in development has grown significantly.

Many of these new organizations are focused on specific issues of hunger, environment, education, health, or children—the so-called vertical funds that have become important. These agencies can promote efficiency by providing specialized expertise and focused results, but they can also reduce effectiveness by complicating efforts to achieve policy coherence and by distorting national priorities.

There is broad recognition that the development architecture must change in response to these global trends. The year 2008 represents the midpoint for achievement of the Millennium Development Goals (MDGs). Ministers and senior officials from over 150 countries will meet in September this year, in Accra, Ghana, at the Third High-Level Forum on Aid Effectiveness to recommend actions to ensure faster, broader, and deeper implementation of the Paris Declaration principles. They will also meet in Doha, Qatar, in December to follow up on the financing for development arrangements initiated at Monterrey, Mexico, in 2002. These two events are likely to highlight that greater urgency is needed to scale up financing for development and improve aid effectiveness.

In 2007 IFIs continued the process of shifting strategies in response to the changed global environment. They defined new priorities for differentiated clients, introduced new lending and nonlending instruments, and added more emphasis to regional and global public goods to complement their country-based approaches. At the same time, the IFIs continue to play their traditional roles in helping countries manage market turbulence and high and volatile commodity prices, as they are currently experiencing, and providing financing, knowledge, and technical assistance to countries.

MDB operations increased in volume in 2007, with a record $49 billion in gross disbursements, reflecting higher concessional flows and nonconcessional, nonguaranteed flows to the private sector. Total net nonconcessional flows turned slightly positive in 2007 after four years of being large and negative. Additional financing was provided by the leverage obtained through cofinancing and guarantee operations, which have been growing.

Replenishment of concessional windows in 2007 constitutes a significant achievement. Growth in MDB nonsovereign, nonguaranteed disbursements shows a shift toward greater support for the private sector. Africa, Asia, infrastructure, and higher education are areas seeing the most rapid increase in financial support. International Development Association (IDA) financing for primary education fell. Evaluations suggest that there has been a significant underinvestment in regional projects.

The IFIs are devoting large and growing amounts of their own and trust-fund resources to knowledge activities and are decentralizing operations to strengthen dissemination. But the practical experiences—both successes and failures—of middle-income developing countries are only just starting to be tapped. There appears to be strong demand for IFI knowledge services from all types of clients, but the business model for financing knowledge needs to evolve. IFI revenues traditionally are based on lending and may not easily be deployed in middle-income countries where lending has declined or for regional and global public knowledge goods.

IFI results improved in 2007, in terms of selectivity, harmonization, and managing for results. But much remains to be done in terms of strengthening relevance and enhancing support to meet the MDGs. Although there are multiple IFI assessments, including self-assessments, these are noncomparable and provide mixed results.

In 2007 there is evident progress toward strengthening developing-country platforms: 13 percent of low-income countries are deemed to have fully developed operational strategies, while another 67 percent have taken action to develop such strategies. In the former group of countries, a shift toward risk management approaches in delivery mechanisms rather than ex ante control mechanisms would permit greater use of country systems and speed disbursements without necessarily sacrificing effectiveness. The issues are more challenging in roughly 20 percent of countries—including most fragile states—where only rudimentary elements of operational development strategies exist. Fiduciary and effectiveness problems limit country capacity to absorb larger IFI resources.

The increased focus on regional and global public goods is welcome but requires that IFIs adapt internal structures to complement country-based approaches. New organizational structures have been developed in 2007, such as departments for regional activities, dedicated climate change teams, and international partnerships for health and trade. Climate change and environmental management issues are being mainstreamed into country strategies. Effectively responding to the expanding global and regional public goods agenda will require continued adaptation and innovation.

New Strategic Frameworks

Each of the IFIs is adapting its strategy in light of global trends and recognition that more is needed to help many countries achieve the MDGs. Most countries face broader options in their financing, but low-income countries still receive little private capital (4 percent on average in 2000–05). Countries are also wrestling with issues of how to manage globalization in an inclusive and sustainable way, prompting them to demand more knowledge services from the IFIs. Globally, public goods in health, trade, financial stability, and the environment have taken on greater prominence, and the IFIs are being called upon to respond.

This year, the Asian Development Bank (ADB) discussed a report of an "eminent persons group" that laid out a long-term vision.[2] The World Bank Group issued a document describing its long-term strategic challenges, and its new president outlined a vision for the institution.[3] In 2006 the International Monetary Fund (IMF) released a medium-term strategy, aimed at modernizing surveillance, strengthening crisis prevention in emerging market countries, and clarifying its role in low-income countries. Building on this initiative, the Fund is currently refocusing its operations while maintaining its strong engagement with low-income countries. The African Development Bank (AfDB) commissioned a high-level panel to advise on a medium-term strategic plan.[4] The European Bank for Reconstruction and Development (EBRD) implemented its Capital Resources Review 3 (approved in 2006). The Inter-American Development Bank (IDB) developed the Opportunities for the Majority and other new strategic initiatives.

Although each institution has tailored its new strategic direction to its own circumstances, there are some common themes. At the heart of the new strategies is a sense of rapid change in the world and of a shifting role of the IFIs to help countries manage change. The EBRD board has been explicit in "acknowledg[ing] the need for a change in the business model of the Bank in order to accomplish these objectives,"[5] but all IFIs have introduced important shifts in strategy in the last year (table 5.1).

These shifts fall under three broad categories:

- A shift in client and business focus to promote inclusive and sustainable globalization
- An orientation toward knowledge and learning services
- A greater emphasis on global and regional public goods

Inclusive and Sustainable Globalization

While many countries have benefited from globalization, the gains are uneven. The IFIs are adapting their strategies to the reality that the benefits of globalization have been unevenly distributed both across countries and within countries. There is more that can be done to connect the "bottom billion" to the global economy.

TABLE 5.1   Strategic shifts by IFIs

IFI	Inclusive and sustainable globalization	Knowledge and learning	Regional and global public goods
International Monetary Fund	Macro management of scaled-up aid Economic recovery assistance program Emergency postconflict assistance	Modernizing surveillance Multilateral and regional consultations Assessing vulnerabilities to capital flows Policy support instrument	Financial stability Sovereign Wealth Funds
World Bank Group	Africa Fragile states Scaling-up aid delivery Middle-income countries Private sector development	Provide world-class knowledge Knowledge sharing and learning between clients Governance and anticorruption	Climate change Health Trade International financial architecture
African Development Bank	Infrastructure Private sector development Middle-income countries Postconflict and postcrisis countries	Governance Economic and financial reforms African experiences and perspectives	Regional integration Environment and climate change
Asian Development Bank	Infrastructure Financial development	Regional knowledge hubs Governance and anticorruption Capacity development	Regional integration Regional financial markets Climate change Regional health programs
European Bank for Reconstruction and Development	Early and intermediate transition countries, the Russian Federation	Life in transition survey	Sustainable Energy Initiative Energy efficiency and climate change team
Inter-American Development Bank	Opportunities for the Majority Initiative Infrastructure Investment Fund Disaster Prevention Fund Water and Sanitation Initiative	New evaluability instrument	Sustainable Energy and Climate Change Initiative

Each of the IFIs is emphasizing selectivity in choosing clients that are most in need of assistance. Both the IMF and the World Bank Group are adapting their assistance to low-income countries to take into account the new challenges faced by these countries; both IFIs also have developed new forms of assistance to fragile states. The IMF is using a new instrument—the Policy Support Instrument—for supporting countries that have become mature stabilizers; this new instrument provides assistance for the development of more advanced regimes and tools for macroeconomic policy

making. The IMF has also reviewed its engagement in postconflict and fragile states and has proposed a systematic medium-term approach under an economic recovery assistance program that would be more closely aligned with specific country conditions and that would give greater emphasis to coordinated support for rebuilding capacity. The World Bank has established a framework for sustained engagement in fragile states and an action plan for Africa. The AfDB is focusing on postconflict and postcrisis countries. The EBRD is shifting its focus away from the EU-8 accession countries to the east and south to early and intermediate transition economies and the Russian Federation. The ADB and the World Bank Group have also reaffirmed the importance of continued assistance to middle-income countries, which still have major concentrations of poor in their lagging regions. The IDB has introduced its Opportunities for the Majority Initiative as a means to create strategic partnerships among key actors to improve the lot of the poorest groups in its borrowing member countries.

A private sector supply response is necessary for countries to reap the full benefits of globalization, and most of the MDBs are strengthening their private sector development programs. The EBRD has traditionally been strong in private sector operations. The International Finance Corporation (IFC) has launched a pilot program with IDA to promote small and medium enterprises in Sub-Saharan Africa. But private sector support can also require specific sectoral approaches. Several MDBs, including the ADB, the World Bank Group, the AfDB, and the IDB, have underscored the priority that needs to be given to infrastructure. The IDB's Infrastructure Investment Fund and the World Bank's Infrastructure Action Plan are examples of how these priorities have been translated into concrete actions. The private sector has also benefited from the reduced macroeconomic uncertainties in poor countries resulting from the consistent application of coherent and sustainable macroeconomic policies and associated structural reforms, debt relief under the Heavily Indebted Poor Countries (HIPC) and the Multilateral Debt Relief Initiatives (MDRI), and the application of the debt sustainability framework by the IMF and the World Bank.

Societies that successfully integrate globally also develop social mechanisms for taking care of the most vulnerable groups. Recently, a rash of natural disasters has underscored the risks that are faced by many of the poorest. The MDBs have become more active in disaster response. In addition to humanitarian assistance, the IDB has established a Disaster Prevention Fund to strengthen country capacity to identify natural disaster risks, design prevention and mitigation investments in high-risk areas, and improve early warning systems. The World Bank Group has established a new Caribbean disaster insurance fund.

Knowledge and Learning

All the IFIs have emphasized their knowledge and learning contributions to development and their desire to shift toward more knowledge-based institutions. But implementation of some of the changes has been controversial. The conventional wisdom about development effectiveness has been challenged both within and outside the IFIs. The IFIs are trying to diversify their instruments and approaches to reflect broader experiences with both success and failure in development, including lessons of experience from today's middle-income and poor countries and from the activities of other development actors like private foundations, international NGOs, and non-DAC (Development Assistance Committee) official donors. Marrying global and local knowledge remains a challenge for the IFIs.

Treatment of governance and corruption has been a more controversial area of the new knowledge and learning strategies. The World Bank, ADB, and the AfDB have elevated these issues to the top of the development discussion and are gaining experience with how to embed the lessons and research into operations, with country and sector selectivity and local capacity building. The World Bank has adopted an implementation plan on governance and anticorruption that has three objectives: promoting capable and accountable states and institutions; providing public services; and combating corruption.[6] It has also launched the Stolen Assets Recovery Initiative (StAR). The ADB's second governance and anticorruption plan has completed its first year of implementation, focusing on the assessment of public financial management, procurement, and corruption risks at the project, sector, and country levels. But the balance between fiduciary soundness and scaling up financing remains hard to manage, and the burden of accountability on MDBs and developing countries for maximizing development results by striking the correct balance is high. The World Bank's recent Detailed Implementation Review of five health projects in India provided valuable insights into the risks of fraud and corruption in development operations, which would be important for all development partners. In their action plans that respond to the review, the Government of India and the World Bank have instituted new procedures and systems to mitigate these risks. In the coming months, similar measures will be agreed upon and rolled out as needed to operations across the World Bank.

In the area of support for economic and financial reforms, the ADB and AfDB are building their capacities to advise countries. The IMF has started to modernize surveillance and hold multilateral and regional consultations. In June 2007 the Fund adopted a new Decision on Bilateral Surveillance over Members' Policies to upgrade the foundations of Fund bilateral surveillance. Under the new decision, the concept of external stability becomes an organizing principle for surveillance, bringing greater clarity and specificity to the principles guiding members' exchange rate policies. The Fund is also strengthening the analysis of linkages between macroeoconomic developments and financial markets and multilateral perspectives in bilateral surveillance. The World Bank has done much to reform the use of development policy lending and to improve support for policy and institutional reforms. Both the World Bank and the IMF have streamlined structural conditionality to reflect experiences with reform. The review of IMF conditionality conducted in 2005 showed that structural conditionality in Fund-supported programs has become more focused on macrocritical issues, more clearly formulated, and more closely linked to the core mandate of the IMF. A recent report by the IMF's Independent Evaluation Office on structural conditionality in Fund-supported programs confirms these findings but identifies scope for further progress, including a more rigorous justification for conditions and a better explanation in program documents of the link between a program's goals and the conditions.

The IFIs are also putting greater focus on evaluation as a tool for generating knowledge. The IDB is developing a new evaluation instrument for its knowledge work. The World Bank Group is implementing a development impact monitoring and evaluation program to learn more rigorously from its project experiences.

Several IFIs have strengthened their efforts to help countries generate transparent statistics on development results and address the perceived gap in the links among inputs, outputs, and outcomes. The EBRD's Life in Transition Survey is a recent example of new data collection. The IMF is leading the way with its Special Data Dissemination Standards and new tools, such as the DataMapper, to make data more accessible and usable. The ADB's Fund for Statistical Capacity Building in Asia Pacific (FASTCAP) is assisting countries with weak capacity by providing long-term technical assistance.

Regional and Global Public Goods

The IFIs are intensifying their work on regional and global public goods through direct interventions and by creating an enabling environment to leverage private sector efforts. Climate change and energy efficiency will receive greater priority from the World Bank Group, the IMF, ADB, and the AfDB. The EBRD has established a sustainable energy initiative and is the first MDB to establish a specialized team to address such issues with its Energy Efficiency and Climate Change Team. The IDB has also adopted a Sustainable Energy and Climate Change Initiative to promote alternative energy sources and clean fuels.

More broadly, the ADB and AfDB have underscored the importance of regional economic integration across a number of sectors and given support to emerging regional institutions. The ADB is paying special attention to regional financial market development, while the AfDB has emphasized infrastructural linkages, especially to give landlocked countries better access to international transport routes. The ADB is also helping to strengthen regional collaboration to address common threats, such as HIV/AIDS and avian influenza. At the global level, the IMF continues to play its role in promoting financial stability with its Global Financial Stability Reports, bilateral and multilateral surveillance, and a strengthened analysis of macrofinancial linkages. The IMF has also stepped up its analysis of the macroeconomic effects of climate change and the contribution fiscal policy can make in mitigation and adaptation to climate change. The World Bank Group is active in global health and trade issues as well.

New Collaborative Approaches

Cutting across these changes in strategic direction are new collaborative approaches being developed by all the IFIs to enhance cooperation with other donors. Many of the new players do not fit easily into existing modalities of donor coordination, which are centered around country-executed plans and programs. New vertical funds have expanded rapidly, disbursing about $7 billion over the last five years. These funds have a limited field presence, however, and set priorities at headquarters. Given the very different business models of the vertical funds, the challenges of coherence have grown. In response, the MDBs have boosted efforts to improve developing-country capacity to articulate national plans and poverty reduction strategies and to embed programs funded by vertical funds into these plans.

The complementarity of approaches can be seen in the World Bank's health sector strategy.[7] That document points to the false dichotomy between a focus on priority diseases (the core objective of health-oriented vertical funds) and a focus on strengthening health systems. Both focuses are required to achieve real health results, defined broadly

as saving and improving people's lives and avoiding extreme financial hardship caused by ill health. The World Bank strategy asserts that "financing no longer drives the relationship with client countries . . . it is the quality of the policy and technical dialogue which will define the Bank's contribution. . . ." The strategy repositions the World Bank to focus on strengthening health systems, where development assistance funds are relatively scarce. It embodies an approach that will be long term, country driven, and focused on institutional change, rather than on specific investment projects and technical, medical support. There is a clear definition of comparative advantage of the World Bank that forms the basis for a more effective division of labor among donors.

There is also considerable room for strengthening collaboration among IFIs. For instance, the main recommendations of the External Review Committee on IMF–World Bank Collaboration are to promote cooperation in crisis management, to improve integration and harmonization of work on fiscal and financial sector development issues, and to better coordinate technical assistance (box 5.1).

Operational Trends and Harmonization

IFIs provide resources for development, nonlending activities, capacity building, and research and evaluation. This section reviews operational trends in these areas and IFI efforts to harmonize and align their operations across agencies.

Financial Resources for Development

Demand for IFI financial services is mixed. With a buoyant global environment, in which private flows to developing countries may have approached $1 trillion in 2007, there has been significant net repayment of IFI loans in the last two years. In 2007 repayments to MDBs were almost the same size as nonconcessional gross flows. The

BOX 5.1 Bank-Fund Collaboration: Joint Management Action Plan

The Malan report, or more formally the report of the External Review Committee on World Bank–IMF Collaboration, released in February 2007, found strong foundations for Bank-Fund collaboration but no room for complacency. The report called for strengthening the culture of collaboration in the two institutions in several areas. Following informal board discussions in the Bank and the Fund, the Development Committee and the International Monetary and Financial Committee (IMFC) communiqués in Spring 2007 welcomed the report and said that ministers looked forward to seeing how the two institutions would take the recommendations forward.

In response, a Joint Management Action Plan (JMAP) has been developed, which draws on a staff survey, recommendations from six staff work streams, and a joint high-level staff retreat. The JMAP enumerated specific steps to strengthen collaboration, building on existing approaches rather than calling for dramatic changes or the addition of bureaucratic layers. The three steps were:

- Improve coordination on country issues through new procedures for country team coordination, including regular meetings on work programs, agreement on instruments and division of labor, and new systems for requesting and tracking inputs from the other institution
- Enhance communications through new electronic platforms for the sharing of focal point names, documents, mission schedules, and other information among staff in the two institutions working on country teams or on the financial sector, fiscal issues, and technical cooperation
- Reflect collaboration in staff and managerial performance reviews and replace the Joint Implementation Committee with an information and monitoring clearinghouse function anchored in central departments.

The JMAP aims to translate identified good-practice approaches to collaboration into standard practices. Of course, important differences will remain between the two institutions—from their distinctive cultures to more specific organizational and administrative differences—and successful implementation will depend on mutual understanding of and respect for these differences.

The JMAP was endorsed by the two boards in October 2007 and welcomed by the IMFC and Development Committee at the Annual Meetings. Implementation of the JMAP has begun. The goal is for most new systems to be operational in time for the preparation of FY09 budgets. The first progress report for the two boards will be prepared in time for the 2009 Annual Meetings.

Source: World Bank and IMF staffs.

share of MDB concessional flows in total ODA has fallen to a low point—just 8 percent in 2007.

But net flows are not an adequate measure of demand for IFI financial services. Overall, MDB gross disbursements in 2007—a proxy for new demand—reached a record volume of almost $49 billion (figure 5.1). Of this, $37 billion was in nonconcessional resources, up from $25 billion in 2005. This is the first sustained increase in demand for nonconcessional loans in the absence of a financial crisis in two decades.

Four stylized facts have emerged from the analysis of recent MDB flows:

- Demand for new nonconcessional sovereign loans remains generally flat, with large fluctuations depending on individual country circumstances.
- Demand for nonconcessional loans and guarantees to nonsovereign entities, mainly to the private sector, by the EBRD, the IFC, and regional development banks' (RDBs) private sector arms, has increased substantially.
- Supply of concessional lending has regained momentum in 2007. Record donor pledges for IDA 15 and the African Development Fund (AfDF) XI and promising replenishment discussions for the Asian Development Fund (AsDF) X suggest this trend should continue over the next years.
- Resources are increasingly flowing to Africa and Asia.

FIGURE 5.1 MDBs' gross disbursements, by type of flow and region, 2000–07

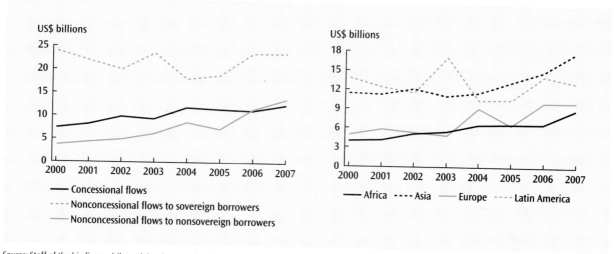

Source: Staff of the big five multilateral development banks

Nonconcessional Sovereign Flows

The IMF, as a provider of balance of payments assistance for countries with external financing difficulties, is expected to be affected most significantly by financial and economic conditions, and a reduction in its lending is a sign of developing-country successes in macroeconomic management. Developing countries repaid the IMF over $7 billion in 2007, for a total of about $135 billion over the last five years. The IMF's outstanding financial support to developing countries declined to about $15 billion at the end of 2007, its lowest level in 25 years and well below its all-time peak of $101 billion in 2003 (box 5.2).

At the same time, even though about 15 countries have seen major terms-of-trade deterioration from oil and other commodity price shocks, there has been no activity in the IMF's Exogenous Shocks Facility. Reasons why countries have not used the facility include access to private capital, use of reserves, and lower demand for oil in some countries as governments often passed through world market price increases to domestic prices. The World Bank has provided financing for longer-term restructuring. Energy Development Policy Lending for Morocco and Senegal this year, for example,

aims to help these countries adapt to high oil prices and improve energy efficiency. Low-income countries have used resources from development policy operations to fill remaining gaps.

MDB gross nonconcessional disbursements to sovereign borrowers were roughly flat in 2007, at a total of $23.4 billion, but this tells only part of the story. The other part is the shifting regional and organizational distribution of such loans. Lending by the International Bank for Reconstruction and Development (IBRD), especially its loans to Latin America, declined. But other regions and regional banks saw rising demand. Taken together, the regional development banks for the first time ever disbursed more than the IBRD in nonconcessional sovereign loans. In the past year, the IBRD took important steps to make the financial terms of its products more competitive, flexible, and transparent. Other enhancements have simplified and improved flexibility of products for delivering customized financial and risk management solutions to clients.

The MDBs also influence financial flows by leveraging other resources: guarantees bring in money from the private sector, and cofinancing and parallel financing bring in funds from other official lenders.

BOX 5.2 Lending by the IMF

The IMF's General Resources Account (GRA) provides nonconcessional financial support to member countries experiencing temporary balance of payments difficulties. The IMF also provides financial support through special GRA facilities, including emergency assistance for natural disasters and postconflict emergency assistance. The IMF provides concessional loans to low-income countries under the Poverty Reduction and Growth Facility (PRGF). At the end of 2007, 23 countries had a PRGF-supported arrangement under which they received subsidized balance of payments support from the IMF. In 2006 repayments of PRGF assistance were boosted by debt relief provided in the context of the MDRI.

Net flows from the IMF to developing countries
US$ millions

Type of flow	2001	2002	2003	2004	2005	2006	2007 est.
Net concessional flows (PRGF loans)	**106**	**567**	**9**	**−179**	**−715**	**−3,587**	**29**
Disbursements	1,111	1,741	1,187	1,204	597	744	485
Repayments	1,005	1,174	1,178	1,383	1,312	4,332	457
Net nonconcessional flows (GRA)	**19,031**	**13,109**	**2,002**	**−14,314**	**−39,802**	**−27,382**	**−5,131**
Disbursements	30,249	32,678	28,429	6,181	3,381	3,486	1,463
Repayments	11,219	19,569	26,427	20,495	43,183	30,868	6,593
Total, net flows	**19,137**	**13,676**	**2,010**	**−14,493**	**−40,517**	**−30,970**	**−5,102**
Of which:							
Total net flows, Sub-Saharan Africa	−181	161	−393	−318	−738	−3,051	117
Gross emergency assistance disbursements	n.a.	35	18	453	189	10	139

Source: IMF staff.
n.a. = Not applicable.

Guarantees. The World Bank Guarantee Program was mainstreamed in 1994 to help extend the reach of private financing to emerging countries, mitigate risks that are beyond the control of the private sector, open new markets, and improve project sustainability. The World Bank offers two basic types of guarantees: Partial Risk Guarantees cover debt service defaults on a loan, normally for a private sector project, when such defaults are caused by a government's failure to meet its contractual obligations related to the project. The IBRD (but not IDA) also offers Partial Credit Guarantees, which cover debt service defaults on a specified portion of a loan, normally for a public sector project, principally to extend maturities and improve market terms. Since 1994, 34 guarantee operations for 31 projects in 25 countries have been approved, for a total amount of financing of about US$27 billion, with an average leverage ratio of almost 10 to 1.[8]

Cofinancing. Cofinancing is a mechanism through which additional financing can be raised to fill unfunded gaps in project or programs and to better calibrate the degree of concessionality to achieve maximum impact. It covers joint and parallel financing. When it takes the form of joint financing, or collaboration on development policy lending and sector-wide approaches (SWAPs), it also establishes formal coordination between donors on country programs, policies, and priorities and provides a cost-effective means by which official agencies can tap into the lead agency's project management expertise. The World Bank has recently heightened attention on joint financing

TABLE 5.2 IBRD cofinancing by types of cofinancier, 1998–2007
US$ millions

Cofinancier	1998	1999	2000	2001	2002	2003	2004	2005	2006	2007
Bilateral	2,436	3,514	1,086	1,514	932	557	2,552	2,415	1,217	2,953
Multilateral	4,925	4,441	5,084	4,042	3,371	2,453	8,845	6,147	3,619	3,931
Total cofinancing	7,361	7,954	6,169	5,556	4,304	3,010	11,398	8,561	4,836	6,884
Selected donors										
JBIC	580	1,746	100	533	359	0	0	0	61	110
DfID	33	12	78	73	91	100	613	609	421	952
KfW	76	66	58	259	85	37	40	59	75	150
EC	69	174	32	98	86	57	641	180	49	449

Source: World Bank staff. Figures for 2007 are estimates.
Note: Total cofinancing includes all sources of cofinancing (concessional or nonconcessional) from bilateral and multilateral agencies.

as an important country-based aid harmonization and partnership instrument, especially with other multilateral agencies. On the bilateral side, the U.K. Department for International Development (DfID) and the Japanese Bank for International Cooperation (JBIC) have been very active in cofinancing with the IBRD. JBIC's activities have declined significantly since 2002, but Japanese cofinancing with the Asian Development Bank looks set to increase substantially under a partnership agreement of May 2007—the Enhanced Sustainable Development for Asia program. In fiscal 2007, World Bank projects were able to leverage an incremental $6.8 billion in cofinancing (table 5.2). Almost half of this amount ($3 billion) went for projects in Africa.

Nonconcessional Flows to Nonsovereign Borrowers

MDB nonsovereign flows (lending and equity investments) have grown sharply in recent years, from $3.1 billion in 2000 to $13.3 billion in 2007, of which half is accounted for by the IFC and the other half by the RDBs, mainly the EBRD. The Inter-American Investment Cooperation (IIC) disbursements in 2007 were almost 10 times their 2000 level while the EBRD quadrupled its disbursements in U.S. dollar terms. For the IIC disbursements, restrictions on private sector lending have been lifted to expand the scope of clients beyond infrastructure, capital markets, and trade finance. Most nonsovereign business is in Europe (56 percent), but the highest growth rate has been in Asia, which has surpassed Latin America for the third straight year. Encouragingly, nonsovereign flows to Africa have more than doubled since 2000.

The MDBs' ability to expand their nonsovereign business with adequately diversified portfolios and acceptable rates of return is a reflection of the better business climate and improved growth prospects in many countries. But improving the business climate and growth prospects is also the development purpose of nonsovereign operations. That outcome, rather than the volume of lending, is a better measure of impact.

Nonsovereign flows provide flexibility in terms of eligible clientele and prices. The MDBs' private sector instruments can price products differentially to allow for varying degrees of country and project risk. In contrast, in the case of sovereign loans, pricing is uniform to reflect the cooperative nature of the institutions. As a consequence, almost half of all business in investment-grade countries of the World Bank Group now consists of IFC and Multilateral Investment Guarantee Agency (MIGA) activities. The IFC is now expanding aggressively into low-income and blend countries.

Subnational lending. Subnational lending is another nonsovereign area with promise. A number of countries have asked for support, extending beyond finance to include enhanced capital market access, especially in cases where administrative responsibilities for basic infrastructure services have been devolved to local governments. The World Bank Group has integrated its approach by offering financial and guarantee products using the IFC balance sheet, but this mechanism has not yet seen significant growth and volumes are still modest.[9] Ten operations with a total exposure of $350 million have mobilized over $1 billion for subnational governments or public service providers in China, Guatemala, Hungary, Mexico, the Philippines, the Russian Federation, and South Africa. With a joint IBRD-IFC team now in place and with management addressing incentive issues within the World Bank Group, project flow is accelerating.

Nonsovereign lending often requires local currency financing, and innovative financial instruments have been developed to meet this market demand. The MDBs already offer swaps and interest and exchange rate hedging instruments. In October 2007 the World Bank Board endorsed a new IBRD-IFC initiative aimed at stimulating domestic bond markets. The Global Emerging Markets Local Currency Bond Fund is an example of market-based innovations customized to fill specific market gaps (box 5.3).

Nonsovereign guarantees. MIGA offers risk insurance for up to 20 years against losses relating to currency transfer restrictions, expropriation, war and civil disturbance, and breach of contract. It covers a broad range of sectors in 147 developing member

---

BOX 5.3 Global Emerging Markets Local Currency Bond Initiative

A new Global Emerging Markets Local Currency Bond Fund (GEMLOC), to be cobranded by IFC, IBRD, and a private partner, is expected to raise $5 billion by early 2008 for investment in up to 40 emerging bond markets. GEMLOC is a "systemic" solution to a market gap. While 70 percent of all emerging market debt is currently denominated in local currency, only 10 percent of the foreign money going into bonds issued by emerging markets is denominated in local currency. Only 2 percent of emerging market local currency debt is benchmarked against existing indexes. There is strong demand among investors for a dedicated fund in emerging markets local currency debt that is broadly diversified. And while about a dozen emerging economies have already developed liquid local currency bond markets, many others would seek to improve liquidity, build market infrastructure, develop efficient tax regimes, and cut red tape. The World Bank is looking for a private fund manager for GEMLOC to raise the funds and to manage a portfolio of investments in local currency bonds across as many as 40 emerging markets. Up to 30 percent of assets could also be invested in subsovereign and corporate bonds.

The fund is not a stand-alone, but a part of a three-part program that also includes an index—the Global Emerging Markets Bond Index (GEMX)—weighted not just by size of market, but by "investability" as well, the latter adjusting for such variables as regulatory and tax regimes and market access rules. The IFC is not new to the business, having launched the first emerging markets equity index two decades ago. The third part of the program is technical assistance, to be provided by the Bank, to help countries develop more investable local bond markets. This technical assistance will be funded by a "development fee" from the fund manager. There is no capital commitment from either the IBRD or the IFC in the project overall; after 10 years the sunset provision kicks in, meaning the *World Bank* name will be removed and the private sector will take over.

Source: World Bank staff.

countries. Since its inception in 1988, MIGA has issued 885 guarantees for projects in 96 developing countries, totaling $17.4 billion in coverage. Two-fifths of MIGA's gross outstanding portfolio is in IDA-eligible countries. Through the first half of fiscal 2008, MIGA has issued $1.2 billion in new coverage, bringing the total active portfolio to the highest level in the agency's history at $5.9 billion. MIGA prices its guarantee premiums based on a calculation of both country and project risk. Equity investments can be covered up to 90 percent and debt up to 95 percent. MIGA may insure up to $200 million, and more can be arranged through syndication.

Concessional Flows

In 2007 gross concessional flows from the MDBs reached a record high, totaling over $12 billion, an increase of 11 percent after two years of stagnation. IDA, which traditionally accounts for 75–80 percent of total concessional flows, was responsible for all of the increase in 2007. Concessional flows from regional development banks were flat. While Asia continued to receive almost half of total concessional gross flows, the fastest rate of increase has been in Africa. MDB support for Sub-Saharan Africa more than doubled between 2000 and 2007. Africa receives 45 percent of total MDB concessional flows today, up from 37 percent in 2000.

Record levels of donor pledges and ongoing discussions for replenishment of MDB concessional windows should allow last year's increase in concessional flows to be sustained. Donor funding commitments to the replenishment cycles of IDA and other concessional arms of the MDBs provide evidence of donor intentions to support the horizontal approach provided by these institutions. IDA's 15th replenishment, concluded in December 2007, resulted in a 30 percent increase over IDA14 (table 5.3). In total, IDA15 will allow for $41.6 billion of new commitments during fiscal 2009–11. New donor pledges will provide $25.1 billion, an increase of $7.4 billion compared with IDA14—the largest expansion in donor funding in IDA's history.[10] Internal transfers from the World Bank Group ($3.9 billion), donor pledges for MDRI debt forgiveness ($6.3 billion) and credit reflows ($6.3 billion) make up the remainder of the replenishment. The IDA15 agreement contained two other "firsts." China became a donor for the first time, along with five other countries, bringing the number of non-DAC contributors to 23 countries. And the United Kingdom became the largest single contributor for the first time.

Regional banks could also see their concessional resources expand significantly. At the AfDF-XI negotiations in December 2007, donors agreed to a record $8.9 billion in support for 2008–10, an increase of 52

TABLE 5.3 Record expansion of IDA

Sources of funds	Special drawing rights			US$		
	IDA 14 (billions)	IDA 15 (billions)	Percent change	IDA 14 (billions)	IDA 15 (billions)	Percent change
New donor pledges	12.1	16.5		17.7	25.1	
Compensation for MDRI debt forgiveness	2.6	4.1		3.8	6.3	
Credit reflows	6.1	4.1		9	6.3	
Agreed IBRD-IFC transfers	1.1	2.6		1.6	3.9	
IDA commitment authority	**21.9**	**27.3**	*25*	**32.1**	**41.6**	*30*
Additional IBRD-IFC transfers	0.3			0.4		
Total actual IDA 14	22.2			32.5		

Source: World Bank staff.

percent over AfDF-X. Negotiations are also under way for the replenishment of the Asian Development Fund for 2009–12 (AsDF X). The ADB is proposing a major increase as this will be the last chance to meaningfully contribute to the MDGs before 2015.

MDRI. The MDRI provides additional debt relief from IDA, the AfDF, the IDB Fund for Special Operations, and the IMF for countries that have reached their HIPC completion points. At the end of 2007, 25 countries (including two non-HIPC countries) had benefited from MDRI relief provided by the IMF. For the MDBs, donors have promised to replace the forgone credit reflows but cannot always provide legally binding commitments so far into the future. IDA has received commitments from 32 of the 34 countries that participate in MDRI funding. IDA expects to forgo credit reflows of special drawing rights (SDR) 24.7 billion ($37.6 billion) between 2006 and 2044, as a result of the MDRI. By September 30, 2007, IDA had provided irrevocable debt reduction commitments to 22 HIPC countries amounting to SDR 19.2 billion, but donors had provided unqualified firm commitments of only SDR 2.9 billion ($4.4 billion), and qualified commitments of a further SDR 14.6 billion ($22.2 billion). This still leaves a gap.

The African Development Fund forgone credit reflows are estimated at Unit of Account (UA) 5.68 billion ($8.5 billion). Only 4.3 percent of the cost of the MDRI will occur before 2011 and 15 percent of the cost before 2016. AfDF has already cancelled debt of UA 4.48 billion for 18 countries, and received UA 4.36 billion ($6.5 billion) in commitments from donors, of which 15 percent are unqualified.

The IDB has four client countries that have already qualified for MDRI debt relief of $4.4 billion. Unlike the other MDBs, IDB will rely only on the internal resources of its Fund for Special Operations (FSO), which has been redesigned to offer blends of highly concessional credits along with nonconcessional loans, with the composition of the blend depending on a debt sustainability analysis for each country. Separately, the IDB has created a grants facility for Haiti to help it reach completion point and obtain debt relief. IDB governors also agreed to consider a replenishment for the FSO by 2013, given that the fund will be able to continue providing concessional credits to its clients only through 2015.

Trust funds. Trust funds are perhaps the most rapidly growing business segment for the MDBs. Donors have sought to use management and program services provided by the MDBs for an increased amount of bilateral funds. Trust funds tend to focus on two broad areas of donor interest. The first consists of programs at the country level to help achieve the MDGs in low-income countries, particularly in Sub-Saharan Africa. These programs also support health, natural disaster relief, and postconflict recovery. The second broad area is global public goods, especially for the environment. This area has seen exponential growth of funds beyond the Global Environment Facility, including the Ozone Phase-Out Fund and carbon funds.

Trust funds vary enormously in size and complexity from multibillion dollar arrangements to much smaller, simpler funds. In 2007 the World Bank trust fund directory listed 100 active arrangements. In 2006 trust fund disbursements by the World Bank had risen to $4.4 billion. The IDB disbursed $215 million, while the AfDB and the ADB committed $85 million and $264 million respectively. By the end of 2007 trust funds under MDB management reached over $20 billion, with the World Bank having the lion's share. Through trust fund arrangements, the MDBs are able to ensure that global initiatives and funds mobilized for specific purposes are integrated with country-based development programs.

Nonlending Activities in Support of the Development Agenda

Knowledge services. Knowledge services—such as country analytical work, technical assistance, and global data and research—are a critical pillar for supporting developing countries in achieving the MDGs. Knowledge services have been growing more important over time as focus on aid effectiveness intensifies. Aid effectiveness is about better development results. It relies on knowledge services to change behavior of recipient countries and donors alike, to monitor and learn about what works, and to provide the support that countries need to enhance their own aid effectiveness. Attention increasingly should be paid to the lessons that low income-countries (and the developmental community) can learn from the middle-income countries' experience. Indeed, the knowledge that some of the IFIs have vis-à-vis other donors derives from their global experience.

Knowledge is the glue that binds different development partners together. Shared knowledge on the development vision, policies, and expenditure frameworks to link programs with budget resources has become indispensable to effective aid, especially in a more complex aid system and with more domestic stakeholders—parliamentarians, civil society, and the private sector. As one example, there are estimated to be 80–100 global health partnerships. Countries with limited capacity to manage and spend aid effectively, dealing with the multiplicity of aid instruments and mechanisms on offer, cannot absorb more money.[11] Knowledge from the IFIs provides countries with the analytic, diagnostic, and capacity-building support required to use aid better, so knowledge services have grown alongside the growth in the volume of aid. For fragile states, where aid volumes tend to be low, knowledge services help create the institutional foundations for effective use of aid.

Knowledge services have been steadily expanding and are increasingly done jointly with partner countries or in a coordinated fashion with other donors, or both. The World Bank, as the largest of the IFIs, tends to produce the greatest volume of knowledge services, with 440 pieces of economic and sector work in fiscal 2007. But all IFIs are committed to enhancing their knowledge

activities. The IFIs participate with 24 other contributors to the Country Analytical Work Web site (table 5.4), a shared portal where reports and best-practice examples are made available to the development community. There are now 3,722 posted reports, with the World Bank providing about one-third.

IFI reports cover a variety of themes. In addition to sectoral themes, there are country strategies and procedures for effective aid management, including public financial management, procurement, and governance and anticorruption. These reports are critical to the system strengthening that lies at the core of the IFI efforts to build and support country-based platforms for aid delivery (box 5.4). Almost all poor countries are now covered by a series of economic memoranda, public expenditure reviews, poverty assessments, and sector strategies, although a number of African countries still have not been able to conduct any household surveys. Between 2003 and 2007, IDA produced 150 poverty and social impact assessments, identifying the impact of policy recommendations and project interventions.

Measuring the relationship among inputs, outputs, and outcomes is central to the achievement of better development results, but the statistical capabilities in countries remain uneven. The IFIs have significant programs for strengthening statistical systems that can improve this situation. At the macroeconomic level, statistics are improving in depth and coverage (box 5.5), but at the sectoral and microeconomic levels much

TABLE 5.4 Reports posted by agency at Country Analytical Work Web site, 2007

Agency	Number of reports
World Bank	1,370
IMF	445
ADB	96
AfDB	48
EBRD	26
IDB	20

Source: www.countryanalyticwork.net.

BOX 5.4 Supporting the preparation of poverty reduction strategies: The case of Mozambique

The analytic products that IDA prepared with the government of Mozambique helped define the policy priorities and institutional systems that underpin the national poverty reduction strategy. The poverty assessment provided the analytic basis for the overall identification of priorities. The Country Economic Memorandum (prepared with the review of the donors of the G-17 coordination group) helped to focus the strategy on the links between key sectors and the overall growth strategy, analyzing how Mozambique's natural resources—land, forests, fisheries, mines, and water—could be better managed to contribute more to overall growth. Reviews of the financial sector, investment climate, and legal and judicial sector contributed to improving the country's institutional foundations for shared growth and helped to form the basis for the strategy's structural reforms. Finally, reviews of public expenditures, financial accountability, and procurement helped form the basis for improving public financial management and the links between the strategy and national systems.

Source: World Bank 2007d.

remains to be done. The IFIs are playing a major role in implementation of the Marrakesh Action Plan for Statistical Capacity Building, a program to support the compilation of data and statistical capacity needed to underpin the MDGs. For instance, the World Bank is cofinancing the activities of PARIS21 (Partnership in Statistics for Development in the 21st Century), which is helping countries develop statistical improvement strategies that are aligned to the statistical needs and priorities of Poverty Reduction Strategy Papers and other development priorities.

As leading global institutions, the IMF and World Bank Group have a comparative advantage in global learning, built on deriving cross-country lessons from country operations. Increasingly they have shifted their approach from one of transferring knowledge from rich countries and development agencies to poor countries to one that emphasizes a process of sharing of experiences between developing countries (box 5.6).

Measuring knowledge generated by an IFI is difficult as knowledge is embedded in a number of different services. The World Bank has several explicit knowledge-related services, such as country analytical work and technical assistance, and budget expenditures on these activities show a steady rise

to almost $450 million in 2007 (figure 5.2). These inputs, however, do not capture implicit knowledge work through convening, coordinating, and catalyzing activities in global programs, partnerships, and trust fund–related work. Nor do they capture knowledge embedded in loans and project supervision. A more detailed breakdown, imputing knowledge services to these other functions, suggests that knowledge inputs could be double the above amounts. Of course, measuring knowledge through its inputs is unsatisfactory in thinking about its impact. Knowledge is a global public good, so inputs on knowledge cannot be compared with inputs on other, excludable services like loans. A different measure looks at utilization of knowledge. Web-based dissemination has become more important for the IFIs; the World Bank Web site now counts over 2 million visitors each month. But internal reviews of World Bank economic and sector work suggest that inadequate attention is paid to dissemination, reducing the impact of the work.

The World Bank's Doing Business project is one of the best known free-standing knowledge services offered by the MDBs. A guide for evaluating regulations on business entry that directly affect economic growth, Doing Business provides a compendium of

BOX 5.5   The IMF's programs for improving statistical capacity

The Special Data Dissemination Standard (SDDS) provides a common standard for international dissemination of economic and financial data. SDDS subscribers provide a National Summary Data Page consisting of a prescribed set of macroeconomic data (including real, fiscal, financial, and external sector data), with given minimum levels of coverage, periodicity, and timeliness. They also provide information about their data dissemination practices and compilation methodologies (metadata) for posting on the IMF's Web site.

Regional representation in the GDDS and SDDS combined

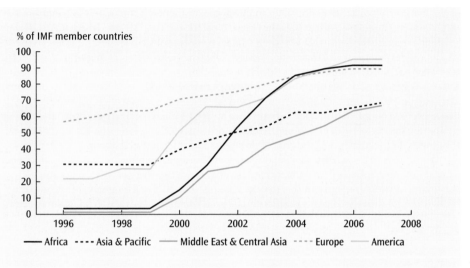

The General Data Dissemination System (GDDS) is a framework to help participating countries improve their macroeconomic and sociodemographic statistics, including relevant MDG indicators. The GDDS facilitates the comparison of a country's current statistical practices with internationally recognized good practices. It guides countries in their efforts to improve statistical systems and to produce and disseminate data in accordance with good-quality standards. The GDDS also promotes the application of established methodological principles, the adoption of sound compilation practices, and the observance of procedures that ensure professionalism and objectivity.

There are currently 64 SDDS subscribers and 90 GDDS participants—a total of about 80 percent of Fund membership. Statistical capacity building, using the GDDS and the Data Quality Assessment Framework, covers both human and institutional elements through knowledge and skills transfers and through organizational and institutional advice. The GDDS, with its incorporation at the center of the PARIS21 program of National Statistical Development Strategies, serves as an important vehicle for donor coordination and leverage of donor funds to bring about improvements in national statistical systems through coordinated technical assistance.

Source: IMF staff.

laws in different countries and cross-country comparisons of these laws. It identifies and champions reformers in developing countries who are trying to improve the business climate. *Doing Business 2008* documented

200 reforms in 98 countries that were introduced between April 2006 and June 2007. Croatia, the Arab Republic of Egypt, Ghana, Georgia, and Macedonia were identified as the top five reformers. For policy purposes,

BOX 5.6 Malaysia-Africa Knowledge Exchange Seminar: An example of South-South knowledge sharing

The Malaysia-Africa Knowledge Exchange Seminar (MAKES) brought together 110 high-level officials from 24 African countries, including 17 ministers, in Kuala Lumpur and Putrajaya, on September 21–22, 2006. The seminar, jointly organized by the Malaysian Ministry of Finance and the World Bank, focused on four themes of relevance to African countries: managing natural resources for economic growth and poverty reduction; fostering export-led growth and a business-friendly investment climate; developing and implementing national plans; and defining the role of government-linked companies.

Honorable Goodall E. Gondwe, the Minister of Finance of Malawi, speaking on behalf of the African ministers, set the tone of the seminar: "We are here not to learn development theory, but to listen to Malaysian officials and understand better how they achieved what is an impressive performance." Several Malaysian cabinet members and the deputy prime minister emphasized Malaysia's inclusiveness, political stability, good economic management, and rapid human development as key factors behind 50 years of strong growth and poverty reduction.

African ministers were particularly impressed by Malaysia's ability to avoid the "natural resource curse." At the center of this success is Petronas, a Fortune 500 oil company created in 1974 with freedom to be managed as a private sector company despite being fully government owned. Transparency seems to have been the decisive factor. The company books are on its Web site, its accounts are audited by certified accountants, and its contributions to the budget are debated in Parliament. Many African ministers asked: Why not Africa? The discussion revolved around the issues of governance and the role of domestic and international actors.

MAKES has started a process of knowledge sharing on national planning, monitoring and evaluation, education (especially higher education), oil resources management, public-private partnerships in infrastructure, management of state-owned enterprises, agriculture, and the investment climate. The Malaysian government has offered free tuition for up to 100 qualified African students a year to pursue graduate studies at three Malaysian universities.

Source: World Bank staff.

FIGURE 5.2   World Bank knowledge service inputs, by type, 2002–07

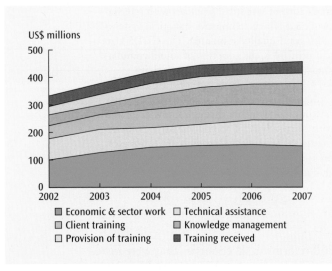

Source: World Bank staff. Figures for 2007 are estimates.
Note: Data include Bank budget, reimbursables, and Bank-executed trust funds.

Doing Business has been complemented by a series of detailed firm-level Enterprise Surveys, supported by many MDBs, and these have become mainstreamed instruments for measuring investment climate reform priorities.

Partnerships. Nonlending services are of particular importance in forming partnerships with others in the development community and in addressing global public goods. The number of active partnerships has mushroomed. The World Bank Group now participates in 125 partnerships, mostly in environment and human development areas. The World Bank itself is the host institution for fewer than half of these partnerships (figure 5.3). The majority are hosted either by the partner or by an independent organization. Over 90 percent of these programs describe themselves as contributing to the brokering of global knowledge.

The MDBs have an important role to play in bridging the gap between partner country priorities and global or regional collective action, especially through country analytical work. Many global public goods are narrowly focused, and the links with a coherent national development strategy need to be elaborated. Poverty reduction strategies, country assistance strategies, and sector strategies can play this role. Sometimes, a regional platform can be useful in intermediating between country and global platforms as well. The linkages provide a two-way communication channel. Global public goods goals are brought into the country dialogue, and, at the same time, the MDBs can be a powerful voice for advocacy of developing-country viewpoints on global public goods at international forums, especially in areas where country capacity for participating in global negotiations is limited. Recent examples of MDB advocacy in trade, aid, and climate change underscore this point.

Harmonization

The commitment of IFIs and the donor community to harmonization of activities was formalized through their participation in the Paris Declaration, setting targets to improve aid effectiveness by 2010. A baseline survey of MDB performance against the Paris targets was undertaken in 2006, with a follow-up survey scheduled for the spring of 2008. The baseline survey showed the MDBs to be ahead of many bilateral agencies, but with some weaknesses. IDA, the ADB, and the AfDB relied too heavily on parallel implementation units. Unpredictability of disbursements was also an issue. The MDBs found the greater use of program approaches and joint missions hard to implement. On the positive side, use of country public financial management and procurement systems, and joint analytical work—more than half for IDA, for example—were progressing well. MDB aid flows were generally aligned with national priorities.[12]

The 2006 monitoring of the Paris targets showed that alignment and harmonization

FIGURE 5.3 World Bank portfolio of global partnership funds *by theme and host institution*

Thematic network	World Bank	Partner org.	Indp. org.	Total no. of funds
Environment & sustainability	27	4	5	36
Human development	8	8	14	30
Infrastructure	12	3	1	16
Finance & economics	6	5	5	16
Poverty reduction & economic management	1	4	3	8
Other	4	5	10	19
TOTAL	58 46%	29 23%	38 30%	125

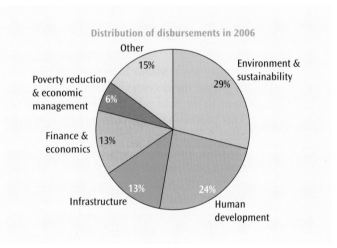

Distribution of disbursements in 2006

- Other 15%
- Environment & sustainability 29%
- Poverty reduction & economic management 6%
- Finance & economics 13%
- Infrastructure 13%
- Human development 24%

Source: World Bank staff.

actions were being undertaken in a growing number of countries. However, in half of the surveyed countries, progress was limited, and countries and development partners still had many opportunities to improve country-level effectiveness. Country-based platforms were the core of the MDB harmonization efforts on strategies and programs, division of labor between agencies, and managing for results. This partnership implies that MDB harmonization efforts are only as good as country efforts, and vice versa (box 5.7).

Experience to date suggests that harmonization has real costs in time and resources. With harmonization efforts being made at the

> ## BOX 5.7   Coordination among donors in Bolivia
>
> The *Grupo de Socios para el Desarrollo de Bolivia* (referred to as GruS) was established to improve the communication between the government of Bolivia and aid donors. GruS's main objective is to help the government better coordinate the tasks of harmonization, development effectiveness, and alignment among aid donors under the framework of the Paris Declaration, the Millennium Development Goals, and Bolivia's National Plan of Development. A coordination mechanism established five thematic areas for coordination (production, social services, democracy, macroeconomics, and harmonization) and calls for monthly meetings between government representatives and donors.
>
> To participate in the GruS, donors must adhere to a few principles: the Bolivian government leads the tasks of harmonization and coordination under the principles of the Paris Declaration; donors will align to the implementation of the objectives of the National Development Plan; donors are represented through their official heads; and the participants in the GruS should support the existing coordination mechanisms at the sector level in order to strengthen them.
>
> GruS terms of reference established that a coordination group consisting of three donors (two bilateral and one multilateral) will lead its activities for three semesters. The IDB will lead the coordination group during the first semester of 2008.
>
> *Source:* IDB staff.

country level, MDBs have found it necessary to pursue the decentralization of their operations to the field with concomitant expenses. This process has advanced quite far. IDA has placed 55 percent of its high-level staff in the field, along with 30 of 40 country directors. Local recruits have risen to 23 percent of the staff complement. Significant progress has also been achieved on decentralization of procurement and financial management staff. The effect of these changes has been to increase the ability of donors to make progress with harmonization on a country-by-country basis, where results are most clearly visible (box 5.8).

The Paris Declaration survey was important in opening a productive dialogue within countries on aid effectiveness. That conversation clearly showed the need to tailor development strategies to each country's priorities and circumstances. But it also pointed to a level of concern in developing countries with the high transaction costs of managing aid and the slow pace of donor reforms.[13] The new survey results will be a guide as to whether these concerns are being adequately met.

While it is early to provide new results from the 2008 survey, there are already indications that progress toward the Paris targets is likely to be mixed. The AfDB reports that its disbursement level might have reached only 60 percent of that scheduled in 2007, and that it still has an average of 6.4 parallel implementation structures per country. IDA has found it difficult to commit jointly to outcomes with other development partners and still maintain clearly defined accountabilities for each partner. It has also found that significant costs are entailed with donor coordination around budget support and sectorwide approaches, with crafting and monitoring memoranda of understanding (MOUs) with other agencies, and with synchronizing staff drafts and management reviews among agencies. A new legal harmonization initiative among the MDBs, plus many bilateral donors, is developing specific understandings about interagency MOUs. Incentives and resources within agencies do not yet reflect these real aspects of harmonization.

Country-based harmonization is nevertheless making progress. As figure 5.4 shows, 13 percent of countries have fully developed operational frameworks and another 67 percent have taken action to develop such frameworks. These figures are higher in countries

> ## BOX 5.8 Recent examples of country-level harmonization with regional development banks
>
> In February 2006 the heads of the seven MDBs set up a joint task force to develop a consistent and harmonized approach to anticorruption work. On the basis of the task force's recommendations, the MDBs agreed to a common framework for fighting fraud and corruption. The joint actions include standardizing the definitions used in sanctioning firms involved in corrupt activities, improving the consistency of investigative rules and procedures, and strengthening information sharing. MDBs will continue to work together to assist countries in strengthening governance and combating corruption in cooperation with civil society, the private sector, the media, and the judiciary. MDBs have also focused attention on the special challenges posed by fragile states and are working on identifying opportunities for increased harmonization in approaches to fragile situations. One of the key recommendations is a proposal to adopt a common approach for identifying fragility, recognizing that it exists at both national and subnational levels, and to partner with the United Nations and other development partners in shared postconflict and postdisaster recovery planning.
>
> Most MDB harmonization activities take place at the country level, with joint country assistance strategies and joint activities. For example, IDA and the ADB have agreed to join efforts in Tajikistan through:
>
> - Joint technical assistance to set up a monitoring system for the Paris Declaration
> - Joint country economic, poverty reduction, and health analytical work
> - Joint support to the health sector's management information system
> - Upgrading the multifunctional role of the joint Development Information Center
> - Adding a common public information window to a joint education portfolio review
> - Joint databases.
>
> In The Gambia, where harmonization and alignment are relatively less advanced, IDA and the AfDB agreed to cooperate closely. Under this joint strategy, the institutions have developed shared objectives and a common platform including joint budget support, joint investments in growth and competitiveness, and joint analytic work in public finance, civil service reform, and governance.
>
> *Source:* World Bank 2007d.

with stronger policies and institutions. The challenge of harmonization and alignment remains high in fragile states, where over half of all countries do not yet have sound operational frameworks. This is not simply a reflection of a legacy of poor policy in fragile states. Analysis suggests that the link between the degree of implementation of Paris Declaration targets and a country's overall policy and institutional score is weak, especially for countries with middle to poor country policy and institutional assessment (CPIA) ratings.[14] The same analysis shows a strong link between resource flows and harmonization and alignment. Those countries with advanced harmonization processes were able to support higher volumes of aid and received higher IDA allocations. The causality could move in either direction. Countries with more aid flows might invest more in harmonization procedures to increase aid effectiveness, or alternatively donors might allocate more aid to countries that have better procedures. The implication is the same. Harmonization does appear to be a critical element in scaling up and enhancing aid effectiveness. IFI efforts to build country capacity can therefore have significant payoffs.

Tracking Results

The IFIs have committed to the Managing for Development Results Initiative (MfDR), an

FIGURE 5.4 Progress toward operational development strategies in low-income countries

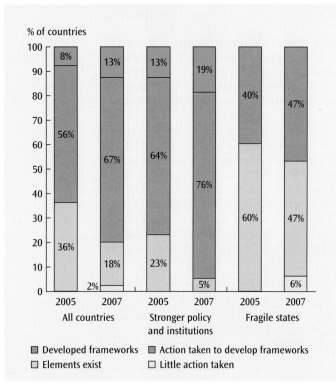

% of countries

Legend:
- ■ Developed frameworks
- ■ Action taken to develop frameworks
- □ Elements exist
- □ Little action taken

Source: World Bank 2007d.
Note: Selected categories are defined in terms of CPIA ratings.

effort to use practical tools for strategic planning, risk management, progress monitoring, and outcome evaluation to direct resources to where the best results are attainable. A *Sourcebook on Emerging Good Practice,* with several country case studies, was finalized by the MfDR secretariat in May 2007. This, along with the Hanoi Roundtable discussion in February 2007, conveys a sense of urgency to improve development results. But that requires a significant upgrading in capacity in many countries. The results agenda is far behind the reforms that have taken place in procurement and financial management systems.

Managing for development results is one of the themes of the Third High-Level Forum on Aid Effectiveness, to be held in Accra on September 2–4, 2008. In addition to ownership, alignment, and harmonization issues, the event will give prominence to the theme

of results orientation. In preparation for the event, the AfDB has been active in planning consultative regional meetings and in the selection of case studies to inform progress.

The heart of the MDB systems lies at the country level. The IDB has launched a new project performance monitoring report for all sovereign guaranteed operations that provides better information on output and outcome indicators against specified targets and baselines and on risks that may affect their achievement. The ADB has been implementing an MfDR Action Plan, 2006–08. It has initiated development effectiveness country briefs. The AfDB has introduced a new results-oriented supervision report format. The World Bank Group and ADB have mainstreamed Results-Based Country Assistance Strategies. The World Bank's Africa Action Plan is based on an outcome-oriented framework to guide the work of the Bank's Africa region to promote country-led efforts in partnership with other donors (box 5.9).

A focus on results is translating into management frameworks that are risk based rather than absolute. Operational manuals can provide guidance to staff, but if recipient countries are responsible for program and project execution and the attainment of development results, then the responsibility of partner agencies is to manage risks inherent in individual transactions and not to prescribe procedures. Better country procurement and financial management systems are already apparent, and the MDBs are active in building capacity to improve these. That will permit more rapid adoption of risk-based procedures.

Selectivity of Financial Resources

As part of the MfDR, the MDBs committed themselves to using more transparent and incentive-improving resource allocation systems aimed at maximizing aid effectiveness and encouraging stronger policies and institutions in recipient countries. At present, the foundation of each of these systems is a formula that calculates the share of the resources that will be allocated to individual countries

---

BOX 5.9   The Africa Action Plan: progress in implementation

The World Bank launched an Africa Action Plan in 2005, and modified it in 2007, to sharpen the focus on results. The Bank believes that good progress is being made in the implementation of the plan. There has been a very encouraging pickup in growth in the region. Africa's growth is continuing to strengthen and could reach 6.3 percent in 2008, according to the *World Economic Outlook* of the IMF. About two-thirds of the region's population now lives in countries that in recent years have achieved average GDP growth of more than 5 percent. Gross primary school enrollment has risen to 96 percent, and gender imbalances in education have been substantially reduced. Thirty-three of 44 countries show a decline in maternal mortality rates.

This broadly positive outlook is clouded by the enormous challenges still facing the region. Despite stronger growth, much of Africa will not meet the MDGs.[a] About 20 countries, many affected by conflict and accounting for about a third of the region's population, remain trapped in low growth. The 2015 target poverty headcount rate of 23 percent will be missed by a sizable degree, with current projections suggesting poverty is on track to decline to only 32 percent in 2015. Primary completion rates are low and child and maternal mortality rates are not coming down fast enough. And aid to Africa, outside debt relief and humanitarian assistance, has not increased at a pace commensurate with the Gleneagles promise.

The Bank Group's contributions are broadly on track with what was expected. Private sector development, infrastructure, HIV/AIDS, and malaria programs are ahead of plan. MIGA and the IFC have made important contributions to private sector development, with the IFC opening a Private Enterprise Partnership for Africa, and raising $31 million in donor contributions. A partnership with Germany and the AfDB to make finance work for Africa was launched in October 2007. Progress is on track in regional integration, with the opening of a new World Bank department to focus on this and export development. But agricultural productivity and gender empowerment programs are behind schedule. African countries have done well in building state capacity, although they could have made faster progress if the World Bank's Capacity Development Management Action Plan had come onstream earlier. Harmonization activities are also well under way at the country level, with money from the Africa Catalytic Growth Fund, designed to crowd in donor resources, fully committed through fiscal 2008.

The World Bank Group has drawn four key lessons from the initial experience with the Africa Action Plan: the country-based model works and should be strengthened; the plan needs to become more selective to be used as an effective management tool; demand from countries should guide selectivity; and accountability for monitoring and results should be strengthened.

Source: World Bank 2007a.
a. On current trends, 13 countries will meet only one MDG, and 23 will not meet any.

---

on the basis of their financial need (proxied by population and income per capita) and policy performance. Each MDB combines these factors somewhat differently in its performance allocation formula and uses different methods to accommodate exceptional circumstances, such as fragile or small states. In the past, the MDBs have taken significant steps to harmonize the CPIA questionnaires that lie behind their policy performance measures. This has led to more harmonization of performance-based allocation systems along the two dimensions of need and policy performance.

The weight ascribed by each MDB to need and policy can be implicitly derived by looking at the coefficients on per capita income

and on CPIA scores in a regression model.[15] These coefficients can be interpreted as the sensitivity of resource allocations to "need" and "policy." Put another way, the coefficients show the selectivity of each agency to these variables. Figure 5.5 shows that most MDBs are quite selective in terms of both policy and need and far more selective than bilateral aid agencies. Poorer countries and countries with better policy scores receive more aid funds. The figure also shows a trend toward greater selectivity in IDA and AfDF. A recent study prepared for the discussion of IDA15 replenishment finds that countries receiving more funds from IDA are those experiencing better results.[16]

FIGURE 5.5 Policy and poverty selectivity of concessional assistance by the MDBs

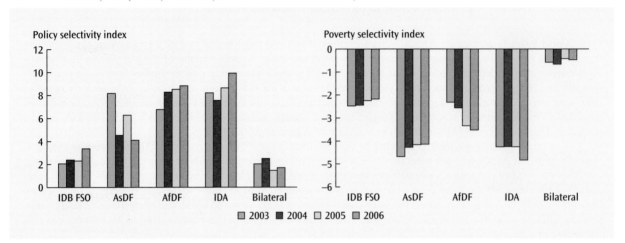

Source: World Bank staff calculations, based on Dollar and Levin (2004).
Note: FSO = Fund for Special Operations.

The contrast between MDB and bilateral donor allocations in terms of their selectivity along the two dimensions of need and policy is partly attributable to the importance placed by bilaterals on historical and cultural ties. But it also reflects differing views on the combination of discretion and rules-based approaches, with bilaterals favoring greater discretion. For example, the U.S. Millennium Challenge Corporation has moved furthest in trying to implement a transparent, performance-oriented system but retains management discretion to deviate from a strict application of its formula. The European Commission has an alternative approach of allocating base funding according to need and performance but with flexibility to deviate if country circumstances so warrant. Discretion in allocation can be used in a number of different ways. It can be used to include political framework conditions, which the MDBs cannot do. But it can also permit greater flexibility in responding to turnaround situations and other special circumstances such as disease burden, landlockedness, or state fragility that are hard to capture in a simple formula. Greater flexibility to respond to some of these conditions may be desirable but comes at a cost in the transparency of allocations.

Concessional flows to fragile states pose a special challenge for MDBs. On the one hand, the likelihood of successful development outcomes from any specific project declines in a fragile state. On the other hand, fragile states have the highest incidence of poverty and are furthest away from reaching the MDGs. The allocation formula provides some flexibility to accommodate exceptional circumstances of fragile states,[17] but recently the share of fragile states in total ODA flows from the MDBs has been relatively stable, despite a sizable increase in the absolute level of MDB lending (table 5.5). As fragile states move from peace building to state building, the MDB role is expected to become larger. IDA has recently spelled out its new parameters for engagement and has systematically worked to reduce the performance gap between fragile and nonfragile states in project outcomes.[18]

Sectoral issues. In line with their changing strategies, MDBs have adjusted the sectoral composition of new commitments. The most striking recent trend is the reemergence of infrastructure as a major sector. The World Bank Group adopted an Infrastructure Action Plan in 2003. Since then it has scaled up financial support considerably, almost doubling its commitments from around $7 billion in fiscal 2003 to around $12.5 billion in fiscal 2007. Figure 5.6 shows how disbursements in infra-

TABLE 5.5 MDB gross disbursements to fragile states, 2002–07
US$millions

Gross disbursement	2002	2003	2004	2005	2006	2007
World Bank	1,107.8	985.3	1,403.2	1,693.4	1,373.7	1,802.7
IDB	2.6	48.0	28.0	70.0	65.7	90.1
AfDB	123.1	216.0	231.5	162.7	165.6	216.9
ADB	318.4	267.8	299.8	330.7	325.6	275.3
Total	*1,552.0*	*1,517.1*	*1,962.5*	*2,256.8*	*1,930.60*	*2,385.0*
Memo items						
Number of countries	36	35	36	36	35	35
Disbursements per capita (in dollars)	2.92	3.05	3.81	4.49	3.94	4.90
Percent of total MDB disbursements	7.9	6.5	11.1	12.3	8.3	10.6

Source: MDB staff. Figures for 2007 are estimates.
Note: Data include debt relief. Fragile states are defined as IDA-eligible countries with either a CPIA rating of 3.2 or below or without a CPIA rating.

structure are already picking up volumes over the last three years. Along with more financing, and leveraging private funds through guarantees and innovative financing mechanisms, the Bank has also made progress in integrating social and environmental concerns into infrastructure operations and strengthening governance and accountability.[19]

A second compositional trend seems less positive. IDA reported an increase in its commitments for education, and an increase in education spending as a whole in recipient

FIGURE 5.6 IBRD and IDA disbursements by sector and themes

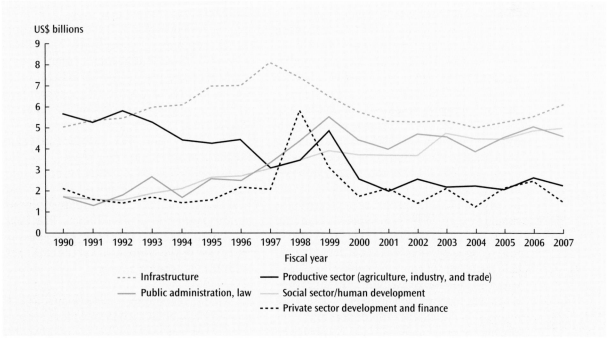

Source: World Bank staff. Figures for 2007 are estimates.

countries, but a continued significant gap in resources for primary education, despite the Fast Track initiative. In fact, IDA's new commitments for basic education have actually fallen by 13 percent in nominal terms in fiscal 2005–07 compared with fiscal 2002–04, while lending for other levels of education rose by 25 percent. These trends hold even for the poorest countries and for Sub-Saharan Africa.[20]

Review of Approaches to Assessing IFI Performance

Several approaches to measuring IFI results have emerged in recent years. The first is internal, developed by each IFI in responding to shareholder concerns. On a parallel track, albeit more focused on performance than results, some MDB shareholders are independently developing their own comparative frameworks for assessing multilateral agencies, generally with a view to fine-tuning their financial support. Third, civil society organizations are monitoring IFI performance in an increasingly systematic manner.

MDB Internal Measurement Systems

IFIs are taking action to improve the result orientation of their own management practices and programs. At the Third Roundtable on Managing for Development, held in Hanoi in February 2007, donors recognized that managing for results should not be seen mainly as a set of measuring and monitoring tools, although statistics and monitoring and evaluation are essential components, but as a management strategy to improve decision making. Internal systems developed by the MDBs to measure results and effectiveness should be seen with this perspective in mind.

Results measurement systems. Efforts to measure the results of concessional lending began with the adoption of the IDA13 Results Measurement System. Much debate, technical analysis, and dialogue with donors and IDA-eligible countries went into the construction of the initial approach, which has since been refined. It uses a two-tiered system to link IDA's contribution to the MDG framework. The first tier looks at key development outcomes, while the second tier looks at intermediate outputs contributed by IDA. The first tier monitors 14 indicators in IDA-recipient countries, grouped into four key areas: growth and poverty reduction; public financial management and investment climate; human development; and infrastructure. The second tier has indicators monitoring IDA performance at project, sector, and country levels.

The AfDF's Results Measurement System is similar in methodology to that of IDA. The assessment of AfDF performance under AfDF-XI will occur at the institutional and country levels through the use of operations quality indexes, changes in country-level indicators based mostly on internationally available statistics, and evaluation findings. The AfDB has examined the outputs and short-term outcomes of more than 140 projects that exited the portfolio over the 2004–07 period. The ADB has also set up a new internal results measurement system.

The IDB is moving toward a culture of results and accountability by designing and implementing various new tools. It is introducing a corporatewide performance framework, supported by steps to implement a results-based budgeting system, a new version of the project performance monitoring report for all sovereign guaranteed operations, and a new project evaluation instrument.

The IMF also has various internal mechanisms for tracking results, starting with regular review by staff and the Independent Evaluation Office of the effectiveness of IMF-supported programs, program conditionality, and surveillance. The Fund also regularly assesses the effectiveness of its advice in the context of surveillance and technical assistance missions.

COMPAS. The common performance assessment system, or COMPAS, was designed as a self-assessment to provide a common source of information on the results orientation of the MDBs' internal practices and operational relations with country and development partners. The focus is on identifying common issues, rather than on individual comparisons among institutions, in order to provide a basis for information exchange and learning about performance and accountability.

Although it is still too early to assess trends, the 2007 COMPAS report attempts to identify the direction of movement since 2006.[21] Overall, the MDBs have improved on four of seven indicators, with the other three remaining stable. The improvement resulted from better performance in assessing and strengthening the capacity of their borrowing member countries to manage for development results; strengthening the results orientation of their respective country strategies; strengthening their various processes related to project and program design and implementation; and better harmonizing their policies and procedures among themselves. Areas where no improvements occurred, but where MDB approaches nevertheless are considered to be in line with current best practices, include allocation of concessional resources, institutional learning from operational experience, and results focus in human resources management.

COMPAS 2007 shows that MDB efforts toward strengthening their results orientation are also reaching their private sector operations in three stages: strategy design and project implementation; ex post evaluation; and learning from operational experience. A major limitation in private sector operations is that not all country strategies include an explicit strategy to promote private sector development.

Among the highlights of the COMPAS 2007 report are the findings of a 12 percent increase in the number of country strategies of the AfDB, independently evaluated ex post, that show satisfactory or better results; an increase of 15 percent in the share of ADB projects that explicitly show baseline data, monitoring indicators, and target outcomes; a 12 percent increase in the proportion of ADB projects with satisfactory or better rat-

ings for development outcomes, based on independent evaluation; an increase in the EBRD disbursement ratio from 55 percent to 60 percent; a 13 percent increase in the number of countries where IDB helped strengthen results management capacity; a 27 percent increase in the share of World Bank projects with baseline data, monitoring indicators, and target outcomes; and a 41 percent increase in the share of World Bank projects receiving a satisfactory or better rating in independent ex post evaluations. The MDBs have formed an Evaluation Cooperation Group (ECG), with the goal of promoting good practices and a focus on project implementation.

MBD Shareholder Comparative Assessments

Several MDB shareholders have set up independent approaches to assess the results and effectiveness of the MDBs. There are now five such systems:

- Multilateral Organizations Performance Assessment Network (MOPAN) promoted by nine donor countries (Austria, Canada, Denmark, Finland, the Netherlands, Norway, Sweden, Switzerland, and the United Kingdom)
- Performance Management Framework of the Danish International Development Agency (DANIDA)
- Multilateral Effectiveness and Relevance Assessment of the Canadian International Development Agency (CIDA)
- Multilateral Effectiveness Framework established by the U.K. Department for International Development
- Multilateral Monitoring Survey System developed by the Netherlands.

These systems differ in objectives, level of assessment focus, sources of data, and tools and methodology (table 5.6). Some focus on strengthening organizational accountability, others on helping guide bilateral financial support. They are based on (nonrepresentative) surveys, checklists, scorecards, or interviews, along with organizational performance measures.

TABLE 5.6 A comparison of MDB assessment systems

Assessment approach	The Common Performance Assessment System	Multilateral Organizations Performance Assessment Network	Danish Performance Management Framework	Canadian Multilateral Effectiveness and Relevance Assessment	British Multilateral Effectiveness Framework	Dutch Multilateral Monitoring Survey System
Area of focus	Self-assessment, harmonization of practices	Perception analysis	Quality assessment of MDBs	Results and management assessment	Organizational effectiveness of MDBs	Perception analysis
Objectives	Gather information on how MDBs are contributing to development results

Monitor and synthesize MBDs progress;

Contribute to lessons learning, accountability, and transparency. | Better information about and understanding of MDBs, their roles and performance by stakeholders in MOPAN member countries

Better dialogue with the MDBs

Engagement of MOPAN country offices in performance assessment

Improvement of overall performance of MDBs at country level | Enhance the quality of Danish development cooperation through stronger focus on results

Improve management and continuous learning through better information and reporting

Strengthen accountability through performance assessments and measurement in the context of an increasingly decentralized management structure | Better information for policy and financial allocation decisions

Improvement of CIDA's accountability

Better identification of areas requiring advancement

Multilateral effectiveness review as part of the Agency Aid Effectiveness agenda | Provide information to strengthen DFID's accountability

Provide inputs to DFID's institutional strategies for engagement with multilaterals

Provide inputs to future financing decisions | Giving an insight into the general perception of a given MDB |
| Level of assessment focus | Country, organization, and global partnership levels | Country level | Corporate (DANIDA), organization, and country levels | Country level. Focused on three themes: relevance, effectiveness, and improvement measures in management | Organization, country and partnership levels | Country level |

The experimentation with assessment frameworks reflects the difficulties of attributing results to individual agencies, more so as harmonization efforts gain strength. Nevertheless, there is demand for a system to help the MDBs improve their comparative strengths and weaknesses through learning. A few common threads appear. The MDBs could increase the attention paid to the quality of monitoring and evaluation practices. Reporting should reflect on progress toward development results, notably the MDGs—that is, real results on the ground—not just process measures. Meanwhile, donors need to harmonize the current ad hoc MDB assessment to provide transparent incentives for institutional change to management.

TABLE 5.6   A comparison of MDB assessment systems (*continued*)

Assessment approach	The Common Performance Assessment System	Multilateral Organizations Performance Assessment Network	Danish Performance Management Framework	Canadian Multilateral Effectiveness and Relevance Assessment	British Multilateral Effectiveness Framework	Dutch Multilateral Monitoring Survey System
Tools, methods	COMPAS is a self-assessment exercise based on process and results indicators. It uses eight categories of data: Country-level capacity development Performance-based concessional financing Country strategies Projects and programs Human resources management Learning and incentives Interagency harmonization Private sector operations	Annual survey: A questionnaire completed by participating MOPAN embassies and country offices for each of the MDBs assessed Country team discussions Country reports summarizing the findings of country teams A synthesis report	A combination of qualitative and quantitative methods, drawing on: Organization strategies Annual results contracts Consultations with each multilateral organization Performance information Perception analyses Evaluation of multilateral organizations Performance reporting systems	A common set of indicators, drawing from multiple sources of information: Evaluations from the institutions themselves Multidonor evaluations Surveys of field staff undertaken by CIDA, MOPAN	Focuses on eight corporate management systems and is based on three main assessment instruments: Checklist with nearly 72 questions or indicators Scorecard rating data in the checklists Summary report presenting the organizations' main strengths and weaknesses	Questionnaires answered by embassy, permanent representation of mission, and constituency offices staff. Performance assessment for the most important UN institutions and IFIs at country level of the 36 Dutch partner countries.

Source: World Bank staff.

Civil Society Monitoring

The third pillar of assessment is through civil society. A number of civil society organizations and Web sites monitor programs conducted by IFIs. These organizations and Web sites provide important feedback—typically quite critical—on IFI activities. They have been strong advocates for more rapid reform of IFIs, stemming from a sense of urgency that many countries are not on track to attain the MDGs. Currently, civil society is organizing to participate in the Accra and Doha conferences, with a focus on five aspects of IFI operations: trade and economic management, conditionality, debt and finance for development, aid, and voice.

Trade and economic management. While civil society groups recognize that there can be differences in views on economic management with IFIs, they have organized strong advocacy efforts to push for change. One issue that is important to these groups is to understand better the poverty and social impact assessment of policy change, especially with respect to trade and employment, the role of safety nets, and trade in agriculture. IFIs have initiated some poverty and social impact assessments, but not to the satisfaction of many critics. These assessments have helped communicate development policies to stakeholders in recipient countries but are not mainstreamed into MDB activity. Nor have they been shown so far to provide benefits in terms of policy choices that out-weigh the costs of additional studies and time delays.

Conditionality. Conditionality is a major channel through which IFIs have encour-aged recipient countries to pursue specific economic policies, and one where civil soci-ety groups have long been critical of the IFIs. This issue is becoming more sensitive as the shift toward program aid, with its attendant conditions, and harmonized approaches gathers momentum. Eurodad, a consor-tium of European NGOs, issued a report on World Bank conditionality in November 2007.[22] That report concluded that although the number of legal conditions in World Bank operations had declined, many con-ditions involved multiple actions. Eurodad claims that when conditions are unbundled into their separate components, there has been no decline (and perhaps an increase in number). Eurodad further claims that sensi-tive conditions—defined as those involving privatization and liberalization—have gone up. At their extreme, civil society groups like Eurodad are advocates for dropping condi-tionality on economic policies completely, on the grounds that it promotes externally induced policies and undermines debate and accountability for policy choice in recipient country political organizations. But in their less extreme form, the critics question the development impact of IFI conditions.

Debt. The process of debt cancellation under the HIPC and MDRI initiatives is one exam-ple of the power of civil society activism and awareness raising. But debt issues have not disappeared. In some instances, countries find themselves again at some risk of debt distress, even after receiving debt relief, because of adverse terms-of-trade shocks, or because of still-outstanding debts held by creditors who have not participated in debt cancellation schemes. A few countries may be in the process of re-indebting them-selves, sometimes outside the framework of the IFIs' debt sustainability analysis. New

lenders have been willing to enter this space. Debt issues, therefore, remain central to the agenda of financing for development.

Aid. Civil society groups are actively moni-toring aid quantity and quality, along with aid effectiveness and new sources of finance. These groups have been strong advocates for more rapid scaling up of aid, as well as encouraging new thinking for making aid more effective.

Voice and accountability. A growing number of voices are being raised about the account-ability of IFIs. While focused on the issues of quotas, shares, and chairs in organizations such as the IMF, there is a broader critique of IFI accountability and an effort to have greater civil society oversight and influence on IFI activities. Civil society voices call for stronger focus of the IFIs on the impact of rich-country policies on development.

Learning from Evaluations

Evaluations are a major element in the IFI results approach. Evaluation is the source of evidence-based learning to improve aid effectiveness. Each of the IFIs has an active evaluation office, conducting annual reviews of key programs. The COMPAS report indi-cates no major changes in learning proce-dures but suggests that the MDB evaluation offices play a greater role in the COMPAS process next year.

The evaluation offices of the IFIs have produced a number of reports in the past year relevant to the themes of strategic repo-sitioning faced by the IFIs.

The Independent Evaluation Group of the World Bank issued a report on middle-income countries. This report found a gener-ally positive view of World Bank engagement in middle-income countries but also found unmet demand from client countries to help them tackle the harder issues of inequal-ity, corruption, and environment. Much work in middle-income countries is oriented toward support of the private sector. The IDB's Office of Evaluation and Oversight found that while most private sector projects achieved their development outcomes, they constituted a weaker performing sector in the IDB. The EBRD evaluation office reported that EBRD operations in providing finance for property development in transition economies had been "partly successful," with poor performance in those economies where market-supporting institutions such as frameworks for property rights were not at an advanced stage.

Other studies looked more broadly at the relevance and impact of the IFIs. The IMF's Independent Evaluation Office found that spillovers and the potential for concerted multilateral action were not given sufficient emphasis in the Fund's reviews of member countries exchange rate policies. The World Bank's evaluators found that regional aid programs offered considerable promise but accounted for only 3 percent of total aid and were weakly linked to country assistance strategies; the evaluators called for a strengthening of the broader aid architecture. The ADB found that its resident missions had "successfully" delivered on their promise to improve the efficiency and effectiveness of operations in client countries but called for a systematic corporate decentralization strategy to respond to future challenges. In another review, the ADB advocated a change in its technical assistance strategy and management to clarify strategic direction at the country level. The AfDB is also conducting a review of its development effectiveness.

These studies suggest that the IFIs have the structures for institutional learning in place. They also suggest, however, that the new strategic directions that the IFIs have outlined are moving the institutions into unfamiliar territory where existing good practices are still evolving.

Promoting Environmental Sustainability

Over the years, the IFIs have vastly expanded the level and scope of their environmental activities. This includes design and imple-

mentation of a variety of environmental products, including projects, policy guidance, research, and training. The IFIs have played a pivotal role in engaging developing countries and international and local organizations on various environmental matters, such as energy development and efficiency, the threat to the ozone layer, greenhouse gas (GHG) emissions, loss of biodiversity, and ocean pollution. Individually and collectively, IFIs are responding to the challenge of climate change by supporting the integration of climate concerns into development policy making and poverty reduction strategies. They have taken major new initiatives to help clients address climate change mitigation and adaptation.

Strategic Framework

In promoting environmental sustainability, the IFIs focus attention on the nexus between environmental conditions, quality of life, and the sustainability of growth and therefore closely align environmental sustainability with the other MDGs. The World Bank's overarching vision for environmental sustainability is laid out in the 2001 Environment Strategy, which outlines policies and actions to promote environmental improvements as fundamental elements of development and poverty reduction strategies.[23] Recognizing the challenge of climate change that confronts all countries and particularly the poorest, the World Bank is currently developing a strategic framework to scale up its work on climate change mitigation and adaptation.

Other IFIs are also paying increased attention to environmental sustainability and the threat of climate change. Environmental sustainability is expected to receive increased emphasis in the ADB's Long-Term Strategic Framework, currently being developed. The ADB's Clean Energy and Environment Program, including the energy efficiency initiative and carbon market initiatives, are focused on environmental sustainability in the energy sector. Similarly, the IDB's strategy for sustainable economic growth outlines actions to promote growth while preserving the natural resource base as well as social and cultural features. The AfDB board approved a new policy on the environment in 2004, which emphasizes environmentally sustainable development. The EBRD plans to expand investments in energy efficiency, renewable energy, and reduction of GHG emissions within its mandate of promoting environmentally sound and sustainable development in all its activities.

The IMF also is paying increased attention to environmental and climate change issues. The Fund stands ready to assist its members in analyzing macroeconomic effects and making the right fiscal policy choices when dealing with environmental issues. The Spring 2008 *World Economic Outlook* examines the macroeconomic implications for the global economy of the potential flows from payments for carbon credits, how countries may best use those revenues, and mitigation and adaptation policy responses to climate change. The IMF will also analyze the fiscal implications of climate change and alternative adaptation mechanisms to deal with its effects.

Environmental Mainstreaming

All IFIs have aimed at mainstreaming environmental issues in their country assistance strategies, sectoral- and policy-lending operations, and analytic activities. The recent review of the World Bank environment strategy documents that mainstreaming of environment issues into the Bank's programs and activities has increased, particularly over the last five years.[24] Similarly, environmental dimensions have been mainstreamed into ADB operations (representing about 12 percent of ADB's annual investments). The ADB has adopted sector-specific policies or strategies on forestry (1995), fisheries (1997), energy (2000), and water (2001). Environmental considerations also figure prominently in key sector policies of the EBRD and the IDB. In addition to increasing investment in traditional environmental sectors, they are placing heightened emphasis on environmental components in economic and social sector operations.

Both the ADB and the EBRD require that a country environmental analysis (CEA) be undertaken every time a country assistance strategy is prepared or revised. This has become a principal mechanism for upstreaming environmental considerations in the context of the Banks' country programming. The CEAs are designed to give an overview of current environmental challenges and the governing legal and institutional framework and to set out the priority investment needs for the country. While not a mandatory requirement, the World Bank and the IDB also have prepared a number of CEAs to inform country operations. These assessments identify sectors and issues that are of highest priority. However, not all CEAs prepared by IFIs so far have achieved tangible outcomes. This could be attributed to a variety of reasons including process of preparation and lack of follow up after completion.

Compliance with Safeguard Policies

The IFIs have over the years developed policies and instruments for mitigation and management of potentially negative environmental impacts of their projects. This has been done through more effective upstream analytical work and dialogue, focused project design and implementation, and strengthened application of environmental safeguards. The environment assessment process has been designed and refined over the years to better assess the economic, social, and environmental aspects of any proposed project. Also, in a number of cases an environmental management plan or mitigation measures have been required to avoid, mitigate, or compensate for a project's harmful effects. Most IFIs have been updating their environmental and social safeguard policies to ensure relevance to changing needs.

There has also been a growing emphasis on harmonization and alignment of safeguard policies and country systems. In 2005, as a part of the Paris Declaration on

Aid Effectiveness, donors and partner countries agreed to foster the better integration of social and environmental considerations into country strategies and programs. The application of safeguard policies to new lending instruments and approaches to development assistance have resulted in several recent safeguards initiatives. These include, for example, the adoption by the World Bank of a new operational policy in 2005 on piloting the use of borrower country systems to address environmental and social issues in Bank-supported projects (box 5.10).

Climate Change Mitigation and Adaptation

IFIs are developing climate change strategies and policies to help client countries mitigate GHG emissions. In regions where the impact of global warming is already apparent, the IFIs are also increasingly helping countries to adapt to the new environment.

The World Bank's Clean Energy for Development Investment Framework is designed to accelerate investments to mitigate GHG emissions by moving to a low-carbon economy. As a follow-up to this framework, the Bank is preparing a new strategy to better integrate climate change in the broader sustainable development objectives.[25] The Bank intends to focus on providing innovative and concessional financing to facilitate both public and private sector investments in low-carbon and adaptation projects; pioneering and advancing new market and trading mechanisms (box 5.11); facilitating technology deployment and transfer to developing

---

BOX 5.10 World Bank country systems pilot

On March 18, 2005, World Bank Executive Directors approved the launch of a pilot program to explore using a country's own environmental and social safeguard systems as an alternative to Bank safeguard policies for selected investment projects. This approach aimed to address what many borrowers viewed as excessive and unnecessary transaction costs of doing business with the Bank, while increasing borrower ownership and facilitating donor harmonization of safeguard policies. The pilot program was adopted in support of the Paris Declaration on Aid Effectiveness, in which donors and borrowers agreed to promote greater use of country systems for financial management, procurement, and environmental and social safeguards. Key to this approach is an increased emphasis by the Bank on capacity building and human resource development. To govern the pilot program the Board approved a new operational policy—Piloting the Use of Borrower Systems to Address Environmental and Social Safeguard Issues in Bank-Supported Projects. The rules define the approach and the criteria for assessing country systems and specify the respective roles of the borrower and the Bank.

Following two years of implementation, the results of the pilot program were evaluated. The evaluation was based on pilots undertaken in Bhutan, the Arab Republic of Egypt, Ghana, Jamaica, Romania, and Tunisia (additional pilots are under way or have been identified in Bhutan, Ghana, India, Morocco, South Africa, Tunisia, and Uganda). Results indicate a substantial potential for use of borrower systems for environmental assessment given strong borrower ownership and capacity to undertake such assessments. For social safeguards, such as involuntary resettlement, there are significant challenges to reconciling differences between Bank and borrower systems. Diligent application of a new analytical tool—the Safeguards Diagnostic Review—will help ensure that Bank safeguards are not diluted in the process of using country systems. Coordination among donors is necessary to mobilize the resources needed to attain and sustain the capacity of borrowers to implement their own systems. The evaluation also identified obstacles, at country level and internally, to more extensive application of the pilot program. As a result, the board in January 2008 approved a proposal to provide more incentives and support for use of country systems for environmental and social safeguards.

BOX 5.11 Carbon Partnership Facility and Forest Carbon Partnership Facility

Since the entry into force of the Kyoto Protocol in 2005, the World Bank has taken a lead role in ensuring that poor countries can benefit from international responses to climate change, including the emerging carbon market for greenhouse gas emission reductions. Significant progress has been made in the development of the carbon markets. The Umbrella Carbon Facility was fully funded in August 2006 with total capital of $1 billion. Two new carbon facilities—the Carbon Partnership Facility (CPF) and the Forest Carbon Partnership Facility (FCPF)—were launched in December 2007 to scale up carbon finance.

The CPF is designed to scale up carbon finance through programmatic and sector-based approaches and support long-term, low-carbon investments by purchasing emission reductions beyond 2012. It is intended to use carbon markets to promote GHG mitigation, enhancing the value of carbon finance to leverage investment for clean energy and the use of lower-carbon technology. The FCPF has been developed in response to requests from developing and industrial countries to explore a framework for piloting activities that would improve livelihoods in forested areas while reducing emissions from deforestation and degradation.

countries; creating an enabling environment to tap the private sector; and expanding research on mitigation and adaptation. The Bank, in partnership with the governments of the United Kingdom and the Netherlands, is leading a global program of research on the economics of adaptation in developing countries, which was launched at the UN Framework Convention on Climate Change meeting in Bali in December 2007.

The regional banks' approaches reflect their regional perspectives. The ADB is focusing on both mitigation and adaptation, including infrastructure development and finance, especially in the energy, transport, agriculture, and water sectors. The EBRD has placed its main emphasis on mitigation and is also developing an approach to adaptation. The EBRD's climate change initiatives include supporting efforts to improve energy efficiency and develop renewable energy sources to reduce the region's dependence on fossil fuels. In May 2006 the EBRD launched a specific initiative, the Sustainable Energy Initiative, to scale up climate change mitigation investment. The objective is to more than double EBRD investment in this area, to €1.5 billion over the period 2006–2008, with a total project value estimated at €5 billion. By the end of 2007, investment by the EBRD under the initiative had exceeded the three-year target of €1.5 billion.

The IDB's Sustainable Energy and Climate Change Initiative, approved in March 2007, is designed to expand the development and use of renewable energy sources, energy efficiency technologies and practices, and carbon finance, as well as to promote climate change adaptation to reduce the region's vulnerability. The IDB has established a team to implement and coordinate activities under this initiative. The AfDB is currently working on a strategy for climate risk management and adaptation as well as developing renewable energy and energy efficiency programs. Work in this area will include partnering with other bilateral and multilateral agencies on climate change for Africa within the "Nairobi Framework." Related initiatives include ongoing discussions on setting up a carbon financing facility and a biofuel support facility.

Financing of Environmental Activities

Environment-related lending has been an increasingly important component of World Bank operations. World Bank investment lending for environment and natural resources management between 2002 and 2007 amounted to $10.2 billion. This constituted about 10.4 percent of total Bank lending. In terms of thematic distribution, pollution management and environmental health activities make up the largest share of the lending (35 percent), followed by water resource management activities (29 percent) (figure 5.7). Besides investment projects, Development Policy Lending is another instrument through which the Bank is supporting environmental policy and institutional reforms. This lending rose sharply, from $59 million in 2004 to $264 million in 2006.

In addition to lending, the Bank administers grant facilities to support the implementation of global environmental agreements and the mainstreaming of their objectives into operations of the Global Environment Facility (GEF). The active portfolio of World Bank–implemented GEF projects at the end of fiscal 2007 included 219 projects, with total net GEF grant commitments of $1.6 billion. In terms of cumulative approvals since 1991, the climate change focal area has received the largest funding ($1.5 billion) followed by biodiversity ($1.3 billion) and international waters ($0.5 billion).

Investments in environment-related projects have also been rising at the regional IFIs. In the past 10 years, the ADB supported 113 investment projects with environmental objectives or elements for a cumulative value of $8.4 billion; these investments averaged $720 million a year and represented about 12 percent of the ADB's overall annual investments. These investments reached a high of 21 percent of the total in 2006. Urban environmental management and natural resources management accounted for more than 80 percent of these investments (figure 5.8). The EBRD's cumulative environmental investments were $3.8 billion between 2002 and 2006 and included projects dealing with municipal environmental infrastructure, energy efficiency, and cleanup operations. Over the same period, the IDB approved 79 environmental loans, investing $2 billion. The focus was primarily on water and sanitation (88 percent). Environmental lending

FIGURE 5.7 Active World Bank environment and natural resource portfolio, by thematic distribution, as of June 30, 2007

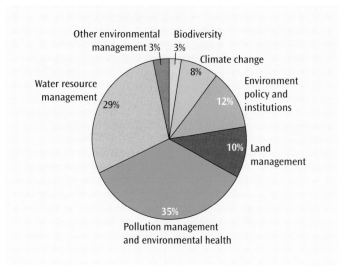

Source: World Bank.

FIGURE 5.8 ADB projects with environmental elements by theme, 2006

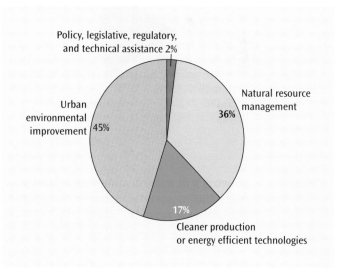

Source: Asian Development Bank.

amounted to about 10 percent of total IDB lending. In addition to these investments in environmental sectors, the IDB, and other regional development banks have been financing environmental components in economic and social sector loans.

Notes

1. IMF 2007 (revised with new purchasing power parity data, January 2008).

2. ADB 2007.

3. World Bank 2007; Zoellick 2007.

4. AfDB 2008.

5. EBRD 2006, p. 4.

6. World Bank 2007e.

7. World Bank 2007c.

8. Financial closure and guarantee effectiveness for four operations are still pending.

9. A municipal fund, which provides loans, guarantees, and equity investments in support of the infrastructure investments of municipalities and other subnational entities without requiring a sovereign guarantee, has been set up at the IFC. The Municipal Fund team also has developed a pipeline of more than 20 projects in all emerging regions.

10. A total of 45 countries made pledges to IDA15, the highest number of donors in IDA's history. Six countries—China, Cyprus, Arab Republic of Egypt, Estonia, Latvia, and Lithuania, are becoming new IDA donors. China and Egypt were once IDA borrowers and have joined the Republic of Korea and Turkey as current donors and prior recipients of IDA's assistance.

7. IDA reports a correlation between country capacity to coordinate aid and total aid received.

8. See detailed analysis in *Global Monitoring Report 2007.*

9. OECD 2007b.

10. World Bank, 2007d, annex 1.

11. Dollar and Levin 2004.

12. World Bank 2007h.

13. Both the AfDB and the World Bank, for instance, have developed an exceptional allocation framework for postconflict countries to allow countries to benefit from additional resources over and above their performance-based allocation for a limited period

14. IDA 2007b.

15. World Bank 2007f.

16. IDA 2007a.

17. The COMPAS report was initiated in 2005, with an initial set of indicators that are intended to constitute the basis for tracking future trends in their performance. The 2006 and 2007 COMPAS reports incorporate some revisions. These changes include slight modifications to a few indicators, the inclusion of performance indicators for the private sector operations of MDBs, the participation of the Islamic Development Bank for the first time, contributions from a group more representative of the bilateral donor community, and greater involvement of MDBs' independent evaluation offices to enhance the objectivity and the credibility of data.

18. Eurodad 2007.

19. World Bank 2001.

20. World Bank 2007b.

21. *Towards a Strategic Framework on Climate Change and Development for the World Bank Group.* World Bank 2008.

II

Special Theme: Environmental Sustainability

A Framework for Monitoring Environmental Sustainability

MDG 7 is simply stated: ensure environmental sustainability. However, the idea of environmental sustainability goes beyond the conservation of nature. Natural resources—and the environment in general—are different from many other economic goods and services in that they constitute simultaneously an integral part of ecological cycles, inputs to production processes, and a source of enjoyment for households and individuals. Environmental goods can be used up or depleted to make space for produced goods (such as transforming a wetland into an urban area). Yet this economic process may entail a permanent loss of environmental goods with a use or an intrinsic value for which no substitute is available. The "art" of balancing nature and development so that

social welfare does not decline over time is at the core of environmental sustainability.

A flow diagram to frame the relationship between the economy and the environment is presented in figure 1. On the right-hand side, production of man-made goods and services takes place and contributes to household well-being. Wealth (the left-hand side of the figure) sustains production and may also contribute directly to well-being. Wealth in such a framework necessarily goes beyond physical and monetary assets to include natural assets and intangibles such as human capital. Production processes may entail the depletion or depreciation of assets, as may the direct use of assets by households, whereas other uses of assets are nondepleting. Production and consumption

PART II

FIGURE 1   Framework for monitoring environmental sustainability

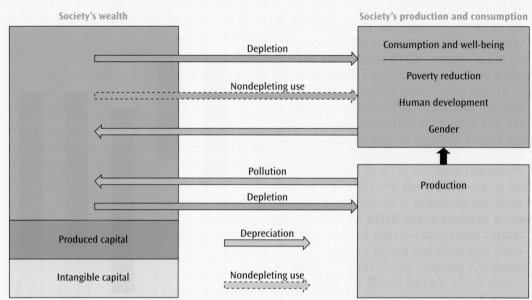

both lead to flows of pollution and waste, which alter the quality of natural assets in particular.

Concerns about environmental sustainability arise because, unlike labor and produced capital, the environment is often an unpriced input into production. This is true for much natural capital. Fisheries and forests in many countries are open access natural resources, as is groundwater. Lack of property rights to these resources prevents them from being used sustainably. Without appropriate institutions, an open-access fishery will be overharvested and habitat for biodiversity will be destroyed. Users of these resources will impose externalities on others. The same is true for air and water as receptors of pollution. In the absence of appropriate institutions, a power plant will impose external costs on households in the form of local air pollutants (such as particulate matter) and also on the earth's climate in the form of carbon dioxide emissions.

Concern about the externalities associated with environmental resources leads to the desire to monitor environmental externalities—levels of local air pollutants and the stock of greenhouse gases in the earth's

atmosphere—as well as stocks of natural capital—forests and fish populations—when these stocks may be used inefficiently. Correcting the externalities associated with environmental resources requires public action. Monitoring environmental sustainability also entails monitoring the ability of local and national governments to allocate environmental resources efficiently and the ability of the nations of the world to use the global commons efficiently.

Chapter 6 of this report monitors environmental sustainability at the local and national levels. It examines environmental pollution and the depletion of natural resources, including forests, water, and land. It also monitors the capacity of countries to deal with local and national environmental problems. Chapter 7 monitors the sustainability of the global commons. Avoiding adverse changes to the earth's climate, protecting biodiversity, and ensuring the sustainability of marine fisheries are three components of ensuring global environmental sustainability. Chapter 7 examines what progress has been made in protecting these environmental public goods, with an emphasis on climate change.

6

Ensuring Environmental Sustainability at the National Level

Achieving environmental sustainability underpins progress on many of the Millenium Development Goals (MDGs). If forests are lost, soils degraded, fisheries depleted, waters polluted, or the air unbreathable, then achievements in poverty reduction may not be sustainable. The evidence in this chapter suggests that developing countries are highly dependent on natural resources and that the mineral and oil-based economies are, in many cases, consuming their national wealth. Deforestation is a fact in many low-income countries, while middle-income countries, and several low-income economies, face high levels of pollution. Water scarcity is a growing problem in countries that are already water-stressed. These trends place a premium on the ability of developing countries to manage their environment and natural resources.

MDG 7—to ensure environmental sustainability—includes four targets (table 6.1). The overarching target, 7.A, presents major challenges for global monitoring. In fact, unlike most of the other MDG targets, its goal is neither quantitative nor time-bound. This chapter takes up the challenge of monitoring progress toward target 7.A, to reverse the loss of environmental resources, by looking at specific indicators of pressure on

the environment, at the broader question of assessing progress toward sustainable development, and at the adequacy of policies and institutions for environmental sustainability in developing countries. Given its global

TABLE 6.1   The targets under MDG 7

Sustainability outcomes	Sustainability policies
Environment Target 7.A: [. . .] Reverse the loss of environmental resources Target 7.B: Reduce biodiversity loss, achieving, by 2010, a significant reduction in the rate of loss	Target 7.A: Integrate the principles of sustainable development into country policies and programmes [. . .]
Infrastructure Target 7.C: Halve, by 2015, the proportion of people without sustainable access to safe drinking water and basic sanitation Target 7.D: By 2020, to have achieved a significant improvement in the lives of at least 100 million slum dwellers	

nature, the biodiversity target, 7.B, is dealt with in chapter 7. Water and sanitation targets are addressed in chapter 2.

Achieving environmental sustainability has both a national and a global character. Some actions, such as reducing particulate matter in urban areas, will have largely local effects. Other actions, such as mitigating greenhouse gas emissions, will affect global sustainability. Other activities, such as reducing deforestation, can have impacts that are both local and global. This chapter focuses primarily on local, national-level actions, but there are inevitable overlaps with chapter 7, which focuses on global environmental sustainability.

Sustainable Development and the MDGs

Table 6.2 highlights the potential links between actions on MDG 7 and other selected MDGs.

Income and poverty reduction. The environment and natural resources constitute a major source of income, especially in the poorest countries: water resources sustain agriculture and industry; forests provide construction materials and energy; mineral exports can generate foreign exchange. In low-income countries natural resources can be an important driver of growth, which in turn can provide the scope for poverty reduction. To make this possible, there is a need for institutions that allow efficient use of public goods and that manage rents equitably. The environmental contribution to income and poverty reduction can be assessed both at the macro and the micro level. The wealth estimates presented in chapter 1 are an example of the former. Microlevel indicators include measures of household dependence on natural resources (the contribution of natural resource income to overall household income; see box 6.1). Natural resources can also serve as a buffer, or insurance, during times of need.

TABLE 6.2 Environmental links to the MDGs

MDG	Environmental action	Policy input
Eradicate extreme poverty and hunger	Improve natural resource management where natural resources contribute a high share of household income	Land titling Market creation
Achieve universal primary education	Reduce education costs of malnutrition by improving environmental conditions	Access to water and sanitation
Promote gender equality and empower women	Reduce time spent collecting water and biomass for cooking and heating Reduce female exposure to pollutants Involve women in environmental and natural resource management	Access to water and sanitation Electrification
Reduce child mortality and improve maternal health Combat HIV/AIDS, malaria, and other infectious diseases	Reduce environmental risk factors	Access to water and sanitation Access to electricity Reduce exposure to indoor air pollution Water resource management in mosquito-infested areas
Foster global partnerships	Agree on a global plan of action to combat climate change	Targets for greenhouse gas emission reduction Development and diffusion of new technologies Development of carbon markets

BOX 6.1 The importance of environmental income to the poor

Wild or uncultivated natural resources contribute to the welfare of the poor, in some cases significantly . While this finding cannot be generalized to all rural households (note the wide ranges in the table below) resource income can contribute over 40 percent of overall household income in some rural areas. This is particularly true for households living on the fringes of forests. Some case studies show that poor households are dependent on natural resources even in areas where those resources are more scarce or less accessible.

Environmental income in resource-poor and resource-rich rural areas
percentage of total incomes

Study	Resource-rich areas		Resource-poor/ low-access areas		Average	
	Poor	Rich	Poor	Rich	Poor	Rich
Jodha 1986					9–26	1–4
Cavendish 2000			44	30		
Vedeld and others 2004					32	17
Narain, vant Veld, and Gupta 2005	41	23	18	18		
Chettri-Khattri 2007	20	14	2	1		

This high dependence on natural resources can exacerbate vulnerability to climate variability. For example, the Intergovernmental Panel on Climate Change estimates that climate change will increase the number of undernourished people in the world by between 40 million and 170 million by 2050. Climate change is likely to exacerbate food insecurity especially in the most malnourished world regions, such as Sub-Saharan Africa.

Source: World Bank 2008b; IPCC 2007.

Education. Educational attainment is lower where lack of water, sanitation, and hygiene is a major cause of malnutrition, as seen in chapter 2. Many studies have documented the effect of early childhood malnutrition on cognitive function, school enrollment, grade repetition, school dropout rates, grade attainment, and test scores among school-age children.[1] A study for the World Bank goes one step further and assesses the effect of lack of water, sanitation, and hygiene on malnutrition and education performance.[2] In Ghana and Pakistan, the study finds that water-related infections cause an annual loss in education performance equivalent to 4.9 and 4.2 percent of GDP, respectively.

Gender equality. The cost of obtaining clean water and energy in developing countries is borne mostly by women and young children. The many hours devoted to these tasks mean less opportunity for women to participate in market-based activities (and thus to earn income independently) and less time for children to go to school. Women performing household tasks are also more exposed to indoor smoke.

Health. Environmental health risks (e.g., lack of water and sanitation and indoor air pollution) are the main cause of child mortality and a major risk factor for maternal health. The World Health Organization

(WHO) shows that an estimated 24 percent of the 2004 global burden of disease and 23 percent of all deaths can be attributed to environmental factors; among children 0-14 years of age, the proportion of deaths attributable to environmental risk factors is 36 percent.[3] The environmental link to infectious diseases is also an important one. HIV-infected people are particularly at risk from unsanitary environments. Malaria and other vector-borne diseases can be prevented by controlling potential breeding grounds such as irrigation systems, poor drainage, and stagnant water.

Global partnerships. Global action for development cannot succeed without coordinated support for provision of global public goods, including environmental goods. Climate change threatens to reverse many achievements in the fight against poverty. Increases in extreme climatic events such as droughts and floods in the poorest countries may also exacerbate conflicts and cross-coun-

try migration. Controlling greenhouse gas emissions constitutes a major challenge for international action and cooperation going forward, as highlighted in chapter 7.

Measuring Progress on Outcomes

The complete set of MDG 7 indicators is shown in box 6.2. The indicators are diverse, aiming to cover a range of pressures on the environment. Environmental issues differ across countries, and their rank as policy priorities may vary depending on specific country circumstances. When it comes to monitoring environmental sustainability, one size does not fit all.

Measuring Progress in Natural Resources Management

Forests. Forests are particularly important natural assets, because they harbor biodiversity, provide environmental services, and

---

BOX 6.2   MDG 7 indicators

Target 7.A: Integrate the principles of sustainable development into country policies and programs and reverse the loss of environmental resources

7.1 Proportion of land area covered by forest
7.2 CO_2 emissions, total, per capita and per \$1 GDP (PPP), and consumption of ozone-depleting substances
7.3 Proportion of fish stocks within safe biological limits
7.4 Proportion of total water resources used

Target 7.B: Reduce biodiversity loss, achieving, by 2010, a significant reduction in the rate of loss

7.5 Proportion of terrestrial and marine areas protected
7.6 Proportion of species threatened with extinction

Target 7.C: Halve, by 2015, the proportion of people without sustainable access to safe drinking water and basic sanitation

7.7 Proportion of population using an improved drinking water source
7.8 Proportion of population using an improved sanitation facility

Target 7.D: By 2020, to have achieved a significant improvement in the lives of at least 100 million slum dwellers

7.9 Proportion of urban population living in slums

Note: GDP (PPP) stands for purchasing power parity–adjusted GDP.

---

sequester carbon dioxide (CO_2). According to the Food and Agriculture Organization (FAO), in 2005 the world average forest endowment was 0.61 hectares of forest per capita, equivalent to the size of five Olympic-size swimming pools. Forest assets are not distributed evenly, however; two-thirds of the global forest area is concentrated in 10 countries, while nearly 140 countries together have less than 5 percent of the world's forests. On average, South Asia has less than 0.06 hectares of forest per capita while the Europe and Central Asia region has 1.94 hectares per capita. Forests are relatively more abundant per capita in richer countries: forest endowments in high-income countries (0.93 hectares per capita) were three times greater than in low-income countries (0.29 hectares per capita) in 2005. High deforestation rates and population growth in the poorest countries have widened this gap over time.

The net loss of forest area in the period 2000–05 is estimated at 73,000 square kilometers a year (an area about the size of Sierra Leone or Panama). Deforestation, mainly from conversion into agricultural land, was very high in low- and middle-income countries, especially in Latin America and the Caribbean and Sub-Saharan Africa (figure 6.1).[4] At the other end of the spectrum is East Asia and the Pacific, where forest area grew between 2000 and 2005 as the result of a major afforestation program in China; this growth masks the situation in Indonesia, which continues to have one of the highest deforestation rates in the world (1.6 percent a year between 2000 and 2005).[5]

Water resources. Monitoring water resources presents major challenges, particularly in the case of groundwater. Information sources are numerous but seldom complete, and access to information on water resources is still sometimes restricted for reasons related to political sensitivities at the local or regional level. Data are available from FAO's AQUASTAT and several World Resources Institute (WRI) compilations.[6] Cross-country comparisons

FIGURE 6.1 Annual deforestation by region and for top 10 countries, 2000–05

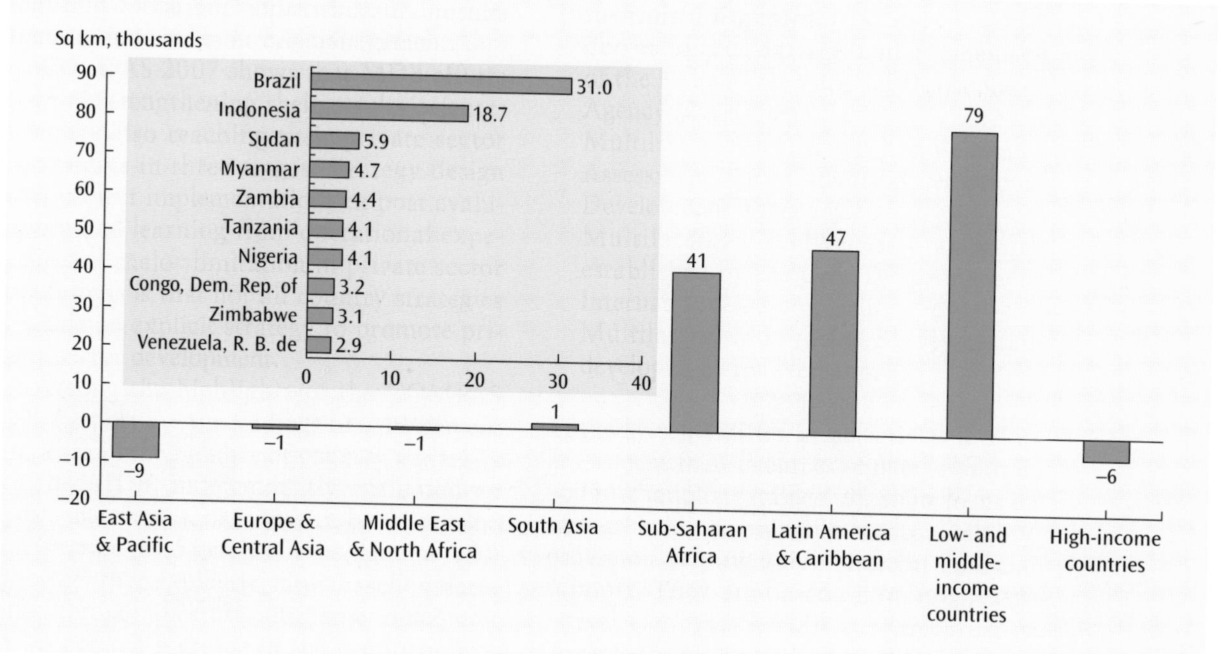

Source: World Bank 2008c.

of water resource data should be made with caution, owing to differing measurement methods and base years.

Water resources are abundant in Latin America and the Caribbean, Europe and Central Asia, and in certain areas of East Asia and the Pacific and Sub-Saharan Africa. The Middle East and North Africa and South Asia regions experience water stress and have a level of internal freshwater resources below 2,000 cubic meters per capita (figure 6.2). The situation is particularly critical in the Middle East and North Africa. Under current projected population growth, water resources per capita are expected to fall below 500 cubic meters per capita in the Middle East by 2050 (figure 6.3).

Worldwide, total annual freshwater withdrawals amount to about 9 percent of freshwater resources available. Agriculture is the largest user of water, accounting worldwide for 70 percent of total withdrawals. This figure rises to 78 percent in low- and middle-income countries and falls to 43 percent in high-income countries (figure 6.4). While most regions have high levels of freshwater surplus, in the Middle East and North Africa region freshwater withdrawals are estimated to be above the level of resources

available. Underground abstraction in some countries substantially exceeds the recharge level, particularly in the Arabian Peninsula, which relies heavily on underground water. Figure 6.5 shows that countries such as Kuwait, Qatar, Saudi Arabia, and the United Arab Emirates, as well as Libya in North Africa, consume more than five times the level of annual available resources.[7] The United Nations Environment Programme predicts that the problem of allocating scarce water resources among competing uses will worsen, despite progress in reforming agricultural policies in some countries.[8] Climate change is likely to contribute to water stress around the world (e.g., through impacts on snowmelt in the Himalayas and the Andean region, which may alter water availability patterns significantly). Chapter 7 provides more details on the projected impacts of global warming.

Energy and mineral resources. Oil, gas, and coal constitute the dominant source of primary energy, and they are expected to continue to dominate energy supply for the foreseeable future. The U.S. Energy Information Administration projects world primary energy demand to grow at an annual

FIGURE 6.2   Internal freshwater resources per capita, by region and income group, 2005

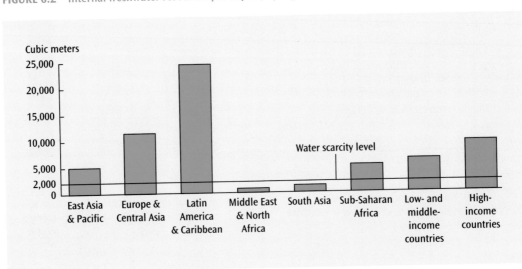

Source: World Bank 2008c.

FIGURE 6.3   Trends and projections in freshwater availability, West Asia

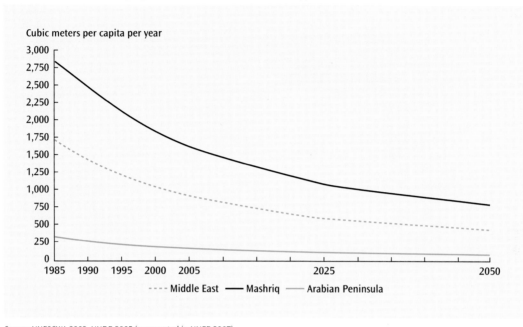

Source: UNESCWA 2003, UNDP 2005 (as reported in UNEP 2007).

FIGURE 6.4   Annual freshwater withdrawals, by region and income group, 2002

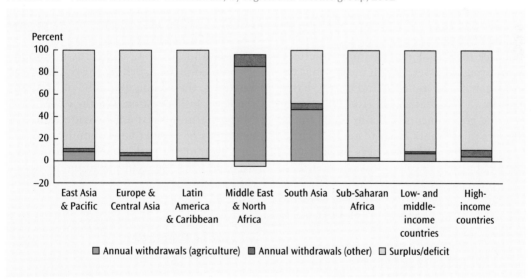

Source: World Bank 2008c.

rate of 1.8 percent a year over the next two decades.[9] Most of the new demand will come from China and India, where consumption is expected to grow by 3.2 percent and 3.6 percent a year, respectively. These rising energy needs will be increasingly met by coal. Coal demand is expected to increase by 73 percent between 2005 and 2030, while oil is expected to increase by 37 percent and gas by 17–22 percent.

FIGURE 6.5   Total water withdrawal relative to renewable water resources, selected countries

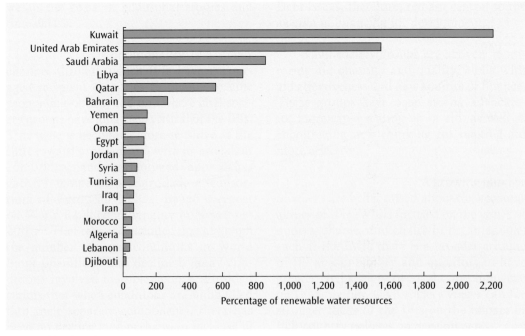

Source: World Bank 2007b.

From the point of view of the resource-exporting country, depleting an exhaustible resource like crude petroleum is, in effect, liquidating an asset, which means that the sustainability of mineral- and energy-based economies is potentially at risk. Oil companies and governments will aim to maximize the stream of rents from resource extraction over time. What matters most from a sustainability point of view is whether these resource rents are invested, rather than consumed, to sustain the income-generating capacity of the economy as nonrenewable resources are depleted.

The question of the sustainability of mineral- and energy-based economies is highlighted in figure 6.6, which combines data on mineral and energy depletion with figures on adjusted net savings (the measure of sustainability introduced in chapter 1). As seen at the top of the figure, the general tendency is for the big resource-extracting economies to have negative adjusted net savings rates (and therefore to be on an unsus-

tainable path). This is true in low-income countries in Sub-Saharan Africa such as Angola and Nigeria, as well as in middle-income countries such as the Syrian Arab Republic, the Islamic Republic of Iran, and the Russian Federation. On the other hand, Malaysia and Vietnam provide excellent examples of extractive economies that are on a sustainable path (that is, their net savings and investments in education more than offset the value of natural resource depletion and environmental degradation).

Measuring Progress in Pollution Management

Pollution emissions are a by-product of economic activity, belonging to the class of problems that economists term *externalities* to reflect the disconnect between the interests of the emitter of the pollution, who wishes to avoid costly pollution abatement expenditures, and the interests of the external parties, who are affected by the pollution through damage to their health or other assets.

Current scientific evidence indicates that urban air pollution causes a wide array of health effects ranging from minor inconvenience to death.[10] Major sources of urban air pollution are emissions from traffic and industrial sources. Nonanthropogenic sources such as dusty winds may also contribute significantly to air pollution in certain cities.

The urban air pollutant with the greatest impact on human health is particulate matter. Typically, this is measured as concentrations of fine, suspended particulates less than 10 microns (PM10) or 2.5 microns (PM2.5) in diameter (the latter are more damaging to health, but are not always monitored in developing countries). These particles are capable of penetrating the respiratory system deep enough to cause health damages. A World Bank study publishes time series of particulate matter concentrations that span the period 1990–2005.[11] The estimates measure the mean annual exposure level of the average urban resident to particulate matter outdoors. Concentrations have been declining across the board since 1990, with the steepest declines taking place in low-income countries, where concentration dropped from 130 micrograms per cubic meter ($\mu g/m^3$) to 77 $\mu g/m^3$ (a 40 percent decline). This decline shows how countries have, to varying degrees, internalized the cost of urban air pollution through policy changes (such as emission standards and pollution taxes). However, concentrations of PM10 in low-income countries continue to be nearly three times higher than those in high-income countries (figure 6.7).

Turning to water pollution, table 6.3 shows the world's top 10 emitters of industrial water pollution (measured in terms of biochemical oxygen demand, or BOD[12]). The data come from an international study of industrial emissions.[13] China heads the list by a wide margin, with 6 million kilograms of emissions a day, followed by the United States, with less than 2 million kilograms of daily emissions. India has a high

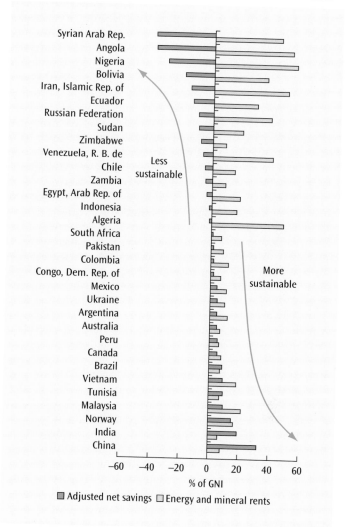

FIGURE 6.6 Sustainability in energy- and mineral-rich economies

Source: World Bank 2008c.

emission intensity, with 20 grams of emissions per day per worker, similar to that of Russia (21 grams per day per worker).

Energy Access, Health, and the Environment

The environment-development trade-off is nowhere more evident than in the case of energy. Without reliable energy, hospitals and health care infrastructure cannot provide dependable services, schools cannot run, and

FIGURE 6.7 Annual particulate matter (PM10) concentrations, 1990–2004

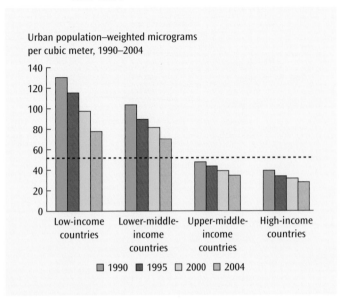

Urban population–weighted micrograms per cubic meter, 1990–2004

☐ 1990 ☑ 1995 ☐ 2000 ☐ 2004

Source: World Bank 2008c.
Note: The dashed line denotes the former (pre-September 2006) EPA standard for annual PM10 concentrations.

TABLE 6.3 Top 10 emitters of industrial water pollution, 2001

Rank	Country	Organic water pollutant (BOD) emissions	
		Kilograms per day	Grams per day per worker
1	China	6,088,663	14
2	United States	1,897,480	13
3	India	1,515,683	20
4	Russian Federation	1,398,496	21
5	Japan	1,279,503	15
6	Germany	982,313	13
7	Indonesia	753,657	18
8	France	616,092	16
9	United Kingdom	599,088	16
10	Italy	493,551	12

Source: World Bank 2008c.

households are forced to use more expensive and inefficient ways of lighting, cooking, and heating. But the generation, transmission, and use of modern energy can have heavy environmental costs. For example, thermal generation plants are major sources of air pollution and CO_2 emissions, and hydropower

can change entire ecosystems and facilitate the spread of vector-borne disease.

Chapter 2 has shown that indoor air pollution is a major cause of mortality in developing countries. This is linked in particular to the lack of energy access. About a quarter of the world population (1.6 billion people) has no access to electricity (table 6.4).[14] The majority of these people live in South Asia, Sub-Saharan Africa, and East Asia and the Pacific. Data at the national level highlight some extreme cases: Afghanistan, Burkina Faso, the Democratic Republic of Congo, and Mozambique have the highest percentage of population without access to electricity, at over 93 percent each.

Lack of access to modern sources of energy is not only a health risk factor, it is a major cause of deforestation as well. Most of the people without access to electricity (1.3 billion, or 81 percent of the total) live in rural areas.[15] Urban-rural differences can be striking. In Malawi 35 percent of urban households are connected compared with only 2 percent of rural households. In Lao People's Democratic Republic access is 44 percent in urban areas and 20 percent in rural areas. Livelihoods of the rural poor depend heavily on the capacity of the ecosystem to provide a sustained source of fuel, and in some regions fuel wood crises loom in the next decade. The loss of forest resources has consequent impacts on biodiversity and the ability of ecosystems to provide key services to the economy, such as regulating water flow.

Progress in improving electricity access in the last 15 years has been slow, with some exceptions. The fastest increase in access rates has taken place in China, which reached almost universal access (99 percent) in 2005. Excluding China, the share of the developing world population without access to electricity has actually increased since 1990. Population growth in particular has offset the modest increases in energy investments. The International Energy Agency estimates that if no new policies are put in place, in 2030 there will still be 1.4 billion people without access to electricity.[16]

TABLE 6.4   Access to electricity, by region, 2005

	Population (millions)	Population without electricity (millions)	Electrification rate (%)	Urban electrification rate (%)	Rural electrification rate (%)
Africa	891	554	37.8	67.9	19.0
North Africa	153	7	95.4	98.7	91.8
Sub-Saharan Africa	738	547	25.9	58.3	8.0
Developing Asia	3418	930	72.8	86.4	65.1
China and East Asia	1951	224	88.5	94.9	84.0
South Asia	1467	706	51.9	69.7	44.7
Latin America	449	45	90.0	98.0	65.6
Middle East	186	41	78.0	86.7	61.8
Developing Countries	4,944	1,570	68.2	85.2	56.4
Transition economies and OECD	1,510	8	99.5	100.0	98.1
World	6,454	1,578	75.6	90.4	61.7

Source: IEA 2006.

In addition to population growth, a major bottleneck in the poorest countries is the infrastructure gap. Sub-Saharan Africa (excluding South Africa) has an installed capacity of 28 gigawatts (GW).[17] About 25 GW of new generation capacity will be needed in the region over the next decade to make up the present shortfall in supply and to meet future demand growth.

The data on the use of traditional biomass products for energy (wood, dung, crop waste, and biogas) show very little progress in the past 10 years. In low-income countries, the use of biomass products and waste as a percent of total energy use has dropped from 55 percent in 1990 to 48 percent in 2004 (figure 6.8). Dependence on biomass products for energy is especially high in Sub-Saharan Africa. Nine of the top 10 biomass-dependent countries are in this region (table 6.5).

Toward a Comprehensive Measure of Sustainability

The sector-specific indicators presented above are crucial for policy making. However, none of them is able to measure environmental sustainability in a comprehensive

way. Building upon the green national accounting literature, this section describes sustainability indicators that are based on a key principle of sustainable development: to sustain well-being it is necessary to ensure that the total value of assets does not decline in real terms.

FIGURE 6.8   Use of biomass products and waste, by income, 1990–2004

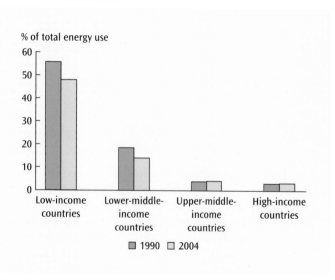

Source: World Bank 2008c.

TABLE 6.5 Top 10 users of biomass products and waste, 1990–2004
percentage of total energy use

	1990	2004
Congo, Dem. Rep. of	84.0	92.5
Tanzania	91.0	91.6
Ethiopia	92.8	90.4
Nepal	93.4	86.8
Mozambique	94.4	84.1
Nigeria	79.8	80.2
Sudan	81.7	79.2
Zambia	73.4	79.1
Cameroon	75.9	77.8
Kenya	78.4	74.1

Source: World Bank 2008c.

The notion that wealth (including natural wealth) is directly related to social welfare is not new. In a seminal paper published in 1961, Samuelson pointed out the inadequacy of income and consumption measures as a proxy for social welfare. The paper argued that the choice of a welfare measure has to be made "in the space of all present and future consumption. . . . [T]he only valid approximation to a measure of welfare comes from computing *wealth-like* magnitudes, not income magnitudes."[18]

A key sustainability indicator, adjusted net savings, was introduced in chapter 1 and will be presented briefly below. The second indicator pertains to a particular component of wealth, the total value of natural resources.

Measuring Changes in Comprehensive Wealth: Adjusted Net Savings

The concept of adjusted net savings is built around the notion that depletion of natural resources, damages to human health caused by pollution, and the resources invested in human capital are all components of national savings. To illustrate this concept, figure 6.9 decomposes saving for Bolivia at two different points in time. In 2002 the policy mix

was broadly sustainable, with net savings and investments in human capital roughly equaling the depletion of natural resources (mostly natural gas); pollution damages turn the adjusted net saving rate slightly negative. In 2005 high natural gas prices provided a windfall for the economy, but gross savings did not adjust fully. The result was that net wealth creation in 2005 turned sharply negative—Bolivia was, in effect, consuming its natural wealth. Maintaining this policy mix would place the economy on an unsustainable development path.

Figures 6.6 and 6.9 show that unsustainable development paths are more than a theoretical possibility. As emphasized previously, a negative saving rate in a country with abundant natural resources is an indication of an opportunity not taken: natural resource rents represent a type of free development finance, and consuming these rents is a process of consuming an inheritance.[19]

Adjusted net savings provides a useful indicator of sustainable development because it measures changes in the economy's total wealth. If population is growing, however, then the relevant sustainability indicator is the change in wealth per capita. In fact, even if total wealth is increasing, population growth may outstrip the growth in total asset value. A World Bank study shows that many developing countries, particularly in Sub-Saharan Africa, have positive adjusted net savings in total but declining wealth per person.[20]

Measuring Natural Capital

While adjusted net savings measures the change in *total* wealth in real terms, there are good reasons to concentrate on the evolution of *natural* wealth over time as well, particularly if there are limits on the substitutability of produced capital for natural capital. This distinction is especially useful in light of the formulation of MDG target 7.A: "reversing the loss of environmental resources."

A recent study by the World Bank disaggregates natural assets into agricultural land

FIGURE 6.9   Adjustments to the saving rate: The case of Bolivia in 2002 and 2005

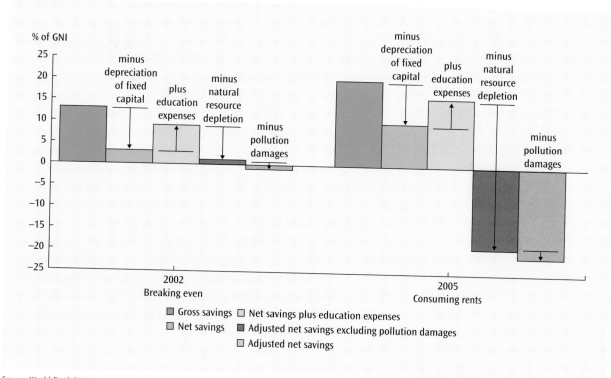

Source: World Bank 2008c.

(crops and pastures), forests (timber and nontimber forest resources), protected areas, and subsoil assets (oil, natural gas, coal, and minerals).[21] Natural capital constitutes a major component of wealth in developing countries, with the average citizen in low-income countries deriving 42 percent of his or her total wealth from some form of natural capital (see chapter 1 and figure 6.10a). This pattern is common to most developing regions, where, with the exception of Latin America and the Caribbean, natural capital accounts for more than a third of total wealth. The share of natural capital is particularly high in the Middle East and North Africa, where subsoil assets play a much larger role than in other regions. As seen in chapter 1, the value of natural capital per capita rises with income level. This is partly a consequence of higher productivity of land in more developed countries (where tech-

nologically advanced production methods allow higher yields per unit of land), partly a consequence of abundant subsoil assets in these countries, and partly a result of relative population sizes.

While high-income countries have more natural capital per person, less wealthy countries are more dependent on their endowments of natural resources, particularly agricultural land (figure 6.10b), as a share of total wealth. So, for example, a person from Sub-Saharan Africa has a total wealth of nearly US$10,000, of which US$2,000 is in the form of agricultural land. On average in low-income countries, the sum of cropland and pastureland accounts for nearly 25 percent of total wealth and 60 percent of natural wealth. This heavy reliance on agricultural land falls as income rises, a natural resource analogue to Engel's Law. Subsoil assets play a major role in natural wealth,

FIGURE 6.10   Relative importance and composition of natural capital, 2005

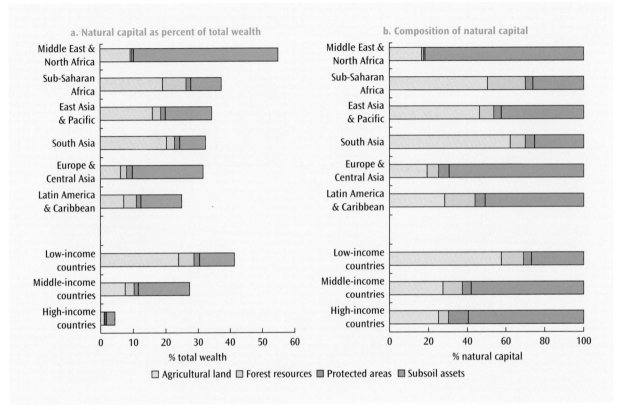

Source: World Bank staff.

particularly in Europe and Central Asia, the Middle East and North Africa, and Latin America and the Caribbean.

The region with the largest value of natural resources per capita is Latin America and the Caribbean (figure 6.11), with US$17,000 per capita. Natural wealth in the region consists mostly of subsoil assets (50 percent) and agricultural land (30 percent). In the Middle East and North Africa, natural resources account for US$12,000 per capita, mostly in the form of oil. Subsoil assets are also very important in Europe and Central Asia, where they account for 68 percent of natural wealth. In East Asia and the Pacific, natural wealth per capita is US$5,600 with a distribution similar to the one in Latin America and the Caribbean. Agricultural land is particularly important in Sub-Saharan Africa (62 percent of the total natural wealth of

US$3,900 per capita). In South Asia, natural wealth is US$2,600 per capita, with most wealth in the form of agricultural land (51 percent), subsoil assets (26 percent), and forests (20 percent).

As seen in figure 6.12, the value of the world's natural capital per capita (measured in 2000 U.S. dollars and deflated using a GDP deflator) increased from 1995 to 2000, largely because of the increase in real energy prices, followed by a slight decline to 2005 (energy prices continued to rise over this period but were more than offset by declines in food prices). In low-income countries, the value of natural capital fell from US$3,400 per capita in 1995 to US$3,100 per capita in 2005 (a 10 percent drop). The decline in value resulted partly from population growth and partly from falling agricultural yields and declining real crop prices. The per cap-

FIGURE 6.11   Natural capital per capita across regions of the world, 2005

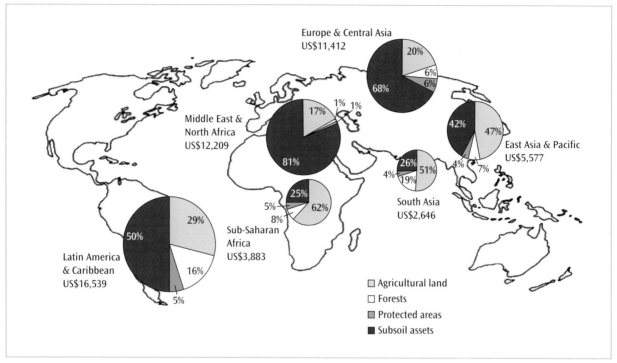

Source: World Bank staff.
Note: The size of each "pie" is proportional to the value of natural wealth per capita.

ita value of agricultural land in low-income countries fell 31 percent in real terms over the same period. Agricultural land values in these countries are also particularly vulnerable to the potential impact of climate change.[22]

Measuring Progress on Policies and Institutions

Public policy is important for protecting the environment and natural resources in most countries. This is because of the public good nature of some assets (such as parks and protected areas) and the market failures inherent in pollution emissions (no one owns the atmosphere, and so everyone is free to pollute it). For open access resources, such as forests and fisheries, governments need to define property rights regimes that will prevent the "tragedy of the commons."

But are good environmental policies something developing countries can afford? It has

been often argued that developing countries should "grow first and clean up later." This is the so-called Environmental Kuznets Curve (EKC), where pollution emissions rise with income until a tipping point is reached, where countries are wealthy enough to wish to invest in environmental quality. A major assumption of the EKC literature is that strong environmental governance is simply not possible for poor countries.

It turns out that a good institutional framework for the environment is not only possible but may improve the quality of growth. In empirical studies, the EKC disappears after controlling for the quality of environmental institutions and the inherent sensitivity of local environments to pollution: poor countries can have good policies and are not fated to be heavily polluted.[23] This is why indicators of environmental governance and institutions are becoming a very important item in the monitoring agenda.

FIGURE 6.12   Evolution of the value of natural capital

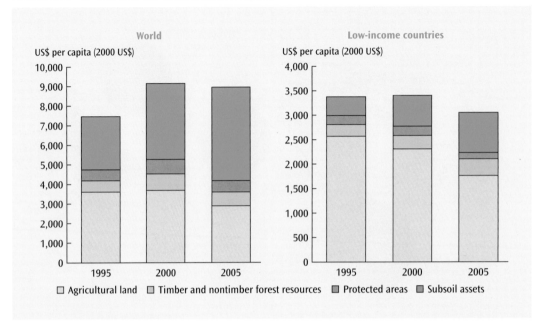

Source: World Bank staff.

A number of measures of policy and institutional quality have been attempted in the recent years. These include:

- Policy outcome indexes (such as the Environmental Performance Index, or EPI), which measure the results of government policy by looking at the distance of any given indicator from a target or appropriately defined benchmark; and
- Policy input indexes (such as the World Bank Country Policy and Institutional Assessment, or CPIA), which track policies for environmental management and assess the quality of institutions intended to enforce them.[24]

The Environmental Performance Index

The EPI is a measure of performance that identifies broadly accepted targets for a set of 25 indicators and measures how close each country comes to meeting these goals. By means of this distance-to-target approach, the EPI provides policy-relevant benchmarks for pollution control and natural resource management. The issue-by-issue rankings facilitate cross-country comparisons both globally and within relevant peer groups. The EPI ranks 149 countries on these indicators tracked across six policy categories: environmental health, air pollution, water resources, biodiversity and habitat, productive natural resources, and climate change.[25]

The EPI is divided into two major subcomponents: environmental health and ecosystem vitality, mirroring the priorities expressed by policy makers. Figure 6.13 shows the results of the 2008 EPI. With some notable exceptions, countries in Sub-Saharan Africa, South Asia, and parts of East Asia and the Pacific have the lowest performance. Higher-income countries on average have higher environmental performance scores than lower-income countries. However, within each income group, including the high-income group, individual country environmental performance var-

FIGURE 6.13 Environmental Performance Index, by income group and region, 2008

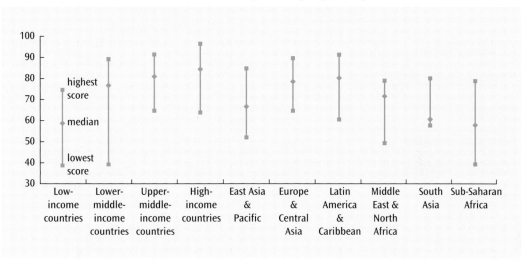

Source: Environmental Performance Index (http://epi.yale.edu/Home).

ies widely. An important factor underlying the low environmental performance of poor countries is these countries' limited capacity to invest in environmental infrastructure (such as water and sanitation systems), pollution control, and systematic natural resource management.

Country Policy and Institutional Assessments

The annual CPIA exercise at the World Bank measures the quality of a country's policy and institutional framework against a set of 16 criteria, including "Policies and Institutions for Environmental Sustainability." Country policies are rated on a scale from 1 to 6 (higher is better); 3.5 is therefore a neutral score representing policies and institutions that are neither particularly strong nor weak. Figure 6.14 shows the evolution of the CPIA environment score since 1999. Excluding South Asia, all regional averages were below the 3.5 midpoint in 1999. In 2006 Europe and Central Asia, Latin America and the Caribbean, and the Middle East and North Africa had exceeded this threshold. The largest increment has taken place in Europe and Central Asia, which moved

from an average score of 3.1 in 1999 to a score of 3.8 in 2006.

The methodology for calculating the environment CPIA score was updated in 2003. The score is obtained by averaging performance in 2 major categories and 10 sub-categories:

- Assessment of the national institutional context
  - Adequacy of prioritization
  - Quality of environmental assessment
  - Cross-sectoral coordination
  - Public information and participation
- Assessment of specific sectors
  - Air pollution
  - Solid and hazardous waste management
  - Freshwater resources
  - Marine and coastal resources
  - Ecosystems and biodiversity
  - Commercial natural resources

Each of the sectors in the second part of the CPIA questionnaire is assessed for the appropriateness of the policy mix and the quality of policy implementation. Figure 6.15a presents Environment CPIA scores for regions for 2006. Sub-Saharan Africa scores

FIGURE 6.14   Evolution of the CPIA environment score, 1999–2006

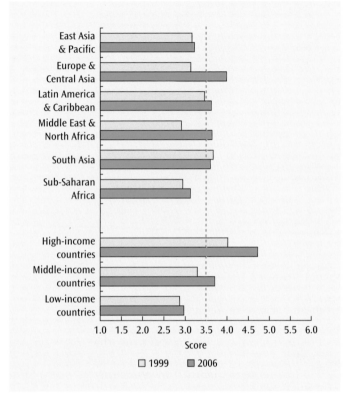

Score

☐ 1999   ■ 2006

Source: World Bank data.

Results on the overall institutional context CPIA subscores show that on average countries perform poorly in terms of public information and participation, particularly in East Asia and the Pacific, and on cross-sectoral coordination, particularly in East Asia and the Pacific and the Middle East and North Africa (figure 6.15b). In contrast, countries are better at identifying priorities, with Europe and Central Asia being a top performer in this area.

Looking at sector-specific policies and institutions, it is evident that upper-middle-income countries have a much stronger performance than low- and lower-middle-income countries (figure 6.15c). The difference is particularly marked in the waste management and water resources management sectors. Low-income countries show a particularly weak performance in air quality management and marine and coastal resources management.

An important distinction should be made between the policies that a country has and its capacity to implement these policies. Figure 6.15d makes this distinction clear, plotting the scores on quality of the policy mix against implementation capacity. Countries score better on establishing standards, regulations, and incentives than on their capacity to actually implement and enforce the policy framework.

Government "policy failure" can be a threat to environmental sustainability, and subsidies are often the source of the problem. Utility subsidies (for water or energy services, for example, where prices may be held artificially low) are often an important element of social programs in developing countries. The result, however, is that water and electricity tariffs in developing countries rarely cover the operational and maintenance costs of utilities. Low tariffs also promote inefficient use of resources. Equally important, utility subsidies have also performed poorly in assisting the needy (box 6.3).

lowest (3.1), while Europe and Central Asia has the highest regional average (3.8). As might be expected, scores vary widely within regions. In Sub-Saharan Africa, scores range from a minimum of 1.1 to a maximum of 4.5. There is also a wide disparity in the environment score between low-income countries (3.0) and upper-middle-income countries (4.1). As shown in *Environment Matters,* resource-poor countries tend to perform better than their resource-rich peers; oil-rich countries, in particular, tend to have lower performance on political stability and rule of law.[26] Overall, there is a high correlation between the CPIA environment score and the CPIA score for property rights and rule-based governance.

FIGURE 6.15 CPIA environment score and its subcomponents, 2006

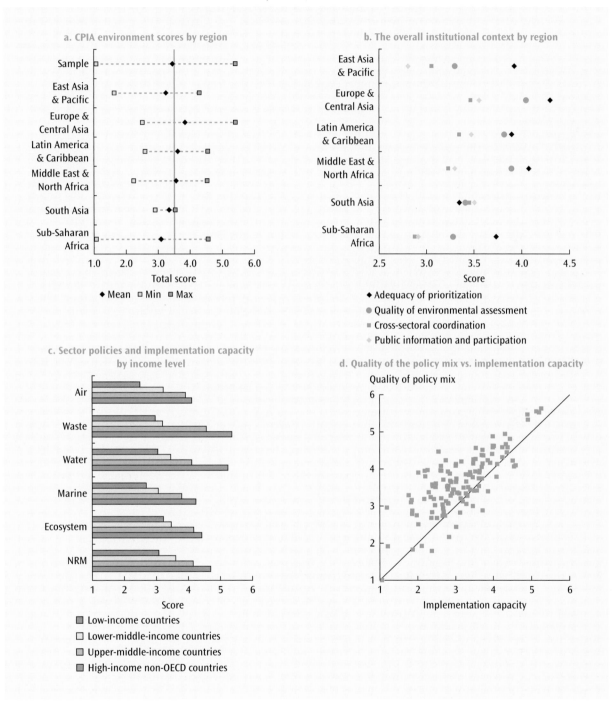

Source: World Bank dataset.
Note: NRM = natural resource management.

BOX 6.3 Assessing the performance of subsidies

From a monitoring point of view, it is important to know whether subsidies actually achieve their poverty targeting goals. The "benefit targeting performance indicator" tries to measure the extent to which energy subsidies effectively target the poor. It does so by measuring the ratio between the share of total subsidies that benefit the poor and the share of poor in total population

$$\Omega = \frac{\text{Subsidy that reaches the poor/Total subsidy}}{\text{Population below poverty line/Total population}}$$

Komives and others show that on a set of quantity-targeted utility subsidies (including water and electricity), the performance indicator is regularly less than 1. What this means is that the poor capture a smaller portion of the subsidy than they would capture if the government decided to distribute the subsidy randomly. That is because those without access to electricity (and hence to the subsidy) belong to the poorest sectors of society. In Sub-Saharan Africa, for example, electricity increasing block tariffs exclude more than 70 percent of the poor.

The performance of subsidies tends to increase with the connection rate. But even in situations where there is universal coverage, subsidies reach at most the neutrality target ($\Omega = 1$). This failure occurs because wealthier households consume considerably more electricity than poorer households, thus capturing a larger share of the subsidy. This is true for all utility subsidies, but it is particularly important in the case of electricity. All this is relevant for analyzing the trade-offs between environment and development. Subsidies place important burdens on the environment since they favor overconsumption, inefficient use of scarce resources, and increased pollution.

Benefit-targeting performance of electricity subsidies in selected developing countries

Country	Type of subsidy	Benefit-targeting performance indicator (Ω)	Error of exclusion (%)
Guatemala	VDT	0.20	55.4
Honduras	VDT	0.49	56.0
Peru	IBT	0.82	59.9
Cape Verde	IBT	0.48	75.6
São Tomé and Principe	IBT	0.41	76.8
Hungary	IBT	0.98	1.7
Rwanda	IBT	0.35	87.2
India (average)	IBT	0.70	21.0

Source: Komives and others 2005.
Note: VDT = volume-differentiated tariffs; IBT = increasing block tariffs. Increasing block tariffs are a price structure in which a commodity is priced at a low initial rate up to a specified volume of use (block), then at a higher or several increasingly higher rates for additional blocks used.

Although increasingly recognized as a development issue for low-income countries, mainstreaming environmental management into Poverty Reduction Strategy Papers and Poverty Reduction Support Credits is evolving slowly. The most recent review for 11 Sub-Saharan African countries shows that attention to environmental priorities ranks low compared with fiscal reforms, macroeconomic stability, and sectoral investments in education and health.[27]

Making Progress on Monitoring

A good indicator should have the following characteristics: policy relevance, analytical soundness, and measurability.[28] Policy relevance is key in the MDG 7 context. Recall that figure 6.3 showed the trends in water availability per capita in the Middle East. While this is an important indicator of an impending problem, it is not particularly policy relevant because it is primarily driven by an endowment, the quantity of water available annually. An indicator that is relevant for decisions about water policy would be some measure of the efficiency with which water is used. Such an indicator would be sensitive to policy actions such as allocating water rights or establishing pricing for water abstraction. In general a policy-relevant indicator should be easy to interpret, show a trend over time, be measurable against a target level, and be responsive to policy changes.

In addition to these characteristics, a good sustainability indicator, or set of indicators, should combine different aspects of sustainable development, such as environmental quality, economic progress, and human and social development. The sustainability indicators currently available in the literature meet this goal to varying degrees. They can be mapped into the following categories:

- Indexes and indicator sets
  - *Weighted indexes,* which combine indicators with an explicit recognition of the relationships between them and their relative importance, such as summing emissions of different greenhouse gases weighted by their individual global warming potentials
  - *Unweighted indexes,* which combine indicators without making explicit assumptions on their relative importance, such as the Living Planet Index (see chapter 7) and the Environmental Performance Index
  - *Indicator sets,* which present indicators separately or group them into logical categories, such as the UN Commission for Sustainable Development indicator set
- *Indicators based on biophysical relationships,* such as the Ecological Footprint

(which accounts for energy use in terms of the land area that would be required to produce the equivalent amount of energy from biofuels)
- *Indicators based on economic accounts,* which employ the national accounting framework to measure changes in well-being and the resources underpinning it over time (for example, the UN System of Environmental and Economic Accounts, adjusted net savings, the Genuine Progress Index, and the Index of Sustainable Economic Welfare).

Aggregate indicators have advantages and disadvantages for monitoring progress. When it comes to measuring environmental sustainability, the core of MDG 7, some degree of aggregation is essential because collections of indicators, usually highly disparate, cannot answer the question of whether social welfare (itself an aggregate concept) is likely to be increasing or decreasing in the future. However, users of indicators are rightly uneasy about aggregate indicators that are effectively a "black box"—that is, if the weights on subaggregates are arbitrary, it is impossible to meaningfully compare aggregates across countries or changes in aggregates across time. National accounts–based indicators have the advantage of using money as a numeraire, having weights (in the form of prices) that relate to social welfare, and using a conceptual framework that provides a rigorous basis for aggregation.[29] Adjusted net savings, introduced in chapter 1 and used in this chapter to measure the sustainability of mineral-based economies, is discussed in more detail in box 6.4.

Indicator sets such as the MDG 7 indicators shown in box 6.2 play an important role in the MDG process. These indicators attempt to span a range of issues—deforestation, extent of protected areas, energy use, and carbon intensity—that are germane to the question of achieving environmental sustainability. It is tempting to propose additional indicators for the set; urban air pollution seems to be a particular gap. But

BOX 6.4   Adjusted net savings as a sustainability indicator

Concerns about sustainable development are fundamentally concerns about the assets that underpin economic development.[a] The overall sustainability of any economy is tied to the management of the portfolio of assets on which the economy depends. Adjusted net (or "genuine") savings is simply the measure of the change in the real value of this portfolio from one year to the next, and economic theory tells us that this change is precisely equal to the change in social welfare.[b] The link between net savings and social welfare is strongest if the accounting of assets is comprehensive, embracing produced capital, natural capital, human capital, and other less tangible forms of wealth such as knowledge, social capital, and quality of institutions.

A unique aspect of adjusted net savings is that it has been tested empirically using the 30+ year time series of estimates published by the World Bank. Ferreira and Vincent show that adjusted net savings is correlated with changes in social welfare for developing countries, but not for developed ones. This makes sense: accumulation of physical assets is an important part of the development process for poorer countries, whereas knowledge creation and innovation (not measured directly in adjusted net savings) are clearly the drivers of growth in rich countries.[c] Ferreira, Hamilton, and Vincent show that this result for developing countries is robust when population growth is taken into account.[d]

Adjusted net savings also has clear links to policy. The policy levers to achieve positive net savings can be applied at the level of the different assets that constitute total national wealth—either the macro policies that influence saving effort, or individual sectoral policies on natural resource management, human resource development, and environmental protection.

Because any measure of saving is likely to be incomplete, a positive adjusted net saving rate needs to be interpreted with caution. Some important assets are omitted from adjusted net savings for methodological and empirical reasons, which may mean that saving rates are only apparently positive. Challenges include lack of data (on subsoil water, land degradation, fish stocks, and diamonds, for example), methodological weaknesses (valuing biodiversity, for example), and measurement errors.

Questions about the degree of substitutability of produced and natural assets can also limit confidence in the link between positive saving and sustainability. There is no technological substitute for the ozone layer as a whole, for example, although in this case it is possible to value marginal losses of ozone according to their incremental impacts on health.

Finally, the step from saving to investment is an important one in the development process. If savings are not channeled to *productive* investments, then they will not be effective in promoting development. This is an important factor in many developing countries, where public sector investments have often been wasteful and where absorptive capacity may be a real constraint.

a. See, for example, Pearce and Atkinson 1993.
b. Hamilton and Clemens 1999.
c. Ferreira and Vincent 2005.
d. Ferreira, Hamilton, and Vincent forthcoming.

when the issue is measuring sustainability, these indicator sets have inherent limitations: each is measuring only a piece of the puzzle, and there is no aggregate measure of progress toward sustainability.

This limitation of indicator sets is one of the primary reasons for emphasizing adjusted net savings in this report. As box 6.4 has suggested, adjusted net savings is by no means a perfect indicator. But it is derived from what is arguably the only sound framework for measuring sustainability, an asset-accounting framework. Investments in better data and methodology can make it a stronger indicator of sustainable development.

The question of potential limits in the substitutability of produced capital for natural capital deserves to be taken seriously. This is an argument, first, for continuing to track changes in the value of total natural capital country by country and, second, for measuring a range of biophysical indicators pertaining to the quality or quantity of critical natural capital.

Conclusions

MDG 7 is arguably the most cross-cutting of the MDGs. Given the high resource dependence of most developing countries, being able to manage the environment and natural resources is fundamental for the sustainability of MDG outcomes—boosting consumption by mining soil nutrients is not a sustainable enterprise, to give just one example. Moreover, sound environmental management can have positive impacts on such key MDG goals as poverty reduction, education, gender equality, and health.

The analysis in this chapter leads to the following findings:

- Natural capital constitutes a major component of wealth in developing countries. The average citizens in low-income countries derive over 40 percent of their wealth from some form of natural capital.
- Owing to falling relative prices, the value of natural capital—including agricultural land, forests, and subsoil assets—has declined over the recent past in those countries that most heavily rely on nature for their well-being. Climate change is likely to exacerbate this situation in the future.
- An area of forest equivalent to the size of Sierra Leone is lost every year to land use changes, particularly in Latin America and the Caribbean and in Sub-Saharan Africa. Most of the world's forest loss takes place in Brazil and Indonesia.
- Population growth will cause per capita water resources to fall below critical levels in the very near future in the Middle East and North Africa and in South Asia. Underground water abstraction is already unsustainable in many Middle Eastern countries, in parts of South Asia, and in Mexico.
- Countries rich in subsoil assets risk being on an unsustainable development path if they primarily consume the rents from natural resource extraction rather than investing them in other forms of capital. This represents lost opportunities for development.
- Low- and lower-middle-income countries are characterized by high levels of urban

air pollution (as measured by particulate matter concentrations), despite the progress made in recent years. Owing to growing rates of urbanization in developing countries, this situation could worsen.

- Progress in improving electricity access in the last 15 years has been slow. In most developing countries, population growth has offset the gains in energy investment. As a consequence of low levels of access, the consumption of biomass fuels is still very high in developing countries, with continuing adverse conequences for forests and human health.
- Progress in institutional and policy performance has been uneven across world regions. The Europe and Central Asia region has been characterized by the sharpest improvements, while South Asia and Sub-Saharan Africa have lagged behind. Good performance in establishing environment and natural resource policies does not necessarily mean good performance in enforcing them, as shown by the disaggregated CPIA scores.

The policy challenges raised by the environment are as diverse as the endowments of natural resources enjoyed by developing countries. Strengthening private or communal property rights to local natural resources has been shown to be an effective tool for many resource management problems. Improving governance is key for many resources that are effectively subject to open access, such as forests and fish. Explicit resource rent policies are often needed; the chain from rent capture to the management and use of resource rents can determine whether rich resource stocks are a source of development finance or a contributor to the "resource curse." Water rights and more explicit treatment of water as an economic good can help to manage water scarcity. Managing pollution starts from the recognition that the marginal damages from pollution emissions far exceed the marginal costs of abatement in many industrializing countries; finding *efficient* solutions to pollution problems is clearly a priority, given competing demands for finance in developing countries. Policies such as energy subsidies, which encourage inefficient use, can exacerbate pollution problems while simultaneously straining fiscal resources.

This chapter has emphasized one of the principal difficulties in meeting MDG 7, the challenge of building stronger institutions. The problem is not unique to the environment and natural resource sectors, of course, but policies and institutions in these sectors are particularly weak. The *Global Monitoring Report 2007* analyzed CPIA data for 2005 to show that environment CPIA scores significantly lag overall CPIA scores.[30]

A key ingredient in resolving institutional weakness is better and more comprehensive data. Public access to environmental data is essential to the process of building public demand for environmental quality. And better data are needed to support policy decisions concerning environment and natural resource management, as well as policy implementation. One of the strengths of the MDG process is this emphasis on data and indicators. This chapter highlights some of the strengths as well as the deficiencies in environment and natural resource data.

Notes

1. See World Bank 2008a for a review.
2. World Bank 2008a.
3. Prüss-Üstün and Corvalán 2006.
4. Deforestation in LAC and SSA is highest also as a percent of total forest resources. Between 1990 and 2005, the annual deforestation rate has been 0.4 and 0.6 percent respectively.
5. The forest cover indicator is not perfect. A major problem with this indicator is that it does not distinguish between natural forests and plantations. This is particularly relevant for biodiversity as well as other natural functions of forests.
6. ACQUASTAT: (http://www.fao.org/nr/water/aquastat/dbase/index.stm); WRI (http://earthtrends.wri.org/searchable_db/index.php?theme=2).
7. World Bank 2007b. While the Middle East and North African region features a critical situation with respect to water, the problem is not unique to the region. In China, for example, parts of the North China Plain and the North East are highly water stressed.
8. UNEP 2007.

9. EIA 2007.
10. Cohen and others 2005.
11. World Bank 2008c.
12. Biochemical oxygen demand refers to the amount of oxygen that bacteria in water will consume in breaking down waste. This indicator measures pollution from organic matter and fertilizers (in general referred to as *nutrients*) thus excluding other important sources of pollution such as sediment, acids and salts, heavy metals, toxic chemicals and other pathogens.
13. Hettige and others 1998.
14. The International Energy Agency (IEA) defines access to electricity as the number of people (in households) who have some form of electricity at home, either commercially purchased or self-generated (when data is available through surveys by national administrators). It excludes unauthorized connections.
15. IEA 2006.
16. IEA 2006.
17. EIA 2007.
18. Samuelson 1961, pp. 50–57.
19. In extreme circumstances, of course, consuming resource rents may the only alternative to starvation.
20. World Bank 2006b.
21. World Bank 2006b.
22. See chapter 7 for an analysis of climate change impacts.
23. Dasgupta and others 2006.
24. A caveat about these measures is in order: because these are indexes consisting of arbitrarily weighted (and highly disparate) subcomponents, the interpretation of the aggregate indexes can be problematic. There is no numeraire to weight the contributions of different aspects of environmental management to social welfare. These indicators are therefore best used to compare close peers at the level of individual subcomponents of environmental management.
25. The EPI has been developed by the Center for Environmental Law and Policy at Yale University and the Center for International Earth Science Information Network (CIESIN) at Columbia University, in collaboration with the World Economic Forum and the Joint Research Centre of the European Commission.
26. World Bank 2006a
27. Kishore 2007.
28. OECD 1994.
29. Hamilton 2003.
30. World Bank 2007a.

7

Global Environmental Sustainability: Protecting the Commons

ustainable management of global environmental resources—the earth's climate, ocean fisheries, and biodiversity— is essential to achieving the Millennium Development Goals (MDGs) and, indeed, to ensuring continued economic progress over the next century. Failure to mitigate the impact of greenhouse gas (GHG) emissions on the earth's climate may lead to disastrous changes in temperature and precipitation and to an increase in extreme weather events. Pollution and overexploitation of marine fisheries can damage or destroy fish populations. Habitat destruction may lead to species extinction. All three global environmental problems, and how the world deals with them, will affect the welfare of the developing world.

The goal of this chapter is to monitor recent progress in dealing with each of the three global environmental problems, with an emphasis on climate change. The chapter begins by describing temperature trends; the relationship between GHG concentrations and climate; and projections, and effects, of future climate change in the absence of any mitigation efforts. The chapter then discusses the sources of and trends in GHG emissions and the opportunities for adapting to changes in climate. Progress in international efforts to develop institutions and policies to deal with climate change is reviewed, and the

chapter ends with a review of trends in biodiversity and the health of marine fisheries.[1]

Climate Change: The Impact of Human Activity on Climate

Deforestation and the burning of fossil fuels produce greenhouse gases that trap incoming solar radiation, leading to a rise in global average surface temperature. Measurements show that the average world temperature has increased since the start of the industrial revolution in the mid-1800s; over the last hundred years, the average temperature has risen 0.74°C.[2] Indeed, eleven of the last twelve years rank among the warmest years on record since 1850. Rising sea levels are consistent with warming. Since 1961 global sea levels have risen at an average rate of 1.8 millimeters (mm) a year and since 1993 at an average rate of 3.1 mm a year.[3] At the same time snow cover has decreased, and ice fields in the Arctic and Antarctic have shrunk drastically. Average temperatures in the Arctic are rising twice as fast as elsewhere in the world. The polar ice cap as a whole is shrinking: satellites show that the area of permanent ice cover is contracting at a rate of 9 percent each decade. If this melting continues, summers in the Arctic could become nearly ice-free by the end of the century.

More important, scientific research suggests that human activities are contributing to the rise in global temperatures. The concentration of carbon dioxide (CO_2) in the atmosphere—the most important GHG—has increased from approximately 277 parts per million volume (ppm) in 1744 to 384 ppm in 2007.[4] Models of the determinants of temperature change that take into account the addition of GHGs into the atmosphere from human activities provide much more accurate estimates of historical trends in temperature than do models that ignore these emissions.[5]

Relationship of GHG Concentrations to Climate Change

The extent of future climate change depends on future GHG emissions and on the relationship between climate and the stock of GHGs in the atmosphere. Table 7.1 shows the likelihood of various changes in mean global surface temperature (relative to levels before the industrial revolution) corresponding to various equilibrium concentrations of GHGs.[6] In 2005 the concentration of all GHGs was approximately 375 ppm CO_2e (carbon dioxide equivalents).[7] Stabilization at 450 ppm CO_2e, as advocated by the UN's *Human Development Report,* would still carry a risk of an increase in mean surface temperature of at least 3°C.[8] Equilibrium GHG concentrations of 650 or 750 ppm

CO_2e, which are consistent with some of the nonmitigation scenarios in the IPCC (Intergovernmental Panel on Climate Change) Fourth Assessment Report, carry a significant risk of an increase in mean global surface temperature of 5°C.[9]

A mean increase in global surface temperature of 5°C would result in disastrous consequences: heat waves throughout the world, increases in heavy precipitation in northern latitudes, and drought and decreases in precipitation in most subtropical regions. It would likely lead to the melting of snowpack in the Himalayas and risk the total disappearance of the West Antarctic ice sheet, which could increase the global sea level by six meters. It would also risk "tipping points"—positive feedbacks that would cause atmospheric GHG concentrations and temperature to rise rapidly. These feedbacks include the release of methane from permafrost as warming occurs, the release of carbon from deep oceans as climate change affects deep-sea circulation, and the increased absorption of solar radiation as polar ice caps melt. Any of these effects could lead to truly catastrophic climate changes.[10]

The Geographic and Temporal Dimensions of Climate Change

How likely are GHG concentrations to reach 650 or 750 ppm, and how fast might this occur? The IPCC in its Fourth Assessment Report estimates the change in the stock of GHGs under various nonmitigation emissions scenarios, together with the corresponding changes in temperature and sea level rise worldwide (table 7.2).[11]

Figure 7.1 shows the geographic distribution of temperature changes for three nonmitigation scenarios: B1, a scenario that results in an increase in mean global temperature of 1.8°C in 2090 (relative to 1980–99 temperatures);[12] A1B, a scenario that results in an increase in mean global temperature of 3.3°C in 2090; and A2, which results in an increase in mean global temperature of

TABLE 7.1 Likelihood of various CO_2e concentrations exceeding various increases in global mean surface temperature
percent

Stabilization level (in ppm CO_2e)	2°C	3°C	4°C	5°C	6°C	7°C
450	78	18	3	1	0	0
500	96	44	11	3	1	0
550	99	69	24	7	2	1
650	100	94	58	24	9	4
750	100	99	82	47	22	9

Source: Stern 2008.

TABLE 7.2 Changes in mean global temperature and sea level associated with various IPCC scenarios

Case[b]	Temperature change (°C at 2090–99 relative to 1980–1999)[a]		Sea level rise (meters at 2090–99 relative to 1980–99)
	Best estimate	Likely range	Model-based range excluding future rapid dynamic changes in ice flow
Constant year 2000 concentrations[c]	0.6	0.3–0.9	Not applicable
B1 scenario	1.8	1.1–2.9	0.18–0.38
A1T scenario	2.4	1.4–3.8	0.20–0.45
B2 scenario	2.4	1.4–3.8	0.20–0.43
A1B scenario	2.8	1.7–4.4	0.21–0.48
A2 scenario	3.4	2.0–5.4	0.23–0.51
A1FI scenario	4.0	2.4–6.4	0.26–0.59

Source: Summary for Policy Makers, Fourth Assessment Report, IPCC 2007b.
a. These estimates are assessed from a hierarchy of models that encompass a simple climate model, several earth system models of intermediate complexity, and a large number of atmosphere-ocean general circulation models (AOGCMs).
b. The six main scenarios for the projections are described as follows:
    B1: Convergent world; low population growth; change toward a service and information economy, clean technologies.
    B2: Regional focus; intermediate population growth; development and technical change; environmental emphasis.
    A1: Convergent world; population peaks at mid-century; rapid growth and introduction of more efficient technologies that are sourced from either:
    A1T: Nonfossil energy sources
    A1B: A balance across all sources
    A1FI: Fossil-intensive
    A2: Heterogeneous world; high population growth; slower economic growth and technical change.
c. Year 2000 constant composition is derived from AOGCMs only.

3.9°C in 2090. The global distribution of temperature changes (figure 7.1) is roughly the same for all three scenarios: temperature increases are greatest in the northern latitudes, but in scenarios A1B and A2, they rise above 4°C in parts of Latin American and Sub-Saharan Africa, as well as in India and the Middle East.

Other effects are likely to accompany these temperature changes. Arid and semi-arid regions will become drier, while areas in the mid-to-high latitudes will become wetter. Heavy precipitation events are very likely to occur in mid-to-high latitudes, while the likelihood of droughts will increase in areas that are currently dry. Storm surges, cyclones, and hurricanes are also likely to increase in frequency throughout the world. Water supplies are likely to be affected: the melting of glaciers will lead to higher spring-time water flows and reduced summertime flows. The majority of the negative effects of climate change are likely to occur in lower latitudes—in the South, rather than the North—implying that developing countries will bear the brunt of these effects.

Climate change is often viewed as a problem for the future, but figure 7.1 suggests otherwise. As the first set of maps indicates, significant temperature changes in Africa and Latin America are likely as early as 2020–29 under the A1B nonmitigation scenario—a scenario of rapid economic and population growth in which the world relies on a combination of fossil fuels and renewable energy sources. More important, avoiding the risk of large temperature changes in 2090–99 requires action now. As the IPCC noted, world GHG emissions would have to decline by 50 to 85 percent of their 2000 levels by 2050 to stabilize concentrations at 450 ppm, depending on the mitigation path chosen.[13] World GHG emissions would have to decrease by as much as 30 percent from 2000 levels by 2050 (depending on the mitigation path chosen) to stabilize concentrations at 550 ppm.

FIGURE 7.1 Projections of surface temperatures for three IPCC scenarios

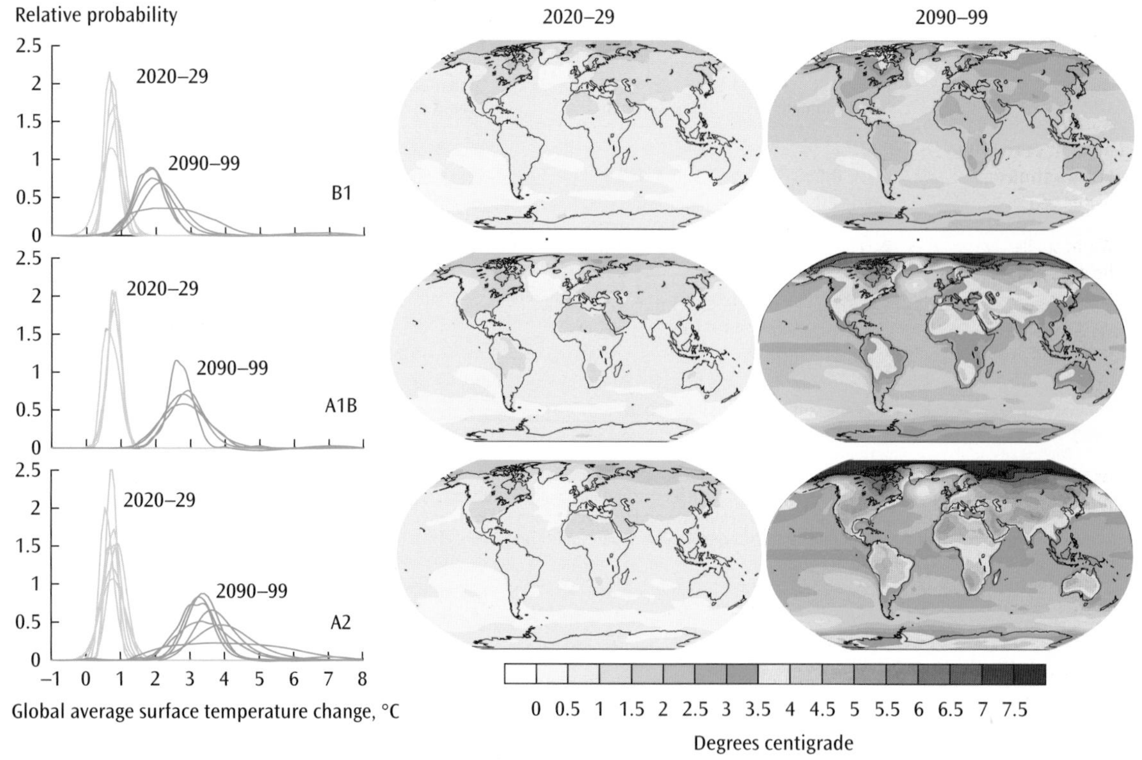

Source: IPCC 2007a.

The Impacts of Climate Change and Opportunities for Adaptation

What impacts would the temperature changes in figure 7.1 have on the economies of developing and developed countries? Table 7.3 describes in qualitative terms some of the likely impacts of climate change on agriculture, forestry and ecosystems, water resources, human health, and human settlements that are expected to occur under the nonmitigation scenarios in figure 7.1. The magnitude of these effects depends on the extent to which countries adapt to them and also on the extent to which mitigation efforts lower GHG emissions. The effects of climate change vary greatly among developing countries—even for countries in the same region. Efforts to adapt to climate change must therefore be tailored to specific country needs.

Impact on Agriculture

There is wide recognition that developing countries in general stand to lose more from the effects of climate change on agriculture than developed countries. Although figure 7.1 suggests that temperatures will rise more in northern than in southern latitudes, temperatures in developing countries are already close to thresholds beyond which further increases in temperature will lower productivity. Developing countries are also likely to have fewer opportunities for adaptation. Moreover, the losses in yields that

TABLE 7.3   Possible impacts of climate change in the mid-to-late-21st century

Phenomenon[a] and direction of trend	Likelihood of future trends[b]	Examples of major projected impacts by sector			
		Agriculture, forestry and ecosystems	Water resources	Human health	Industry, settlement, and society
Over most land areas, warmer and fewer cold days and nights, warmer and more frequent hot days and nights	Virtually certain[c]	Increased yields in colder environments; decreased yields in warmer environments; increased insect outbreaks	Effects on water resources relying on snow melt; effects on some water supplies	Reduced human mortality from decreased cold exposure	Reduced energy demand for heating; increased demand for cooling; declining air quality in cities; reduced disruption to transport from snow, ice; effects on winter tourism
Warm spells/ heat waves. Frequency increases over most land areas	Very likely	Reduced yields in warmer regions from heat stress; increased danger of wildfire	Increased water demand; water quality problems, such as algal blooms	Increased risk of heat-related mortality, especially for the elderly, chronically sick, very young, and socially isolated	Reduction in quality of life for people in warm areas without appropriate housing; impacts on the elderly, very young, and poor
Heavy precipitation events. Frequency increases over most areas	Very likely	Damage to crops; soil erosion, inability to cultivate land because of waterlogged soils	Adverse effects on quality of surface and groundwater; contamination of water supply; water scarcity may be relieved	Increased risk of deaths, injuries, and infectious, respiratory and skin diseases	Disruption of settlements, commerce, transport, and societies from flooding; pressures on urban and rural infrastructures; loss of property
Area affected by drought increases	Likely	Land degradation; lower yields, crop damage, and failure; increased livestock deaths; increased risk of wildfire	More widespread water stress	Increased risk of food and water shortages; increased risk of malnutrition; increased risk of water- and food-borne diseases	Water shortages for settlements, industry, and societies; reduced hydropower generation potentials; potential for population migration
Intense tropical cyclone activity increases	Likely	Damage to crops; windthrow (uprooting) of trees; damage to coral reefs	Power outages causing disruption of public water supply	Increased risk of deaths, injuries, water- and food-borne diseases; post-traumatic stress disorders	Disruption by flood and high winds; withdrawal of private risk insurance coverage in vulnerable areas; potential for population migrations; loss of property
Increased incidence of extreme high sea level (excludes tsunamis)[d]	Likely[e]	Salinization of irrigation water, estuaries, and freshwater systems	Decreased freshwater availability from saltwater intrusion	Increased risk of deaths and injuries by drowning in floods; migration-related health effects	Costs of coastal protection versus costs of land-use relocation; potential for movement of populations and infrastructure; also see effects of tropical cyclones above

Source: IPCC 2007b.
a. See Working Group I Fourth Assessment table 3.7 for further details regarding definitions.
b. Based on projections for 21st century using scenarios in table 7.2.
c. Warming of the most extreme days and nights each year.
d. Extreme high sea level depends on average sea level and on regional weather systems. It is defined as the highest 1 percent of hourly values of observed sea level at a station for a given reference period.
e. In all scenarios, the projected global average sea level in 2100 is higher than in the reference period. The effect of changes in regional weather systems on sea level extremes has not been assessed.

occur in developing countries are likely to affect a larger number of people—especially the poor—because of the greater importance of agriculture in the livelihoods of people in developing countries.[14]

Cline presents estimates of the impact on agriculture of a 4.4°C increase in mean global temperature and a 2.9 percent mean increase in precipitation occurring during the period 2070–99.[15] His estimates combine results from the two main strands of the literature—cross-sectional studies of land values or net revenues (the Ricardian approach) and crop models. The estimates of impacts on yields shown in figure 7.2 incorporate carbon fertilization effects—that is, they allow for the fact that increased carbon in the atmosphere will increase yields by promoting photosynthesis and reducing plant water loss.[16] As figure 7.2 clearly shows, the largest agricultural losses will occur in parts of Africa, in South Asia, and in parts of Latin America. In contrast, the United States and Canada, Europe, and China will, in general, benefit under the nonmitigation climate scenario.

Why do the estimated impacts differ significantly across countries in Africa and Latin America? The answer in part lies in adaptation: yields on irrigated farmland decrease less than on rain-fed land; in some areas, yields increase. In Africa the value of output per hectare declines less for farmers who can substitute livestock for crops. Two points about adaptation should be noted, however. One is that the Ricardian approach, which allows farmers in different climatic zones to adapt to climate, assumes that prices in the future will remain unchanged. If water shortages increase the price of irrigation, yields may fall more than indicated in figure 7.2. Second, it is the impact of climate change on net revenues that should be measured rather than the impact on yields. Adaptation is costly, and the impact of climate change should be measured as the sum of damages after adaptation plus the costs of adaptation. As Cline notes, output in southwest India falls by approximately 37 percent under the nonmitigation climate scenario, but net revenues fall by 55 percent.[17]

FIGURE 7.2 Impacts of increases in temperature and precipitation on agricultural yields, 2079–99

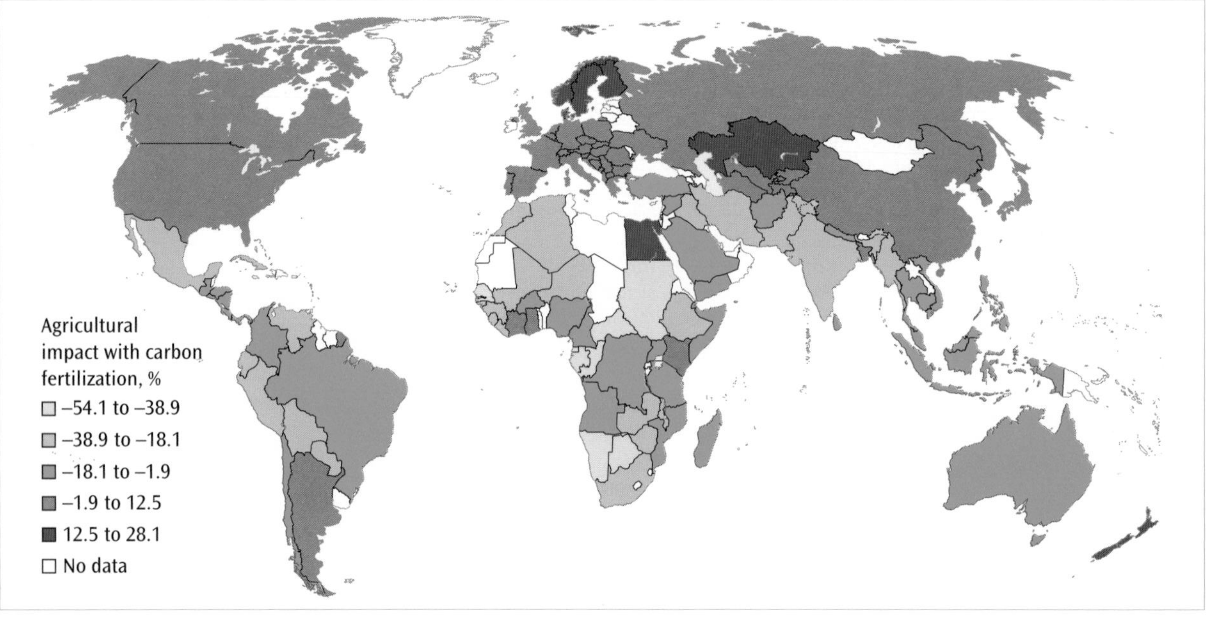

Source: Cline 2007.

Impacts on Health

Climate change may affect human health both directly and indirectly. Increased warming in cold climates may reduce cardiovascular and respiratory deaths, but heat waves in both warm and cold climates are likely to increase cardiovascular deaths. Changes in temperature and precipitation also affect diarrheal disease—the second-leading cause of death among children between one and five years. Extreme weather events—hurricanes, floods, and tornadoes—are likely to raise accidental deaths and injuries. Equally important to the poor in developing countries are the indirect effects of climate change on health. As figure 7.2 suggests, climate change, through its impact on agricultural yields, may lower food security and lead to malnutrition. Increased temperatures and precipitation in low latitudes may increase the incidence of malaria and other vector-borne diseases.

The largest impacts of climate change on mortality and morbidity occur through malnutrition, diarrhea, and malaria, and the largest effects geographically are felt in Sub-Saharan Africa, South Asia, and the Middle East. Simply put, the health burden of climate change is borne by the children of the developing world. Table 7.4 shows estimated disability-adjusted life years (DALYs) attributable to climate change in 2000; figure 7.3 shows the distribution of deaths. Climate change in 2000 is associated, worldwide, with 166,000 deaths—77,000 associated with malnutrition, 47,000 with diarrhea, and 27,000 with malaria. The highest number of deaths (per 100,000 persons) occurs in Africa, parts of South Asia (SEAR-D), and the Middle East. The impact of climate change on the United States, Canada, and Europe is negligible, with cardiovascular deaths associated with heat waves cancelling out the benefits of milder winter temperatures.

The future impacts of climate change are more dramatic than those in 2000. In 2030, assuming that GHG emissions are stabilized at 750 ppm by 2210, the risk of malnutrition is predicted to be 11 percent higher in Latin

TABLE 7.4 Estimated DALYs attributed to climate change in 2000, by cause and subregion
thousands, unless otherwise indicated

WHO subregion	Malnutrition	Diarrhea	Malaria	Floods	All causes	Total DALYs (per 1 million population)
AFR-D	293	154	178	1	626	2,186
AFR-E	323	260	682	3	1,267	3,840
AMR-A	0	0	0	4	4	12
AMR-B	0	0	3	67	71	167
AMR-D	0	17	0	5	23	324
EMR-B	0	14	0	6	20	148
EMR-D	313	277	112	46	748	2,146
EUR-A	0	0	0	3	3	7
EUR-B	0	6	0	4	10	48
EUR-C	0	3	0	1	4	15
SEAR-B	0	28	0	6	34	117
SEAR-D	1,918	612	0	8	2,538	2,081
WPR-A	0	0	0	1	1	9
WPR-B	0	89	43	37	169	111
World	2,846	1,459	1,018	193	5,517	925

Source: McMichael and others 2004.

FIGURE 7.3 Estimated death rate from climate change in 2000, by WHO subregion

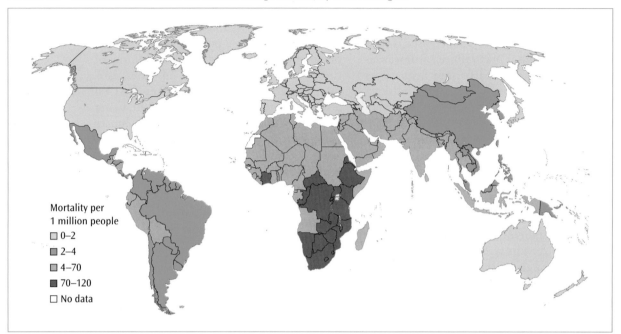

Mortality per
1 million people
☐ 0–2
■ 2–4
■ 4–70
■ 70–120
☐ No data

Source: Map created by Center for Sustainability and the Global Environment, University of Wisconsin, using data from McMichael and others 2004.
Note: Change in climate compared to baseline, 1961–90.

America than it was in 1990, and 17 percent higher in South Asia (SEAR-D). The risk of diarrhea is predicted to be 6 percent higher in Sub-Saharan Africa and 7 percent higher in South Asia (SEAR-D) than in 1990. It should be emphasized that these increased risks apply to large exposed populations.

These calculations assume little adaptation to climate change—for example, a program that eliminated the anopheles mosquito from Sub-Saharan Africa, or the development of an effective malaria vaccine, would of course reduce malaria risks. A program to improve food security in the region would reduce deaths caused by malnutrition.

Sea Level Rise

Although the mean increases in sea level rise associated with the IPCC nonmitigation scenarios are modest—ranging from 0.2 to 0.5 meters during this century (see table 7.2)—these estimates exclude future rapid

dynamic changes in ice flow. Velicogna and Wahr have measured variations in the Antarctic ice sheet during 2002–05.[18] Their results indicate that the mass of the West Antarctic ice sheet decreased significantly, at a rate several times greater than assumed by the IPCC in its Third Assessment Report. Climate change could possibly cause the West Antarctic ice sheet to slide into the ocean, which would raise average sea level by approximately five to six meters, even if the ice sheet did not melt.

Measuring the vulnerability of developing countries to rising sea levels—given the current location of settlements—provides a useful starting point for measuring the benefits of adaptation. Dasgupta and others estimate the impact of various possible increases in sea level on 84 coastal developing countries.[19] Using Geographic Information System techniques, they estimate the fraction of land area, agricultural land, wetlands, urban land area, population, and GDP that would be affected by increases in sea level of one to five meters. These calculations pertain to current land uses and assume no adaptation.

Figure 7.4 shows the share of various classes of land area, population, and GDP affected by sea level rise, by World Bank region. The impacts of sea level rise are greatest—in virtually all dimensions—in East Asia and the Pacific, followed by the Middle East and North Africa. Effects, however, vary significantly among countries within each region. Table 7.5 shows the ten countries most affected by an increase in sea level of one meter for four dimensions of vulnerability. With no adaptation Vietnam would lose 10 percent of its GDP; the Arab Republic of Egypt, over 6 percent. Egypt would stand to lose 13 percent of its agricultural land (not shown), and Vietnam 28 percent of its wetlands. Twelve percent of the Bahamas would be submerged. As table 7.5 indicates, Vietnam ranks among the top five countries most affected by a one meter rise in sea level; the Bahamas, Egypt, and Suriname also rank among the countries most vulnerable to sea level rise.

Extreme Weather Events

Although regional forecasts of climate change are uncertain, it is likely that weather variability will increase, and with it, extreme weather events. To the extent that future events follow historical patterns, the damages from past weather events—such as droughts, heat waves, and floods—provide an additional index of vulnerability to climate change. Buys and others have compiled a country vulnerability index based on droughts, heat waves, floods, wildfires, and wind storms that occurred between 1960 and 2002.[20] The index gives persons killed in these events a weight of 1,000, persons rendered homeless a weight of 10, and persons affected by each event a weight of 1. This sum is divided by population for 1980 (the midpoint of the period) to develop an index of population impact relative to population size.

Table 7.6 presents the index of vulnerability to extreme weather events, showing the 10 most vulnerable countries in each World Bank region. Again, the differences across countries are striking: in per capita terms, Bangladesh is affected more than three times as much as India by extreme weather events—on a par with Ethiopia. Countries in East Asia are—in per capita terms—affected much less than countries in South Asia or Africa, although total damages are high.

Adaptation to Climate Change

Nobel laureate Tom Schelling has argued that the best way for developing countries to adapt to climate change is to develop.[21] In many ways this prescription is correct. Preventing the health impacts of climate change means making progress toward reducing malnutrition, eliminating diarrhea as a leading cause of death among children under five years of age, and eradicating malaria. Achieving MDGs 1, 4, and 6 would constitute effective adaptation to the most adverse health effects of climate change. Development also would reduce the impacts of climate change by helping developing countries to diversify their economies. Agricultural economies are more vulnerable to the effects of climate change than economies where employment is concentrated primarily in manufacturing and services. The yield impacts pictured in figure 7.2 would be less serious in a world in which a smaller share of employment and GDP in developing countries depended on agriculture than is currently the case.[22]

Economic growth would also reduce the damages associated with extreme weather events.[23] Yohe and Tol explain variation across countries in the fraction of the population affected by extreme weather events between 1990 and 2000.[24] They find that the fraction of the population affected by natural disasters decreases with increases in

FIGURE 7.4 Vulnerability to sea level rise

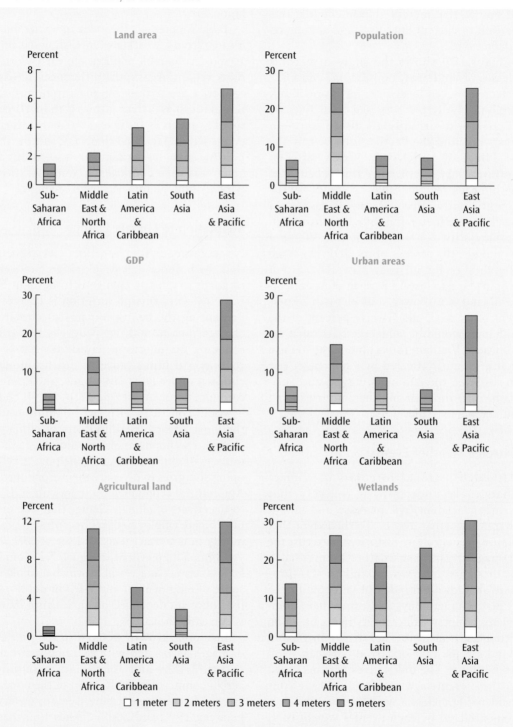

Source: Dasgupta and others 2007.

TABLE 7.5 Ten countries most affected by a one meter rise in sea level
percentage affected

Rank	Population	GDP	Urban areas	Wetlands
1	Vietnam (10.79)	Vietnam (10.21)	Vietnam (10.74)	Vietnam (28.67)
2	Egypt, Arab Rep. of (9.28)	Mauritania (9.35)	Guyana (10.02)	Jamaica (28.16)
3	Mauritania (7.95)	Egypt, Arab Rep. of (6.44)	French Guiana (7.76)	Belize (27.76)
4	Suriname (7.00)	Suriname (6.35)	Mauritania (7.50)	Qatar (21.75)
5	Guyana (6.30)	Benin (5.64)	Egypt, Arab Rep. of (5.52)	The Bahamas (17.75)
6	French Guiana (5.42)	The Bahamas (4.74)	Libya (5.39)	Libya (15.83)
7	Tunisia (4.89)	Guyana (4.64)	United Arab Emirates (4.80)	Uruguay (15.14)
8	United Arab Emirates (4.59)	French Guiana (3.02)	Tunisia (4.50)	Mexico (14.85)
9	The Bahamas (4.56)	Tunisia (2.93)	Suriname (4.20)	Benin (13.78)
10	Benin (3.93)	Ecuador (2.66)	The Bahamas (3.99)	Taiwan, China (11.70)

Source: Dasgupta and others 2007.

TABLE 7.6 Weather damage index (WDI), by country and region

Sub-Saharan Africa	WDI	East Asia & Pacific	WDI	Latin America & the Caribbean	WDI	Middle East & North Africa	WDI	South Asia	WDI
Ethiopia	1809	Tonga	698	Honduras	819	Iran, Islamic Rep. of	183	Bangladesh	1940
Mozambique	1134	Samoa	589	Antigua Barbados	387	Jordan	32.9	India	566
Sudan	999	Laos PDR	573	Belize	385	Tunisia	29.3	Sri Lanka	318
Djibouti	586	Solomon Islands	416	Haiti	254	Yemen, Rep. of	27.5	Pakistan	172
Botswana	536	Philippines	392	Nicaragua	242	Syrian Arab Rep.	18.4	Maldives	151
Somalia	497	Vanuatu	340	Venezuela, R. B. de	215	Algeria	17.6	Nepal	84.4
Mauritania	433	Fiji	310	St. Lucia	212	Oman	14.5	Afghanistan	73.5
Malawi	411	Vietnam	235	Dominican Republic	191	Morocco	13.3	Bhutan	64.5
Zimbabwe	394	China	223	Dominica	182	Iraq	11.1		
Swaziland	352	Cambodia	213	Bolivia	124	Lebanon	5.6		

Source: Buys and others 2007.

per capita income (elasticity = –1); increases with increases in income inequality (elasticity = 2.2), and increases with increases in population density (elasticity = 0.24).

In addition to pursuing economic growth, developing countries will also have to adapt to climate change. People in developing countries are already adapting to annual variations in temperature and precipitation, as well as to droughts, floods, and cyclones. In agriculture adaptation to temperature is reflected in crop choice. In Africa, for example, farmers select sorghum and maize-millet in cooler regions; maize-beans, maize-groundnut, and maize in moderately warm regions; and cowpea, cowpea-sorghum, and millet-groundnut in hot regions. As precipitation increases or decreases, farmers shift toward water-loving or drought-tolerant crops.[25] In the Indian state of Orissa, champeswar rice—a flood-resistant strain—is grown to provide insurance against agricultural losses. Farmers in the Mekong Delta build dikes to control flood waters.[26] And community microinsurance schemes have been implemented in India's Andra Pradesh to provide insurance against natural disasters.[27]

Climate change means that the need for this sort of adaptation will become greater. Much adaptation to climate change is a private good. But government actions to strengthen private adaptation to climate change will be needed in four areas: to provide those inputs to adaptation that are public goods—information about climate impacts, early warning systems for heat waves and floods, and construction of defensive public infrastructure; to take climate impacts into account in designing roads, bridges, dams, and other public infrastructure that may be affected by climate; to correct market failures that may impede adaptation; and to provide social safety nets that will sustain the poor through natural disasters.

Information about expected precipitation or early warnings about floods and heat waves can help people adjust to adverse weather conditions. In Mali the national meteorological service distributes information about precipitation and soil moisture through a network of farmers' organizations and local governments. This information is transmitted throughout the growing season to allow farmers to adjust production practices. Obtaining information about weather risks depends on having enough monitoring stations and an adequate budget for collecting meteorological data, which can be facilitated by donor contributions and through transfer of technology for predicting weather events.[28]

Defensive infrastructure includes sea walls to protect against storm surges and irrigation systems that store monsoon rains. The Stern Review reports that expenditures of $3.15 billion on flood control in China between 1960 and 2000 avoided losses of $12 billion, while flood control projects in Rio de Janeiro yielded an internal rate of return of over 50 percent. Climate-proofing of roads, dams, and other infrastructure that may be affected by climate changes can also yield high returns. In dam construction in Bangladesh and South Africa, benefit-cost analyses have determined that it pays to increase the size of reservoirs to accommodate increased water runoff.[29] Studies by the World Bank and Asian Development Bank have helped to identify cost-effective measures to climate-proof infrastructure in small island states.[30]

Governments can also help promote efficient market responses to climate risks. These include promoting insurance markets and making sure that credit is available, especially to the poor, to finance private adaptation. In high-income countries, one-third of losses associated with natural disasters are insured, compared with only 3 percent of losses in developing countries.[31] Governments can promote weather insurance when private markets fail. The development of weather-index insurance to reduce farmers' vulnerability to weather shocks is another example of the use of insurance markets to reduce climate risk (box 7.1).

In addition, governments can build institutions to help with disaster relief and create social programs to cushion households from income shocks. The Maharashtra Employment Guarantee Scheme, which was developed in the 1970s to help households cope with crop losses and other negative income shocks, is an excellent example of this, as are the employment creation programs adopted in Indonesia in 1997.[32]

BOX 7.1 Weather-index insurance

One of the biggest problems faced by farmers in developing countries is dealing with weather shocks and adverse weather conditions, a problem that will only be exacerbated by climate change. The problem is especially acute for small farmers who are the most vulnerable to the increased frequency and magnitude of droughts, cyclones, and floods. Public programs to deal with weather risk include crop insurance, which reimburses farmers for yield losses and, more recently, weather-index insurance (WII). Weather-index insurance differs from traditional crop insurance because it pays farmers based on realizations of an index that is highly correlated with farm-level yields and can be used as a proxy for production losses. The index is based on the objective measurement of weather variables, such as the deficit of precipitation at a weather station or the trajectory and wind speed of a tropical cyclone. Weather-index insurance has several advantages over traditional crop insurance: adverse selection and information asymmetries are reduced since both the insurer and the insured can observe the same weather index; farmers cannot influence the results of the index (as opposed to the yield in their fields), and index-based payouts reduce administrative costs since a field-based loss assessment is not required. The success of WII depends on the availability of sufficient meteorological stations, which may be a problem, especially in Sub-Saharan Africa.

Weather index insurance has recently been researched or introduced in pilot projects in Ethiopia, India, Kenya, Malawi, Mexico, Morocco, Nicaragua, Peru, Thailand, Tunisia, and Ukraine. The introduction in India of rainfall insurance by BASIX and ICICI Lombard in 2003 was the first index insurance initiative launched at the farmer level in the developing world, and this insurance is now expanding in the Indian private and public insurance sectors.[a] A World Bank initiative in Malawi has succeeded in reaching small-scale farmers of maize and groundnuts. Policies sold to farmers are based on a rainfall index calibrated to the rainfall needs of the crop. The Malawi WII has been bundled with credit to allow farmers to repay input loans in the face of severe drought.

a. Manuamorn 2005.

The extent to which these activities will be undertaken depends on institutional capacities in developing countries and on the availability of funding. Determining what should be done requires planning. The heterogeneity in climate impacts described above and highlighted in box 7.2 suggests the need for impact studies and benefit-cost analyses of specific adaptation strategies at the country level. Even though some of the most severe climate impacts may not occur until the second half of the century, developing countries are already vulnerable to variations in temperature and precipitation and extreme weather events. Projects that cushion these shocks are likely to have positive net benefits, although further studies are required.

Many studies are already under way. The development of National Adaptation Programmes of Action (NAPAs) by the United Nations Framework Convention on Climate Change (UNFCCC) is an attempt to help developing countries cope with the adverse effects of climate change. Each NAPA takes into account existing coping strategies at the grassroots level and builds upon them to identify priority activities. Currently 46 countries are preparing (or have prepared) NAPAs, with financial assistance from the UNFCCC's Least-Developed Countries Fund (UNFCCC 2008). Multilateral development banks are also sponsoring studies: adaptation strategies are currently being prepared by the World Bank for each World Bank region. The Asian Development Bank,

BOX 7.2 Adaptation to climate change

The heterogeneity in climate change impacts across countries suggests that country-level studies are required to measure climate effects and to assess the benefits and costs of various adaptation measures in each individual country.

The three figures below depict the distribution of temperature and precipitation impacts in agriculture, the percent of population affected by a three meter rise in sea level, and the distribution of flood risk damages across countries.

The distribution of agricultural productivity losses, which assume no carbon fertilization effect, suggests that 20 developing countries would suffer yield losses of 30 percent or more. Adaptive agriculture programs should be examined in countries facing large agricultural productivity losses, such as India, Mexico, Senegal, and Sudan. Broader micro-insurance coverage for the poor should also be part of these programs.

The distribution of losses from sea level rise is highly skewed. Countries facing huge losses from rising sea levels, such as Egypt, Suriname, and Vietnam, will need to examine the net benefits of adaptive infrastructure and urbanization programs.

The distribution of flood risks (shown on a per capita basis) is also highly skewed. Programs combining adaptive infrastructure and micro-insurance should be the focus for countries facing high risk of flood disaster, such as Bangladesh, Benin, Cambodia, Honduras, Jamaica, and Mozambique.

Distribution of climate change impacts in developing countries

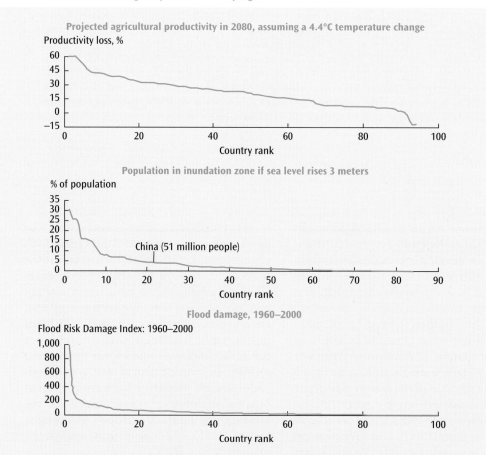

Source: Wheeler 2007, based on Cline 2007, Dasgupta and others 2007, and Buys and others 2007.
Note: The term "country rank" refers to the ranking of countries by size of damages, going from the country with the largest damages (first country) to the country with the smallest damages. In the top panel, the country with the largest agricultural losses (number 1) suffers yield declines of about 60 percent, while the country ranked 20th loses about 30 percent of its output.

following its case studies of adaptation options in Micronesia and the Cook Islands has, with the World Bank, initiated a study of climate change impacts in four Asian coastal cities (Bangkok, Ho Chi Minh City, Kolkata, Manila).[33] This study is tied to the Southeast Asia "mini-Stern" review, one of several regional climate impact studies currently in progress.

Resources, beyond traditional development assistance, are available to help finance adaptation. The UNFCCC Special Climate Change Fund (SCCF) was established in 2001 to finance projects relating to adaptation, technology transfer, and capacity building. The UNFCCC Adaptation Fund, established in December 2007, will provide funds for adaptation by taxing emission reduction credits generated under the Clean Development Mechanism (box 7.3). These funds are small, however; currently the SCCF is approximately $60 million and the Adaptation Fund, $45 million.

Emission Trends and Progress toward Mitigation

Although differences of opinion exist about stabilization targets and means of achieving them, there is broad agreement that GHG emissions must be reduced over the coming decades to avoid serious alternation of the earth's climate. GHG emissions have continued to increase since 1990, although the rate of increase in emissions has slowed for some sectors.

GHG Sources and Distribution

Figure 7.5 and table 7.7 show the breakdown of world GHG emissions in 2000 by sector.[34] Approximately 65 percent of GHG emissions come from energy consumption and industrial processes, 18 percent from land use change (deforestation), and the remaining 17 percent from agriculture and waste. Deforestation and fossil fuel consumption primarily produce CO_2, while agriculture and waste are the main source of methane

FIGURE 7.5 World GHG emissions, by sector, 2000

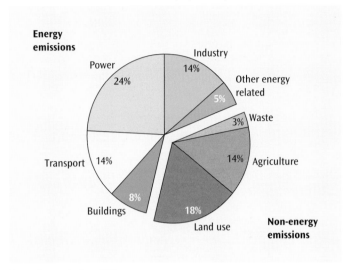

Source: Stern and others 2006.

and nitrous oxide emissions.[35] When GHG emissions from energy are broken down by sector, over one-third of energy emissions are from power generation, approximately 22 percent from industry, and 22 percent from transportation.[36]

The source of GHGs by sector varies widely across countries and regions (table 7.7). For the very poorest countries, most GHG emissions come from agriculture and changes in land use. Indeed, for the International Development Association (IDA) countries, only 29 percent of GHG emissions come from energy use.[37] The ranking of the world's largest emitters of CO_2 depends on whether emissions from land use change are counted in the total. When they are not, the top 10 emitters account for 73 percent of CO_2 emissions, and China and India are the only developing countries in the top 10. When emissions from land use change are included, the top 10 emitters account for two-thirds of CO_2 emissions, and three developing countries—Brazil, Indonesia, and Malaysia—join China and India in the list of top 10 emitters.[38]

The rank of emitters based on per capita emissions is quite different. In 2004 world emissions per capita were 4.5 tons of CO_2

TABLE 7.7   GHG emissions, by sector and region, 2000
metric tons of CO_2e

	Energy	Industrial processes	Agriculture	Land use change and forestry	Waste	Total
East Asia & Pacific	4,009	428	1,402	3,536	239	9,613
	(42)	(4)	(15)	(37)	(2)	(100)
South Asia	1,206	65	550	145	151	2,117
	(57)	(3)	(26)	(7)	(7)	(100)
Middle East & North Africa	868	49	78	22	42	1,059
	(82)	(5)	(7)	(2)	(4)	(100)
Europe & Central Asia	3,504	101	354	86	146	4,190
	(84)	(2)	(8)	(2)	(3)	(100)
Latin America & the Caribbean	1,361	82	1,009	2,357	134	4,943
	(28)	(2)	(20)	(48)	(3)	(100)
Sub-Saharan Africa	553	23	294	1,379	59	2,307
	(24)	(1)	(13)	(60)	(3)	(100)
High-Income countries	15,481	622	2,043	93	591	18,830
	(82)	(3)	(11)	(0)	(3)	(100)
World	26,980	1,369	5,729	7,619	1,361	43,058
	(63)	(3)	(13)	(18)	(3)	

Source: WRI.
Note: The figures in parentheses are percentages of total emissions.

per person from the burning of fossil fuel. The average emissions were 13.3 tons per person in high-income countries, 4.0 in middle-income countries, and only 0.9 tons per person in low-income countries. The map in figure 7.6 illustrates the striking disparity in per capita CO_2 emissions between developing and developed countries, even when land use change is included as a source of emissions.

How have emissions changed over time, and how are they likely to change if no steps are taken to reduce GHGs? Figures 7.7 and 7.8 show historic CO_2 emissions from fossil fuel combustion and project them into the future under the IPCC A1FI scenario, which assumes high reliance on fossil fuels and rapid economic and population growth (see table 7.2). Emissions are broken down between those countries that agreed to limit GHG emissions under the UNFCCC—labeled Annex I countries— and the developing world (non-Annex I

countries). Table 7.8 shows complementary information for emissions of all GHGs in 2000, broken down by Annex I and non-Annex I countries.

Carbon emissions by both high-income (Annex I) and developing countries have continued to increase and are predicted to increase—by over 60 percent by 2035 from 2004 levels under the A1FI scenario. Moreover, developing countries' CO2 emissions from fossil fuel will soon equal those of high-income countries (figure 7.7). Indeed, by 2035 developing countries will equal high-income countries in their contribution to the stock of CO_2 in the atmosphere if the world follows the A1FI trajectory (figure 7.8). If all sources of GHGs are included, non-Annex I countries already emit more GHGs than Annex I countries (table 7.8). This does not imply that the total emissions of developing countries should immediately be reduced, but it does indicate that their magnitude cannot be ignored.

FIGURE 7.6   Per capita GHG emissions in 2000, including emissions from land use change

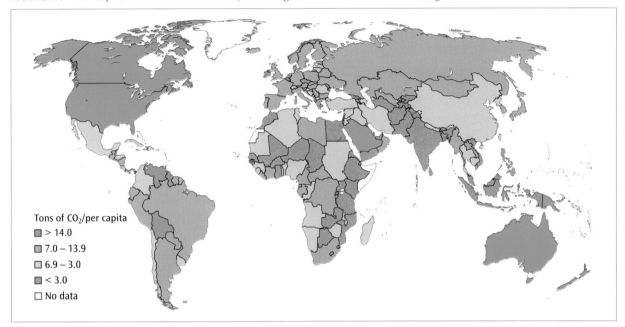

Tons of CO$_2$/per capita
- ■ > 14.0
- ■ 7.0 – 13.9
- □ 6.9 – 3.0
- ■ < 3.0
- □ No data

Source: Map created by Vinny Burgoo (http://commons.wikimedia.org/wiki/Image:GHG_per_capita_2000.svg) using CAIT 4.0 database of WRI.

Understanding Sources of Change in CO$_2$ Emissions from Fossil Fuel

To better understand sources of growth in CO$_2$ emissions, it is useful to decompose the change in CO$_2$ emissions into three components: the change in CO$_2$ per unit of GDP (carbon intensity of output); the change in per capita income; and the change in population.[39] For emissions to decline as population, per capita incomes, or both rise, the CO$_2$ intensity of output must decrease. A recent World Bank study decomposes the change in fossil fuel emissions for the 70 largest emitters of CO$_2$ from fossil fuel over the period 1994–2004 to see which countries were able to offset some of the growth in emissions that results from income (GDP) growth by reducing the carbon intensity of output.[40]

For the 70 countries as a whole, which accounted for about 95 percent of global CO$_2$ emissions from fossil fuel in 2004, CO$_2$ emissions from fossil fuel increased by approximately 5,000 million metric tons between 1994 and 2004. This change can be decomposed into a per capita GDP effect equal to 5,735 metric tons, a population effect of 2,665 tons, and a carbon intensity effect of –3,400 tons. This implies that the largest factor behind CO$_2$ growth was the growth in per capita incomes. The effect of population growth was about half as large. Improvements in carbon intensity, however, offset 40 percent (–3,400/8,400) of the growth in CO$_2$ from growth in population and per capita incomes.

How did reductions in the carbon intensity of output vary across countries? Figure 7.9 groups countries according to the percentage of increase in CO$_2$ emissions from GDP growth (growth in GDP per capita plus growth in population) that was offset by a decline in the carbon intensity of output. In 15 countries, shown in the right bar of the figure, the percentage decline in the carbon intensity of output was greater than the percentage increase in GDP, implying that more

FIGURE 7.7 Annual CO$_2$ emissions under the A1FI scenario, 1965–2035

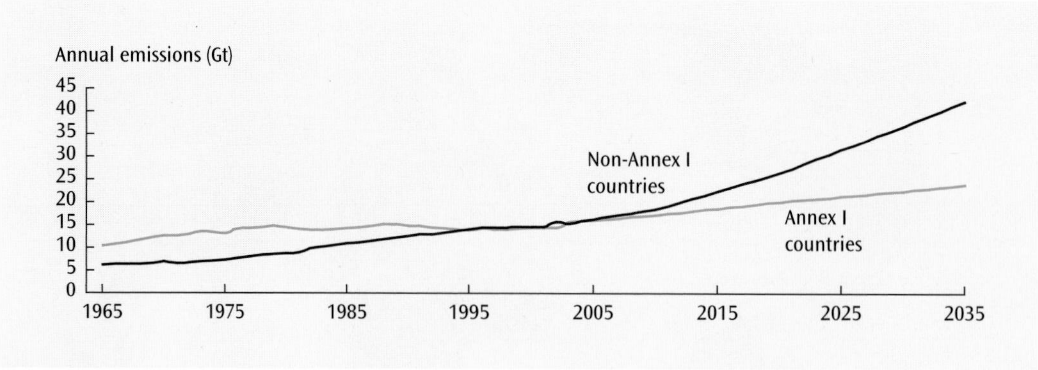

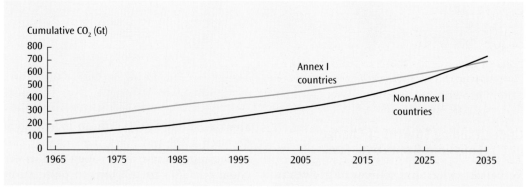

Source: Wheeler and Ummel 2007.

FIGURE 7.8 Cumulative atmospheric CO$_2$ under the A1FI scenario, 1965–2035

Source: Wheeler and Ummel 2007.

than 100 percent of the increase in CO$_2$ emissions due to GDP growth was offset. In these countries, which include Denmark, Germany, the Russian Federation, and Sweden, and some other countries that were part of the former Soviet Union, CO$_2$ emissions actually declined between 1994 and 2004. Of the world's 10 top emitters of CO$_2$, only 2 countries (Germany and the Russian Federation) were in this group. For 36 countries (reflected in the middle bar of figure 7.9) the carbon intensity of output declined, but the percentage decrease in carbon intensity was smaller than the percentage increase in GDP, implying offsetting between 0 and 100 percent. For the remaining 19 countries, the carbon intensity of output actually increased, implying no offsetting.

What figure 7.9 makes clear is that the declines in CO$_2$ emissions by the countries in the right bar of the figure were swamped by the increases in emissions of the other two groups. Countries in the middle group, in spite of reductions in the carbon intensity of their output, increased carbon emissions substantially—by nearly 4 billion tons a year in the aggregate. Countries whose carbon intensity increased caused world emissions to rise by 1.24 billion tons a year. In contrast, countries in the right bar caused annual emissions to drop by only 200 million tons a year.

Although the carbon intensity of GDP fell for 51 out of the 70 largest emitters of CO$_2$ between 1994 and 2004, it must fall even faster if world carbon emissions are to

TABLE 7.8 Comparison of GHG emissions for Annex I and non-Annex I countries

Category	Measurement	Annex I	Non-Annex I
GHG emissions in 2000: CO_2, CH_4, N_2O, PFCs, HFCs, SF_6 (including land use change)	Percent of total emissions	42.0	58.0
	Tons of CO_2e per person	13.9	4.9
Cumulative CO_2 emissions, 1950–2000 (including land use change)	Percent of total emissions	52.5	47.5
	Tons of CO_2 per person	457	103
Carbon intensity of electricity production	Grams of CO_2/kilowatt hour	436	679
CO_2 intensity of economy (excluding land use change)	Tons of CO_2/ million $PPP GDP	491	569

Source: WRI 2007.

decrease. For developing countries, carbon per unit of GDP must decrease even if their total carbon emissions are allowed to increase. Suppose, for example, that the carbon emissions of developing countries are allowed to double over the next 20 years, implying an annual growth rate in emissions of 3.5 percent. For carbon emissions to grow at a rate of 3.5 percent a year when GDP is growing at a rate of 10 percent a year—growth rates that India and China have recently experienced—carbon per dollar of GDP must fall at a rate of 6.5 percent a year.

Balancing Economic Growth and Reductions in Carbon Intensity

How can the carbon intensity of GDP be reduced as countries continue to grow? This must occur by reducing either the energy intensity of GDP (the energy used per unit of output), the fossil fuel intensity of energy (the fossil fuel used per unit of energy), or the carbon intensity of fossil fuel (the amount of carbon in a unit of fossil fuel), or by some combination of the three. Between 1994 and 2004 the reduction in the carbon intensity of GDP came almost entirely from reductions in the energy intensity of GDP. The carbon intensity of fossil fuel decreased slightly, reflecting a shift from coal to natural gas, but this reduction was offset by an increase in the fossil fuel intensity of energy.

FIGURE 7.9 Change in annual CO_2 emissions by carbon intensity class, 1994–2004

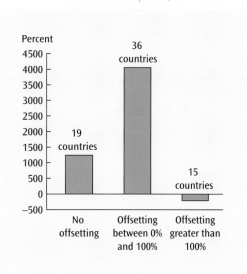

Source: Derived from Bacon and Bhattacharya 2007.
Note: Countries are categorized according to whether changes in carbon intensity of output offset growth in GDP. Offsetting greater than 100 percent indicates that reductions in carbon intensity of output more than offset emissions from GDP growth, resulting in a decline in total emissions; offsetting between 0 and 100 percent indicates that some fraction of emissions from GDP growth was offset by reductions in carbon intensity; and "no offsetting" indicates that carbon intensity of output increased, adding to the increase in emissions from GDP growth.

Improving energy efficiency. Figure 7.10 shows the energy intensity of GDP for World Bank regions. Eastern Europe and Central Asia had the highest energy intensity in 2004, largely because of the continued use of old, inefficient production equipment across various industries, dilapidated heating systems in cities and towns, high transmission and distribution losses, and inefficient stocks of household appliances. In China the widespread use of inefficient, coal-based power plants and small boilers for heating has offset an increasing trend in efficiency in other sectors. In both China and India a large proportion of small- and medium-scale industries continues to use old and inefficient technologies that contribute to high energy-intensity levels. Even though Sub-Saharan Africa's energy use is small on a global scale (it used only 4 percent of global energy supply in 2004), as the industrial sector in the region develops, the adoption of new technologies will be needed if energy intensity is to improve.

How great is the technical scope for improving energy efficiency in developing countries? The International Energy Agency has recently completed a global analysis of energy efficiency in manufacturing.[41] The study found that manufacturing accounts for about a third of world energy consumption, and three industries—chemicals and petrochemicals, iron and steel, and nonmetallic minerals—account for over half of manufacturing energy use and over 70 percent of CO_2 emissions from manufacturing. Table 7.9 compares the energy efficiency of three production processes in various countries with each other and with best-available technology. There is clear variation in energy efficiency across countries: China, the world's largest producer of cement, is less efficient than India or Japan. However, the energy efficiency of cement production could be increased even in Europe and Japan. Similar gains in efficiency could be realized in steel and ammonia production. Overall, the IEA study estimates that between 18 and 26 percent of world industrial energy use could be reduced by using best-practice technologies. This would reduce CO_2 emissions by between 1.9 billion and 3.2 billion tons a year.

Improving energy efficiency in power generation will also reduce energy CO_2 intensities, especially in countries such as India and

FIGURE 7.10 Energy intensity by region, 2004

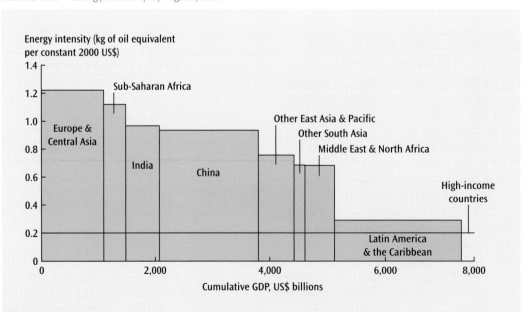

Source: World Bank 2007a.

China that depend on coal for power generation. The average thermal efficiency (the amount of power produced per unit of heat input) of power plants in India and China is between 29 and 30 percent, compared with 36 percent in developed countries. Supercritical plants can achieve efficiencies up to 45 percent. In China, installed capacity is expected to double—from 500 to 1,000 gigawatts (GW) between 2007 and 2015. India is expected to add 100 GW of capacity over the same period.[42] Installing thermal power plants with an efficiency of 38 percent in China would reduce carbon emissions at a typical plant by 22 percent. Emission reductions of up to 92 percent could be achieved by building supercritical plants with carbon capture and storage.[43]

The adoption of some low-carbon options will clearly require external financing and a positive shadow price for carbon. There are, however, some "no regrets," win-win options for improving energy efficiency that would pay for themselves in fuel savings if subsidies to energy consumption and production were removed.[44] These include reducing losses in the transmission and distribution of electricity, some improvements in power plant efficiency, insulation of buildings and improvements in appliance and vehicle efficiency. In many developing countries, demand-side incentives to improve energy efficiency are weak because electricity is not priced to recover the costs of generation. Failure to reform the electricity sector may also hamper access to financing more efficient power plants.

Low-carbon investments that would not pay for themselves in fuel savings or ancillary benefits could be financed by selling the emission reduction credits in a world in which long-term commitments to reduce CO_2 emissions establish a price path for carbon. This is now possible under the Kyoto Protocol's Clean Development Mechanism (box 7.3); however, because the Kyoto Protocol ends in 2012, the Clean Development Mechanism does not currently provide long-term financing opportunities. With donor

TABLE 7.9 Comparison of industrial energy efficiency across countries

	Energy consumption per unit produced (100 = most efficient country)		
	Steel	Cement	Ammonia
Japan	100	100	n.a.
Europe	110	120	100
United States	120	145	105
China	150	160	133
India	150	135	120
Best-available technology	75	90	60

Source: Watson and others 2007.
n.a. = Not available.

support, international financial institutions are attempting to fill this market void. Currently, the World Bank manages nine carbon funds totaling more than $2.5 billion. The International Finance Corporation and European Bank for Reconstruction and Development manage three additional carbon funds. These funds support more fuel-efficient thermal power generation as well as renewable energy sources.[45]

Reducing the carbon intensity of energy use. The carbon intensity of energy used by the top 70 emitters of CO_2 did not improve over the 1994–2004 period—although the carbon intensity of fossil fuel decreased slightly, the share of fossil fuel in energy increased. Substituting renewable energy sources for fossil fuels does, however, represent another means of reducing the carbon intensity of GDP. Although many sources of renewable energy may not be cost-effective at current energy prices, the potential for tapping these sources exists in many developing countries. And, given a functioning carbon market, these sources would likely be exploited eventually.

A recent World Bank study has estimated the potential for developing five sources of renewable energy—solar power, wind power, hydro power, geothermal energy, and biofuels—in developing and developed countries.[46] In each case potential energy supply is expressed as a fraction of current energy consumption. Table 7.10 shows the availability of renewable energy sources, relative to current consumption, for developing countries by World Bank region. The opportunities for renewable energy are greatest in Sub-Saharan Africa and parts of Latin America. Of the top 35 countries in the world with the most solar energy potential, 17 are in Sub-Saharan Africa and 7 in Latin America. Of the top 35 countries in the world with the most biofuel potential, 25 are in Sub-Saharan Africa. Note that table 7.10 measures the technical potential for developing renewable energy sources. For such development to be economically feasible, the world would have to make a significant commitment to GHG reduction. In the case of biofuels, the implications of their development on land use and food security must also be considered.[47]

Reducing deforestation. Land use change currently accounts for 18 percent of GHG emissions. As figure 7.11 shows, CO_2 emissions from changes in land use increased more or less steadily from 1850 until 2000. Since the early 20th century emissions from land use change in developing countries have dominated emissions from Annex I countries. In recent years two countries—Brazil and Indonesia—have produced over half of all world emissions from land use change. In Brazil, forests in the Amazon have been cleared to make way for pasture and cropland. The ultimate drivers of deforestation in Brazil are the demand for beef, soybeans, and lumber. Deforestation in Indonesia has been driven by the demand for timber and pulp and for land for palm oil plantations.[48] In both countries, deforestation has been undertaken by large corporate interests as well as by small-holders. Although the data pictured in figure 7.11 stop in 2000,

TABLE 7.10 Availability of renewable resources relative to current consumption, by World Bank region
annual renewable energy potential in years of current energy consumption

Sub-Saharan Africa		East Asia and Pacific		Latin America and the Caribbean		South Asia	
Namibia	100.5	Mongolia	514.9	Bolivia	37.5	Nepal	2.8
Central African Republic	90.9	Papua New Guinea	12.6	Uruguay	31.7	Pakistan	1.9
Mauritania	86.2	Solomon Islands	9.3	Argentina	27.5	Sri Lanka	1.2
Chad	77.3	Lao PDR	8.8	Guyana	19.3	Bangladesh	1.1
Mali	58.4	Cambodia	4.9	Paraguay	19.1	India	0.9
Niger	50.4	Myanmar	3.9	Peru	6.7		
Congo, Rep. of	43.6	Vanuatu	3.3	Brazil	6.4		
Angola	27.9	Fiji	1.5	Chile	5.5		
Sudan	27.6	China	1.2	Colombia	4.4		
Zambia	25.2	Indonesia	0.8	Nicaragua	3.8		
Congo, Dem. Rep.	24.7	Vietnam	0.7	Belize	3.8		
Mozambique	23.4	Thailand	0.6	Venezuela. R. B. de	2.6		
Botswana	22.4	Philippines	0.6	Ecuador	2.6		
Gabon	20.3	Malaysia	0.6	Honduras	2.2		
Burkina Faso	15.9			Panama	1.9		
Madagascar	14.6			Costa Rica	1.8		
Guinea-Bissau	14.2			Guatemala	1.3		
Tanzania	14.1			Mexico	1.1		
Cameroon	12.7						
Senegal	12.5						
Benin	12.5						
Sierra Leone	10.1						

Source: Buys and others 2007.

annual hectares deforested in Indonesia were approximately the same between 2000 and 2005 as between 1990 and 2000.[49] In Brazil hectares deforested actually increased from 2.7 million annually between 1990 and 2000 to 3.1 million annually between 2000 and 2005.

As many have observed, the continued conversion of the world's forests for agriculture would not be economical if there were a well-functioning carbon market.[50] The present value of a hectare of crop- or pastureland in the Brazilian Amazon is worth between $100 and $200.[51] Clearing a hectare of dense rainforest could release 500 tons of CO_2. At a carbon price of even $10 per ton of CO_2, an asset worth $5,000 is being destroyed for a land use that is one-twentieth as valuable.

Currently the carbon market does not extend to avoided deforestation. The Clean Development Mechanism allows parties to the Kyoto Protocol to purchase emission reduction credits from projects in developing countries that reduce CO_2 emissions (box 7.3). These reductions must be *additional* to what would have occurred under business as usual and can include reforestation projects. The mechanism, however, does not allow developing countries to create emission reduction credits from avoided deforestation.

A new carbon credit program is currently under negotiation within the UNFCCC that would compensate countries with carbon credits for avoided deforestation (see box 7.3). This complements donor efforts to fund avoided deforestation, including the World Bank's Forest Carbon Partnership Facility, which will help developing countries improve their estimates of forest carbon stocks and fund pilot projects to reduce deforestation, and the Bank's BioCarbon Funds.

Progress on Institutions and Policies to Deal with Climate Change

Because the abatement of greenhouse gases is a global public good, policies to reduce GHGs require international coordination. Beginning with the formation of the IPCC in 1988 and continuing with the establishment

FIGURE 7.11 CO_2 emissions from land use change, 1850–2000

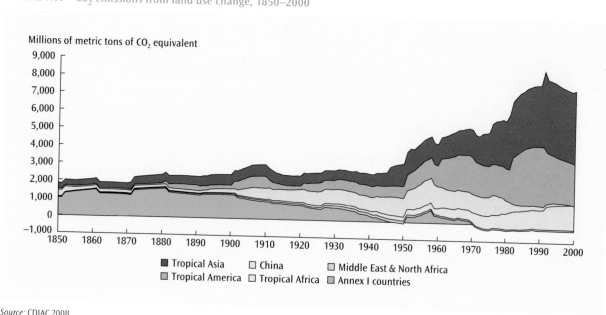

Source: CDIAC 2008.

BOX 7.3   Sources of carbon finance under the UNFCCC

Under the Clean Development Mechanism (CDM), parties to the Kyoto Protocol can meet their obligations to reduce GHG emissions by purchasing emission reduction credits (ERCs) from projects in developing countries. An ERC is generated if a project reduces its carbon emissions below what would have occurred without the CDM. The credits must be certified by the UNFCCC before they can be used to meet obligations under the Kyoto Protocol.

The CDM market is growing rapidly. As of January 2008, the UNFCCC had registered 901 projects with ERCs totaling 1.15 billion tons of CO_2 equivalent. Most of these projects have originated in Asia or Latin America, with fewer than 3 percent originating in Africa. If projects are weighted by the number of ERCs delivered, China was the largest seller of ERCs in transactions that occurred between January 2005 and September 2006, accounting for 61 percent of credits sold.[a] Most transactions have involved energy and manufacturing projects. Under the Marrakesh accords, land use projects are limited to afforestatation and reforestation projects.

A new carbon credit program is under negotiation within the UNFCCC—Reducing Emissions in Deforestation and Forest Degradation (REDD)—that would compensate countries with carbon credits for their efforts in reducing CO_2 emissions through forest conservation and by controlling forest degradation. A recent study by the Woods Hole Research Center[b] develops a conceptual framework of the costs to tropical countries of implementing REDD programs. It estimates that, in the Brazilian Amazon, approximately 90 percent of the opportunity costs of maintaining existing forest could be compensated for $3 per ton of carbon (approximately $1 per ton of CO_2). Under the program, forest families would double their incomes, fire-related damages would be avoided, and carbon emissions would be reduced over 30 years by 6.3 billion tons, equivalent to 23 billion tons of CO_2.

a. Lecocq and Ambrosi 2007.
b. Woods Hole Research Center 2007.

of the UNFCCC in 1992, the nations of the world have taken steps to address the effects of human actions on the earth's climate. Progress in establishing a link between human actions and climate change—and drawing public attention to this fact—is the first step in formulating effective public policies. The successful regulation of ozone-depleting substances under the Montreal Protocol would never have occurred had scientists not demonstrated that 40 percent of the stratospheric ozone layer had disappeared between 1957 and 1984 and linked pictures of the hole in the ozone layer to emissions of chlorofluorocarbons (CFCs) and other ozone-depleting substances.

International policies to deal with climate change have been organized under the United Nations Framework Convention on Climate Change, which was signed in Rio de Janeiro in 1992, went into force in 1994, and has been ratified by 190 countries. The UNFCCC created an international frame-work for climate change policy consisting of four elements: a long-term goal of stabilizing GHG concentrations in the atmosphere at a level that would prevent dangerous interference with the climate system; a short-term goal for developed (Annex I) countries to stabilize their emissions at 1990 levels by 2000; a principle of "common but differentiated responsibilities," suggesting that developing countries should not be expected to undertake the same obligations as developed countries; and opportunities for realizing more cost-effective reductions in GHG emissions through joint implementation.[52] Under joint implementation developed countries were allowed to invest in emission-reducing projects in developing countries to meet their 2000 emission reduction goals. Although only a few Annex I countries had met their emissions goals by 2000, the Rio accords established important principles that continue to be reflected in policy discussions.

The Kyoto Protocol

The Kyoto Protocol, which came into force in February 2005, committed most industrial countries and some transition economies (referred to as the Annex B countries) to specific GHG emissions targets. Over 2008–12, the total emissions of Annex B countries are to be reduced 5 percent below 1990 levels. Countries can either reduce GHG emissions or enhance the amount of carbon captured in "carbon sinks" (by sequestering GHG from the atmosphere) such as reforestation programs. The protocol also allows countries to buy emission rights from other Annex B countries whose emissions are below their limits and to assist non–Annex B countries to implement projects that reduce GHG emissions through the Clean Development Mechanism (see box 7.3).

The Kyoto Protocol represents a major attempt by the international community to come to grips with climate change. By signaling the intention of many countries to reduce GHG emissions, it may encourage investors to adopt more efficient, low-carbon technologies. Through provisions for carbon trading and the Clean Development Mechanism, the protocol helps to establish the principle that emissions reductions should be achieved in a cost-effective manner. It is also equitable, in the sense that it imposes no restrictions on the emissions of developing countries, which on a per capita basis have contributed less to the existing stock of greenhouse gases than developed countries.

The Kyoto Protocol has nevertheless been subject to many criticisms. For one thing, it does not limit the emissions of three of the world's five largest emitters of greenhouse gases—the United States, China, and India. The United States did not ratify the treaty, and the Kyoto Protocol does not extend to developing countries. It is too early to judge compliance (obligations to curtail are legally binding only for the 2008–12 period), but transition economies have more than satisfied their Kyoto targets because of a major

decline in economic activity after 1990, while most developed-country parties to the Protocol have thus far not met their targets (figure 7.12).[53]

Beyond Kyoto

International agreements to deal with climate change in the future will have to deal with several issues. Progress toward global environmental sustainability will depend on how agreements measure up against the following criteria.[54] First, an agreement must achieve a desirable environmental outcome. This could be stated as an emissions (or concentration) target or as a temperature goal. Second, the agreement should be efficient— it should achieve the environmental outcome at least cost, both in the timing of actions and in minimizing the costs of abatement across countries. Third, the obligations and results of the policies should be viewed as equitable, both across countries and, given the long-term nature of climate change, across generations. Fourth, the policies should be flexible—they should be able to accommodate changes in information about climate science. And, finally, the agreement should encourage wide participation and compliance among countries.

Whatever form an international agreement takes, it will have to provide incentives to reduce GHG emissions and an institution to collect and verify information on GHG emissions so that progress toward mitigation goals can be monitored.[55] The verification and publicizing of GHG emissions at the country level is necessary for the enforcement of an international agreement, will signal the willingness of countries to participate in the agreement, and will provide the means for stakeholders to put pressure on major emitters.[56] To provide an incentive to reduce GHG emissions, emissions must be priced, whether through a carbon tax, a permit market, or some combination of the two. The agreement will also have to make some provisions for the accelerated development of clean

FIGURE 7.12 Kyoto targets and changes in GHG emissions for Annex B countries

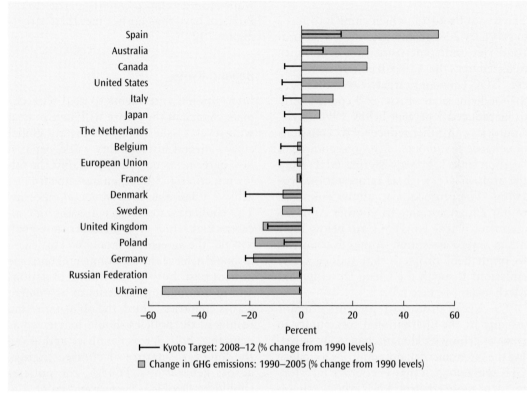

Source: UNFCCC 2008, EEA.

technologies, including clean energy technologies, carbon capture and storage, and geo-engineering, and it will need to finance the diffusion of these technologies in developing countries. Finally, the agreement will need to support developing-country adaptation to the impacts of unavoidable climate change.

Recent Trends in Biodiversity and Marine Fisheries

The global commons includes the animal and plant species that inhabit the planet, as well as the earth's climate. Protecting the diversity of animal and plant life is important for both economic and noneconomic reasons: humans attach a value to the existence of diversity per se, quite apart from the role that biological organisms play in the production of goods and services. At the same time,

continued diversity of animal and plant species is important to the world's economy, and especially to the lives of the poor in developing countries. Ocean fisheries, in particular, constitute an important source of food, and of livelihoods, for developing countries.

Biodiversity

One of the targets of MDG 7 is to reduce biodiversity loss. The two indicators associated with this target are the proportion of terrestrial and marine areas that are protected, and the proportion of the earth's species that are threatened with extinction. Figure 7.13 depicts trends in protected areas from 1990 to 2005. As the figure shows, the percent of area protected in all World Bank regions has increased since 1990. On average, approximately 15 of territorial area is

FIGURE 7.13 Proportion of terrestrial and marine area protected

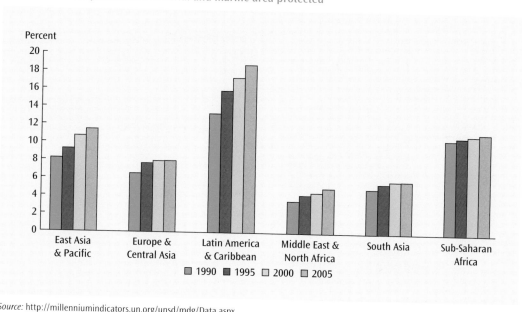

Source: http://millenniumindicators.un.org/unsd/mdg/Data.aspx.

protected worldwide, although the percent protected varies considerably across countries and regions.

Measuring the health of a wide variety of animal and plant species is inherently more difficult than measuring the fraction of land that is protected. Data on birds and mammals come from sightings of individual members of populations in a limited numbers of locations. The size of fish populations is often inferred from the ratio of harvests to effort (such as number of boat days) and is likewise subject to error, especially for individual species. Obtaining reliable data on the proportion of individual species threatened with extinction (indicator 7.6) is therefore difficult. The World Wildlife Fund (WWF) summarizes changes in populations of vertebrate species in its Living Planet Index (LPI)—the index measures trends in the planet's biodiversity by tracking over 3,600 populations of 1,313 vertebrate species.[57] Separate indexes are computed for terrestrial, marine, and freshwater organisms using data from a variety of sources. Indexes are also computed for different biogeographic regions of the world.

The LPI (figure 7.14) decreased from a value of 1.0 in 1970 to 0.71 in 2003, suggesting a downward trend in vertebrate populations overall. Each of the three component indexes also declined by approximately 30 percent. These aggregate trends, however, mask important regional changes in biodiversity (figure 7.15). The decline in the terrestrial index reflects a slight increase in the population of temperate species, but

FIGURE 7.14 Living Planet Index, 1970–2003

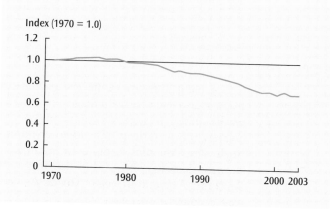

Source: WWF 2006.

FIGURE 7.15   Living Planet Indexes for terrestrial, marine, and freshwater organisms

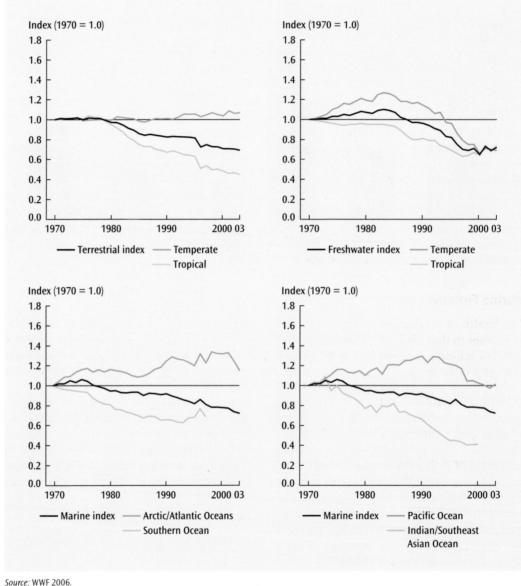

Source: WWF 2006.

a 55 percent decrease in the populations of tropical species. The rapid decline in the terrestrial index in tropical regions reflects the conversion of natural habitat to cropland or pasture. The most rapid conversion over the past 20 years occurred in the forests of Southeast Asia and in South America.

The marine subindex declined overall by 27 percent between 1970 and 2003,

but trends in the four ocean basins varied greatly. Monitored populations in the Atlantic-Arctic oceans actually increased, while populations in the Pacific were at approximately the same levels in 2003 as in 1970. In contrast, marine populations in the Indian Ocean declined by 55 percent, while populations in the Southern Ocean decreased by 30 percent. The relative stability of populations in the Pacific, the world's largest commercial fishery, masks declines in economically important species such as cod and tuna as a result of overfishing.

The freshwater index shows that species populations in this group declined by 30 percent between 1970 and 2003. This represents a stable trend in bird populations, but a 50 percent decline in fish species, attributable to habitat destruction, overfishing, and pollution. The damming of rivers for industrial and domestic use is likely responsible for much of the habitat destruction. The alteration of natural river flows alters the migration and dispersal of fish. More than 70 percent of large river systems (measured by catchment area) in virtually all biomes have been disrupted, primarily for irrigation.[58]

Marine Fisheries

The health of marine fisheries is especially important to developing countries. Fish provide 2.6 billion people with over 20 percent of their protein intake.[59] Two-thirds of world

fisheries production comes from marine and freshwater fish capture; the remainder comes from aquaculture. Developing countries are among the top 10 countries in fish capture: together China, Peru, Chile, Indonesia, and India accounted for 45 percent of inland and marine fish catches in 2004.[60] While the number of fishers has been declining in most high-income countries, it has increased in China, Peru, and Indonesia since 1990.

Indicator 7.3 of MDG 7 calls for monitoring the proportion of fish populations within safe biological limits. The Food and Agriculture Organization (FAO) has monitored the world's marine stocks since 1974. As figure 7.16 reveals, about half of all stocks are fully exploited, implying that production is close to maximum sustained yield. The share of fish stocks that are moderately exploited or underexploited has fallen, from 40 percent in 1974 to 25 percent in 2006, while the share of overexploited fish populations has increased, from 10 percent in 1974 to 25 percent. The increase in the number of over-exploited stocks occurred primarily during

FIGURE 7.16 Global trends in the world's marine stocks since 1974

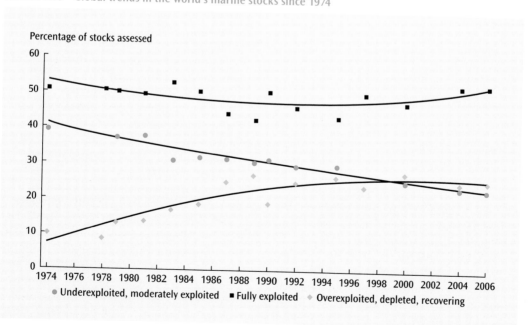

Source: FAO 2007.

the 1970s and 1980s, however, and the share overexploited has stabilized since 1990.

The data in figure 7.16 are consistent with trends in capture fisheries production. Production from marine and inland fisheries increased rapidly from 1950 until 1970, grew more slowly from 1970 until 1990, and has stabilized since then.[61] Since the world's fishing fleet has also been approximately stable between 1990 and 2004, the stable catch is consistent with fish populations that are, in the aggregate, stable.

This does not, however, mean that there is no cause for concern. The most commercially successful species are all fully exploited or overexploited. Examples of the latter include the blue whiting in the Northeast Atlantic and the Chilean jack mackerel and some anchoveta stocks in the Southeast Pacific. The percent of stocks that are overexploited varies by area. The areas with the highest proportion (46–60 percent) of overexploited species are the Southeast Atlantic, the Southeast Pacific, the Northeast Atlantic, and the high seas. The FAO suggests that deep water species in the high seas are at particular risk of exploitation because of their slow growth rates and late age at first maturity.[62]

Conclusions

Following are the key points summarizing the findings of this chapter:

- The world has been warming since the industrial revolution as a result of human emissions of greenhouse gases. This effect has accelerated in the second half of the 20th century and especially since 1990. If past trends in emissions continue, the world could experience mean global temperature increases of 2 to 6 degrees centigrade by the end of the century.
- These temperature increases, and accompanying changes in precipitation, sea level rise, and extreme weather events will not be evenly distributed across countries. Temperatures will rise more in north-

ern latitudes than in subtropical regions. But temperature increases in subtropical regions will reach levels where agricultural productivity is likely to decline. Heat waves will be more likely in both southern and northern latitudes. Dry areas are likely to become drier and wet areas wetter.
- Poor countries will suffer the most from, and are able to adapt the least to, the effects of climate change. These include impacts on agriculture and human health and effects caused by rising sea levels and extreme weather events. However, vulnerability to climate impacts varies widely among developing countries, suggesting that adaptation planning must be country-specific.
- For developing countries, the best way to adapt to climate change is to promote inclusive development. This will help to reduce vulnerability to climate impacts through economic diversification and by providing the poor with the resources they need to adapt. Achieving MDGs 1, 4, and 6 would constitute effective adaptation to the health effects of climate change.
- Although much adaptation is a private good, governments have a role to play in fostering adaptation: they can help provide information, including weather forecasts; they can facilitate infrastructure investments; they can promote efficient market responses to climate change—such as weather-index and flood insurance; and they can build institutions to help with disaster relief and set up social programs to cushion households from income shocks.
- Preventing dangerous changes in climate will necessarily involve mitigation of GHGs. This includes CO_2 from fossil fuel use, but also mitigation of CO_2 from deforestation and reduction of methane and nitrous oxide from agriculture. Better data are needed on GHG emissions from land use and agriculture, as these sources currently account for one-third of GHG emissions.

- CO_2 emissions from fossil fuel can be reduced by reducing the energy intensity of output and the carbon intensity of energy. Studies of the technical feasibility of improving energy efficiency indicate considerable scope for improving energy efficiency and for replacing fossil fuels with renewable energy sources.
- The use of technologies that are more energy efficient and the tapping of renewable energy sources will depend in part on the world's making a commitment to reduce GHG emissions. If carbon is priced, then the reductions in carbon emissions in developing countries could be sold on the carbon market to finance low-carbon technologies. This approach, however, would require a long-term commitment since low-carbon capital investments will yield carbon reductions over a long horizon. International financial institutions may be able to bridge the gap between current schemes (such as the Clean Development Mechanism) and those that will replace them in the longer term.
- Carbon finance can also help reduce emissions from deforestation. Using carbon finance to protect forests will require the development of institutions to monitor and protect forests at the national level, as well as funding from developed countries, through a carbon market or other forms of assistance.
- The world has made progress in dealing with climate change in the past 20 years, most notably by establishing the IPCC and UNFCCC. The UNFCCC has established important principles in dealing with climate change: that the world should stabilize GHG concentrations in the atmosphere at a level that would prevent dangerous interference with the climate system; that this goal should be achieved through "common but differentiated responsibilities," suggesting that developing countries should not be expected to undertake the same obligations as industrialized countries; and that reductions in GHG emissions should be achieved in a cost-effective manner.
- The formulation of an international architecture to deal with climate change is an ongoing process. Despite its limitations, the Kyoto Protocol has helped establish a foundation for global collective action to build on. Future agreements will be judged according to their ability to limit GHG emissions significantly, to do so in a cost-effective and equitable manner, and to ensure widespread compliance.

Notes

1. In this respect the chapter has a very different objective from the UNDP's 2007 *Human Development Report,* which discusses the impacts of climate change and the costs of mitigation and argues for specific emissions targets, and the Stern Review (Stern and others 2006), which presents a detailed analysis of the economics of climate change. The International Monetary Fund (2008) in chapter 4 of the April 2008 *World Economic Outlook* discusses the macroeconomic implications of climate change, including the costs of GHG mitigation and their fiscal implications.
2. IPCC 2007b.
3. IPCC 2007b.
4. CDIAC 2008; NOAA 2008. Other GHGs include methane (CH_4), nitrous oxide (N_2O), fluorocarbons (perfluorocarbon (PFC), hydrofluorocarbon (HFC), and sulphur hexafluoride (SF_6). The concentrations of these GHGs in the atmosphere are described in terms of CO_2 equivalents. Equivalent CO_2 (CO_2e) is the concentration of CO_2 that would cause the same level of radiative forcing as a given type and concentration of greenhouse gas.
5. IPCC 2007b, figure SPM.4.
6. A change of 2°C relative to pre-industrial times represents a change of 1.5°C relative to 1980–99 levels.
7. IPCC 2007b, figure SPM 6. The CO_2 equivalent concentration of 375 ppm reflects the effects of aerosols as well as long-lived GHGs.
8. UNDP 2007.
9. IPCC 2007a.
10. Weitzman (2007) has recently emphasized this point.
11. IPCC 2007b.
12. Or 2.3°C compared with pre-industrial levels.
13. 2007b, table SPM.6.

14. World Bank 2007d.
15. Cline 2007.
16. The carbon fertilization effect raises yields approximately 15 percent for crops such as rice, wheat, and soybeans.
17. Cline 2007, table 6.2. It should be noted that Cline's analysis ignores the effects of yield changes on agricultural prices.
18. Velicogna and Wahr 2006.
19. Dasgupta and others 2007. The impacts of sea level rise on GDP are calculated by attributing current GDP to each square mile of a country's surface area. The percent of GDP affected by sea level rise is calculated based on this attribution and ignores the macroeconomic impacts of sea level rise on GDP.
20. Buys and others 2007. The data for the index come from the Emergency Disasters Database (EM-DAT) at the Center for Research on the Epidemiology of Disasters, Université Catholique de Louvain.
21. Schelling 1992.
22. In 2004, 55 percent of the labor force in South Asia, and 58 percent of the labor force in Sub-Saharan Africa and East Asia and the Pacific were employed in agriculture (World Bank 2007a). On average, the share of agriculture in GDP in 2004 was 22 percent in low-income countries and only 2 percent in high-income countries.
23. Kahn 2005.
24. Yohe and Tol 2002.
25. Kurukulasuriya and Mendelsohn 2007.
26. UNDP 2007.
27. Stern and others 2006.
28. UNDP 2007.
29. Stern and others 2006.
30. Bettencourt and others 2006; ADB 2005.
31. Stern and others 2006.
32. Suryahadi, Sumarto, and Pritchett 2003.
33. ADB 2005.
34. Information on CO_2 emissions from land use, based on Houghton (2003), have been published for 1850–2000. Data on non-CO_2 gases are available from the U.S. Environmental Protection Agency for 1990, 1995, and 2000 (WRI 2007).
35. In terms of CO_2 equivalents (see note 4), carbon dioxide accounts for approximately 78 percent, methane for 14 percent, and nitrous oxide for 7 percent of GHG emissions. Fluorocarbons and sulphur hexafluoride account for the remaining GHG emissions.
36. There are various possible sectoral breakdowns, depending on whether or not electricity is attributed to end users (such as agriculture and the residential sector).
37. World Bank 2007b.
38. WRI 2007.
39. Formally, emissions = carbon intensity effect + per capita GDP effect + population effect. The carbon intensity effect = emissions * [rate of growth carbon intensity/rate of growth in emissions]. Other effects are defined similarly.
40. Note that CO_2 intensity is calculated using PPP (purchasing power parity) GDP; however, using GDP at market exchange rates makes little difference in the rates of change computed in the study (Bacon and Bhattacharya 2007).
41. IEA 2007.
42. UNDP 2007.
43. Watson and others 2007.
44. World Bank 2006.
45. For more on external financing of climate change mitigation and adaptation in developing countries, see chapter 3.
46. Buys and others 2007.
47. World Bank 2007d.
48. Chomitz and others 2007.
49. FAO 2008.
50. Chomitz and others 2007; UNDP 2007.
51. Chomitz and others 2007.
52. Aldy and Stavins 2007.
53. The penalties for noncompliance are not likely to change behavior. Countries that fail to meet their targets in 2008–12 must make up for this shortfall in the subsequent commitment period, plus a 30 percent penalty. A country liable for the penalty could fail to ratify the extension or insist on raising its emissions limit as a condition of participation.
54. Aldy and others 2003; Aldy and Stavins 2007.
55. Wheeler 2007
56. Currently the UNFCCC reviews the GHG inventories of Annex I countries. For a description of the review process, see (http://unfccc.int/national_reports/annex_i_ghg_inventories/review_process/items/2762.php).
57. WWF 2006.
58. WWF 2006.
59. FAO 2007.
60. FAO 2007.
61. The yearly variation in production between 1990 and 2004 is due almost entirely to variation in production from the Peruvian anchovy fishery and is associated with El Niño.
62. FAO 2007.

References

Chapter 1

Adams Jr., R.H. and J. Page. 2003. "International migration, remittances and poverty in developing countries", *World Bank Policy Research Working Paper,* No. 3179, Washington.

Alfaro, Laura, and Andrew Charlton. 2007. "Growth and the Quality of Foreign Direct Investment: Is All FDI Equal?" Harvard Business School Working Paper 07-072.

Alvaro, Gonzalez, Ernesto Lopez-Cardova, and Elio Valladares. 2007. "The Incidence of Graft on Developing Country Firms." World Bank Policy Research Working Paper No. 4394. World Bank, Washington, DC.

Aterido, Reyes, Mary Hallward-Driemeier, and Giuseppi Iarossi. 2007. "From Benchmarking to Impact: Identifying Which Dimensions Matter." In *Africa Competitiveness Report 2007,* Report of the World Economic Forum on Africa, Cape Town, SA, June 13–15, World Bank, Washington.

Aterido, Reyes, Mary Hallward-Driemeier, and Carmen Pages. 2007. "Investment Climate and Employment Growth: The Impact of Access to Finance, Corruption and Regulations Across Firms." IZA Discussion

Chowdhury, Abdur, and George Mavrotas. 2006. "FDI and Growth: What Causes What?" *World Economy* 29 (1): 9–19.

Dasgupta, Partha. 2001. *Human Well-Being and the Natural Environment.* Oxford, U.K.: Oxford University Press.

de Renzio, Paolo, and Bill Dorotinsky. 2007. "Tracking Progress in the Quality of PFM Systems in HIPCs: An Update on Past Assessments Using PEFA Data." Public Expenditure and Financial Accountability Secretariat, World Bank, Washington, DC.

Dorsey, T. 2008. "The Landscape of Capital Flows to Low-Income Countries." IMF Working Paper 08/51. International Monetary Fund, Washington, DC.

Dudine, Paolo, James John, Mark Lewis, Luzmaria Monasi, Helaway Tadesse, and Joerg Zeuner. 2006. "Weathering the Storm So Far: *The Impact of the 2003-05 Oil Shock on Low-Income Countries,"* IMF Working Paper 06/171, International Monetary Fund, Washington, DC.

Ferreira, S., K. Hamilton, and J. R. Vincent. Forthcoming. "Comprehensive Wealth and Future Consumption: Accounting for Population Growth." *World Bank Economic Review.*

Ferreira, S., and J. Vincent. 2005. "Genuine Savings: Leading Indicator of Sustainable Development?" *Economic Development and Cultural Change* 53: 737–54.

Gupta, Sanjeev, Catherine Pattillo, and Smita Wagh. 2007. "Impact of Remittances on Poverty and Financial Development in Sub-Saharan Africa." IMF Working Paper 07/38, International Monetary Fund, Washington, DC.

Hamilton, K., and J. M. Hartwick. 2005. "Investing Exhaustible Resource Rents and the Path of

Consumption." *Canadian Journal of Economics* 38 (2): 615–21.

Hansen, Henrik, and John Rand. 2006. "On the Causal Links Between FDI and Growth in Developing Countries." *World Economy* V29 (1): 21–41.

International Monetary Fund. 2007. *World Economic Outlook*. Washington, DC: IMF.

Kaplan, David, Eduardo Piedra, and Enrique Seira. 2007. "Entry Regulation and Business Start-Ups: Evidence from Mexico." Policy Research Working Paper No. 4322, World Bank, Washington, DC.

Kireyev, A. 2008. "The Macroeconomics of Remittances." IMF Working Paper 06/02, International Monetary Fund, Washington, DC.

Klapper, Leora, Raphael Amit, Mauro F. Guillén, and Juan Manuel Quesada. 2007. "Entrepreneurship and Firm Formation Across Countries." Policy Research Working Paper No. 4313, World Bank, Washington, DC.

Klapper, Leora, Luc Laeven, and Raghuram Rajan. 2006. "Entry Regulation as a Barrier to Entrepreneurship." *Journal of Financial Economics* 82 (3): 591–629.

Özden, Çağlar and Maurice Schiff. 2005. *International Migration, Remittances, and the Brain Drain*. Washington, DC: World Bank.

———. 2007. *International Migration, Economic Development and Policy*. Washington, DC: World Bank.

Safavian, Mehnaz, and Siddharth Sharma. 2007. "When Do Creditor Rights Work?" Policy Research Working Paper No. 4296, World Bank, Washington, DC.

World Bank. 2006. *Where Is the Wealth of Nations? Measuring Capital for the XXI Century*. Washington, DC: World Bank.

———. 2006 *World Development Report*. Washington, DC: World Bank.

———. 2007. *Economic Growth in Latin America and the Caribbean: A Microeconomic Approach*. Washington, DC: World Bank.

———. 2007. *World Development Indicators*. Washington, DC: World Bank.

———. *Doing Business 2008: Comparing Regulation in 178 Economies,*, Washington, DC: World Bank.

Chapter 2

Alderman, Harold H., Jere R. Behrman, and John F. Hoddinott. 2007. "Economic and Nutritional Analyses Offer Substantial Synergies for Understanding Human Nutrition." *Journal of Nutrition* 137 (3): 537–44.

Alderman, Harold H., Jere R. Behrman, Victor C. Lavy, and Rekha Menon. 2001. "Child Health and School Enrollment: A Longitudinal Analysis." *Journal of Human Resources* 36 (1): 185–205.

Alderman, Harold H., John F. Hoddinott, and Bill Kinsey. 2006. "Long-Term Consequences of Early Childhood Malnutrition." *Oxford Economic Papers* 58 (3): 450–74.

Alderman, Harold H., Hans Hoogeveen, and Mariacristina Rossi. 2006. "Reducing Child Malnutrition in Tanzania: Combined Effects of Income Growth and Program Interventions." *Economics and Human Biology* 4 (1): 1–23.

Alderman, Harold, and Victor Lavy. 1996. "Household Responses to Public Health Services: Cost and Quality Tradeoffs." *World Bank Research Observer* 11 (1): 3–22.

Anwar, A. T. M. Iqbal, Japhet Killewo, Mahbub-E-Elahi K. Chowdhury, and Sushil Kanta Dasgupta. 2005. "Bangladesh: Inequalities in Utilization of Maternal Health Care Services—Evidence from Matlab." In Gwatkin, Wagstaff, and Yazbeck 2005.

Armar-Klemesu, Margaret, Marie T. Ruel, Daniel G. Maxwell, Carol E. Levin, and Saul S. Morris. 2000. "Poor Maternal Schooling Is the Main Constraint to Good Child Care Practices in Accra." *Journal of Nutrition* 130 (6): 1597–1607.

Banerjee, Abhijit, Angus S. Deaton, and Esther Duflo. 2004. "Wealth, Health, and Health Services in Rural Rajasthan." *American Economic Review* 94 (2): 326–30.

Banerjee, Sudeshna, Quentin Wodon, Amadou Bassirou Diallo, Taras Pushak, M. Helal Uddin, Clarence Tsimpo, and Vivien Foster. 2008. "Access, Affordability, and Alternatives: Modern Infrastructure Services in Sub-Saharan Africa." *Africa Infrastructure Country Diagnostic Study*. Washington, DC: World Bank.

Barber, Sarah L., Stefano M. Bertozzi, and Paul J. Gertler. 2007. "Variations in Prenatal Care Quality for the Rural Poor in Mexico." *Health Affairs* 26 (3): w310–w323.

Barış, Enis and Majid Ezzati, eds. 2007. *Household Energy, Indoor Air Pollution and Health: A Multisectoral Intervention Program in Rural China.* Washington, DC: World Bank ESMAP.

Behrman, Jere, Harold H. Alderman, and John F. Hoddinott. 2004. "Hunger and Malnutrition." In *Global Crises, Global Solutions,* ed. Bjørn Lomborg, 363–420. Cambridge, U.K.: Cambridge University Press.

Bhutta, Zulfiqar A., Tahmeed Ahmed, Robert E. Black, Simon Cousens, Kathryn Dewey, Elsa Giugliani, Batool A. Haider, Betty Kirkwood, Saul S. Morris, H. P. S. Sachdev, and Meera Shekar. 2008. "What Works? Interventions for Maternal and Child Undernutrition and Survival." *The Lancet* 371 (9610): 417–40.

Black, Robert E., Lindsay H. Allen, Zulfiqar A. Bhutta, Laura E. Caulfield, Mercedes de Onis, Majid Ezzati, Colin Mathers, and Juan Rivera. 2008. "Maternal and Child Undernutrition: Global and Regional Exposures and Health Consequences." *The Lancet* 371 (9608): 243–60.

Bokhari, Farasat A. S., Yunwei Gai, and Pablo Gottret. 2007. "Government Health Expenditures and Health Outcomes." *Health Economics* 16 (3): 257–73.

Bruce, Nigel, Eva Rehfuess, Sumi Mehta, Guy Hutton, and Kirk Smith. 2006. "Indoor Air Pollution." In Jamison et al. 2006, 793–817.

Campbell-Lendrum, Diarmid, and Rosalie Woodruff. 2007. "Climate Change: Quantifying the Health Impact at National and Local Levels." WHO Environmental Burden of Disease Series 14, World Health Organization, Geneva, Switzerland.

Coady, David P., Deon P. Filmer, and Davidson R. Gwatkin. 2005. "PROGRESA for Progress: Mexico's Health, Nutrition, and Education Program." *World Bank Institute Development Outreach.* Washington, DC: The World Bank.

Confalonieri, Ulisses, Bettina Menne, Rais Akhtar, Kristie L. Ebi, Maria Hauengue, R. Sari Kovats, Boris Revich, and Alastair Woodward. 2007. "Human Health." In *Contribution of Working Group II to the Fourth Assessment Report of the Intergovernmental Panel on Climate Change,* ed. Martin L. Parry, Osvaldo F. Canziani, Jean P. Palutikof, Paul J. van der Linden, and Clair E. Hanson, 391–431. Cambridge, U.K.: Cambridge University Press.

Chaudhury, Nazmul, Jeffrey S. Hammer, Michael Kremer, Karthik Muralidharan, and F. Halsey Rogers. 2006. "Missing in Action: Teacher and Health Worker Absence in Developing Countries." *Journal of Economic Perspectives* 20 (1): 91–116.

Collier, Paul, Stefan Dercon, and John Mackinnon. 2002. "Density versus Quality in Health Care Provision: Using Household Data to Make Budgetary Choices in Ethiopia." *World Bank Economic Review* 16 (3): 425–48.

Danel, Isabella, and Gerard La Forgia. 2005. "Contracting for Basic Health Care in Rural Guatemala—Comparison of the Performance of Three Delivery Models." In *Health System Innovations in Central America: Lessons and Impact of New Approaches,* ed. Gerard La Forgia, 49–88. Washington, DC: World Bank

Dasgupta, Susmita, Mainul Huq, M. Khaliquzzaman, Kiran Pandey, and David R. Wheeler. 2004. "Who Suffers from Indoor Air Pollution? Evidence from Bangladesh." Policy Research Working Paper No. 3428, World Bank, Washington, DC.

Das, Jishnu, and Jeffrey S. Hammer. 2007. "Location, Location, Location: Residence, Wealth, and the Quality of Medical Care in Delhi, India." *Health Affairs* 26 (3): w338–w351.

Das, Jishnu, Jeffrey S. Hammer, and Kenneth L. Leonard. 2008. "The Quality of Medical Advice in Low-Income Countries." Policy Research Working Paper No. 4501, World Bank, Washington, DC.

de Garbino, J. Pronczuk, ed. 2004. *Children's Health and the Environment: A Global Perspective.* Geneva, Switzerland: World Health Organization.

de Onis, Mercedes, Monika Blössner, Elaine Borghi, Richard Morris, and Edward A. Frongillo. 2004. "Methodology for Estimating Regional and Global Trends of Child Malnutrition." *International Journal of Epidemiology* 33 (6): 1260–70.

Donabedian, Avedis. 2005. "Evaluating the Quality of Medical Care." *The Milbank Quarterly* 83 (4): 691–729 (Orig. pub. 1966).

Filmer, Deon. 2003. "The Incidence of Public Expenditures on Health and Education." Background note for *World Development Report 2004: Making Services Work for Poor People.* World Bank, Washington, DC.

Filmer, Deon, and Lant Pritchett. 1999. "The Impact of Public Spending on Health: Does Money Matter?" *Social Science and Medicine* 49 (10): 1309–23.

Franco, Lynne Miller, Diana R. Silimperi, Tisna Veldhuyzen van Zanten, Catherine MacAulay, Karen Askov, Bruno Bouchet, and Lani Marquez. 2002. "Sustaining Quality of Healthcare: Institutionalization of Quality Assurance." *QA Monograph Series* 2 (1): 1–59.

Glewwe, Paul, and Elizabeth M. King. 2001. "The Impact of Early Childhood Nutritional Status on Cognitive Development: Does the Timing of Malnutrition Matter?" *World Bank Research Observer* 15 (1): 81–113.

Grabowsky, Mark, Nick Farrell, John Chimumbwa, Theresa Nobiya, Adam Wolkon, and Joel Selanikio. 2005. "Ghana and Zambia: Achieving Equity in the Distribution of Insecticide-Treated Bednets through Links with Measles Vaccination Campaigns." In Gwatkin, Wagstaff, and Yazbeck 2005.

Grantham-McGregor, Sally, Yin Bun Cheung, Santiago Cueto, Paul Glewwe, Linda Richter, Barbara Strupp, and the International Child Development Steering Group. 2007. "Developmental Potential in the First 5 Years for Children in Developing Countries." *The Lancet* 369 (9555): 60–70.

Gwatkin, Davidson R., Adam Wagstaff, and Abdo S. Yazbeck. 2005. *Reaching the Poor with Health, Nutrition, and Population Services: What Works, What Doesn't, and Why.* Washington, DC: World Bank.

Gwatkin, Davidson R., Shea Rutstein, Kiersten Johnson, Eldaw Suliman, Adam Wagstaff, and Agbessi Amouzou. 2007. *Socio-Economic Differences in Health, Nutrition, and Population Within Developing Countries: An Overview.* Washington, DC: World Bank.

Haddad, Lawrence, Harold H. Alderman, Simon Appleton, Lina Song, and Yisehac Yohannes.

2003. "Reducing Child Malnutrition: How Far Does Income Growth Take Us?" *World Bank Economic Review* 17 (1): 107–31.

Hanushek, Eric A., and Ludger Woessmann. 2007. "The Role of Education Quality for Economic Growth." Policy Research Working Paper No. 4122, World Bank, Washington, DC.

Hoddinott, John F., John A. Maluccio, Jere R. Behrman, Rafael Flores, and Reynaldo Martorell. 2008. "Effect of a Nutrition Intervention During Early Childhood on Economic Productivity in Guatemalan Adults." *The Lancet* 371 (9610): 411–16.

Jack, William and Maureen Lewis. 2007. "Health Investments and Economic Growth." Paper presented at the Growth Commission's Health and Growth Workshop, October 16, Washington, DC

Jamison, Dean T., Joel G. Breman, Anthony R. Measham, George Alleyne, Mariam Claeson, David B. Evans, Prabhat Jha, Anne Mills, and Philip Musgrove. 2006. *Disease Control Priorities in Developing Countries*, 2nd ed. New York: Oxford University Press.

Johnson, Ian, and Kseniya Lvovsky. 2001. "Double Burden." *Our Planet* 12 (2).

King, Elizabeth M., and Dominique van der Walle. 2007. "Girls in Lao PDR: Ethnic Affiliation, Poverty, and Location." In Lewis and Lockheed 2007b, 31–70.

Kjellström, Tord, Madhumita Lodh, Tony McMichael, Geeta Ranmuthugala, Rupendra Shrestha, and Sally Kingsland. 2006. "Air and Water Pollution: Burden and Strategies for Control." In Jamison et al. 2006, 817–32.

Lavy, Victor C., John Strauss, Duncan Thomas, and Philippe de Vreyer. 1996. "Quality of Health Care, Survival, and Health Outcomes in Ghana." *Journal of Health Economics* 15 (3): 333–57.

Lengeler, Christian P. 2004. "Insecticide-Treated Bed Nets and Curtains for Preventing Malaria." *Cochrane Database of Systematic Reviews* 2004 (2): CD000363.

Leonard, Kenneth L. 2007. "Variations in the Quality of Care Accessible to Rural Communities in Tanzania." *Health Affairs* 26 (3): w380–w392.

Leonard, Kenneth L., and David K. Leonard. 2004. "The Political Economy of Improving Health Care for the Poor in Rural Africa: Institutional Solutions to the Principal-Agent Problem." *Journal of Development Studies* 40 (4): 50–77.

Leonard, Kenneth L., Gilbert R. Mliga, and Damen Haile Mariam. 2002. "Bypassing Health Centres in Tanzania: Revealed Preferences for Quality." *Journal of African Economies* 11 (4): 441–71.

Lewis, Maureen A. 2006. "Governance and Corruption in Public Health Care Systems." CGD Working Paper 78, Center for Global Development, Washington, DC.

Lewis, Maureen A., and Marlaine E. Lockheed. 2007b. *Exclusion, Gender and Education: Case Studies from the Developing World.* Washington, DC: Brookings Institution Press.

Lvovsky, Kseniya. 2001. "Health and Environment." Environment Strategy Paper No. 1, World Bank, Washington, DC.

Maluccio, John A., John F. Hoddinott, Jere R. Behrman, Reynaldo Martorell, and Agnes R. Quisumbing. 2006. "The Impact of an Experimental Nutritional Intervention in Childhood on Education among Guatemalan Adults." Food Consumption and Nutrition Division Discussion Paper No. 207, International Food Policy Research Institute, Washington, DC.

Mason, John, Jonathan Rivers, and Carol Helwig. 2005. "Recent Trends in Malnutrition in Developing Regions: Vitamin A Deficiency, Anemia, Iodine Deficiency, and Child Underweight." *Food and Nutrition Bulletin* 26(1): 57–162.

McMichael, Anthony, Diarmind Campbell-Lendrum, Sari Kovats, Sally Edwards, Paul Wilkinson, Theresa Wilson, Robert Nicholls, Simon Hales, Frank Tanser, David Le Sueur, Michael Schlesinger, and Natasha Andronova. 2004. "Global Climate Change." In *Comparative Quantification of Health Risks: Global and Regional Burden of Disease Attributable to Selected Major Risk Factors,* vol. 1, ed. Majid Ezzati, Alan D. Lopez, Anthony Rodgers, and Christopher J. L. Murray, 1543–1650. Geneva, Switzerland: World Health Organization.

Narayan, Deepa, Robert Chambers, Meera K. Shah, and Patti Petesch. 2000. *Voices of the Poor: Crying Out for Change.* Washington, DC: World Bank.

O'Donnell, Owen, Eddy van Doorslaer, Ravi P. Rannan-Eliya, Aparnaa Somanathan, Shiva Raj Adhikari, Deni Harbianto, Charu C. Garg, Piya Hanvoravongchai, Mohammed N. Huq, Anup Karan, Gabriel M. Leung, Chiu Wan Ng, Badri Raj Pande, Keith Tin, Kanjana Tisayaticom, Laksono Trisnantoro, Yuhui Zhang, and Yuxin Zhao. 2007. "The Incidence of Public Spending on Health Care: Comparative Evidence from Asia." *World Bank Economic Review* 21 (1): 93–123.

O'Donnell, Owen, Eddy van Doorslaer, Adam Wagstaff, and Magnus Lindelow. 2008. *Analyzing Health Equity Using Household Data: A Guide to Techniques and Their Implementation.* Washington, DC: World Bank.

Peabody, John W., Paul J. Gertler, and Arleen Leibowitz. 1998. "The Policy Implications of Better Structure and Process on Birth Outcomes in Jamaica." *Health Policy* 43 (1): 1–13.

Peabody, John W., and Anli Liu. 2007. "A Cross-National Comparison of the Quality of Clinical Care Using Vignettes." *Health Policy and Planning* 22 (5): 294–302.

Prevost, Christophe. 2008. Personal Communication. January 9.

Prüss-Üstün, Annette, and Carlos Corvalán. 2006. *Preventing Disease through Healthy Environments: Towards an Estimate of the Environmental Burden of Disease.* Geneva, Switzerland: World Health Organization.

Prüss-Üstün, Annette, David Kay, Lorna Fewtrell, and Jamie Bartram. 2004. "Unsafe Water, Sanitation and Hygiene." In *Comparative Quantification of Health Risks: Global and Regional Burden of Disease Attributable to Selected Major Risk Factors,* vol. 1, ed. Majid Ezzati, Alan D. Lopez, Anthony Rodgers, and Christopher J. L. Murray, 1321–52. Geneva, Switzerland: World Health Organization.

Ranson, M. Kent, Palak Joshi, Mittal Shah, and Yasmin Shaikh. 2005. "India: Assessing the Reach of Three SEWA Health Services Among the Poor." In Gwatkin, Wagstaff, and Yazbeck 2005.

Reinikka, Ritva, and Jakob Svensson. 2007. "Working for God? Evidence from a Change in Financing of Not-for-Profit Health Care Providers in Uganda." IIES Seminar Paper No. 754, Institute for International Economic Studies, Stockholm, Sweden.

Roemer, Milton I. and Carlos Montoya-Aguilar. 1988. "Quality Assessment and Assurance in Primary Health Care." *WHO Offset Publication* 105. Geneva, Switzerland: World Health Organization.

Sameroff, Arnold J., Ronald Seifer, Alfred Baldwin, and Clara Baldwin. 1993. "Stability of Intelligence from Preschool to Adolescence: The Influence of Social and Family Risk Factors." *Child Development* 64 (1): 80–97.

Schwartz, J. Brad, and Indu Bhushan. 2005. "Cambodia: Using Contracting to Reduce Inequity in Primary Health Care Delivery." In Gwatkin, Wagstaff, and Yazbeck 2005.

Smith, Lisa C., and Lawrence Haddad. 2000. *Explaining Child Malnutrition in Developing Countries: A Cross-Country Analysis.* Washington, DC: International Food Policy Research Institute.

Thomas, Duncan, Victor C. Lavy, and John Strauss. 1996. "Public Policy and Anthropometric Outcomes in the Cote d'Ivoire." *Journal of Public Economics* 61(2): 155–92.

Verhoef, Hans, Clive E. West, Nico Bleichrodt, Peter H. Dekker, and Marise P. Born. 2003. "Effects of Micronutrients during Pregnancy and Early Infancy on Mental and Psychomotor Development." In *Micronutrient Deficiencies in the First Months of Life,* ed. François M. Delange and Keith P. West, Jr., 327–57. Basel, Switzerland: Karger and Nestlé Nutrition Institute.

Victora, Cesar G., Adam Wagstaff, Joanna Armstrong Schellenberg, Davidson Gwatkin, Mariam Claeson, and Jean-Pierre Habicht. 2003. "Applying an Equity Lens to Child Health and Mortality: More of the Same Is Not Enough." *The Lancet* 362 (9379): 233–41.

Victora, Cesar G., Linda Adair, Caroline Fall, Pedro C. Hallal, Reynaldo Martorell, Linda Richter, and Harshpal Singh Sanchdev. 2008. "Maternal and Child Undernutrition: Consequences for Adult Health and Human Capital." *The Lancet* 371 (9609): 340–57.

Wagstaff, Adam and Mariam Claeson. 2004. *The Millennium Development Goals for Health: Rising to the Challenges.* Washington, DC: The World Bank

Walker, Susan P., Susan M. Chang, Christine A. Powell, and Sally M. Grantham-McGregor. 2005. "Effects of Early Childhood Psychosocial Stimulation and Nutritional Supplementation on Cognition and Education in Growth-Stunted Jamaican Children: Prospective Cohort Study." *The Lancet* 366 (9499): 1804–07.

———. 2006b. *Pakistan: Strategic Country Environment Assessment 1.* Report No. 36946-PK. Washington, DC: World Bank.

———. 2006c. *Repositioning Nutrition as Central to Development: A Strategy for Large-Scale Action.* Washington, DC: World Bank.

———. 2008. *Environmental Health and Child Survival: Epidemiology, Economics, Experiences.* Washington, DC: World Bank.

WHO (World Health Organization). 2002. *World Health Report 2002: Reducing Risks, Promoting Healthy Life.* Geneva, Switzerland: World Health Organization.

———. 2005. *The World Health Report 2005: Make Every Mother and Child Count.* Geneva, Switzerland: World Health Organization.

———. 2007. "Environmental Health." http://www.who.int/topics/environmental_health/en/ (accessed January 22, 2008).

WHO and United Nations Children's Fund. 2006. *Meeting the MDG Drinking-Water and Sanitation Target: The Urban and Rural Challenge of the Decade.* Geneva, Switzerland: World Health Organization.

Wößmann, Ludger and Paul E. Peterson, eds. 2007. *Schools and the Equal Opportunity Problem.* Cambridge, MA: MIT Press

Young, Mary Eming, and Linda M. Richardson, eds. 2007. *Early Child Development from Measurement to Action—A Priority for Growth and Equity.* Washington, DC: World Bank.

Chapter 3

Birdsall, Nancy, William D. Savedoff, and Katherine Vyborny. 2007. "Progress-Based Aid for Education: A Hands-Off Approach." Center for Global Development, Washington, DC.

Brook, Penelope, and Murray Petrie. 2007. "Output-Based Aid: Precedents, Promises, and Challenges." Global Partnership on Output-Based Aid, World Bank Group. http://www.gpoba.org.

Cavalcanti, Carlos. 2007. "Reducing the Transaction Costs of Development Assistance Ghana's Multi-Donor Budget Support (MDBS) Experience from 2003 to 2007." Policy Research Working Paper No. 4409, World Bank, Washington, DC.

Celasun, Oya and Jan Walliser. 2008. "Predictability of aid: Do fickle donors undermine the predictability of aid?" Forthcoming in *Economic Policy*.

Center for the Study of Global Governance. 2004. *Global Civil Society Yearbook 2004/5*. Anheier, Helmut, Marlies Glasius, and Mary Kaldor, eds. London: Sage.

Cerrell, Joe. 2007. "Making Markets Work." *Finance and Development* 44 (4).

Claessens, Stijn, Danny Cassimon, and Bjorn van Campenhout. 2007. "Empirical Evidence on the New International Aid Architecture." IMF Working Paper WP/07/277, IMF, Washington, DC.

Cliffe, Sarah, and Gary Milante. 2008. "Financing Post-crisis Recovery." forthcoming in the *General Review of Strategy*.

Collier, Paul, Anke Hoeffler, and Mans Soderbom. 2006. "Post-Conflict Risks." Working Paper 256, Centre for the Study of African Economies, Oxford University. http://www.bepress.com/csae/paper256.

Development Initiatives. 2006. "Global Humanitarian Assistance 2006." Somerset, U.K., Development Initiatives.

European Commission. 2007. "Technical Discussion Paper on a 'MDG Contract'—A Proposal for Longer-Term and More Predictable General Budget Support (June 19)." EC DG Development, Brussels.

The Gates Foundation. 2007. *Annual Report 2006*. Seattle, WA: The Bill & Melinda Gates Foundation. http://www.gatesfoundation.org/nr/AnnualReports/annualreport06/index.html.

Global Fund. 2007. "Donors Provide US$9.7 Billion to the Global Fund." Press release, September 27. http://www.theglobalfund.org/en/media_center/press/pr_070927.asp.

GPOBA (Global Partnership on Output-Based Aid). 2005. "Output-Based Aid." OBApproaches Note No. 05. GPOBA, Washington, DC.

Government of Ethiopia, Irish Aid, UNICEF, USAID, and the World Bank. 2007. "Reaching the Health MDGs in Ethiopia: Facing or Escaping the Scaling Up Challenge." Study prepared as part of the follow up to the High Level Forum on the health MDGs, World Bank, Washington, DC.

Government of Tanzania, Tanzania Development Partners Group, and the World Bank. "Joint Assistance Strategy for the United Republic of Tanzania FY2007-FY2010." World Bank, Washington, DC.

Hudson Institute. 2007. "The Index of Global Philanthropy." Hudson Institute, Washington, DC.

IDA (International Development Association). 2006. "A Review of Output-Based Aid Approaches." World Bank, Washington, DC.

———. 2007. "Country Assistance Strategy for Ghana FY08-11." Report No. 39822-GH, World Bank, Washington, DC.

IMF (International Monetary Fund). 2007. "Fiscal Policy Response to Scaled-Up Aid." IMF, Washington, DC.

IMF and World Bank. 2007. "Heavily Indebted Poor Countries (HIPC) Initiative and Multilateral Debt Relief Initiative (MDRI). Status of Implementation." IMF and World Bank, Washington, DC.

International Health Partnership. 2007. "Scaling up for better health. IHP+ work plan of the eight international health agencies." Available at http://www.who.int/healthsystems/ihp/en/index1.html

International Health Partnership. 2008. "Update on the International Health Partnership and Related Initiatives (IHP+)." Prepared for the H 8 Meeting. Available at www.who.int/healthsystems/IHP+progress_report_H8.pdf

Kerlin, J., and S. Thanasombat. 2006. "The International Charitable Nonprofit Sector." Urban Institute Policy Brief No. 2, Urban Institute, Washington, DC.

Kharas, Homi. 2007a. "The New Reality of Aid." Wolfensohn Center for Development, Brookings Institution, Washington, DC.

———. 2007b. "Trends and Issues in Development Aid." Wolfensohn Center for Development, Brookings Institution, Washington, DC.

———. 2008. "Measuring the cost of aid volatility." Wolfensohn Center for Development Working Paper, The Brookings Institution, Washington, DC.

Lane, Christopher, and Amanda Glassman. 2007. "Bigger and Better? Scaling Up and Innovation in Health Aid." *Health Affairs* 26 (4): 935–48.

Lee, Linda. 2008. "Humanitarian Aid." Background Paper for the 2008 *Global Monitoring Report*.

Lewis, Maureen. 2005. "Addressing the Challenge of HIV/AIDS: Macroeconomic, Fiscal and Institutional Issues." CDG Working Paper 58, Center for Global Development , Washington, DC.

Manning, Richard. 2006. "Will 'Emerging Donors' Change the Face of International Co-operation?" *Development Policy Review* 24 (4): 371–85.

Michaud, Catherine. 2008. "Trends in Development Assistance to the Health Sector." Tables provided for *The Global Monitoring Report* prepared at the Harvard School of Public Health.

Moon, Allister. 2007. "Aid Predictability in Tanzania." Presentation at a PREM session on Improving the Predictability of Aid: Experiences at the Country Level, World Bank, Washington, DC.

OECD (Organisation for Economic Co-operation and Development). 2007a. "2006 Survey on Monitoring the Paris Declaration overview of the Results." OECD, Paris.

———. 2008a. "Development Cooperation Report 2007." OECD, Paris.

———. 2008b. "ODA in 2007." Press release, April 4, 2008. Paris.

OECD DCD (Development Co-operation Directorate). 2006. "Draft Good Practice Guidance for Integration and Effectiveness of Global Programs at the Country Level." (COM/DCD/DEV(2006)9, November 24, OECD, Paris.

———. 2007a. "Donor Practices on Forward Planning of Aid Expenditures." OECD, Paris.

———. 2007b. "Scaling Up: Commitments and Performance." DAC Senior Level Meeting, Development Co-operation Directorate, Paris, December 11–12.

———. 2007c. "Towards Better Division of Labour: Concentration and Fragmentation of Aid." OECD, Paris.

Republic of Rwanda. 2006. "Scaling Up to Achieve the Health MDGs in Rwanda." Background study for the OECD DAC High-Level Forum Meeting in Tunis, June 12–13.

Sambanis, Nicholas. 2007. "Short-Term and Long-Term Effects of United Nations Peace Operations." Policy Research Working Paper 4207, World Bank, Washington, DC.

Schieber, George, Lisa Fleischer, and Pablo Gottret. 2006. "Getting Real on Health Financing." *Finance and Development* 43 (4).

Strategic Partnership with Africa. 2008. "Survey of Budget Support 2007 Volume 1."

Stromberg, David. 2007. "Natural Disasters, Economic Development, and Humanitarian aid." *Journal of Economic Perspectives*, Volume 21, Number 3: 199-222.

UNDP (United Nations Development Programme). 2007. *Human Development Report 2007*. New York: UNDP.

World Bank. 2007a. "Country-Based Scaling Up: Assessment of Progress and Agenda for Action." World Bank, Development Committee Meeting, Washington, DC.

———. 2007b. "Enhancing Linkages Between Aid Modalities and Country Strategies: The Views of Partner Countries." Summary of workshop held in Mauritius, June 20–21, 2007,

———. 2007c. "Enhancing Linkages Between Aid Modalities and Country Strategies: Mozambique Country Consultation Report." Study prepared for an upcoming workshop on global programs, World Bank, D.C.

Chapter 4

Anderson, Kym, ed. Forthcoming. *Distortions to Agricultural Incentives: A Global Perspective.* London: Palgrave Macmillan; Washington, DC: World Bank.

Anderson, Kym, and Will Martin, eds. Forthcoming. *Distortions to Agricultural Incentives in Asia.* Washington, DC: World Bank..

Anderson, Kym, and William Masters, eds. Forthcoming. *Distortions to Agricultural Incentives in Africa.* Washington, DC: World Bank.

Anderson, Kym, and Johan Swinnen, eds. Forthcoming. *Distortions to Agricultural Incentives in Europe's Transition Economics.* Washington, DC: World Bank.

Anderson, Kym, and Alberto Valdés, eds. Forthcoming. *Distortions to Agricultural Incentives in Latin America and the Caribbean.* Washington, DC: World Bank.

Brenton, Paul, Gareth Edwards-Jones, and Michael Friis Jensen. 2008. "Carbon Labeling and Low Income Country Exports: A Look at the Issues." Mimeo. World Bank, Washington, DC.

Brewer, Thomas L. 2008. "U.S. Climate Change Policy and International Trade Policy Intersections: Issues Needing Innovation for a Rapidly Expanding Agenda" Paper Prepared for a Seminar of the Center for Business and Public Policy Georgetown University - February 12, 2008

Djankov, Simeon, Caroline Freund, and Cong Pham. 2006. "Time Costs as a Barrier to Trade." Policy Research Working Paper No. 3909, World Bank, Washington, DC.

Findlay, Ronald, and Kevin O'Rourke. 2007. *Power and Plenty: Trade, War and the World Economy in the Second Millennium*. Princeton, NJ: Princeton University Press.

Francois, Joseph, Bernard Hoekman, and Miriam Manchin. 2006. "Preference Erosion and Multilateral Trade Liberalization." *World Bank Economic Review* 20 (2): 197–216.

Gootiz, Batshur, and Aaditya Mattoo. 2008. "Restrictions on Services Trade and FDI in Developing Countries." Mimeo. World Bank, Washington, DC.

Harrison, Ann, ed. 2006. *Globalization and Poverty.* Chicago: University of Chicago Press.

Hertel, Thomas, and Alan Winters, eds. 2006. *Poverty and the WTO. Impacts of the Doha Development Agenda.* Washington, DC: World Bank.

Hoekman, Bernard. 2006. "Liberalizing Trade in Services: A Survey." Policy Research Working Paper No. 4030, World Bank, Washington, DC.

Hoekman, Bernard, and Aaditya Mattoo. 2008. "Services Trade and Growth." Policy Research Working Paper 4461. World Bank, Washington, DC.

Hoekman, Bernard, and Marcelo Olarreaga, eds. 2007. *Global Trade and Poor Nations. The Poverty Impacts and Policy Implications of Liberalization.* Washington, DC: Brookings Institution.

Kee, Hiau Looi, Alessandro Nicita, and Marcelo Olarreaga. Forthcoming. "Estimating Trade Restrictiveness Indices." *The Economic Journal.*

Mattoo, Aaditya, and Lucy Payton, eds. 2007. *Services Trade and Development: The Experience of Zambia.* Washington, DC: Palgrave Macmillan/World Bank.

Mattoo, Aaditya, Robert M. Stern, and Gianni Zanini, eds. 2008. *A Handbook on International Trade in Services.* Oxford, U.K.: Oxford University Press.

OECD (Organisation for Economic Co-operation and Development). 2007. *Agricultural Policies in OECD Countries: Monitoring and Evaluation.* Paris: OECD.

Stern, Nicholas. 2007. *The Economics of Climate Change: The Stern Review.* Cambridge, U.K.: Cambridge University Press.

UNFCCC (United Nations Framework Convention on Climate Change) Secretariat. 2007. "Synthesis Report on Technologies for Adaptation Identified in the Submissions from Parties and Relevant Organizations." http://www.unfccc.int. Complete link is: http://unfccc.int/resource/docs/2007/sbsta/eng/06.pdf

World Bank. 2007a. "Connecting to Compete. Trade logistics in the global economy" World Bank, Washington, DC.

World Bank. 2007b. *International Trade and Climate Change: Economic, Legal, and Institutional Perspectives.* World Bank, Washington, DC.

World Bank. 2008. Finance for All? *Policies and Pitfalls on Expanding Access.* Policy Research Paper. World Bank: Washington, DC.

WTO (World Trade Organization). 2007. *World Trade Report 2007: Six Decades of Multilateral Trade Cooperation.*www.wto.org

Chapter 5

ADB (Asian Development Bank). 2007. Toward a New Asian Development Bank in a New Asia Report of the Eminent Persons Group to the President of the Asian Development Bank." ADB, Manila, Philippines.

AfDB (African Development Bank). 2008. "Investing in Africa's Future: The AfDB in the 21st Century. Report of the High Level Panel." African Development Bank, Cote d'Ivoire.

Dollar, David, and Victoria Levin. 2004. "The Increasing Selectivity of Foreign Aid, 1984–2002." Policy Research Working Paper No. 3299, World Bank, Washington, DC.

EBRD (European Bank for Reconstruction and Development). 2006. "Capital Resources Review 3," EBRD, London. www.ebrd.org

Eurodad. 2007. "Untying the Knots: How the World Bank Is Failing to Deliver Real Change on Conditionality." Eurodad, Brussels.

IDA (International Development Agency). 2007a. "Education for All—Fast Track Initiative." www.worldbank.org

———. 2007b. "Operational Approaches and Financing in Fragile States." www.worldbank.org

IMF (International Monetary Fund). 2007/2008. *World Economic Outlook.*. Washington, DC: IMF.

InWEnt, OECD. 2007. "Performance and Coherence in Multilateral Development Finance, Summary Report." German Ministry for Economic Co-operation and Development Informal Experts Workshop, Berlin, Germany, January 29–30.

OECD (Organisation for Economic Co-operation and Development). 2007a. *Multilateral Organisations Performance Assessment: Towards a Harmonised Approach.* Paris: OECD.

———. 2007b. *The 2005 Survey Results on Monitoring the Paris Declaration.* Vol. 1. Paris: OECD.

Scott, Alison. 2004. *Assessing Multilateral Effectiveness.* London: DFID.

———. 2005: "*DFID'S Assessment of Multilateral Organisational Effectiveness: An Overview of Results.*" London: DFID.

World Bank. 2000. *Making Sustainable Commitments: An Environment Strategy for the World Bank.* Washington, DC: World Bank.

———. 2005. *Infrastructure and the World Bank: An Update.* Board Document DC 2005-0015. Washington, DC: World Bank.

———. 2007a. *Accelerating Development Outcomes in Africa:- Progress and Change in the Africa Action Plan.* Washington, DC: World Bank.

———. 2007b. "Environment Strategy Update: Adjusting Environmental Priorities, Maximizing Effectiveness, Focusing on Results." Unpublished. World Bank, Washington, DC.

———. 2007c. "Healthy Development." World Bank, Washington, DC.

———. 2007d. "IDA's Role in Aid Effectiveness." World Bank, Washington, DC

———. 2007e. "Implementation Plan for Strengthening World Bank Engagement on Governance and Anticorruption." World Bank, Washington, DC.

———. 2007f. *Meeting the Challenges of Global Development. A Long-Term Strategic Exercise for the World Bank Group,* Washington, DC: World Bank.

———. 2007g. *Infrastructure Action Plan Implementation Update.* Washington, DC: World Bank.

Chapter 6

Cavendish, W. 2000. Empirical Regularities in the Poverty-Environment Relationship of Rural Households: Evidence from Zimbabwe. *World Development* 28 (11): 1979–2003.

Chettri-Khattri, Arun. 2007. "Who Pays for Conservation: Evidence from Forestry in Nepal." In *Promise, Trust and Evolution: Managing the Commons of South Asia,* ed. R. Ghate, N. C. Jodha, and P. Mukhopadhyay. Oxford: Oxford University Press.

Cohen, A. J., H. R. Anderson, B. Ostro, K. D. Pandey, M. Krzyzanowski, N. Kuenzli, K. Gutschmidt, A. Pope, I. Romieu, J. M. Samet, and K. Smith. 2005. "The Global Burden of Disease Due to Outdoor Air Pollution." *Journal of Toxicology and Environmental Health, Part A,* 68: 1301–07.

Dasgupta, S., K. Hamilton, K. D. Pandey, and D. Wheeler. 2006. "Environment During Growth: Accounting for Governance and Vulnerability." *World Development* 34 (9): 1597–1611.

Energy Information Administration. 2007. *International Energy Annual 2005.* Washington, DC: EIA.

FAO (Food and Agriculture Organization of the United Nations). 2005. *Forest Resource Assessment.* Rome: FAO.

Ferreira, S., and J. Vincent. 2005. "Genuine Savings: Leading Indicator of Sustainable Development?" *Economic Development and Cultural Change* 53: 737–54.

Ferreira, S., K. Hamilton, and J. Vincent. Forthcoming. "Comprehensive Wealth and Future Consumption: Accounting for Population Growth." *World Bank Economic Review.*

Hamilton, K. 2003. "Accounting for Sustainability." Mimeo. Environment Department, World Bank, Washington, DC.

Hamilton, K., and M. Clemens. 1999. "Genuine Savings Rates in Developing Countries." *World Bank Economic Review* 13 (2): 333–56.

Hettige, H., M. Mani, and D. Wheeler. 1998. "Industrial Pollution in Economic Development:

Kuznets Revisited." Policy Research Working Paper No. 1876, World Bank, Washington, DC.

IEA (International Energy Agency). 2006. *World Energy Outlook 2006.* Paris: IEA.

———. 2007, *World Energy Outlook 2007: China and India Insights.* Paris: IEA.

IPCC (Intergovernmental Panel on Climate Change). 2007. "Climate Change 2007—Impacts, Adaptation and Vulnerability." Contribution of Working Group II to the Fourth Assessment Report of the IPCC. Cambridge University Press, Cambridge, U.K.

Jodha, N. S. 1986. "Common Property Resources and the Rural Poor in Dry Regions of India." *Economic and Political Weekly* 21 (27): 1169–81.

Kishore, S. 2007. "Mainstreaming Environment in the Implementation of PRSPs in Sub-Saharan Africa." Environment Department Paper N. 112, World Bank, Washington, DC.

Komives, K., V. Foster, J. Halpern, and Q. Wodon. 2005. *Water, Electricity, and the Poor: Who Benefits from Utility Subsidies?* Washington, DC: World Bank.

Narain, Urvashi, Klaas vant Veld, and Shreekant Gupta. 2005. "Poverty and the Environment: Exploring the Relationship Between Household Incomes, Private Assets, and Natural Assets." Resources for the Future Discussion Paper 05-18, Washington, DC.

OECD (Organisation for Economic Co-operation and Development). 1994. *Environmental Indicators–OECD Core Set.* Paris: OECD.

Pearce, D. W., and G. Atkinson. 1993. "Capital Theory and the Measurement of Sustainable Development: An Indicator of Weak Sustainability." *Ecological Economics* 8 (2): 103–08.

Samuelson, P. 1961. "The Evaluation of Social Income: Capital Formation and Wealth." In *The Theory of Capital,* ed. F. A. Lutz and D. C. Hague. New York: St. Martin's Press.

UNDP (United Nations Development Programme). 2005. "Environmental Sustainability in 100 Millennium Development Goals Country Reports." UNDP, New York. http://www.unep.org/dec/docs/UNDP_review_of_Environmental_Sustainability.doc.

UNEP (United Nations Environment Programme). 2007. *Global Environment Outlook 4: Environment for Development.* Nairobi: UNEP.

UNESCWA (United Nations Economic and Social Commissions for Western Asia). 2003. "Sectoral Water Allocation Policies in Selected UNESCWA Member Countries: An Evaluation of the Economic, Social and Drought Related Impact." E/UNESCWA/SDPD/2003/13, UNESCWA, Beirut, Lebanon.

Prüss-Üstün, A., and C. Corvalán. 2006 *Preventing Disease through Healthy Environments: Towards an Estimate of the Environmental Burden of Disease.* Geneva, Switzerland: World Health Organization.

Vedeld, Paul, Arild Angelsen, Espen Sjaastad, and Gertrude K. Berg. 2004. "Counting on the Environment: Forest Incomes and the Rural Poor." Environment Department Paper 98, World Bank, Washington, DC.Narain, vant Veld, and Gupta 2005

World Bank 2006a. "From Curse to Blessing – Natural Resources and Institutional Quality", *Environment Matters 2006: Good Governance and Environmental Management,* Washington DC: World Bank

———. 2006b. *Where Is the Wealth of Nations? Measuring Capital for the XXI Century.* Washington, DC: World Bank.

———. 2007a. *Global Monitoring Report.*

———. 2007b. "Making the Most of Scarcity Accountability for Better Water Management Results in the Middle East and North Africa." *MENA Development Report.* Washington, DC: World Bank.

———. 2008a. *Environmental Health and Child Survival: Epidemiology, Economics, and Experiences.* Washington, DC: World Bank.

———. 2008b. *Poverty and Environment: Understanding Linkages at the Household Level.* Washington, DC: World Bank.

———. 2008c. *World Development Indicators.* Washington, DC: World Bank.

Chapter 7

ADB (Asian Development Bank). 2005. "Climate Proofing: A Risk-Based Approach to Adaptation." Asian Development Bank, Manila.

Aldy, Joseph E., and Robert N. Stavins, eds. 2007. *Architectures for Agreement: Addressing Global Climate Change in the Post-Kyoto World.* Cambridge, U.K.: Cambridge University Press.

Bacon, Robert W., and Soma Bhattacharya. 2007. "Growth and CO_2 Emissions: How Do Different Countries Fare?" Environment Department Paper, Climate Change Series, No. 113, World Bank, Washington, DC.

Barrett, Scott. 2005. "The Theory of International Environmental Agreements." In *Handbook of Environmental Economics;* vol. 3, 1457–1516, ed. K. G. Mäler and J. Vincent. Amsterdam: Elsevier.

Bettencourt, Sofia, Richard Croad, Paul Freeman, John Hay, Roger Jones, Peter King, Padma Lal, Alan Mearns, Geoff Miller, Idah Pswarayi-Riddihough, Alf Simpson, Nakibae Teuatabo, Ulric Trotz, and Maarten Van Aalst. 2006. "Not If, But When: Adapting to natural hazards in the Pacific Islands Region." Policy Note, World Bank, Washington, DC.

Buys, Piet, Uwe Deichmann, Craig Meisner, Thao Ton That, and David Wheeler. 2007. "Country Stakes in Climate Negotiations: Two Dimensions of Vulnerability." Policy Research Working Paper No. 4300, World Bank, Washington, DC.

Capoor, Karan, and Philippe Ambrosi. 2007. "State and Trends of the Carbon Market 2007."World Bank, with IETA (International Emissions Trading Association), Washington, DC.

CDIAC (Carbon Dioxide Information Analysis Center). 2008. http://cdiac.ornl.gov/trends/co2/.

Chomitz, Kenneth M. 2002. "Baseline, Leakage, and Measurement Issues: How Do Forestry and Energy Projects Compare?" *Climate Policy* 2 (1): 35–49.

Chomitz, Kenneth M., Piet Buys, Giacomo De Luca, Timothy S. Thomas, and Sheila Wertz-Kanounnikoff. 2007. "At Loggerheads? Agricultural Expansion, Poverty Reduction, and Environment in the Tropical Forests." World Bank, Washington, DC.

Cline, William R. 2007. "Global Warming and Agriculture: Impact Estimates by Country." Peterson Institute, Washington, DC.

Commission of the European Communities. 2005. "Winning the Battle Against Global Climate Change." Communication from the Commission to the Council, the European Parliament the European Economic and Social Committee, and the Committee of the Regions COM(2005)35, European Union, Brussels. http://europa.

eu.int/eur-lex/lex/LexUriServ/site/en/com/2005/com2005_0035en01.pdf.

Dasgupta, Susmita, Benoit Laplante, Craig Meisner, David Wheeler, and David Jianping Yan. 2007. "The Impact of Sea Level Rise on Developing Countries: A Comparative Analysis." Policy Research Working Paper No. 4136, World Bank, Washington, DC.

Dinar, Ariel, Robert Mendelsohn, Robert Evenson, Jyoti Parikh, Apurva Sanghi, Kavi Kumar, James McKinsey, and Stephen Lonergan. 1998. "Measuring the Impact of Climate Change on Indian Agriculture." Technical Paper No. 402, World Bank, Washington, DC.

FAO (Food and Agriculture Organization of the United Nations). 2007. *The State of World Fisheries and Aquaculture 2006.* Rome: FAO.

———. 2008. "Change in Extent of Forest and Other Wooded Land, 1900–2005." Table in Global Forest Resources Assessment. http://www.fao.org/forestry/site/32033/en/.

Houghton, R. A. 2003. "Revised Estimates of the Annual Net Flux of Carbon to the Atmosphere from Changes in Land Use and Land Management 1850–2000." *Tellus* 55B: 378–90.

IEA (International Energy Agency). 2007. *World Energy Outlook 2007.* Paris: IEA.

IMF (International Monetary Fund). 2008 (April). *World Economic Outlook.*" Washington, DC: IMF.

IPCC (Intergovernmental Panel on Climate Change). 2007a. "Climate Change 2007: The Physical Science Basis." Contribution of Working Group I to the Fourth Assessment Report of the Intergovernmental Panel on Climate Change. Cambridge University Press, Cambridge, U.K., and New York.

———. 2007b. "Climate Change 2007: Synthesis Report." Summary for Policymakers, *Fourth Assessment Report of the Intergovernmental Panel on Climate Change.* Cambridge University Press, Cambridge, United Kingdom and New York, NY, USA.

Kahn, Matthew E. 2005. "The Death Toll from Natural Disasters: The Role of Income, Geography, and Institutions." *Review of Economics and Statistics* 87 (2): 271–84.

Kurukulasuriya, Pradeep, and Robert O. Mendelsohn. 2007. "Crop Selection: Adapting to Climate Change in Africa." Policy Research

Working Paper No. 4307, World Bank, Washington, DC.

Kurukulasuriya, Pradeep, Robert Mendelsohn, Rashid Hassan, James Benhin, Temesgen Deressa, Mbaye Diop, Helmy Mohamed Eid, K. Yerfi Fosu, Glwadys Gbetibouo, Suman Jain, Ali Mahamadou, Renneth Mano, Jane Kabubo-Mariara, Samia El-Marsafawy, Ernest Molua, Samiha Ouda, Mathieu Ouedraogo, Isidor Séne, David Maddison, S. Niggol Seo, and Ariel Dinar. 2006. "Will African Agriculture Survive Climate Change?" *World Bank Economic Review* 20 (3): 367–88.

Lecocq, Franck, and Philippe Ambrosi. 2007. "The Clean Development Mechanism: History, Status, and Prospects." *Review of Environmental Economics and Policy* 1 (1): 134–51.

Lopez, Alan. 2006. "Global and Regional Burden of Disease and Risk Factors, 2001: Systematic Analysis of Population Health Data." *The Lancet* 367: 174757.

Manuamorn, Ornsaran Pomme. 2005. "Scaling-Up Micro Insurance. The Case of Weather Insurance for Smallholders in India," World Bank, Washington, DC.

McMichael, Anthony J., Diarmid Campbell-Lendrum, Sari Kovats, Sally Edwards, Paul Wilkinson, Theresa Wilson, Robert Nicholls, Simon Hales, Frank Tanser, David Le Sueur, Michael Schlesinger, and Natasha Andronova. 2004. "Global Climate Change." In *Comparative Quantification of Health Risks: Global and Regional Burden of Disease Due to Selected Major Risk Factors,* ed. M. J. Ezzati, et al. 1543–1649. Geneva, Switzerland: World Health Organization.

Murdoch, James C., and Todd Sandler. 1997. "Voluntary Cutbacks and Pre-Treaty Behavior: The Helsinki Protocol and Sulfur Emissions." *Public Finance Quarterly* 25 (2): 139–62.

NOAA (National Oceanic and Atmospheric Administration). 2008. "Trends in Atmospheric Carbon Dioxide." Earth System Research Laboratory, Global Monitoring Division. http://www.esrl.noaa.gov/gmd/ccgg/trends/.

Parry, M., C. Rosenzweig, A. Iglesias, M. Livermore, and G. Fischer. 2004. "Effects of Climate Change on Global Food Production under SRES Emissions and Socio-Economic Scenarios." *Global Environmental Change* 11 (3): 1–3.

Schelling, Thomas. 1992. "Some Economics of Global Warming." *American Economic Review* 82 (1): 1–14.

Stern, Nicholas 2008. Richard T. Ely Lecture, American Economic Association.

Stern, N., S. Peters, V. Bakhshi, A. Bowen, C. Cameron, S. Catovsky, D. Crane, S. Cruickshank, S. Dietz, N. Edmonson, S.-L. Garbett, L. Hamid, G. Hoffman, D. Ingram, B. Jones, N. Patmore, H. Radcliffe, R. Sathiyarajah, M. Stock, C. Taylor, T. Vernon, H. Wanjie, and D. Zenghelis. 2006. "Stern Review on the Economics of Climate Change." HM Treasury, London. http://www.hm-treasury.gov.uk/independent_reviews/stern_review_economics_climate_change/stern_review_report.cfm

Sunstein, Carl R. 2007. *Worst-Case Scenarios.* Cambridge, MA: Harvard University Press.

Suryahadi, Asep, Sudarno Sumarto, and Lant Pritchett. 2003. "Evolution of Poverty during the Crisis in Indonesia," *Asian Economic Journal* 17 (3): 221–41.

UNFCCC. 2008. http://unfccc.int/2860.php

UNDP (United Nations Development Programme). 2007. *Human Development Report 2007/2008— Fighting Climate Change: Human Solidarity in a Divided World.* New York: UNDP.

U.S. EPA (U.S. Environmental Protection Agency). 1999. *The Benefits and Costs of the Clean Air Act: 1990–2010.* Washington, DC: Office of Policy Analysis, U.S. EPA.

Velicogna, Isabella, and John Wahr. 2006. "Measurements of Time-Variable Gravity Show Mass Loss in Antarctica." *Science* 311 (5768): 1754–56.

Watson, Jim, Gordon MacKerron, David Ockwell, and Tao Wang. 2007. "Technology and Carbon Mitigation in Developing Countries: Are Cleaner Coal Technologies a Viable Option?" Occasional Paper 2007/16, Human Development Report Office, UNDP, New York.

Weitzman, Martin L. 2007. "Role of Uncertainty in the Economics of Catastrophic Climate Change." Working Paper No. 07-11, AEI Center for Regulatory and Market Studies (formerly AEI-Brookings Joint Center), Washington, DC.

Wheeler, David. 2007. "Greenhouse Emissions and Climate Change: Implications for Developing Countries and Public Policy." Mimeo. Center for Global Development, Washington, DC.

Wheeler, David, and Kevin Ummel. 2007. "Another Inconvenient Truth: A Carbon-Intensive South Faces Environmental Disaster, No Matter What the North Does." CGD Working Paper 134, Center for Global Development, Washington, DC.

Woods Hole Research Center. 2007. "Reducing Emissions from Deforestation and Forest Degradation (REDD): The Costs and Benefits of Reducing Carbon Emissions from Deforestation and Forest Degradation in the Brazilian Amazon." A Report for the United Nations Framework Convention on Climate Change (UNFCCC) Conference of the Parties (COP), Thirteenth Session, Bali, Indonesia, December 3–14, 2007.

World Bank. 2006. Clean Energy and Development: Towards an Investment Framework. April 23, 2006.

World Bank. 2007a. *World Development Indicators 2007*. Washington, DC: World Bank.

———. 2007b. "IDA and Climate Change: Making Climate Action Work for Development." World Bank, Washington, DC.

———. 2007c. "Global Economic Prospects 2007: Managing the Next Wave of Globalization." World Bank, Washington, DC.

———. 2007d. *World Development Report 2008: Agriculture for Development*. Washington, DC: World Bank.

WWF (World Wildlife Fund). 2006. *Living Planet Report 2006*. Geneva, Switzerland: WWF International; London: Institute of Zoology; Oakland, CA: Global Footprint Network.

WRI (World Resources Institute). 2007. "Climate Analysis Indicators Tool (CAIT) database 5.0." World Resources Institute, Washington, DC.

Yohe, G.W. and R.S.J. Tol 2002. "Indicators for Social and Economic Coping Capacity – Moving Towards a Working Definition of Adaptive Capacity." *Global Environmental Change*, 12 (1), 25-40.

Monitoring the MDGs: Selected Indicators

Goals and Targets from the Millennium Declaration

GOAL 1	ERADICATE EXTREME POVERTY AND HUNGER
TARGET 1.A	Halve, between 1990 and 2015, the proportion of people whose income is less than $1 a day
TARGET 1.B	Achieve full and productive employment and decent work for all, including women and young people
TARGET 1.C	Halve, between 1990 and 2015, the proportion of people who suffer from hunger

GOAL 2	ACHIEVE UNIVERSAL PRIMARY EDUCATION
TARGET 2.A	Ensure that by 2015, children everywhere, boys and girls alike, will be able to complete a full course of primary schooling

GOAL 3	PROMOTE GENDER EQUALITY AND EMPOWER WOMEN
TARGET 3.A	Eliminate gender disparity in primary and secondary education, preferably by 2005, and at all levels of education no later than 2015

GOAL 4	REDUCE CHILD MORTALITY
TARGET 4.A	Reduce by two-thirds, between 1990 and 2015, the under-five mortality rate

GOAL 5	IMPROVE MATERNAL HEALTH
TARGET 5.A	Reduce by three-quarters, between 1990 and 2015, the maternal mortality ratio
TARGET 5.B	Achieve by 2015 universal access to reproductive health

GOAL 6	COMBAT HIV/AIDS, MALARIA, AND OTHER DISEASES
TARGET 6.A	Have halted by 2015 and begun to reverse the spread of HIV/AIDS
TARGET 6.B	Achieve by 2010 universal access to treatment for HIV/AIDS for all those who need it
TARGET 6.C	Have halted by 2015 and begun to reverse the incidence of malaria and other major diseases

GOAL 7	ENSURE ENVIRONMENTAL SUSTAINABILITY
TARGET 7.A	Integrate the principles of sustainable development into country policies and programs and reverse the loss of environmental resources
TARGET 7.B	Reduce biodiversity loss, achieving by 2010 a significant reduction in the rate of loss
TARGET 7.C	Halve by 2015 the proportion of people without sustainable access to safe drinking water and basic sanitation
TARGET 7.D	Have achieved a significant improvement by 2020 in the lives of at least 100 million slum dwellers

GOAL 8	DEVELOP A GLOBAL PARTNERSHIP FOR DEVELOPMENT
TARGET 8.A	Develop further an open, rule-based, predictable, nondiscriminatory trading and financial system (including a commitment to good governance, development, and poverty reduction, nationally and internationally)
TARGET 8.B	Address the special needs of the least-developed countries (including tariff- and quota-free access for exports of the least-developed countries; enhanced debt relief for heavily indebted poor countries and cancellation of official bilateral debt; and more generous official development assistance for countries committed to reducing poverty)
TARGET 8.C	Address the special needs of landlocked countries and small island developing states (through the Programme of Action for the Sustainable Development of Small Island Developing States and the outcome of the 22nd special session of the General Assembly)
TARGET 8.D	Deal comprehensively with the debt problems of developing countries through national and international measures to make debt sustainable in the long term
TARGET 8.E	In cooperation with pharmaceutical companies, provide access to affordable, essential drugs in developing countries
TARGET 8.F	In cooperation with the private sector, make available the benefits of new technologies, especially information and communications

Source: United Nations. 2008. *Report of the Secretary-General on the indicators for monitoring the Millennium Development Goals.* E/CN.3/2008/29. New York.
Note: The Millennium Development Goals and targets come from the Millennium Declaration, signed by 189 countries, including 147 heads of State and Government, in September 2000 (http://www.un.org/millennium/declaration/ares552e.htm) and from further agreement by member states at the 2005 World Summit (Resolution adopted by the General Assembly - A/RES/60/1). The goals and targets are interrelated and should be seen as a whole. They represent a partnership between the developed countries and the developing countries "to create an environment – at the national and global levels alike – which is conducive to development and the elimination of poverty."

Eradicate Extreme Poverty and Hunger

Most recent global poverty projections anticipate that the proportion of people living in extreme poverty—on less than $1 a day—will fall from 29 percent in 1990 to 10 percent in 2015. Recently estimated purchasing parities for 2005 will inevitably affect calculation of poverty levels in developing countries but are not expected to change them significantly. Although extreme poverty has been reduced substantially since 1990, trends vary among the regions, with Sub-Saharan Africa lagging far behind the other regions in attaining MDG 1.

MDG 1 FIGURE 1   Share of people living on less than $1 or $2 a day in 2004, and projections for 2015

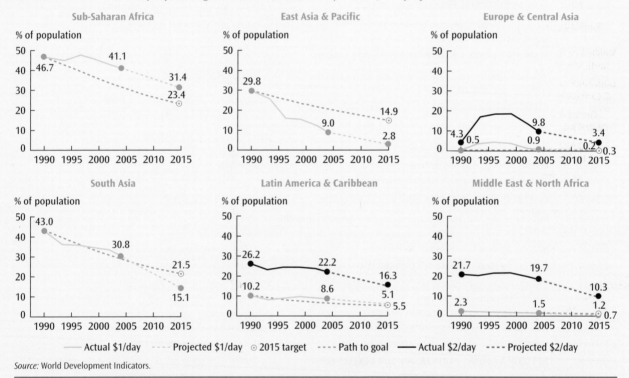

Source: World Development Indicators.

▲ Extreme poverty is defined as the proportion of individuals in developing countries who live on less than $1 a day (based on purchasing power parity 1993 constant prices). Poverty estimates are computed based on data covering 93 percent of developing countries' population. MDG 1 Figure 1 shows that all regions except Sub-Saharan Africa are on track to halve that proportion between 1990 and 2015. On current trends, this region will reduce poverty by only 33 percent between 1990 and 2015. In 1990 South Asia had the second-highest proportion of people living on less than $1 a day (43 percent) but has made substantial progress in reducing poverty and on current trends may surpass the target in 2015. Most of the progress in this region can be attributed to India's rapid growth over the past decade.

MDG 1 FIGURE 2   Share of poorest and richest quintiles in national consumption

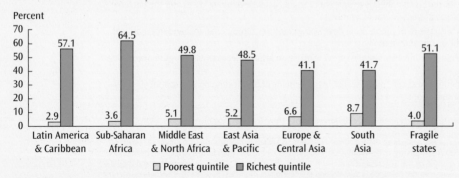

◄ Consumption data reveal the inequality that exists between the richest and poorest population quintiles in different regions. Individual countries' income distribution data is compiled together to create regional income distribution data, so both inter- and intracountry inequality can be assessed. The data use purchasing power parities based on 2005 prices and cover 93 percent of developing countries' total population.

Source: World Bank staff estimates.

TARGET 1.A Halve, between 1990 and 2015, the proportion of people whose income is less than $1 a day

TARGET 1.B Achieve full and productive employment and decent work for all, including women and young people

TARGET 1.C Halve, between 1990 and 2015, the proportion of people who suffer from hunger

MDG 1 FIGURE 3 Proportion of countries on track to achieve the poverty reduction target

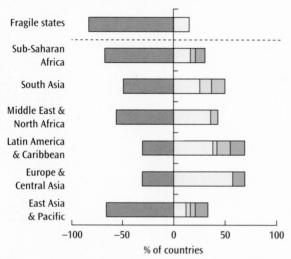

% of countries

■ No data □ Seriously off track □ Off track ■ On track ■ Achieved

Source: World Development Indicators.

▲ Of the 71 countries with available data (out of 149), 24 have already achieved or are on track to meet the poverty reduction target, but 47 are either off track or seriously off track. Fifteen of 18 countries in Europe and Central Asia, and 11 of 20 countries in Latin America and the Caribbean, are seriously off track. Since the 5 fragile states with available data are all seriously off track, there is no evidence to suggest that even 1 fragile state will meet MDG 1. Fragile states are low-income countries or territories with no CPIA score or a CPIA score of 3.2 or less.

MDG 1 FIGURE 5 Proportion of countries on track to reduce under-five malnutrition by half

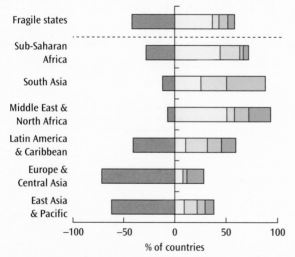

% of countries

■ No data □ Seriously off track □ Off track ■ On track ■ Achieved

Source: World Development Indicators.

MDG 1 FIGURE 4 Annual changes in vulnerable employment, 34 countries, 1990–2005

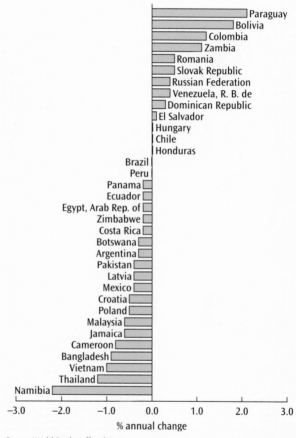

% annual change

Source: World Bank staff estimates.

▲ Vulnerable employment is the sum of contributing family workers and own-account workers as a percentage of total employment. Data available at two points in time between 1990 and 2005 for 34 low- and middle-income countries highlight the diversity of patterns. Some countries witnessed a decline in vulnerable employment over time, while others experienced substantial increases. Countries that have faced severe shocks, such as financial crises in East Asia and the Pacific or Latin America and the Caribbean, over the period can be found in both groups. Transition economies can also be found in both groups.

◄ The prevalence of child malnutrition is measured by the percentage of children under the age of five whose weight-to-age ratio is more than two standard deviations below the international median. Standards of child growth are currently being updated, but preliminary figures suggest that the global picture of malnutrition should not be significantly altered. The data covers 97 percent of developing countries' total population and suggests that many countries in Sub-Saharan Africa and the Middle East and North Africa are seriously off track. However, most countries in South Asia are on track.

Achieve Universal Primary Education

On the primary school completion rate target, Sub-Saharan Africa is off track for both males and females, while South Asia is on track for females but off track for males. Nevertheless, net enrollment rates for male and female children in both regions have been steadily increasing since 1990. The other four regions are on track to achieve the primary school completion rate target for both males and females; 46 countries in these regions have already achieved

full primary completion. In East Asia and the Pacific, Europe and Central Asia, and Latin America and the Caribbean, where primary school completion rates are already close to 100 percent, literacy rates for youth ages 15 to 24 are also close to 100 percent. Since 1990 significant progress has been observed in literacy rates, along with enrollment and primary school completion, in the Middle East and North Africa, Sub-Saharan Africa, and South Asia.

MDG 2 FIGURE 1 Primary school completion rates

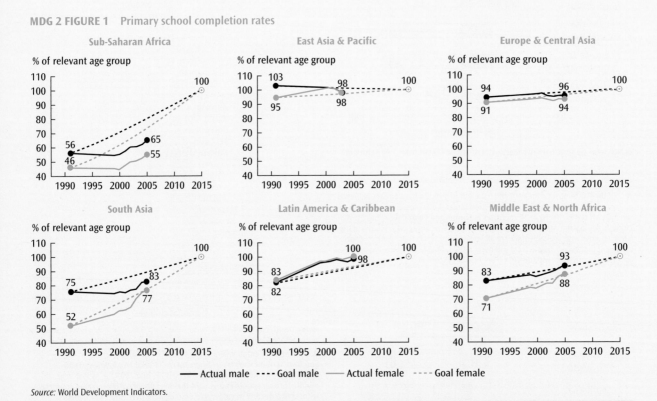

Source: World Development Indicators.

▲ The primary school completion rate is the percentage of children completing the last year of primary schooling. It is computed by dividing the total number of students in the last grade of primary school, minus repeaters in that grade, by the total number of children of official completing age. Under certain circumstances, the computation can overestimate the actual proportion of a given cohort completing primary school and sometimes exceeds 100 percent. Country data used to compute regional primary completion rates cover 65 percent of total developing countries' population.

TARGET 2.A Ensure that by 2015, children everywhere, boys and girls alike, will be able to complete a full course of primary schooling

MDG 2 FIGURE 2 Proportion of countries on track to meet the primary education target

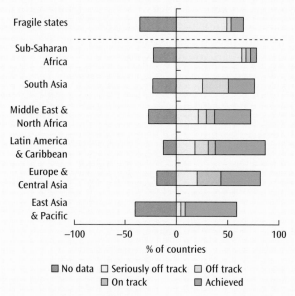

% of countries

■ No data □ Seriously off track □ Off track
□ On track ■ Achieved

Source: World Development Indicators.

▲ Twelve of 14 countries in East Asia and the Pacific (for which data exist) have already achieved the target, but data are still missing for the other 10 countries. Sixteen of 25 countries in Latin America and the Caribbean and 16 of 21 countries in Europe and Central Asia (for which data exist) have already met or are on track to meet the target. Conversely, most countries in Sub-Saharan Africa and South Asia are off track. In the Middle East and North Africa, 6 out of 10 countries (for which data exist) have already met or are on track to meet the target, but data are missing for the other 4 countries in this region. Fragile states and Sub-Saharan Africa record the largest proportions of countries off track or without data.

MDG 2 FIGURE 3 Net enrollment rates in primary education

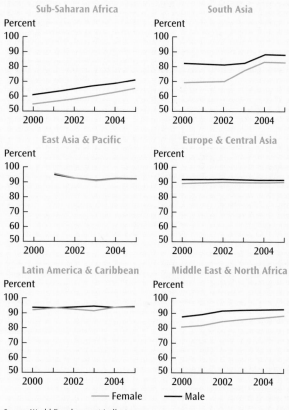

— Female   — Male

Source: World Development Indicators.

▲ Primary school net enrollment rates measure the proportion of children of official school age who are enrolled in school, but the rates ignore effective attendance, repetitions, or the fact that children can start school above the official age as long as they enter school before the official age of completion. Net enrollment rates for male and female children have slightly decreased in East Asia and the Pacific but have remained stable or increased in the other regions since 2000. In South Asia and the Middle East and North Africa the gap between male and female net enrollment has narrowed, but enrollment rates for females are still lower than for males. In Sub-Saharan Africa net enrollment rates have risen steadily since 1990, but the gap between males and females has not significantly narrowed.

MDG 2 FIGURE 4 Literacy rates, ages 15–24

% of youths 15–24 who are literate

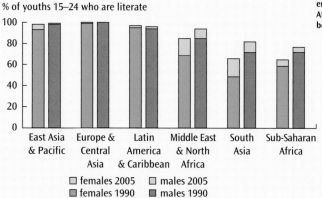

□ females 2005   □ males 2005
■ females 1990   ■ males 1990

Source: World Development Indicators.

◄ The youth literacy rate is the percentage of people ages 15–24 that can, with comprehension, both read and write a short, simple statement about their everyday life. Literacy rates for males and females have increased in all regions, especially in regions starting from lower levels. For females in South Asia, the literacy rate increased from 48 percent in 1990 to 65 percent in 2005, which complements the progress for this group in net enrollment and completion rates in primary education.

Promote Gender Equality and Empower Women

Significant progress has been achieved since 1990 in reducing developing countries' gender disparity in primary and secondary education. All regions except Sub-Saharan Africa are broadly on track to meet MDG 3 by 2015, even if some countries in these regions remain off track. However, gender gaps in wages and labor participation rates remain substantial, and there is little statistical evidence to suggest that these gaps are narrowing.

MDG 3 FIGURE 1   Ratio of girls to boys enrolled in primary and secondary education

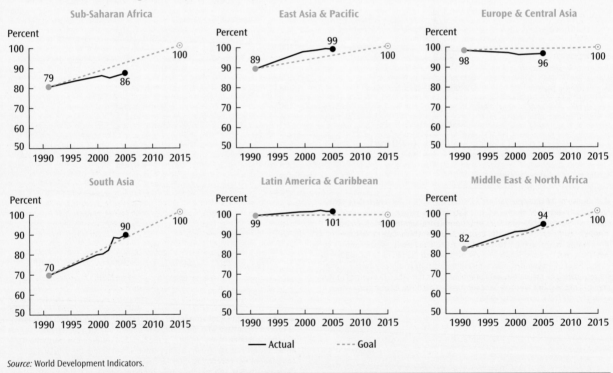

Source: World Development Indicators.

▲   Gender disparity is measured by the ratio of girls to boys enrolled in schools, whether at the primary, secondary, or tertiary levels. Country data used to compute regional rates cover 92 percent of developing countries' total population. The original target aimed to eliminate gender disparity in primary and secondary education by 2005, but this target was achieved only in Latin America and the Caribbean; East Asia and the Pacific came close to meeting that target.

TARGET 3.A Eliminate gender disparity in primary and secondary education, preferably by 2005, and in all levels of education no later than 2015

MDG 3 FIGURE 2   Proportion of countries on track to achieve gender parity in primary and secondary education

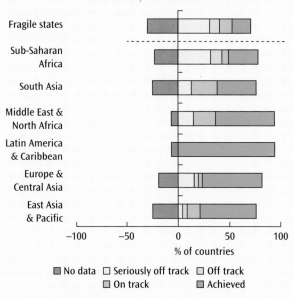

% of countries

■ No data   □ Seriously off track   □ Off track
□ On track   ■ Achieved

Source: World Development Indicators.

▲ All 27 countries (for which data exist) in Latin America and the Caribbean have achieved gender parity in primary and secondary education. For the countries with available data, 2 of 18 countries in East Asia and the Pacific and 3 of 21 countries in Europe and Central Asia are not on track to meet this goal. Thirteen countries in these three regions still lack data. In Sub-Saharan Africa, 18 of 37 countries (for which data exist) are not on track, and another 11 countries lack data. Eleven of 23 fragile states (for which data exist) are off track, while another 10 countries lack data for assessing progress.

MDG 3 FIGURE 3   Gender differences in hourly wages

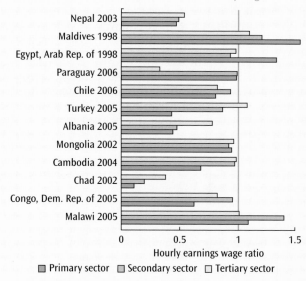

Hourly earnings wage ratio

□ Primary sector   □ Secondary sector   □ Tertiary sector

Source: World Bank staff calculations based on national household surveys.

▲ Women generally receive lower wages than their male counterparts in the primary (agriculture and mining), secondary (manufacturing and construction), and tertiary (services) sectors of the economy. The wage ratio, used to analyze inequality in earnings, divides the female wage by the male wage. Chad's primary sector had a wage ratio of 0.11 in 2002, indicating that men's hourly earnings were almost ten times higher than women's. In Albania men earned around double the hourly earnings of women in the primary sector. However, in some countries, such as the Arab Republic of Egypt, Malawi, and the Maldives, the wage ratio was higher than 1.0, indicating that women's hourly earnings were higher than men's. Overall, the data do not suggest strong patterns in terms of wage gaps by sectors. In some countries, such as Albania, Cambodia, Democratic Republic of Congo, or Turkey, wage gaps have been more pronounced in the primary sector than in the other two sectors. In others, such as the Maldives or Paraguay, wage gaps have been more pronounced in the tertiary sector.

MDG 3 FIGURE 4   Share of men and women participating in the labor force, 1990–2006

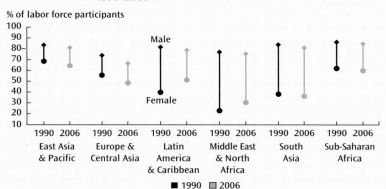

■ 1990   □ 2006

Source: World Development Indicators.

◄ The labor force participation rate measures the proportion of the population between ages 15 and 64 that is economically active, that is, employed or actively seeking a job. Labor participation rates in all regions are lower for females than for males. Gender gaps in 2006 were the widest in the Middle East and North Africa and South Asia (47 percent and 46 percent, respectively). In all regions male labor participation rates declined between 1990 and 2006, to some extent because longer periods of education delayed entry into the labor market. In four of the six regions in the developing world, female labor participation rates declined in similar proportions, leaving gender gaps basically unchanged. In Latin America and the Caribbean and the Middle East and North Africa, the combination of decreasing male participation rates and increasing female participation rates has narrowed the gender gap.

Reduce Child Mortality

Most child mortalities can be prevented through proper nutrition, care, and simple medical treatment. In 1990, 13 million children in developing countries died before age five from diseases such as pneumonia, diarrhea, malaria, measles, and AIDS. By 2006 that number had dropped to 10 million, and under-five mortality rates had declined in all regions. Sub-Saharan Africa had the highest under-five mortality rate in 2006, at 158 per 1,000. Ten of the 11 developing countries with rates above 200

are in Sub-Saharan Africa, including Sierra Leone (270) and Angola (260), and child mortality rates have increased, rather than decreased, in 12 countries in the region since 1990. The spread of the HIV/AIDS epidemic has contributed to this phenomenon. South Asia is also off track for reaching the MDG child mortality target. Even in the regions that are broadly on track to achieve the target, many countries remain off track.

MDG 4 FIGURE 1   Under-five mortality rate

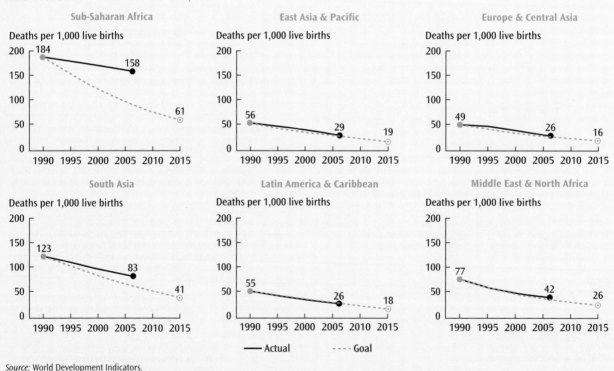

Source: World Development Indicators.

▲   A commonly used measure of child mortality is the under-five mortality rate, which is the probability that a newborn will die before reaching age five (expressed as a rate per 1,000). Regional estimates of child mortality are based on countries' data covering 99.9 percent of developing countries' total population.

TARGET 4.A Reduce by two-thirds, between 1990 and 2015, the under-five mortality rate

MDG 4 FIGURE 2 Proportion of countries on track to achieve the child mortality target

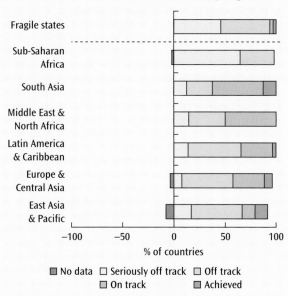

◀ One hundred and seven out of 145 developing countries with available data are either off track or seriously off track to reduce the under-five mortality rate by two thirds by 2015. In fact, a few on-track countries have a large influence on global and regional indicators. No country in Sub-Saharan Africa is on track or has reached the target. Only 2 of the 33 fragile states have achieved or are on track to reduce by two-thirds the under-five mortality rate they recorded in 1990.

Source: World Development Indicators.

MDG 4 FIGURE 3 Increase in measles vaccination coverage, 1992–2006

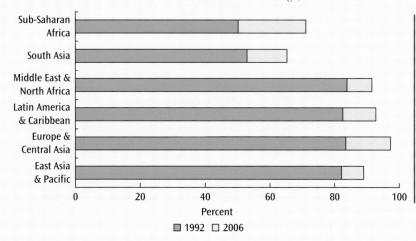

◀ Although many countries are not on track to reach the MDG child mortality target, inexpensive medical treatments have nonetheless helped reduce the number of child deaths. Oral rehydration tablets have mitigated dehydration from diarrhea, antibiotics have treated respiratory infections, mosquito nets have helped to prevent malaria, and measles vaccinations have protected children from the disease. Since 1992 the coverage of measles vaccinations has increased in all six regions, with the greatest change occurring in Sub-Saharan Africa, which now has greater coverage than South Asia. Measles vaccination coverage in Sub-Saharan Africa went from 50 percent in 1992 to 71 percent in 2006. Measles vaccination coverage is defined as the percentage of children ages 12–23 months who received measles vaccinations before 12 months or at any time before the survey.

Source: World Development Indicators.

Improve Maternal Health

An estimated 536,000 maternal deaths occurred worldwide in 2005, over 99 percent of them in developing countries. Difficulties during pregnancy and childbirth are the primary cause of death for women of childbearing age in these countries. Sub-Saharan Africa is the region with the highest maternal mortality rate—more than twenty times higher than the mortality rate for Europe and Central Asia.

Although all regions have increased the percentage of births attended by skilled health staff, the statistics still remain low for South Asia (41 percent) and Sub-Saharan Africa (46 percent). Adult fertility rates have declined over the past 10 years in all regions, and 87 percent of countries with available data have increased contraceptive prevalence rates.

MDG 5 FIGURE 1   Maternal mortality rates

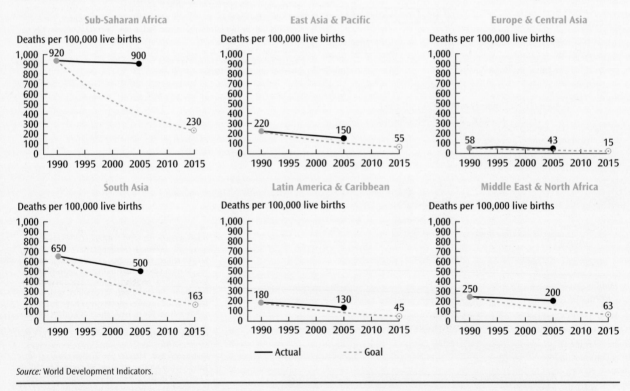

Source: World Development Indicators.

▲   The maternal mortality rate is the number of women who die either during pregnancy or delivery due to pregnancy-related complications, per 100,000 live births. Such statistics are very difficult to collect through surveys, and data reported here rely on modeling techniques developed by the World Health Organization, United Nations Children's Fund, and United Nations Population Fund.

TARGET 5.A Reduce by three-quarters, between 1990 and 2015, the maternal mortality ratio

TARGET 5.B Achieve by 2015 universal access to reproductive health

MDG 5 FIGURE 2 Births attended by skilled personnel

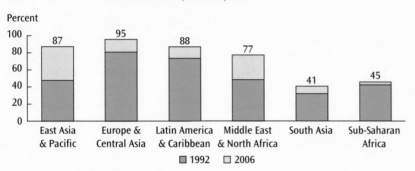

Source: World Development Indicators.

◄ The high maternal mortality rate in developing countries is correlated with poor health care during pregnancy and childbirth. Since 1990 the proportion of births attended by skilled health personnel has increased across all regions, most noticeably in East Asia and the Pacific, where it almost doubled from its 1992 level of 47 percent, to reach 87 percent in 2006. Conversely, the proportion of attended births by skilled personnel increased only one percentage point in Sub-Saharan Africa, where the maternal mortality rate remains the highest. Regional estimates reported here are based on country data covering 90 percent of developing countries' total population.

MDG 5 FIGURE 3 Contraceptive prevalence: Annual change for 89 countries, various dates 1988–2006

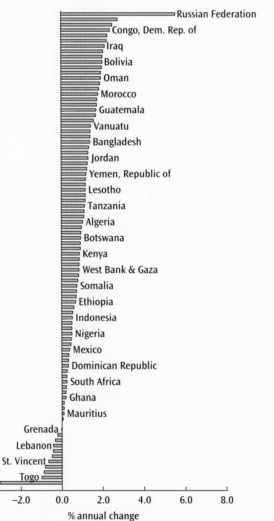

Source: World Development Indicators.

◄ The contraceptive prevalence rate is the percentage of married women ages 15–49 who use, or whose sexual partners use, any form of contraception. In most of the 89 countries that have two data points between 1988 and 2006, contraceptive use increased.

MDG 5 FIGURE 4 Fertility rate for women ages 15–19, 1997–2008

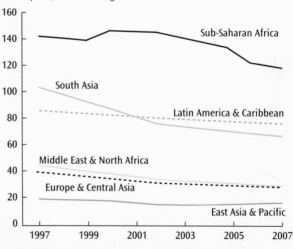

Source: World Development Indicators.

▲ Adolescent fertility rates, or the number of births per 1,000 women ages 15–19, have decreased in all regions since 1997, but the 2007 rate in Sub-Saharan Africa (119) is more than seven times greater than the rate in East Asia and the Pacific (16).

Combat HIV/AIDS, Malaria, and Other Diseases

It is estimated that 99 percent of individuals who die from AIDS, tuberculosis, and malaria reside in the developing world. In 2007, 33 million individuals were living with HIV, 2.5 million were newly infected, and 2.1 million died from AIDS. As the estimated number of people living with HIV increases each year, the AIDS epidemic has become one of the greatest challenges to public health and requires improved access to HIV prevention and treatment

services. Prevalence rates have stabilized since 2001 and have now started to decline, although moderately. Progress is most pronounced in Sub-Saharan Africa, where the proportion of population living with HIV has declined by a full percentage point since 2000. However, other regions that had started from much lower levels conversely record increases in prevalence rates, mostly within high-risk populations.

MDG 6 FIGURE 1   Tuberculosis incidence and prevalence rates, 1990–2005

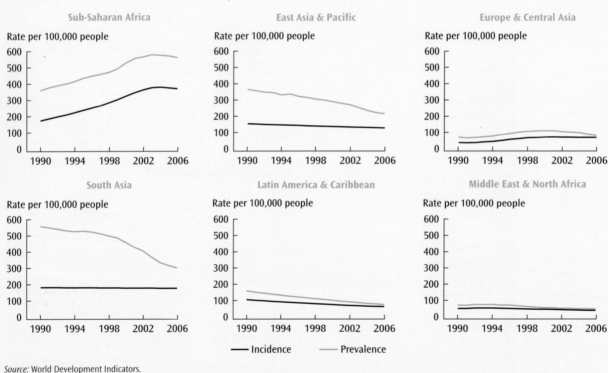

Source: World Development Indicators.

▲   Tuberculosis (TB) incidence rates measure the percentage of the population that is newly infected with TB (pulmonary, smear positive, and extrapulmonary), while prevalence rates measure the percentage of individuals in a population who have TB. Both are measured per 100,000 people. Both the incidence and prevalence rates for TB have either remained level or declined from 1990 to 2005 in every region except Sub-Saharan Africa and Europe and Central Asia, where it has been leveling off since the early 2000s. Following earlier declines in prevalence rates for TB, the incidence rate for the different regions has now stabilized or has been decreasing, but population growth has been offsetting the slow fall in incidence rates.

TARGET 6.A Have halted by 2015 and begun to reverse the spread of HIV/AIDS

TARGET 6.B Achieve by 2010 universal access to treatment for HIV/AIDS for all those who need it

TARGET 6.C Have halted by 2015 and begun to reverse the incidence of malaria and other major diseases

MDG 6 FIGURE 2   Estimated HIV prevalence trends for ages 15–49

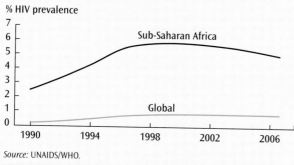

Source: UNAIDS/WHO.

▲   The HIV prevalence rate measures the percentage of individuals in a population who are infected with the HIV virus. The global prevalence rate has remained level since 2001. In many Sub-Saharan African countries, the national prevalence rate has either leveled off or decreased.

MDG 6 FIGURE 4   Rates of condom use and HIV knowledge in Sub-Saharan Africa

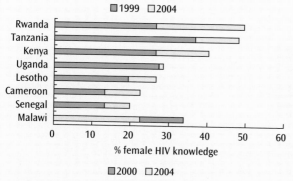

Source: World Development Indicators.

MDG 6 FIGURE 3   HIV prevalence rates, 2003–05

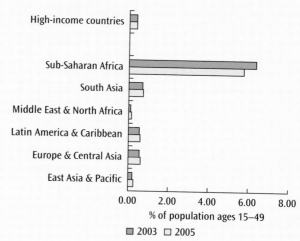

Source: World Development Indicators.

▲   Sub-Saharan Africa, the region with the highest HIV prevalence rates, had a decrease from 6.36 in 2003 to 5.76 in 2005. In 2005 the prevalence rates in other regions were much lower, ranging from 0.15 (in the Middle East and North Africa) to 0.71 (in South Asia). High-income countries recorded a prevalence rate of 0.36 in both 2003 and 2005. From 2003 to 2005, 69 countries had positive annual changes in HIV prevalence rates, while 51 had annual decreases during that time.

◄   Condom use and knowledge about HIV can help to decrease the number of individuals who become infected by HIV. The rate of condom use is defined as the percentage of the population between the ages of 15 to 24 who use a condom (or in the case of females, whose partner uses a condom), and the rate of HIV knowledge is defined as the percentage of individuals (in this case female) who have comprehensive, correct knowledge about HIV (ability to describe two ways to prevent infection and to reject three misconceptions concerning HIV). Condom use for females' partners increased in all Sub-Saharan African countries with available data except Zimbabwe, where usage is estimated to have decreased from 11 to 10 percent between 1999 and 2004. Usage sharply increased in South Africa, from 25 percent in 1999 to 60 percent in 2004. Female HIV knowledge also increased in most countries in Sub-Saharan Africa, most notably in Rwanda, where knowledge went from 26 to 48 percent between 1990 and 2004. But gains can also be reversed, as observed in Malawi, where HIV knowledge receded.

Ensure Environmental Sustainability

Access to clean potable water and basic sanitation is one of the targets to ensuring environmental sustainability and a key indicator for human development. Over 1 billion individuals lack access to safe drinking water, and 2.6 billion individuals lack access to basic sanitation. Improvements in these two areas could help to reduce dramatically the burden of disease, particularly diarrhea, which contributes to approximately 1.8 million deaths annually. In addition, deforestation and greenhouse gas emissions, such as carbon dioxide, threaten biodiversity and drive climate change through global warming. In most regions adjusted net savings is negative or on the decline, indicating that countries are not saving enough to offset resource depletion and environmental degradation, thus clouding prospects of sustainable development.

MDG 7 FIGURE 1 Population without access to an improved water source or sanitation facilities

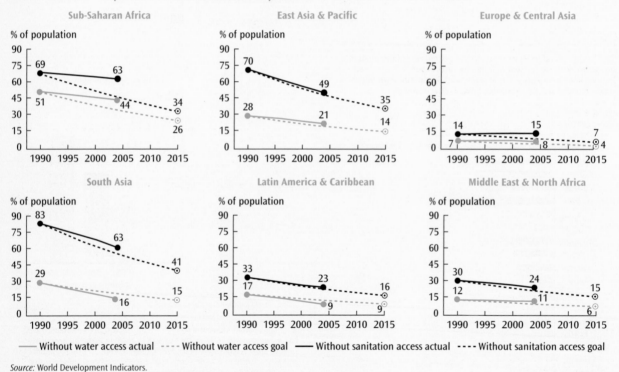

Source: World Development Indicators.

MDG 7 FIGURE 2 Regions' contributions to global deforestation, 1990–2005

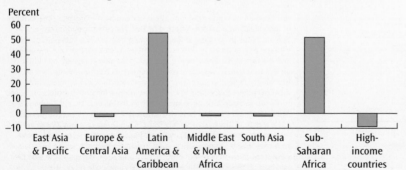

◄ Forests act as carbon sinks and absorb carbon dioxide in the atmosphere. Deforestation thus hinders sustainable development because it results in higher levels of greenhouse gas emissions as well as loss of biodiversity. Between 1990 and 2005 the global surface of forests was reduced by 1.3 million square kilometers, or 3 percent of its total. Forty percent of the world's forests are located in Latin America and Sub-Saharan Africa, which were the two most important regional contributors to global deforestation. Latin America and the Caribbean lost 7 percent of its forests in 15 years; Sub-Saharan Africa, 9 percent.

Source: World Development Indicators.

TARGET 7.A Integrate the principles of sustainable development into country policies and programs and reverse the loss of environmental resources

TARGET 7.B Reduce biodiversity loss, achieving by 2010 a significant reduction in the rate of loss

TARGET 7.C Halve by 2015 the proportion of people without sustainable access to safe drinking water and basic sanitation

TARGET 7.D Have achieved a significant improvement by 2020 in the lives of at least 100 million slum dwellers

◄ Access to sanitation refers to the percentage of population with at least adequate access to excreta facilities (private or shared, but not public) that can effectively prevent human, animal, and insect contact with excreta. Regional estimates are computed using country data covering 99 percent of developing countries' total population. Access to improved sources of water refers to the percentage of population with reasonable access to a permanent source of safe water in their dwelling or within a reasonable distance from it. Regional estimates are computed using country data covering 98 percent of developing countries' total population. Latin America and the Caribbean and East Asia and the Pacific were broadly on track by 2004 to halve the proportion of people without access to an improved source of water and sanitation facilities by 2015. South Asia was on track to meet the water access goal, but off track for reaching the sanitation access goal. The Middle East and North Africa, Sub-Saharan Africa, and Europe and Central Asia were off track on both goals; the transition economies record the lowest proportion of people lacking access to both water and sanitation.

MDG 7 FIGURE 3 CO₂ emissions per capita, 1995–2004

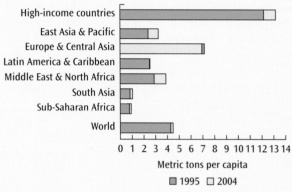

Source: World Development Indicators.

▲ Carbon dioxide (CO₂) emissions are derived from fossil energy use and cement manufacture, which tends to rise with incomes. Thus per capita CO₂ emissions are greatest in high-income countries, which record levels more than five times those of developing countries. The Middle East and North Africa, East Asia and the Pacific, South Asia, and Sub-Saharan Africa have recorded increases.

MDG 7 FIGURE 4 Adjusted net savings, 1995–2005

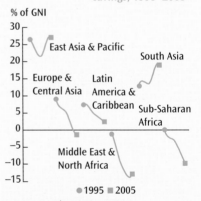

Source: World Development Indicators.

▲ Adjusted net savings measures the saving rate in an economy after adjustments are made for educational expenditure, capital depreciation, natural resource depletion, and carbon dioxide and particulate emissions damage. A negative saving rate indicates that an economy is on an unsustainable future path of economic growth. Europe and Central Asia, the Middle East and North Africa, and Sub-Saharan Africa have all exhibited a downward trend in adjusted net saving since 1995 and had negative adjusted net saving rates in 2005. Latin America and the Caribbean had a positive 2005 adjusted net saving rate but also had declining adjusted net saving levels. In recent years, only the Asian regions seem to have both an upward trend in adjusted net savings and a positive saving rate.

MDG 7 FIGURE 5 Proportion of countries on track to achieve the targets for access to improved water and sanitation

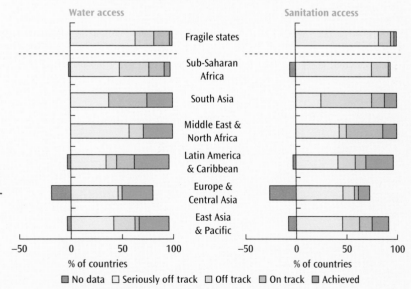

Source: World Development Indicators.

▲ Thirty-five percent of the developing countries (with available data) have achieved or are on track to achieve the improved water target, while 24 percent have achieved or are on track to achieve the improved sanitation target. Fifty-seven percent of countries (with available data) in the Middle East and North Africa and in Europe and Central Asia are seriously off track in improving access to safe drinking water. Conditions are worse for the improved sanitation target, where 12 of 19 European and Central Asian countries and 36 of 45 Sub-Saharan African countries (with available data) are seriously off track.

Develop a Global Partnership for Development

Official development assistance (ODA) from Development Assistance Committee (DAC) countries of the Organisation for Economic Co-operation and Development has increased steadily in the last decade, with a large jump in 2005, mostly attributable to debt-relief initiatives. Aid today is more flexible and more aligned to national priorities. It is also more selective, that is, more responsive to needs, as well as to the quality of policies and institutions.

Aid from DAC countries, as measured by per capita income levels, still falls short of the United Nations target of 0.7 percent of gross national income (GNI). Moreover, multilateral trade discussions have not yet delivered tangible results, even if market access for developing countries' exports has slightly improved. With decreasing costs, information technologies are spreading very rapidly across the world, but the digital divide still remains a concerning reality.

MDG 8 FIGURE 1   Evolution of global aid in DAC countries, 1990–2006

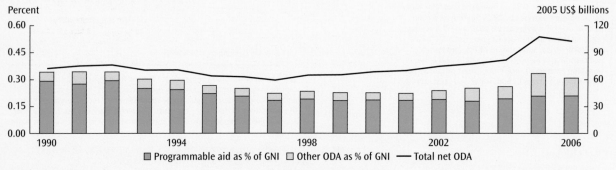

Source: OECD DAC database.

▲   One of the indicators for MDG 8 is the ratio of total net ODA to DAC donors' GNI. The ODA-to-GNI ratio for DAC donors stood at 0.31 percent in 2006, below the level of the early 1990s. The level of programmable aid, which can be more rapidly and effectively aligned to national priorities, has increased since 1990, but the percentage of ODA considered programmable aid has fallen. Programmable aid is total ODA excluding bilateral humanitarian aid, debt relief, administration costs, in-donor country refugee costs, and imputed student costs. Non-DAC ODA, which is estimated to be growing rapidly, has not yet been monitored on a systematic basis.

MDG 8 FIGURE 2   Evolution of global DAC aid by income category

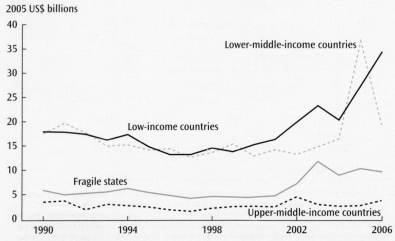

◄   The amount of ODA disbursed by DAC donors to low-income countries grew by 124 percent from 2000 to 2006. Owing to debt-relief initiatives, ODA to lower-middle-income countries rose by 175 percent from 2002 to 2005 but sharply decreased, by 47 percent, in 2006.

Source: OECD DAC database.

TARGET 8.A Develop further an open, rule-based, predictable, nondiscriminatory trading and financial system

TARGET 8.B Address the special needs of the least developed countries

TARGET 8.C Address the special needs of landlocked developing countries and small island developing states

TARGET 8.D Deal comprehensively with the debt problems of developing countries through national and international measures in order to make debt sustainable in the long term

TARGET 8.E In cooperation with pharmaceutical companies, provide access to affordable essential drugs in developing countries

TARGET 8.F In cooperation with the private sector, make available the benefits of new technologies, especially information and communications

MDG 8 FIGURE 3 Trade restrictiveness and market access by income groups

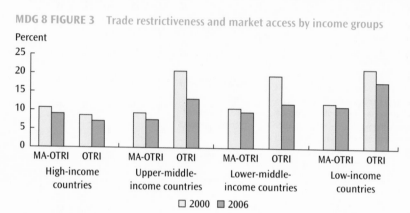

Source: World Bank Staff calculations.

◀ The Overall Trade Restrictiveness Index (OTRI) measures the overall restrictiveness (including non-tariff measures) faced by imports while the Market Access Overall Trade Restrictiveness Index (MA-OTRI) measures the overall restrictiveness (including non-tariff measures) faced by exports. Despite limited progress in the Doha round of multilateral trade negotiations, low- and middle-income countries benefited from a slight improvement between 2000 and 2006 in market access for their products. However, low-income countries, given their specialization in agriculture, still face the lowest levels of access to exports markets. Symmetrically, low-income countries still impose larger restrictions on imports than any other group of countries, despite significant progress between 2000 and 2006. Over the same period, trade liberalization in middle-income countries was more pronounced.

MDG 8 FIGURE 4 Debt sustainability 2006–08

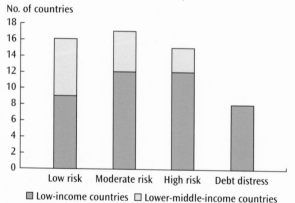

Source: IMF.

▲ With the adoption of the MDGs and recent multilateral debt-relief initiatives, the international community is committed to monitoring more closely external (and domestic) debt-sustainability indicators, primarily in low-income and lower-middle-income countries. A country is said to experience debt-stress risk if its debt-burden indicator exceeds its indicative threshold over a 20-year projection period. Low risk indicates that all the debt-burden indicators are far below the baseline scenario threshold; moderate risk indicates that debt-burden indicators currently below the threshold could increase from external shocks or unexpected macroeconomic policy changes; high risk indicates that at least one debt-burden indicator has surpassed the threshold, and debt distress indicates that a country is already having repayment difficulties. For the 56 countries that have reliable data, eight low-income countries were in debt distress as of early 2008.

MDG 8 FIGURE 5 Growth in Internet affordability and use

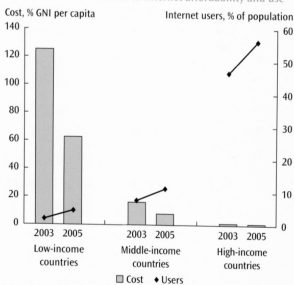

Source: World Development Indicators.

▲ Internet costs are dropping rapidly but are still very expensive for users in developing countries, low-income countries in particular, where a one-year subscription cost was equivalent to 62 percent of GNI per capita in 2005. The proportion of users doubled in low-income countries between 2003 and 2005 but remains low, at 4 percent of the population. In contrast, the proportion of users in high-income countries increased from 46 to 56 percent over the same period.